# SEVEN HUNDRED YEARS

## A HISTORY OF SINGAPORE

# SEVEN HUNDRED YEARS

## A HISTORY OF SINGAPORE

Kwa Chong Guan

Derek Heng

Peter Borschberg

Tan Tai Yong

Supported by

 National Library Board Singapore

 Marshall Cavendish Editions

 SG Bicentennial From Singapore to Singaporean

Published by

**National Library Board, Singapore**
100 Victoria Street
#14-01 National Library Building
Singapore 188064
www.nlb.gov.sg
ref@nlb.gov.sg

In partnership with

**Marshall Cavendish International (Asia)**
1 New Industrial Road
Singapore 536196
Tel: (65) 6213 9300
genref@sg.marshallcavendish.com
www.marshallcavendish.com/genref

Supported by

**Singapore Bicentennial Office**
100 Victoria Street
#09-02 National Library Building
Singapore 188064
singapore_bicentennial@pmo.gov.sg
www.bicentennial.sg

**National Library Board, Singapore Cataloguing in Publication Data**

Name(s): Kwa, Chong Guan. | Heng, Derek Thiam Soon, author. | Borschberg, Peter, author. | Tan, Tai Yong, author.
Title: Seven Hundred Years : A History of Singapore / Kwa Chong Guan, Derek Heng, Peter Borschberg, Tan Tai Yong.
Description: Singapore : National Library Board, Singapore : Marshall Cavendish Editions, [2019]. | Includes bibliographical references and index.
Identifier(s): OCN 1098154065 |
ISBN 978-981-48-6820-4 (hardback) ISBN 978-981-48-2810-9 (paperback)
Subject(s): LCSH: Singapore–History.
Classification: DDC 959.57–dc23

Printed in Singapore by Oxford Graphic Printers Pte Ltd

# CONTENTS

# PREFACE

This book offers a complete rewrite of *Singapore: A 700-Year History – From Early Emporium to World City*, published exactly ten years ago. The original authors, now joined by Peter Borschberg, felt that the occasion of the Bicentennial Commemoration warranted a reminder that Singapore has a history pre-dating the arrival of Stamford Raffles by some five centuries. This volume presents a possible approach to rethinking the significance of Raffles' establishment of a British station on Singapore.

We thank the Singapore Bicentennial Office for supporting our effort in bringing out this new volume. Without the encouragement and unstinting support of its Executive Director, Gene Tan, and his staff, the gestation of this book would have been prolonged. In particular, we single out the editorial skills of Yap Koon Hong in weaving the disparate styles of the four co-authors into a cogent and readable narrative. Additional writing of box stories was contributed by staff of the Bicentennial Office's Content team, including Koon Hong, Joshua Sim and Syafiqah Jaffar. We also appreciate Chang Yueh Siang's efforts in coordinating the final stages of the book's production. We thank the National Library Board, who led the project management, for their support and supervision of the publication process. We are grateful to Lee Geok Boi and Tan Li Jen for their editorial assistance in working on the many drafts that eventually led to the final version. Finally, Glenn Wray efficiently and sympathetically coordinated Marshall Cavendish's production of our book, for which we are grateful.

This book sums up the evidence we have been collecting on the long history of Singapore, our reflections, and writing on that material. We are now in a position to propose a more defined linear-cyclical time frame and more in-depth historical information for narrating this 700-year history of Singapore than ten years ago. We hope this book provides a more convincing response to K.G. Tregonning's and C.M. Turnbull's challenge to connect Singapore's historical development before 1800 to its development after 1800.

We have also sought to rise to Tregonning's other challenge of writing our history from an Asian perspective, rather than a European one that makes Singapore's past a part of British colonial history. Our close reading of the evidence suggests that the underlying plot or theme of an autonomous history of Singapore may lie in the shifting and evolving harbours or ports around which a settlement or city developed. Writing Singapore's history has focused largely on the city that emerged to service the growing port Raffles established. Our reconstruction shows, however, that at least twice in Singapore's long history there were thriving ports or harbours with their supporting settlements on this island. What connected these harbour-settlements and port-cities, or aspiring global city today, are the long cycles of the maritime history of the South China Sea and the Indian Ocean. This history of Singapore therefore attempts to look at Singapore from the sea.

For the images illustrating this volume, we have attempted to draw the majority of them from the collections of the National Archives, the National Library and the museums of the National Heritage Board. These illustrations demonstrate the extent and depth of our national collections on our history. The images, especially the maps, are not supplements or illustrations adorning the text, but critical evidence for our reconstruction of Singapore's history. Contained in these maps and images are a history of Singapore.

Kwa Chong Guan
Derek Heng
Peter Borschberg
Tan Tai Yong

27 April 2019

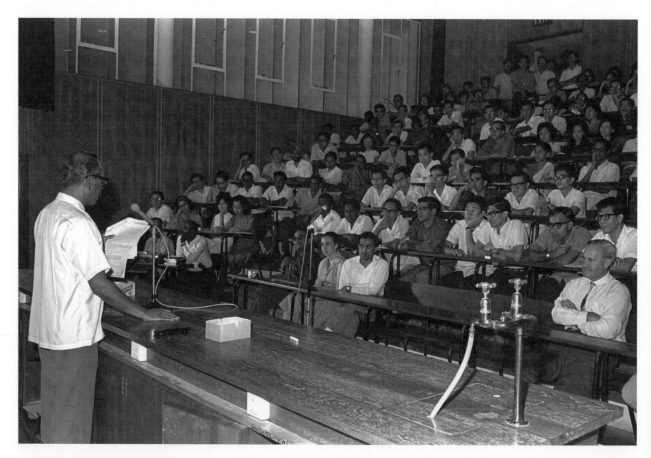

S. Rajaratnam addressing the University of Singapore History Society in 1964. Rajaratnam wrote history as he witnessed it and was participant to its making. His writing the history of the People's Action Party's role in the struggle for Singapore's independence became the beginnings of today's "Singapore story". Raffles Professor of History K.G. Tregonning is seated on the extreme right of the front row.

# INTRODUCTION

# Writing Singapore's History

*odern Singapore began in 1819. Nothing that occurred on the island prior to this has particular relevance to an understanding of the contemporary scene; it is of antiquarian interest only.*

In 1969, K.G. Tregonning, who was Raffles Professor of History at the University of Singapore, made the above declaration in his contribution to a volume commemorating the 150th anniversary of Sir Stamford Raffles' arrival and the establishment of a British trading station in Singapore.

Professor Tregonning's remarks reflected the prevailing perception held by historians of Singapore's past as recently as 50 years ago. They echoed the British template of Singapore's history, which had been articulated by, among others, Straits Settlements Governor Sir Frank Swettenham, who in 1906 pronounced that without Raffles, Singapore could not have become the crowning port jewel of the "Eastern Seas".

The view that Singapore was historically unsubstantial prior to 1819 was not confined to colonial luminaries or their comparatively more arcane counterparts in academia. In fact, it gained popular currency after it was reaffirmed as late as some 20 years after independence. In 1987, S. Rajaratnam, a founding member of the People's Action Party (PAP), attributed Singapore's beginnings entirely to Raffles' arrival: "Nothing very much appears to have happened in Singapore... before Raffles landed in this unpromising island".

Is this still our understanding of Singapore's history as we commemorate the bicentennial of Raffles' arrival in Singapore? This Introduction reviews the background to Tregonning's declaration and explores where we are today in our understanding and writing of Singapore's history.

## Colonial Beginnings

For colonial administrator Sir Richard Winstedt, the foremost scholar of the time on Malay history, language and literature, Singapore had no local history until the end of World War II, when Britain returned to Malaya to reorganise the Malayan states constitutionally as the Malayan Union. Singapore was excluded from the proposed Malayan Union, and became a separate Crown Colony. It was only then that Singapore had, for Malayan Civil Service officers such as Winstedt and later, C.M. Turnbull, its own administration, and with that, its own history separate from that of the Federation of Malaya, which they could write about.

As a historian, Winstedt was well aware that Singapore had a past before Raffles. In 1928, he published the first description of 14th-century gold ornaments found at Fort Canning, which have since become a national treasure. Four years later, his groundbreaking history of Malaya articulated Singapore as a part of Johor. His 1938 transcription of a seminal Melaka court chronicle, the *Sejarah Melayu*, or *Malay Annals*, acknowledged Singapore even earlier, as a 15th-century Melaka fiefdom.

Why were Winstedt and his Malayan Civil Service colleagues unable to connect the history they read in the *Malay Annals* and the Fort Canning Hill ornaments with the 20th-century British Malaya they were administering? The issue can be traced back to the time of Raffles. In several letters, Raffles attributed his journey towards Singapore to his study of Malay history. He saw Singapore as the "ancient Maritime Capital of the Malays", which had apparently been abandoned for 600 years before he arrived. John Crawfurd, Singapore's second Resident, agreed. In his 1856 *Descriptive Dictionary of the Indian Islands & Adjacent Countries*, he stated:

> Singapore is the name of an island, which with the exception of a single village of poor and predatory Malay fishermen, and that only formed in 1811, was covered with a primeval forest down to the 6th day of February 1819.... [F]or a period of about five centuries and a half, there is no record of Singapore having been occupied, and it was only the occasional resort of pirates.

This became the template of Singapore's history – that it began on 6 February 1819, when Raffles established a British station on a desolate, depopulated island. Crawfurd's citation that British governance propelled Singapore's rapid rise – to fourth place among "the European emporia of India" – reflects this historical mantra.

## Writing Singapore's Colonial History

Singapore's template as a British Empire port-city that grew into the capital of British Malaya by 1919 came to be detailed by a generation of students trained by the History Department of the University of Malaya, established in 1949. These students learnt that the histories of Malaya and Singapore that they were researching and writing had to be underpinned by the archived records of the British East India Company (EIC) and the Colonial Office. These records were the multigenerational product of colonial servants like Winstedt who hewed largely to their view of British rule. Inevitably, these students described a Singapore that was incorporated within the EIC and the British Empire, and not as part of an Asian world.

Tregonning and his colleagues, including the notable historian of Singapore, C.M. Turnbull, articulated Singapore's – and Malaya's – place in a waning empire after World War II. Their histories examined Britain's preparation for Malaya and Singapore's independence and the respective local responses to this impending power transfer. In 1975, Turnbull published her pioneering *History of Singapore: 1819–1975*, framing Singapore's history, which she had observed for 20 years as a Malayan Civil Service officer and subsequently as a university lecturer, as a positive outcome of British colonialism.

Indeed, Britain's place in modern Singapore's origins was acknowledged by its founding leaders, including Rajaratnam, who served as Singapore's first Foreign Minister. In 1984, he declared:

> *After attaining independence in 1965 there was a debate as to who should be declared the founding fathers of Singapore. The debate was brought to an abrupt end when the government fixed responsibility for this on Sir Stamford Raffles and officially declared him the founder of Singapore…. [I]n nominating Raffles as the founder of modern Singapore we are accepting a fact of history. To pretend otherwise is to falsify history – about as honest as claiming descent from the sun or the moon or the wolves or licentious Greek gods.*

In other words, independent Singapore existed because of one EIC officer's initiative.

### From Colonial to National Histories and Beyond

Rajaratnam was a visionary politician with a deep empathy for the past. He sought to shape public perceptions of Singapore's colonial history and its implications for the present. In a 1987 address, he conceded:

> *Though our history began in 1819, this brief past is what made Singapore and its people what they are today, and it is this Singapore past which will shape their future and furnish the ingredients for a national identity.*

For Rajaratnam and his colleagues, who were schooled in the colonial history of Singapore as an integral part of British Malaya, the 1963 merger to form Malaysia negated Britain's disastrous detachment of Singapore from Malaya in 1945 under the Malayan Union. The ensuing separation of Singapore from Malaysia in 1965 was a tragedy that Rajaratnam's generation had to overcome. They had to exorcise the ghost of separation by disproving the deeply held assumption that a decoupled Singapore would collapse and "crawl back to Malaysia" – a prospect that Lee Kuan Yew, Singapore's founding Prime Minister, feared.

So, Singapore's survival against the odds became the basis of a national history. Rajaratnam could, in 1973, write that Singapore had survived because it managed to transform itself from a "trading city of Southeast Asia, the market place of the region" into a "new kind of city – the global city". Rajaratnam was prescient in declaring thus, because it would be another 20 years before a new cycle of globalisation and a world economy networked around several global cities, spurred by the end of the Cold War, would emerge.

In Lee Kuan Yew's 1998 memoirs, *The Singapore Story*, we see the transformation of Singapore's colonial history into a national narrative. Like other national histories, *The Singapore Story* reflects an earlier European vogue, going back to the mid-19th century, following the French Revolution. The historians of this era, including Thomas Macaulay (1800–59), Jules Michelet (1798–1874) and George Bancroft (1800–91), worked their respective national histories by co-opting the past's immediacy to the present. Theirs was a passionate argument for the changes and reforms – some traumatic – that they were experiencing. Macaulay was an early and energetic promoter of the Whig interpretation of British history as the story of human progress. A similar spirit of economic development, progress and modernisation since 1819 underpins *The Singapore Story*.

*The Singapore Story* has served Singapore well in explaining its rise from the Third World to the First World. Yet, embedded in the story's transformational success are questions about Singapore's history as a nation and as a city-state. One set of issues centres around questions such as: What kind of nation state is emerging from this successful economic development and progress? Is it a liberal-capitalist and democratic one, or is it a modern Asian state that privileges Asian values of communitarian rights over individuals?

Another set of issues centres around whether Singapore's history as a successful city-state can be compatible with its emerging history as an aspiring world city in a globalising world. Singapore's history as a nation and city-state is the creation of an anti-colonial and nationalist struggle for independence which began with its colonial founding in 1819, and which has no connection to any earlier history. But is 1819 also the beginning of Singapore's emerging history as a global city? Much would depend on how a global city is defined and rooted historically.

Cities that are also states have an illustrious history, harking to Greek city-states like Athens, early modern Italian cities like Venice, the Hanseatic League in the North Sea and Nordic region, and arguably, the cities of ancient China's Spring-Autumn and Warring States periods. But what is their place and role in the modern world? What is Singapore's future as only the third city-state today, after the Vatican City and Monaco?

This issue worried Rajaratnam's colleague, Goh Keng Swee, the Deputy Prime Minister and independent Singapore's economic architect. In an underappreciated 1967 essay, "Cities as Modernisers", Goh argued that late 20th-century Asian capitals began as beach-heads of European imperialism. To Goh, such cities should "transform themselves under their independent national governments into beach-heads of a dynamic modernisation process to transform the countryside". Cities, he added, are not the creations of their hinterland, but the reverse: their creators.

Goh recalled that the Malay Peninsula's development as Singapore's economic hinterland was financed by Singapore capital and nurtured by Singapore's "management skills"; and that Singapore continued in 1967 to be the natural trading centre for Malaysia, Sumatra and Kalimantan. He regretted that Singapore could not persuade its neighbours to continue using its services and not try to develop their own at greater cost. "While we will do everything possible to retain our trade links with our hinterland," Goh concluded, "it will only be prudent if we try to broaden our external economic ties by attempting to provide services and goods to countries outside the immediate region."

### Singapore's History as a Port and City

This volume traces its roots to a study module offered by the National University of Singapore's History Department. Its focus was on Singapore's history as a British port-city that morphed successfully into a global metropolis in the 1990s. The module asked whether this narrative of Singapore's transformation from colonial port-city to aspiring global city was a better template for understanding its past. Subsequently, the module explored whether the port-city model could be applied to the pre-1800s. Fresh historical tools and sources like archaeological data from excavations on and around Fort Canning Hill since 1984 offered evidence of a 14th-century port-city in Singapore. Fresh research by Peter Borschberg, the fourth writer joining the original trio of writers, into Portuguese, Spanish and Dutch records and maps, attests to the existence of a thriving harbour-settlement on Singapore from the late-16th to late-17th century and Portuguese and Dutch proposals to establish forts on Singapore to protect their ships sailing to and from China.

This volume narrates Singapore's chronological history from its earliest documented settlement to the present. It casts Singapore's narrative over 700 years, between the late 13th century and the 21st, situating developments within the context of local, regional and global events.

How we perceive and think about history is influenced by the ways we study and write it. Several approaches come to mind. One is via a continuous, successive history based on dynastic rule; this is seen in the detailing of Chinese history, for instance, or the Melakans' genealogy of their kings, the *Sulalat'us-Salatin*, or *Malay Annals*. Another is teleological – crafting narratives that culminate in the successes of state and society, such as in the case of canonical and Whig history in 19th- and 20th-century Britain, as well as the Singapore story. A third way focuses history through the fixed star of a geographic location around which the vicissitudes of societies and individuals wax and wane over the *longue durée*, as in the case of the history of the Mediterranean littoral as written by the French Annales school.

For Singapore, casting a narrative spanning seven centuries presents critical challenges. First, there is the challenge of the nation state. Can Singapore survive independently in the long term based on its past 60 years of self-rule? Can Singaporeans continue to exercise some degree of political autonomy, which is in turn closely linked to independent economic and demographic sustainability? Ultimately, can Singapore's story be constructed on a history anchored by the notion of centrality? Derek Heng, one of this book's original writers, argues that the pivotal reason for a nation state's existence after colonial freedom lies in its citizens' ability to identify their uniqueness through a set of sociocultural norms, exercise suzerainty within its borders, and determine its own external affairs.

In this respect, some scholars have applied geographic models of analysis to Singapore's past, particularly its economic history. John Miksic and Wong Lin Ken have reconstructed Singapore in the 14th and 19th–21st centuries as a port-city, reminiscent of Karl Polanyi's "port of trade" template, in which an autonomous space is provided by an independent state equipped with a specialised administration and a set of rules governing trade and commerce.

Others, including Chiang Hai Ding and C.M. Turnbull, representing historians working on the 19th and 20th centuries using traditional archival sources, have structured Singapore's economic history within a branching, dendritic model. Under this model, populations located at collection centres and feeder points in the Malay Peninsula, east Sumatra and the Riau-Lingga Archipelago harnessed the produce of their respective surroundings and channelled them to a key export emporium: Singapore. In return, the same emporium despatched resources obtainable only from international markets, including foreign goods and human resources, to these collection centres and feeder points.

More recently, conceptual models have argued for the centrality of Singapore's past. Anthony Reid, for example, postulates Singapore as a cosmopolis. Drawing from studies of Singapore's demographics in the past two centuries, he suggests that the cosmopolitan nature of Singapore's settlements can be evidenced by how it was populated across 700 years. First, as a port-polity in the 14th century, it had sojourning foreigners living among the inhabitants. Then, as a colonial port-city in the past two centuries, it had a population drawn from maritime Asia and the British Empire's territories. And most recently, it has seen new waves of migration arriving mainly from South Asia and China.

While geographical models enable arguments for the centrality of Singapore's settlement history, which is often tied to its strategic location and hence its functions, they do not address the second challenge – that human habitation was discontinuous and did not experience the passage of historical events, or *histoire événementielle*.

The challenge, therefore, has been to rationalise the chronological span of Singapore's past. Scholars like Peter Coclanis suggest framing Singapore's historical trajectory and disjointed settlement histories as a series of cycles echoing repetitively, thereby providing continuity and rationality for joining the discordant periods. Inspired by the historical concept of the *longue durée*, this approach is premised on the timelessness of Singapore's geographical location set in the natural environment of maritime Asia. So, its fixed location provides the rationale for its chronological depth and continuity. Coclanis has identified three cycles anchored by economic globalisation over the past 700 years:

1. The 14th to early 17th centuries, characterised by the rise of Ming China and the entry of European trading nations into maritime Asia;

2. The early 19th to early 20th centuries, marked by the importance of the China trade to Europe, European imperialism and the establishment of imperial economies globally, as well as technological developments that shrank distances; and

3. The 1950s to the present, with an American-led world economic order and the lowering of barriers to transnational movements of trade and people. This cycle has also been witness to the alignment of commercial laws and adjudication processes across boundaries, and the advent of transportation and information technologies that have further compressed geography and, importantly, helped to craft transregional and transnational identities.

In a similar economic vein, Borschberg identifies three different up-cycles: in 14th-century Temasek; under the Johor Sultanate (16th to 17th centuries), when Singapore had a port run by the Shahbandar, or harbour master; and since 1819, under the British Empire and subsequently in independent Singapore.

By contrast, Kwa Chong Guan, the first-named of this book's quartet of writers, argues that Singapore's settlement history comprises a series of cyclical echoes centred on the sociocultural idea embedded in the port-cities of the Melaka Straits. The series began with Sriwijaya in Palembang, southeast Sumatra (late 7th century), followed by Temasek (14th century), Melaka (15th century), Johor (16th to 18th centuries), and finally Singapore (since the 19th century). In this regard, Singapore may be seen as part of the cyclical history of a larger geographical and cultural sphere.

Kwa's key criterion is the role of the central point in a transregional setting, whereby Singapore's history pertained directly to how its role was projected regionally. So, in the case of economic globalisation, Singapore was a commercial nodal point; in terms of a consistent sociocultural notion of Malay regional leadership, it was a port-city with a ruler exercising autonomy and wielding influence (*daulat*) regionally over its inhabitants (*rakyat*).

But the *longue durée* exacts a trade-off. Its broad-brush sweep rationalises Singapore's chronological depth but blurs narrative nuances. While economic globalisation explains Singapore's history between the late 13th and early 17th centuries as a single cycle, the differences between at least three settlement phases during those 300 years are rendered opaque. Similarly, while Singapore's history may be understood within the regional cyclical pattern of successive port-polity rule, this framework casts all the port-cities in the same mould.

Second, the approach creates distinct, repetitive historical trajectories with multiple narratives, instead of a single arc traversing a singular timeline that results in a single narrative. Here, the *longue durée* converges with the argument made by Karl Hack, Jean-Louis Margolin and Karine Delaye (*Singapore from Temasek to the 21st Century*) that Singapore's past may have to be cast as a series of successive or concurrent disjointed histories.

To reconcile these narrative breaks, historians must connect two key scenarios in Singapore's past: autonomous societies and settlements on the one hand, and societies and settlements as part of larger entities on the other.

Autonomous societies in Singapore have occurred thrice thus far: during the Temasek period (late 13th to 14th centuries), the EIC Straits Settlement period (1819–58), and the post-independence era (1965 onwards). In all three periods, the societies were self-governing, exercised considerable economic independence, and determined the constitution of their membership.

By contrast, in all other periods, Singapore, its inhabitants and its waterways were framed as part of a larger entity: under the Melaka and Johor sultanates (15th to 17th centuries); as the fief of the Temenggong of the Straits of Singapore under the Riau-Lingga Sultanate (late 18th to early 19th centuries); as British Malaya's export gateway and administrative centre during colonial rule (1864–1963); and as a state under federal authority during the short-lived Greater Malaysia period (1963–65).

This view of Singapore's history highlights two critical counterpoints. With a past partly dominated by periods when it was subsumed under larger political entities, any historical narrative over the *longue durée* must accommodate this subordinate, even if at times ancillary, history. But by the same measure, the recognition that Singapore also experienced fairly regular autonomous periods suggests that it had a nation-state history prior to post-colonial independence.

By approaching Singapore's past as an oscillation between these two scenarios, we can cast a singular historical trajectory for Singapore, instead of a cycle of repetitions of the rise and fall of its fortunes, or as several discordant, unrelated histories. Importantly, this conjoined approach acknowledges that the periods when Singapore was part of a larger entity have a rightful place in the Singapore story and should be addressed frontally, instead of being footnoted within larger regional or international histories.

A third challenge remains: the gaps in Singapore's settlement records. While Singapore's history may have begun in the late 13th century, it is not the absence of any settlement prior to that, but the absence of historically worthy evidence of any settlement that is the key determinant of this starting point. Similarly, from the 15th century onwards, Singapore's habitation history enters the Dark Ages, when settlement records range from scarce to none. Borschberg points out that while this era's records, including European accounts and cartography, mention extant settlements cursorily, no detailed description animates them.

This does not mean that Singapore's past consequently paled before regional and global history. Significant geopolitical changes in the western Java Sea, Straits of Melaka and the southern Gulf of Siam, as well as strategic maritime contests between European powers and Southeast Asian kingdoms, occurred between the 16th and early 19th centuries. Southeast and East Asia also felt the impact of geostrategic and economic rivalry and armed conflict in Europe and the Middle East.

And, as Heng has argued, between the late first and second millennia AD, significant economic and geopolitical developments began in Southeast Asia and the Melaka Straits from at least the late 7th century with the rise of thalassocratic Sriwijaya, which lasted 600 years. These developments may be superimposed upon larger maritime Asian developments, including the rise and naval expansion of the South Asian Chola dynasty (late 10th to early 11th centuries), Song China (late 10th century) and the accompanying development of Chinese maritime trade and shipping (11th to 13th centuries). The latter period also witnessed the rise and fall of powerful eastern Java states, including Kediri, Singhasari and Majapahit. Singapore and the waters around it, located at the nexus of the Java Sea, the South China Sea and the Bay of Bengal, would have experienced – and were likely a part of – these developments, even as the island seemed to have no significant settlement then.

For the past 10 years, historians have sought to integrate these periods of sparse settlement into Singapore's past. Borschberg's original work in processing hitherto unknown textual accounts and maps about Singapore between the 16th and 18th centuries offers a "strategic location/contested space" approach. He suggests framing Singapore's past as a series of confluences and conflicts playing out in the waters around the island as well as on the island itself. Singapore's history and its surrounding waterways, he suggests, do not necessarily require the presence of human agency as a critical factor.

In this regard, Singapore's history may be understood as an account based on the evidence of cultural influences, economic flows of goods and logistics networks, and strategic considerations with respect to military installations and naval conflicts around the geographical space of Singapore. The resulting human experiences may thus be viewed as "evental" outcomes rather than prime causes (*prima causa*). These approaches collectively premise a way by which Singapore's past may be rationalised historically in its multiple layers and complexities.

### Fresh Sources

These varied methods of casting the Singapore story are possible because of the breadth of sources of historical information available today. While archives were the only historical source in the 1970s, the range of sources has since broadened to include four key sets: textual and archival materials, archaeological finds and data, cartographic materials, and scientific data.

Textual and archival materials have been the dominant historical source of information. Traditionally, the archives of the British were the vanguard of information on the modern era of Singapore's history, even as some pre-1819 information surfaced occasionally. Over the past two decades, materials on Singapore's history before 1819 have been discovered in Portuguese, Spanish and Dutch archives. These caches have been instrumental in illuminating largely unknown experiences, particularly between the 16th and late 18th centuries. Finally, over the past decade, declassified US records, particularly by the State Department, have offered fresh information on Singapore's post-World War II era.

While archives have provided the informational mother lode for recrafting structural histories or histories from the state's perspective, there have been, since the 1990s, concerted efforts at using other types of written materials to illuminate Singapore's history from the societal perspective. Histories of the interstices, sociocultural histories, and histories of marginalised groups have emerged through the use of more grassroots sources. These include newspapers, many of which were owned by individuals or interest groups and addressed specific audiences.

Other sources include coroners' records, which reveal details on the lives of the destitute and working classes in colonial Singapore, and literary products, including those of the Singapore Peranakan community. Lastly, oral interviews have played a significant role in gathering information about ordinary people in more recent times. These include grassroots experiences of World War II, migratory and economic experiences of the early 20th century, and social experiences of the post-war and post-independence years.

One group of writings has been gaining stature as historical source material. These encompass pre-19th-century regional texts, including codified volumes like the *Sejarah Melayu* and *Hikayat Hang Tuah*, as well as modern-era accounts. Previously, these were regarded by historians as unviable historical documents because of their unproven veracity and their interlacing of fantastical stories. Today, these texts are used as a portal into the indigenous or local perspectives of historical events occurring in and around Singapore, particularly from a cultural viewpoint. Even 19th-century texts such as the *Hikayat Abdullah* and *Tuhfat al-Nafis* offer indigenous counterpoints to contemporaneous European accounts. In this regard, such literary sources have allowed historians to gain local perspectives and reconstruct the indigenous zeitgeist that may have surrounded key events.

Archaeological research constitutes the second set of historical sources. While archaeological finds were sporadic between the 19th and early

20th centuries, archaeology has now become an established field of historical research since taking off in the 1980s. Much of the research in the 1980s and 1990s focused on Singapore's human history in the 14th century, primarily in the area encompassing Fort Canning Hill and the north bank of the Singapore River. Since the turn of the millennium, archaeological research into Singapore's colonial era has grown increasingly important, with excavations in downtown Singapore, the outskirts of colonial Singapore Town (including Adam Park, the Botanic Gardens and Tiong Bahru) and offshore islands like Pulau Ubin and Sentosa.

The recovered materials comprise small finds such as ceramics, small metal items, organic fauna remains, glass shards and beads; excavations of colonial period sites have also uncovered built forms. In all, they provide the raw material for generating data to help historians reconstruct at least three aspects of Singapore's past. First, they shine a light on Singapore's urban settlement history, including space usage and the location of different demographic groups. Second, the material cultural history of the inhabitants, including their economic activities and aesthetics, gains further definition. And third, the regional and international links maintained by the inhabitants can be inferred, based on the overseas sources from which these finds originated.

In the past decade, cartography has become a third and increasingly vital source, especially for periods when written records remain sparse and evidence of material culture absent. Maps can be challenging to process, requiring a competent grasp of the lens through which the subject (i.e., the place) was viewed, understood, interpreted and rendered graphically by the observer (i.e., the cartographer).

Maps provide three key types of data. First, as macro-level renderings of interlinked spaces, they encapsulate regional and global perspectives of a given space and the information their users considered important – for example, knowledge of waterways, ports and harbours for anchorage and trade, riverine access into inland areas, and economic products available from specific areas.

Second, maps with micro-level data related to space usage – such as cartographies of urban centres, or maps illustrating land ownership – provide a glimpse of the nature of cities and settlements. As multiple maps of the same spaces are made available, they provide a sense of the changes experienced by the inhabitants over time. Planning and architectural blueprints are also part of this set.

Third, we have maps relating to imaginations of space. In these maps, the size and location of land masses and islands, including empty spaces that have yet to be filled in, become the ground for the cartographer's subjective imagination, as well as sources of information for the cartographer to draw from. These are important because they reveal the map commissioners' perceptions of future challenges, their agendas in co-opting new spaces, and their ideas of optimum usage. They also illustrate the limits of the commissioners' knowledge, specifically regarding the level of habitation and the usage of space by the local residents, even as the outsiders may regard the same space as vacant or unused.

Scientific data, the fourth recent source, includes environmental data such as tree-ring records, which reveal historical changes in climate. It also includes landscape archaeological information, such as stratigraphic data from beach caves, which offers insights on the occurrence of tsunamis or major storms. Even from glacial ice cores, we are able to derive information on pollen activity levels, which in turn reflect the nature of world climate systems and their correlation with flora growth globally. This source is important as such data complements the geopolitical and sociocultural factors which historians previously held up as the primary factors for historicity. There is growing awareness that environmental facets converge with human factors to fundamentally affect the nature of human experience – in the past as well as in the present.

Together, these four groups of sources provide a firm base of knowledge from which a sophisticated history of Singapore may be constructed.

**About This Book**
The present volume details a chronological account of Singapore's history over the past 700 years and rests on the collective shoulders of the historians of the past six decades. It coalesces the most current scholarship available with the aim of demonstrating the correlation between Singapore's past, the extent of external influence on critical developments in Singapore and its surrounding maritime environment, and the impact of Singapore and its people externally.

The story is related in seven chapters, each narrating about 100 years of history. At first glance, this division seems simply chronologically convenient, but in fact it mirrors the major developments in Singapore and externally. In this regard, the chapters seek to locate Singapore's historical experiences regionally and globally, and to demonstrate that while there may be disjunctures, there are historical cords that bind Singapore's chronological account across seven centuries.

Chapter One explores Singapore's earliest known settlements and the conditions under which coastal land settlements arose in the riparian environment of maritime Southeast Asia during the first and early second millennia AD. The chapter reconstructs Temasek, Singapore's first historically recorded settlement, and examines the geopolitical and economic circumstances in maritime Asia that created the autonomous port-polity, the nature and composition of the urban settlement, and its political and social features. It concludes by looking at the factors leading to the end of Temasek's autonomy around the late 14th century, including environmental exigencies, geopolitical shifts in China, and the rise of regional powers in the Gulf of Siam littoral and Java.

Chapter Two situates Singapore within the Melaka Sultanate between the 15th and early 16th centuries. The chapter begins with Singapore's incorporation into the Melaka Sultanate as Singapore loses political autonomy in the face of the geopolitical manoeuvrings of regional powers – Siamese Ayutthaya and Javanese Majapahit – and an ascendant Ming China.

The chapter explores how Singapore's inhabitants, in particular the Orang Laut, became integrated as part of the larger Malay body politic, with leaders constituted in the Melakan court, while Singapore was relegated to being a lesser feeder port serving the Melaka emporium. In the process, the chapter tries to reconcile three major, yet seemingly contradictory, historical sources of information on the Melaka Straits, and Singapore's place in this historiographical conundrum.

Chapter Three takes up Singapore's history as the 16th century opens, after Melaka falls to the Portuguese in 1511 and with the Johor Sultanate succeeding Melaka. Singapore's history starts to assume a dual nature – within the context of the rivalry between Johor and Aceh for trade and political prestige in the Melaka Straits, and in relation to the emergent presence of the Portuguese-Spanish trading empire and the Dutch East India Company in Southeast Asia and across the South China Sea littoral.

The chapter describes Singapore's challenges as a base of the Shahbandar's collection centre within the nexus of the Johor Sultanate, and as home to a naval armada. As the East-West trade becomes increasingly integrated through state-sponsored Portuguese, Spanish and Dutch commercial networks, the waters around Singapore become increasingly important. At the same time, the frontiers of Western cartographic and navigational knowledge are systematically pushed forward. These developments culminate, as the 17th century begins, in intense conflict and competition in the waters around Singapore.

Chapter Four captures Singapore's geostrategic history as an arena of maritime conflict between European naval powers – Portugal, Spain and the Dutch Republic – and its role in European and global conflict, including the Eighty Years' War (1567–1648) and the Thirty Years' War (1618–48). The chapter describes the paradox of Singapore's increasingly strategic military attraction for European powers against the ebb tide of its human history. Cursory cartographic and fragmentary archaeological evidence from the early 17th century of the existence of a port on Singapore's southern coast gives way, by the mid-17th century, to the absence of recorded settlement activity – an absence that coincides with the discovery of Governor's Strait farther south of Singapore. Singapore's history pivots to a maritime narrative involving conflict and competition.

The century of conflict among the European powers and the Melaka Straits polities of Aceh and Johor results, by the early 18th century, in the recession of Spanish Philippines and the dimming of Portuguese-Spanish commercial and naval power in Southeast Asia. This century witnesses the rise of Batavia-based Dutch hegemony in the Indonesian Archipelago. The Johor court is riven by political divisions, which leads to the transfer of its capital to the Riau islands by the late 17th century. The consequent shift of maritime shipping networks from the southern end of the Melaka Straits farther south to the Sunda Straits–Riau-Lingga Archipelago nexus leads to Aceh's decline as a trading centre and the dilution of the strategic relevance of Singapore waters to international shipping and commerce.

Chapter Five recounts the overall decline of the Melaka Straits region, Dutch control in the Riau-Lingga Archipelago, and the regional context for the rivalry between the British and the Dutch in the early 19th century, on the cusp of Raffles' arrival in Singapore. Dutch hegemony takes hold in the Malay Archipelago, creating a flux within the Malay political world, while Britain rises in the Indian Ocean and seeks to establish a footing in the China trade with Lord Macartney's mission to the Qing court in 1793. Finally, the 19th century opens with European geopolitical rivalry projected through the Napoleonic Wars (1803–15).

Chapter Six begins with the founding of the EIC factory in Singapore in 1819, and traces Singapore's growth in three areas: its role as a port connected to the regional, East Asian and European trading worlds; the populating of Singapore, fed by the diasporic networks facilitated by British imperialism; and the island's rise as the British Empire's colonial administrative centre in the Far East. The chapter's conclusion considers Singapore's development as a centre of pan-Asian intellectualism, arising from its function as a critical node of the British Empire and its cosmopolitan migrant population.

Finally, Chapter Seven examines Singapore as Britain's Far East administrative centre, as well as its role as the international export gateway of the primary economy of the Malay Peninsula and north Borneo, as the 20th century arrives. The chapter analyses Singapore's challenges as the world undergoes regional and global nationalist movements, with the island experiencing the twists of economic globalisation, total war and ideological conflict. Through the course of the century, Singapore's society becomes embroiled in ideological polemics: loyalty to the empire versus nationalism, Western democratic values versus socialism, British-sanctioned decolonisation versus communalism. The chapter ends with Singapore redefining itself as a nation state and a centre of commerce, anchored in the region and connected to the maritime Asian and international economy.

Gold armlet and earrings recovered on Fort
Canning Hill in 1926. They were found at a
depth of 3 metres near the summit of the
hill, west of the Keramat Iskandar Shah. The
moulded face on the armlet is the demoniac
Kala, the "All-Destroyer", an epithet of
Siva and, more often, Yama, the god of
death. The decorative style is reminiscent
of Majapahit craftsmanship of the 14th
century. These ornaments may have been
lost or left behind by a resident of 14th-
century Fort Canning. They give an insight
into the religious beliefs and aesthetic
tastes of the time.

# CHAPTER ONE

# The 14th Century
## Advent of a "Great City"

The location of the place: it is connected to Longyamen. The hill in the rear is like a coiled headdress [i.e., a turban], truncated [i.e., terraced], rising to a concaved [i.e., two peaks] and plateaued peak. Hence, the people live around it. The fields are poor, and the cereals are sparse. The weather is not consistent. In summer, due to a lot of rain, it is a little cold. The customs and nature [of the people]: Their hair is short and worn down [i.e., not tied up]. Satin and brocade [are used] to wrap their heads, and red oil cloth to wrap their bodies. Sea water is boiled to produce salt. Rice is fermented to produce wine, which is called "mingjia". There is a tribal chief. The place produces top-quality hornbill casques, middle-quality lakawood and cotton. Goods used for trade are silk cloth, iron bars, local printed cloth, chi jin [lit., "red gold"], porcelain wares, iron cauldrons and the like.

Wang Dayuan, *Daoyi Zhilue*, c. 1349

### In the Beginning: The Kingdom on the Hill

Singapore's earliest history can be traced to the end of the 13th century, when a settlement emerged on the north bank of the Singapore River basin. Known in Chinese historical texts as Danmaxi (Temasek) and in indigenous Malay texts as Singapura, this settlement was a port-polity in that it possessed a port, was engaged in regional and international trade, and was administered by its own ruler.

To date, there is little evidence of settlement activities in Singapore prior to the late 13th century. Scholars such as Paul Wheatley, Roland Braddell and Hsu Yun-ts'iao have found some 24 possible references to Singapore in Chinese, Middle Eastern, South Asian and Southeast Asian texts. However, none of these references is definitive, even as they variously refer to the likelihood of a settlement located at the southern end of the Malay Peninsula, and to places sharing similar toponyms as the later settlement in Singapore.

Archaeologically, a very small body of material recovered from the islands near Singapore suggests that human habitation likely took place very early on. Lithic finds, including several stone tools, were found on Pulau Ubin and in the vicinity of Keppel Straits in the early 20th century, but apart from those, no finds have been recovered at any other site in Singapore. Habitation in Singapore, if it occurred, was likely to have been very sparse.

The absence of traces of settlement activities may be tied to the geography of maritime Southeast Asia and the resulting societies. Whereas land-based agrarian societies are typically identifiable through such physical remains as agricultural lands, hydrological works, and monumental, political and domestic architecture, sea-based societies on the other hand are much more elusive.

Societies that occupied the coastlines of such places as Singapore – with life taking place on vessels that were highly mobile, moving as the seasons changed, constantly in search of marine food supplies – would have left very little in the way of material deposits. With such a light footprint on the natural environment, such societies would be impossible to detect through scientific methods currently available. Mobility would also explain the absence of a human footprint, apart from the occasional ethnographic mention, in historical texts.

It was only when the coastal and land-based societies came together that a more "detectable" settlement pattern emerged. These riparian societies typically engaged in a combination of land-based activities – including port trade, domestic market trade, small-scale material processing, agriculture and architectural building – and sea-based activities, such as marine resource harvesting and shipping activities. Such settlements are therefore identifiable archaeologically.

That said, riparian settlements are still harder to detect than purely land-based settlements. Because of the absence of large-scale manipulation of the natural landscape, most of their physical remains are small finds, comprising material cultural deposits like ceramic sherds and metal items, and organic remains. Nevertheless, riparian settlements, being more permanent in their location, and situated at strategic points along the coastline of Southeast Asia, would have been more visible to – and hence noted and documented by – those traversing the region.

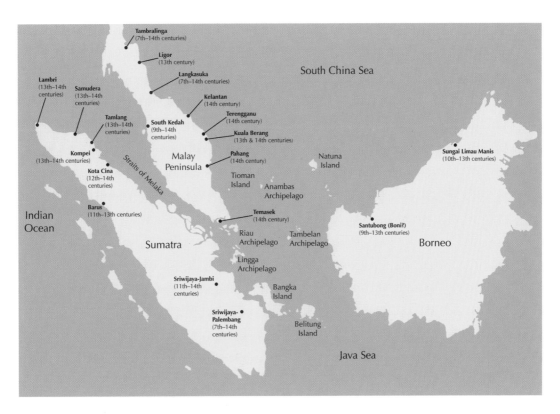

Such a riparian society emerged on the southern coast of Singapore, in the vicinity of the Singapore River basin, at the end of the 13th century. At the time, the Straits of Melaka – along with the Singapore Straits and the waters around the southeastern tip of the Malay Peninsula and the Riau Archipelago – constituted an important maritime highway for ships from the Indian Ocean, Southeast Asia and China. The numerous coastal societies that inhabited the coasts of these waterways would likely have been known to sailors and traders. However, it was only when a port-settlement appeared on the coastline that these navigators and traders began to take note of Singapore.

Map of port-settlements that existed in the Melaka Straits region during the 7th to 14th centuries. The locations of the port-settlements caused them to be oriented towards different major economic zones. Ports in the northern Straits region interacted primarily with the Indian Ocean market, while those in the southern Straits region interacted with the South China Sea and Java Sea markets.

### Singapore's First Land-based Settlement Emerges

Why did a port-settlement emerge in Singapore at the end of the 13th century? In the part of Southeast Asia where Singapore is located, the international economy that held sway involved primarily the Chinese landmass, Java, Sumatra and the Indian subcontinent.

Substantial economic, diplomatic and sociocultural interactions between the countries in these three areas took place throughout the first and early second millennia AD. Java and Sumatra, for example, periodically sent diplomatic missions to China, while Chinese pilgrims travelled to Southeast Asia and the Indian subcontinent in pursuit of Buddhist texts. Historical documents from China, South Asia, the Middle East and Southeast Asia provide vivid details of these interactions. Archaeological data from both shipwrecks and land settlements paint a rich picture of the material cultural exchanges and communication networks involved.

For much of the first millennium AD, right through to the end of the Tang dynasty (618–906), the Chinese court, through the state bureaucracy, dominated trade. Tribute missions, or state-level exchanges, constituted the main channel for the exchange of goods, with Guangzhou the key port of call where such activities were centred. The Chinese people themselves were not permitted to venture into Southeast Asia or the Indian Ocean to garner foreign products in a private capacity.

For the Malay region and the Melaka Straits, 7th-century Sriwijaya, a port-polity located on the southeast coast of Sumatra near present-day Palembang, became the regional hub for shipping and trade. The pre-eminent position of Sriwijaya's ports depended on the particular nature of maritime trade in the South China Sea and the Indian Ocean – one that was conducive to the establishment of a hegemonic economic, and therefore political, order in the Straits region.

Consequently, the international maritime trade necessitated the existence of a trans-shipment hub in the region to facilitate the exchange of goods between China and the Indian Ocean littoral. It was therefore natural that one main entrepôt port would emerge in the Melaka Straits region. The region's other ports subsumed themselves as feeder ports under this entrepôt port, servicing its economic needs.

Along with the establishment of a regional hub, this period saw the development of Southeast Asian shipping, which, along with other shipping networks, such as those from the Middle East, sought to trans-ship foreign products in high demand between the Chinese, South Asian, maritime Southeast Asian and Middle Eastern markets as a means of facilitating the international economic exchange.

The *Jewel of Muscat*. Built in Oman and gifted to Singapore in 2010, this vessel is a replica of a 9th-century Middle Eastern dhow, similar to one that sank off Belitung island in the Java Sea with its large cargo of Tang ceramics and other goods.

As the 10th century came to a close, however, the nature of Asia's maritime economy began to change dramatically. The ban on Chinese private maritime trade was gradually relaxed, starting from 972, such that by the 1070s, approximately two-thirds of the Chinese trade in foreign products imported into China had devolved into private hands. The Chinese market, as opposed to the Chinese state, now dictated the nature of demand for foreign products. While imports had previously consisted of relatively small volumes of high-quality and rare goods, such as frankincense, camphor and benzoin, the Chinese market was now able to project its mass consumption needs abroad. This resulted in a switch to low-quality and relatively cheap goods – including aromatic woods such as lakawood, and raw materials for furniture construction such as rattan – that were consumed in vast quantities. Southeast Asia became the most important source of these products.

Another major policy change – the one that had the greatest impact on the Melaka Straits region's ports – was the lifting of the long-standing ban on Chinese private shipping venturing abroad for trade. In 990 this ban was partially lifted, with the requirement for ships wanting to embark on a foreign journey having to register themselves at just three ports – Guangzhou, Hangzhou and Mingzhou (present-day Ningbo). Initially, Chinese maritime shipping did not expand significantly, and foreign shipping networks continued to carry the bulk of international trade to China's shores.

By the late 11th century, Song China had developed the technology to construct large oceangoing junks. These junks plied the routes between South China and maritime Southeast Asia, and by the 15th century they had reached as far as India and the east coast of Africa.

All this changed in 1090, when the Song court decreed that Chinese vessels were henceforth allowed to depart on overseas voyages from any prefecture along the Chinese coastline, so long as their departure was officially registered by the local administration, and a permit for the trip issued. Chinese international shipping boomed. Over the course of the next two centuries, Chinese ships came to dominate international shipping in the South China Sea, maritime Southeast Asia and, by the 14th century, the Bay of Bengal as well.

Concurrently, South India, under the Chola Kingdom, had begun to move aggressively across the Bay of Bengal into the Melaka Straits. Beginning in the 10th century, Tamil merchant guilds had established their presence in Sumatra, the Malay Peninsula and Java. In the early 11th century, presumably to bolster its position in the Straits, the Chola Kingdom launched a series of naval campaigns against the region's port-cities. Whereas previously the port-polities in the Melaka Straits would despatch ships to the Indian subcontinent to maintain trade with the kingdoms and ports there, these Indian states were now proactively entering Southeast Asia to trade as well as to draw the Melaka Straits port-polities into their orbit.

Taken together, by the 13th century, the need for a trans-shipment hub to act as the crossroads between the markets in the Indian Ocean and the South China Sea was no longer present. In such circumstances, the key port of Sriwijaya began to decline. At the same time, ports in the Melaka Straits began decoupling from

Sriwijaya's hierarchical structure and turned to pursue their economic and political fortunes independently. They began to hawk the produce of their immediate hinterlands to international traders and became known individually for very specific products.

With the collapse of Sriwijaya's capital in 1275, and the apparent availability of economic opportunities for the taking, new port-settlements began to mushroom in the late 13th and 14th centuries – at Aru, Sungei Bujang, Kelantan, Pahang, Terengganu, Brunei, Sarawak, Sabah and Pulau Tioman. It was at this juncture in history that Singapore's first port-settlement emerged.

### A Wealth of Historical Sources

Today, when we think of the pre-modern history of Singapore, there is a tendency to believe that historical information on the earliest port-settlement is sparse and sporadic. It would therefore surprise many that when the first British colonials arrived on the island, they did in fact register the presence of substantial urban remains. Stamford Raffles himself, having landed on 29 January 1819 as agent of the British East India Company (EIC), noted on 12 February:

> *The place in which I have fixed our Establishment is Singapour the ancient Capital of the Malay Kings and the Rival of the great State of Menangkabau in Sumatra.*

Raffles was acknowledging not only the remains that were present, but also the historical legacy of the port-settlement that had been eulogised in such important Malay historical texts as the *Sejarah Melayu*, or *Malay Annals*. Of the earliest colonial-era sources of information, the most detailed is the travelogue of John Crawfurd, Singapore's second Resident (1823–26). The travelogue provides an account of pre-19th-century urban remains on the north bank of the Singapore River, including building remains and small finds on Fort Canning Hill, a freshwater rivulet, a dry moat and an earth rampart. The travelogue also describes a 3-metre-tall sandstone boulder at the eastern tip of the river's south bank – commonly known as the Singapore Stone – which bore a lengthy inscription in a language that Crawfurd was unable to identify with certainty.

Unfortunately, almost all of these remains were destroyed by the British town planners. The bricks from the remains on Fort Canning Hill were dismantled and used to construct the first governor's

Fragment of the large boulder (estimated to be about 3 metres tall, 60–150 centimetres thick and 2.7 metres in length) that once stood at the mouth of the Singapore River. An inscription of some 50 lines, in a script that has been identified as East Javanese, was engraved on the stone.

residence on the hill in 1822, while the earth rampart was demolished to make way for the northward sprawl of the town within the first 10 years of the EIC settlement's founding. In 1848, one of the most devastating losses of these pre-modern remains occurred when British engineers, who were clearing the site to build a fortified position, demolished the inscribed boulder. Three fragments of the boulder were eventually recovered by the British, of which only one is presently extant.

Apart from colonial-era accounts, two other categories of historical data provide us with information on the earliest documented settlements in Singapore. The first pertains to historical documents. The Vietnamese annals indicate that in 1330, Malay envoys were despatched by a kingdom called Sach-ma-tich (Temasek) to the Vietnamese court, and were received by a prince who could speak the native language of the Malays. The *Yuanshi* (Official History of the Yuan Dynasty, c. 1370) mentions a mission being sent to Longyamen in the 1320s to procure tame elephants for the Mongol court. The *Nagarakatagama*, a Javanese court poem composed in 1365, mentions Temasek in a list of vassals under Majapahit, the kingdom and regional power that was located in Java during the 14th century. Another poem, the 16th-century *Pararaton*, which recounts events purported to have taken place at the courts of Singhasari and Majapahit, describes Temasek as one of the petty kingdoms that Gajah Mada, a prime minister of the 14th century, had taken an oath to conquer.

Two texts stand out. The *Daoyi Zhilue* (c. 1349) by Wang Dayuan, who travelled in Southeast Asia during the 14th century, describes the settlements, inhabitants and items traded at every location he visited in the Malay region. According to Wang, there were two trading settlements in Singapore – one named Banzu, located on and around Fort Canning Hill, and the other named Longyamen (proposed by historians to have been located at present-day Keppel Straits) – that were apparently linked. His descriptions provide information on the politics of the settlements, as well as the nature of habitation on the slopes of Fort Canning Hill.

The other key text, the *Malay Annals*, is a 17th-century Malay text comprising a series of loosely linked episodes and anecdotes about the Melaka court and its continuation in the Johor court. Temasek is recounted in the first six chapters as the precursor of the Melaka Sultanate. The account begins with the arrival of a Malay prince named Sri Tri Buana (also known as Sang Nila Utama) from Palembang, who, after encountering a magnificent creature, founds a port-city on the island and names it Singapura. The text then narrates the reign of the four succeeding rulers, covering Singapura's international relations, its rivalry with the kingdoms of the Bay of Bengal, the Melaka Straits and the western Java Sea, and anecdotal stories such as the erecting of a stone memorial at the mouth of the Singapore River.

The other category of sources that historians have drawn on is archaeological data. Some of the earliest archaeological finds in Singapore emerged in the early 20th century. In 1926, a cache of gold jewellery was found while a hole for a septic tank was being dug on the north slope of Fort Canning Hill near the summit. Richard Winstedt, a noted colonial scholar of Malay history and literature, identified the style of the jewellery as being of Majapahit origin. Unfortunately, no attempt was made to establish their archaeological context or to extract information from the site.

Archaeological research on Singapore's early history started only in 1984, when archaeologist John N. Miksic, at the invitation of the National Museum, conducted a limited excavation to ascertain the historicity of texts such as the *Malay Annals* and *Daoyi Zhilue*. The artefacts recovered from this first excavation, on the east slope of Fort Canning Hill near the Keramat Iskandar Shah, pointed to the existence of a late-13th to 14th-century settlement on the hill. More than 10 excavations have since followed in the area bounded by the north bank of the Singapore River basin, Fort Canning Hill and Stamford Road. The archaeological remains, though consisting entirely of small finds, demonstrate that a vibrant port-city existed in this area from the end of the 13th through the 14th centuries, with the settlement continuing into the 16th century.

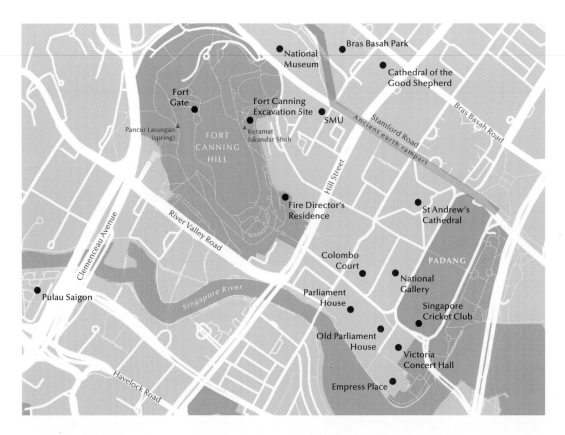

At least 10 large-scale excavations have been conducted in downtown Singapore. They have yielded materials from as early as the late 13th century.

Collectively, the colonial period accounts, pre-colonial historical documents and archaeological research over the last four decades allow us to piece together a cogent and sophisticated reconstruction of the port-settlement on the north bank of the Singapore River basin during the 14th century.

The history of the Melaka Straits region in the classical period is characterised by a remarkable sense of continuity, from the advent of Sriwijaya as a regional polity until the end of the Melaka Sultanate in 1511. As the first Malay emporium in the region, Sriwijaya with its capital in Palembang appears to have been a reference point for the political, social and economic culture of the region's polities in subsequent centuries. Up-and-coming polities tended to take their cue from bigger and more important Malay centres.

As such, the physical features, society and culture of Singapore's 14th-century port-settlement would most likely have been cast in the mould of a classical Malay port-city. Another important similarity was in the choice of locations for these settlements, where the requisite features included a hill, a foothill plain and a river drainage. These features provided for the two major spaces within a Malay port-city – the ritual and political centre, and the main settlement area.

### The Palace on the Hill

At the core of a Malay port-city was the ritual-political centre, which was also the kingdom's cosmological centre. The physical characteristics of such a space in pre-Islamic times had to replicate Mount Meru, the centre of Hindu-Buddhist cosmology. In Southeast Asian cultures, this was generally achieved through the construction of man-made temple pyramids or raised terraced platforms, such as the ones in Angkor, Cambodia, and the temple complexes at Prambanan, Java. In the Melaka Straits region, the scarcity of manpower limited the construction of such massive projects. Instead, natural geographical features such as hills were often used to replicate Mount Meru for siting the polity's ritual centre and palace precinct. Examples of such hills include Bukit Seguntang in Palembang and St John's Hill in Melaka.

Archaeological data coupled with Crawfurd's account suggest that the whole of Fort Canning Hill formed the ritual centre and palace precinct of Temasek. The spaces on the hill were used for various different purposes. Firstly, there appears to have been an artisans' quarter. Excavations conducted in 1984 and 1988 on the lower east slope of the hill, near the present location of the Keramat Iskandar Shah, revealed an area with a high concentration of glass fragments, beads and ceramic moulds that appear to have been used in the production of glass bangles, as well as resin that was

Glass fragments (*below left*) appear to have been melted down and used in the production of glass beads (*below*) and bangles on the lower east slope of Fort Canning Hill.

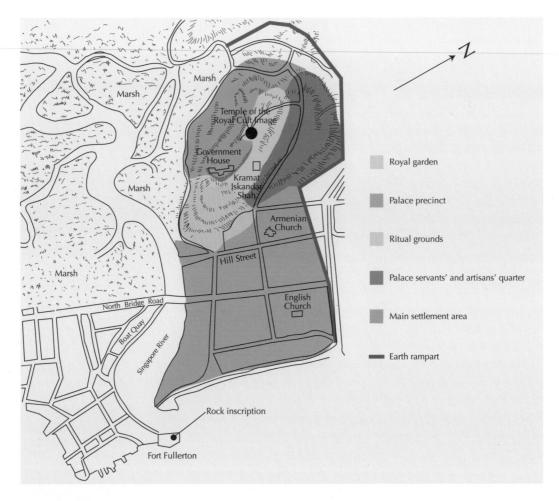

Royal garden

Palace precinct

Ritual grounds

Palace servants' and artisans' quarter

Main settlement area

Earth rampart

A hypothetical reconstruction of the layout and usage of spaces in the Temasek settlement in the late 13th and 14th centuries. It is based on information from Malay and Chinese classical texts, colonial accounts and maps of the early 19th century, as well as archaeological research conducted since 1984. The reconstruction is superimposed on a map of Singapore drawn in the 1830s.

used for starting fires. These finds suggest that glass-making activities took place in this area, together with, quite possibly, other artisan activities such as jewellery-making.

The location of the artisans' quarter here makes topographical sense, as the east slope presented the easiest way for the inhabitants on the north bank of the Singapore River to approach and ascend the hill. Such ease of access would have facilitated the employment of inhabitants in the artisans' quarter.

This route would also have given inhabitants open access to the ritual grounds. As Crawfurd noted, the greater parts of the north and east slopes were covered by the remains of building foundations, including a number that were constructed of baked bricks. These foundations probably belonged to structures of religious significance, given that non-perishable building materials were only used for such buildings as temples, sanctuaries and tombs. The absence of a deliberate layout of these buildings suggests that they were likely erected over time, and in an organic fashion, as communal acts of merit-making, rather than as a planned socio-political project.

According to Crawfurd, the passage through the area of religious buildings eventually led to a terrace on the northern slope near the summit of the hill. This terrace was the site of the most impressive of the building platforms still extant in 1822 when he visited. Measuring approximately 12 metres on each side and constructed of sandstone, the platform had several post-holes, presumably to hold up the pillars supporting a superstructure that towered over the platform. This structure could well have been a thatched *meru* – a multi-tiered roof structure that was fairly common throughout maritime Southeast Asia and similar to those depicted in the wall reliefs of such East Javanese temples as Candi Jago, Jawi, Surawana and Panataran.

The uniqueness of this building, its prominent position, and the presence of an enclosed space at its centre, suggest that it was likely a building of politico-religious significance. Could it have housed the cult image of the rulers of Temasek?

The *Malay Annals* records that the founder of Temasek, Sri Tri Buana, whose name is a Buddhist appellation meaning "Lord of the Three Worlds", was one who possessed the attributes of a *cakravatin* or "universal ruler", rode a white elephant and wore a crown studded with precious stones. Being the earthly manifestation of Avalokitesvara – the Bodhisattva of universal rule – it would have been imperative for Sri Tri Buana, having been newly settled in Singapura, to legitimise his rule by establishing the Mount Meru of his new universe. The elevated position of Fort Canning Hill would have made it a natural Mount Meru, while the cosmological centre would have been established through the consecration of the royal cult image at the summit. The inhabitants of the port-settlement could then ascend "Mount Meru" to pay obeisance to the sacred image of their ruler.

Apart from these accessible spaces, the hill would have also been the site of certain restricted zones. Two important ones – the royal garden and palace – would have been located on the south and west slopes of the hill. Gardens were was an integral feature of

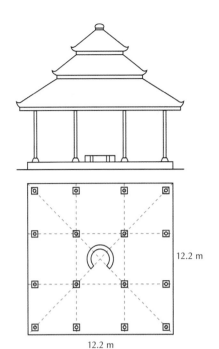

12.2 m

12.2 m

A hypothetical reconstruction of the main temple platform and superstructure, based on the description provided by John Crawfurd when he toured Fort Canning Hill in 1822. From Crawfurd's description, the base platform would resemble those discovered at the Padang Lawas site in Sumatra, and at Pengkalan Bujang and Sungei Mas in south Kedah. The architectural style of the superstructure could have been influenced by Javanese architectural forms of the 14th century.

Duku (*Lansium domesticum*), from the William Farquhar Collection of Natural History Drawings. Duku trees, among other fruit trees, were noted by both Crawfurd and Munshi Abdullah on the southern slope of Fort Canning Hill, supporting the possibility of the existence of a royal garden at that location in former times.

Malay palace precincts. A large number of fruit trees were noted on the lower reaches of the south slope of Fort Canning Hill in the early 1820s. Munshi Abdullah bin Abdul Kadir, a Malay scribe and translator for the EIC in Singapore in the 1820s and 1830s, recorded that there were such fruit trees as the durian, duku, lime, langsat, petai, jering and pomelo. Crawfurd also noted that the southern slope was forested with fruit trees of great size, albeit degenerated because of their old age.

With the likely location of the royal garden on the lower reaches of the south slope, the palace itself was most likely found on the upper south and west slopes of Fort Canning Hill. The higher of the two plateaus of Fort Canning Hill was located on the south side, and would have given the ruler of Temasek and his royal court a panoramic view of the port-settlement to the south, and vistas of the island in the other directions. The residences of the ruler's ministers and their retinue would also have been found in this area; in accordance with Malay political protocol, their locations would have reflected their relative position vis-à-vis the ruler.

The palace precinct was likely surrounded by a perimeter defence structure, much like the royal residences of Melaka, Aceh and Jogjakarta. Not only did such a structure demarcate the space occupied by the settlement's sociopolitical elite, it would also have offered them protection. The *Daoyi Zhilue* notes that when the settlement was besieged by the Tai people (likely from Sukothai), the inhabitants of Temasek defended themselves by staying within a fenced area of the settlement. A similar defensive tactic is described in the *Malay Annals*, where a siege by Majapahit forces was only overcome by the inhabitants shutting the city gates and remaining within the fortified area of the settlement.

### People of the Plain

The plain below Fort Canning Hill, on the north bank of the Singapore River, was the location of the main settlement. While no urban architectural remains are left of the settlement today, a number of features of this urban space may be gleaned from the *Malay Annals*. These include streets formed by houses on either side, markets where commerce took place, and a perimeter wall, with gates, that enclosed the settlement and protected it from external threats. In addition, there was a harbour for maritime trade, the entrance to which was protected by a chain boom stretched across the mouth of the river.

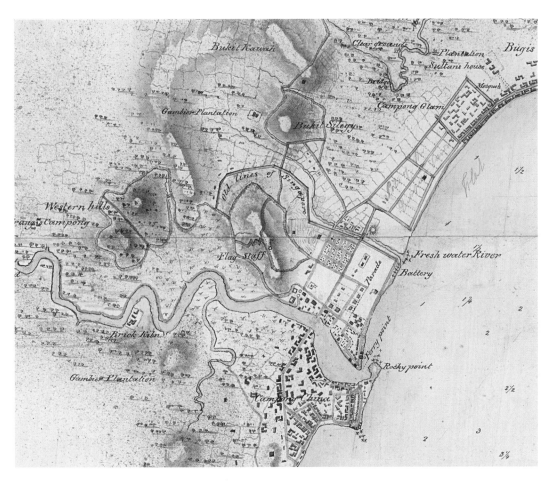

The only built forms that the early British accounts recorded were an earth rampart and moat that circumscribed a sizeable area of the north bank. Referred to as the "Old Malay Lines" or "Old Lines of Singapore", the rampart was approximately 5 metres wide at its base and 3 metres high. It began near the coastline, following the course of present-day Stamford Road, and as it reached the foot of Fort Canning Hill, it circumvented the foot of the hill before eventually ending at the salt marshes at the northwestern foot of the hill. The rampart was bordered by a rivulet, but where the rampart circumvented the hill and moved along a higher elevation, the rivulet continued along the course of the rampart in the form of a dry moat.

If the rampart and moat are taken to have demarcated the extent of the settlement area, the total land area would have been approximately 74 hectares, with the plain area accounting for roughly 54 hectares. The supposition that the settlement ended at

Several features that may be dated to the Temasek period of Singapore's history were recorded in an 1825 map. These include the "Old Lines of Singapore", denoting the earth rampart, and the "Fresh Water River", denoting the moat that ran alongside it.

the rampart is supported by archaeological research – Temasek-period artefacts unearthed thus far have been found exclusively within this space, and none beyond.

In the absence of textual information on the plain area, archaeological information presents itself as the most important set of data for our understanding of the activities that took place in this part of the settlement. Approximately 10 tons of materials have been recovered over three decades of excavations. While the bulk of the finds remain to be analysed, small samples from several sites – notably the St Andrew's Cathedral site (2004), Empress Place site (1998), Old Parliament House site (2002) and Singapore Cricket Club site (2003) – have been classified, with quantitative data accompanying them.

Ceramic sherds form the largest group of finds, and can be divided into three general categories: earthenware, coarse stoneware, and fine stoneware and porcelain. The earthenware used by the Temasek inhabitants was most likely made locally, with some also imported from maritime Southeast Asia, including Sumatra and Java. These imports may have included water containers and cooking pots – common earthenware forms produced by maritime Southeast Asian cultures.

The coarse stoneware ceramics, on the other hand, were all imported, and they provide information on the culinary activities that took place in the port-settlement. Highly vitrified vessels, such as small-mouthed jars from Fujian kilns and bottles from Jiangsu kilns, had clay bodies that were impervious to liquids and would therefore have been used to contain such items as wine and sauces. Buff ceramics, produced primarily by kilns in Guangdong, were heavily potted with clay that contained minimal grit and inclusions; these robust jars would have been used to carry wet foodstuffs and items of relatively high densities, including preserved foods. Buff ceramics also included mortars and basins, which would have been used as food preparation equipment.

Large, thinly potted storage jars, primarily the products of South Fujian kilns, would have been used to carry items of fairly low densities, such as dehydrated plant-based foodstuffs. A small number of the jars recovered were products of the Sukothai kilns of Thailand, dating to around the 15th century. These jars, as evidenced by the remains of shipwrecks in Southeast Asia, such as

the Belitung (early 9th century), Pulau Buaya (early 12th century) and Turiang (late 14th century) wrecks, were used to store foodstuffs and carry small fragile items such as fine ceramics.

Finally, the fine stoneware and porcelain found in the settlement were entirely of Chinese origin. These included white ware (*shufu*, *qingbai* and Dehua), green ware (including celadon-glazed ware) and blue-and-white ceramics, and were mostly the products of provincial kilns in Guangdong and Fujian, although a sizeable proportion originated from well-known kilns in Zhejiang, Fujian and Jiangsu. Blue-and-white porcelain, arguably the most expensive type of ceramics produced in China during the 14th century, constitute only a tiny fraction of this type of find, while green ware form the majority. The main forms of all three types of fine stoneware and porcelain were bowls and dishes, although some rare forms like stem-cups, ladles and jarlets have also been recovered, primarily on Fort Canning Hill.

The fine stoneware ceramics provide insight into the material consumption patterns and aesthetic tastes of Temasek's inhabitants. Among the more unique finds are large celadon platters that were exported to West Asia, small figurines such as Bodhisattvas in *qingbai* glaze, and white-glazed figurines of a couple in a copulating position, mounted on the inside of a small ceramic box.

Apart from ceramics, a number of metal finds have also been recovered, including copper prills (a copper processing by-product) and

(*Above left*) Fragments of a celadon platter, produced in the Longquan kilns of Zhejiang province, China. Items such as these were in great demand in Southeast Asia and West Asia.

(*Above*) A *qingbai* figure of a Bodhisattva in repose, with the head missing. A number of these figures were recovered during a 2015 excavation at Empress Place, suggesting that Buddhism may have been practised by the people of Temasek and its trading partners.

(*Above*) Fragment of an underglazed blue-and-white porcelain stem-cup excavated on Fort Canning Hill.

(*Above centre and right*) A complete example of a similar stem-cup produced at Jingdezhen during the Yuan dynasty. This not only provides evidence of the extensive trade between Temasek and Yuan China, but also supports the conclusion that the residents of Fort Canning Hill could afford to import some of the finer ceramic products being made in China.

hooks, iron slag, gold fragments and a silver priest's bell – all at the New Parliament House excavation site. At the Empress Place site, a bronze spear point and a lead figurine of a rider on horseback, most likely of Javanese origin, have been recovered.

The variations in the quantities of these finds at different locations tell us several things about land usage in the plain area of Temasek. First, it is likely that different activities were concentrated at specific areas. For example, the proportion of coarse stoneware ceramics relative to the overall quantities of finds was highest at the Empress Place site, suggesting that this was where imported goods were typically brought ashore or traded. Similarly, the recovery of copper items and iron slag at the New Parliament House site – and nowhere else – suggests a concentration of metal-working activities there.

Finally, the highest concentration of Chinese copper coin finds occurs at the Empress Place site, followed by the New Parliament House, the National Gallery and the Singapore Cricket Club sites, suggesting that activities related to the usage of Chinese copper coins and other coinages, including those from Sri Lanka and Java, primarily occurred in this part of the settlement, with the likelihood of a market located in this area.

The variations point to cultural and possibly demographic differences between the groups that occupied the various parts of the settlement. For example, the quantity of small-mouthed jar sherds as a proportion of the total quantity of coarse stoneware finds excavated is uniquely low at the Empress Place site, while the proportion of such jar sherds recovered at the Old Parliament

House site and at the St Andrew's Cathedral site are higher and similar to each other. The proportion of such sherds recovered at Fort Canning Hill is even higher – double that found at the Old Parliament House and St Andrew's Cathedral sites.

This information suggests that the inhabitants occupying the river bank near the mouth of the Singapore River consumed significantly less of the liquids that these jars held, including alcohol, than did the inhabitants of the upper reaches of the river bank or the foot plains at St Andrew's Cathedral. In the same vein, the occupants of the hill likely consumed substantially more of these liquids than anyone else in the settlement.

An example of a small-mouthed jar. A large number of these jars were recovered from the grounds of the Old Parliament House in 2002, suggesting that the location was designated as the commercial district of the Temasek settlement.

Similarly, the proportion of buff ceramics, which were used in the preparatory stages of culinary production (including washing, grinding and mincing, and the use of wet foodstuffs), is highest at the St Andrew's Cathedral site, and lowest at Fort Canning Hill, with the proportions at the river bank sites somewhere in the middle.

This suggests that the occupants of the foot plains at St Andrew's Cathedral were likely heavily engaged in culinary activities, possibly even servicing the culinary needs of the Fort Canning Hill occupants. Thus, the inhabitants of the area around St Andrew's Cathedral and those on Fort Canning Hill may have been closely connected in their economic co-dependency, while the occupants along the river bank were likely distinct, even as they were part of the Temasek settlement. The occupants of Fort Canning Hill were also likely to have occupied a more elite position, given that the material evidence for such mundane activities as cooking was proportionally lower, and the density of finds on the hill is also significantly less. There were, overall, fewer people occupying Fort Canning Hill than the plain area and river bank.

### Agriculture and Food

The archaeological finds suggest that the inhabitants of Temasek led a materially rich existence. Most of the archaeological remains originate from imported items and only a small proportion comes from local products. This is likely to have applied to the settlement's food supplies too.

The Melaka Sultanate – and the Johor Sultanate that succeeded it – has generally been taken as the model for food sustainability in the region. While Melaka's hinterland yielded produce such as fruits and possibly some cereal staples, the supply would have been insufficient to sustain the city's approximate population of 10,000 to 30,000 inhabitants. Melaka used its port connections to bring in rice from regional sources such as Thailand and Java. The population of Temasek, given a settlement area of about 74 hectares, could have numbered around 500 to 2,000, similar to that of Melaka in the first decade after its founding in 1405. Because Temasek has traditionally been studied in the framework of a Malay port-city, it has always been assumed that the bulk of its food supplies was imported. But given that the ability to ensure a sustainable food supply would have been important to the survival and well-being of its inhabitants, could Temasek have assigned some of its land to agriculture?

One of the settlement's most notable built features was the moat that stretched for about 1 kilometre from the shoreline, running along what would be the eastern fringe of the Padang in a southeast-to-northwest direction, before extending farther northwest between Mount Sophia, Selegie Hill and the present Istana grounds on one side and Fort Canning Hill on the other.

Maps of Singapore of the early 1820s, as well as Captain Daniel Ross' 1819 drawings of the coastline, show the moat as a freshwater stream. It appears to have been constructed as a catchment, drawing water from the hills in the vicinity. This would have been similar to the moated irrigation systems built in the Gulf of Siam and central Thailand in the first and early second millennia AD, such as at Satingpra, Nakhon Si Thammarat, U Thong and Nakhon Pathom. The availability of water would have enabled Temasek's inhabitants to develop a more concerted and intentional agricultural base than merely the incidental cultivation of fruit and vegetable gardens.

The soil in the area bounded by Stamford Road and Bras Basah Road would have been ideal for rice cultivation. Paleo-geological research has revealed that clay, with substantial organic material likely derived from an ancient mangrove swamp, formed the soil stratification of the land in that area, making it similar to such coastal locations as Kelantan, Terengganu, Nakhon Si Thammarat and Satingpra that supported rice planting. In fact, cereal production was alluded to by such visitors as Wang Dayuan, who noted that the fields at Temasek, while not fertile, nonetheless showed

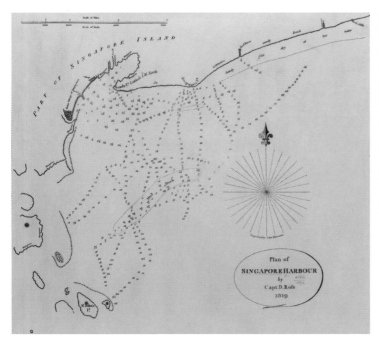

Captain Daniel Ross' "Plan of Singapore Harbour, 1819" (*left, and detail above*) shows the moat as a freshwater stream.

similar productivity levels to those he saw at Langkasuka (Patani, Thailand), Kelantan and Terengganu.

Other built structures point to efforts by Temasek's inhabitants to develop and maintain arable lands. The earth rampart has been postulated to be part of a defensive feature; however, as an earthwork, the stretch bordering the northeast foothill of Fort Canning Hill, which corresponds to the side with the gentlest grade, would have had the effect of stemming systemic soil erosion while enhancing ground moisture retention. This would be similar to the soil-retention techniques used at settlements such as Khao Sam Kheo (east Isthmus of Kra, early first millennium) and Si Pamutung (north Sumatra, 14th to 19th centuries). Apart from creating an area suitable for buildings to be erected, it would have supported agriculture as well.

**Open and Connected: Cosmopolitanism and Cultural Influences**
Archaeological finds point to a cosmopolitan society in Temasek. The general characteristics of its imported material culture were shared by the port-cities of the Malay region during this pre-Islamic period. At such settlements as Sungei Mas, Pengkalan Bujang and Kota Cina, for example, the earthenware ceramics used by the inhabitants were mostly produced locally, with a small proportion imported from nearby production centres. In the case of Temasek,

Earthenware sherds recovered from the Empress Place site in Singapore. Their presence in the Temasek settlement suggests social, economic and cultural links with the other population centres in maritime Southeast Asia, including Sumatra, Java and Borneo.

they were sourced from north Sumatra, north Borneo and the Gulf of Siam littoral.

As for the stoneware ceramics used by Temasek's inhabitants, these were mostly imported from China. Items that were not readily produced within the Malay region were sourced from the economies of the extended economic spheres towards which the settlements of the Melaka Straits were most inclined. A similar consumption pattern may be noted at Kota Cina and south Kedah, where imported ceramics were similarly recovered, the majority of which were sourced from the Bay of Bengal littoral. In this regard, Temasek fell within the South China Sea littoral economic sphere, which included the mainland Southeast Asian states and South China. Notable South Chinese trading ports with which Temasek maintained commercial links included Guangzhou, Quanzhou, and to a lesser extent, Hangzhou.

The use of imported food ingredients suggests that the inhabitants' culinary consumption patterns may have been influenced to some extent by foreign cultures. This would have led to a diversity of culinary traditions, and possibly the formation of a hybridised culinary culture over time. Again, judging from the ceramic remains, the primary source of these ingredients used in Temasek was South China.

In terms of its spatial layout and built forms, while Temasek likely bore the typical attributes of a regional city of the classical Malay period, there are hints of other possible sources of influence. The brick building foundations on the north side of Fort Canning Hill, for example, may have been inspired by architectural practices from farther afield. Crawfurd noted that the brick bases did not appear to have any order to them, suggesting a series of building projects that took place organically over a long period of time, using locally available building materials. In terms of the possible external influences, the geographical distribution of brick foundations, absent of a superstructure, may primarily be seen at places such as Si Pamutung, south Kedah, Takuapa (southwest Thailand), and the east coast of the Isthmus of Kra.

However, the practice of building individual religious structures over a long period of time, often reflecting communal acts of merit-making, stands in contrast to singular building projects to create a cosmological setting, which would have been politically motivated. The former practice has similarities with cultural traditions in Southeast Asia that adhered to Theravada Buddhism, including Bagan (modern-day Myanmar), sites of the Dvaravati tradition in south and central Thailand, and sites along the Isthmus of Kra in the first half of the second millennium AD. In other words, the Temasek inhabitants' practice of building religious structures may have been drawn from two regional sources, not merely one.

The earth rampart and accompanying moat, too, may owe their existence to mainland Southeast Asian influence. As a defensive feature, earth ramparts only began to be built in the Malay region during the late 15th century; prior to that, ramparts were only built as part of religious complexes, such as the 7th-century site of Kota Kapur (Bangka Island, Indonesia), and were characterised by symmetrical forms.

Irregularly shaped ramparts dating to the 14th century and before, like the one at Singapore, are primarily found in the Gulf of Siam littoral, where they possibly served as soil retention and water catchment features. These include Khao Sam Kheo (early first millennium); major Dvaravati urban centres such as U Thong and Nakhon Pathom (mid- to late first millennium); and Isthmus of Kra sites such as Tambralinga (Nakhon Si Thammarat) and Langkasuka (Patani) in the second millennium.

In the Melaka Straits region, only Si Pamutung has an earth rampart possibly constructed for flood prevention purposes, although

## Earth Embankment

The largest man-made structure of the settlement was an earth embankment that began at the coastline, followed the course of present-day Stamford Road, and as it reached Fort Canning Hill, circumvented the base of the hill, eventually ending at the salt marshes along the Singapore River. Approximately 5 metres wide at its base and 3 metres high, the embankment was likely a hydrological feature. It enabled fresh water from the catchment areas comprising present-day Orchard Road and Selegie Hill to be collected into a moat or freshwater stream (present-day Stamford Canal). It also served as a soil retention feature, minimising soil erosion on the east slope of Fort Canning Hill. A possible secondary function of the embankment was as a defensive wall to protect the settlement from external threats.

Servants' quarter

Artisans' quarter

mple

## Perimeter Fence

The palace precinct was likely surrounded by a perimeter defence structure, much like the royal residences of Melaka, Aceh and Jogjakarta. Not only did such a structure demarcate the space occupied by the settlement's sociopolitical elite, it would also have offered them protection.

Royal residence

Royal garden

## Royal Garden

A garden was an integral feature of Malay palace precincts. A large number of fruit trees were noted on the lower reaches of the south slope of Fort Canning Hill in the early 1820s. Munshi Abdullah recorded that there were such trees as the durian, duku, lime, langsat, petai, jering and pomelo. Crawfurd also noted that this slope was forested with fruit trees of great size, albeit degenerated because of their old age.

# Singapore 700 Years Ago: A Reconstruction

In the 14th century, a thriving port-settlement was located in the area comprising the north bank of the Singapore River and present-day Fort Canning Hill. Historical accounts and important archaeological discoveries have shed light on the physical features, economic activities and social nature of this settlement, enabling us to visualise what life in Singapore might have been like seven centuries ago.

## Artisans' Quarter

Archaeological discoveries on the lower east slope of the hill include a high concentration of glass fragments, beads, ceramic moulds and resins, indicating that glass-related activities probably took place here. The location of the artisans' quarter here makes topographical sense, as the east slope presented the easiest way for the inhabitants of the plain to approach and ascend the hill.

Dry moat

Earth embankment

## Temple

According to Crawfurd, the north and east slopes of the hill were littered with a number of brick building platforms. On the north plateau stood the most impressive of these, a square platform measuring 12 metres on each side, with post-holes along its perimeter and a circular enclosure at its centre. The uniqueness of this building and its prominent location suggest that it was likely of politico-religious significance to the settlement's inhabitants.

## Royal Bath

A royal bath is believed to have been located on the western foot of the hill. An untitled map of Singapore Town from 1825 shows a freshwater spring at the northern part of the west slope; the bottom end of the spring would have been the probable location of the royal bath. It is likely that the bath was formed by a natural embankment helping to pool the water, and features such as trees or artificial structures might have helped conceal the bathing activities from unwelcome eyes.

Royal bath

## Royal Residence

A royal precinct was most likely located on the upper south and west slopes of Fort Canning Hill. Of the two plateaus of the hill, the south plateau was the higher, and would have accorded the ruler and his court a panoramic view of the port-settlement, the adjacent islands and the hinterland of Singapore. The residences of the ruler's ministers would also have been found in this area.

# The Kingdom on

There are several accounts of Singapore's first settlement on Fort Canning Hill from as early as the 1300s. But the most detailed account is found in John Crawfurd's travelogue published in 1828, *Journal of an Embassy from the Governor-General of India to the Courts of Siam and Cochin-China*. Crawfurd, who would later serve as the second Resident of Singapore, was on his way to Siam on a diplomatic mission in 1822 when he stopped over in Singapore for several days. He toured the newly founded English East India Company factory, and recorded all that he saw there. What Crawfurd observed has come to form one of the most crucial sources upon which all subsequent research and scholarship on Singapore, both historical and archaeological, have been based. (Note: Based on the known locations of the features on Fort Canning Hill, there is reason to believe that Crawfurd got some of his compass directions mixed up. The corrected directions are provided below where relevant.)

## 3 February 1822

*I walked this morning round the walls and limits of the ancient town of Singapore, for such in reality had been the site of our modern settlement. It was bounded to the east by the sea, to the north by a wall, and to the west by a salt creek or inlet of the sea. The inclosed space is a plain, ending in a hill of considerable extent, and a hundred and fifty feet in height. The whole is a kind of triangle, of which the base is the sea-side, about a mile in length. The wall, which is about sixteen feet in breadth at its base, and at present about eight or nine in height, runs very near a mile from the sea-coast to the base of the hill, until it meets a salt marsh. As long as it continues in the plain, it is skirted by a little rivulet running at the foot of it, and forming a kind of moat; and where it attains the elevated side of the hill, there are apparent the remains of a dry ditch. On the western side, which extends from the termination of the wall to the sea, the distance, like that of the northern side, is very near a mile. This last has the natural and strong defence of a salt marsh, overflown at high-water, and of a deep and broad creek. In the wall there are no traces of embrasures or loop-holes; and neither on the sea-side, nor on that skirted by the creek and marsh, is there any appearance whatever of artificial defences. We may conclude from these circumstances, that the works of Singapore were not intended against fire-arms, or an attack by sea; or that if the latter, the inhabitants considered themselves strong in their naval force, and therefore thought any other defences in that quarter superfluous.*

## 4 February 1822

*On the stony point which forms the western side of the entrance on the salt creek, on which the modern town of Singapore is building, there was discovered, two years ago, a tolerably hard block of sand-stone, with an inscription upon it. This I examined early this morning. The stone, in shape, is a rude mass, and formed of the one-half of a great nodule broken into two nearly equal parts by artificial means; for the two portions now face each other, separated at the base by a distance of not more than two feet and a half, and reclining opposite to each other at an angle of about forty degrees. It is upon the inner surface of the stone that the inscription is engraved. The workmanship is far ruder than any thing of the kind that I have seen in Java or India; and the writing, perhaps from time, in some degree, but more from the natural decomposition of the rock, so much obliterated as to be quite illegible as a composition. Here and there, however, a few letters seem distinct enough. The character is rather round than square. It is probably the Pali, or religious character used by the followers of Buddha,* the feature likely post-dates the 14th century. In this regard, the construction of the rampart and moat in Temasek may be a reflection of influences in agrarian land management practices originating from the Gulf of Siam littoral.

At the same time that Temasek society absorbed influences from the Gulf of Siam and the north Melaka Straits, a high culture exhibiting Javanese characteristics appears to have been consciously cultivated. This would have been part of Temasek's articulation of its position in the cultural, and possibly political, sphere of its neighbouring regional power, Majapahit.

Language would have been one of the aspects through which this was done. To begin with, the only evidence of writing in Temasek available to date is the inscription on the Singapore Stone. Located at the mouth of the Singapore River, the inscription would have been visible to all maritime traffic. The script appears to be a variant of Old Javanese, with a possible date of around the 10th to 12th centuries, or possibly Sanskrit, which was used in Sumatra up to the 12th century. Epigraphists have postulated that the script may represent a Javanese-inspired language that falls between the phases of Early Kawi (c. 925–1250) and Majapahit Kawi (c. 14th century). The absence of writing anywhere else in Temasek suggests that written language may have been used to demonstrate Temasek's place within the Javanese cultural sphere.

The decorated metal finds recovered in Temasek point towards the same possibility. The gold jewellery cache discovered on Fort Canning Hill exhibits motifs such as the Kala head and goose, which are reminiscent of Javanese decorative art up to the 15th century. Archaeologist P.V. van Stein Callenfels has suggested that these decorative icons mirror the best in 14th-century Javanese gold craftsmanship. These items appear to have been imported into Temasek, as evidence of local production has so far not been discovered.

Crucially, such motifs and decorative elements have not been found in any other artefacts recovered in Temasek, suggesting that they were never adopted as part of the local artisans' vocabulary. Instead, these items likely saw very selective use, which was tied to the functions of the demographic groups that inhabited the areas in which they were found. In regard to the gold jewellery, these were likely intended as displays of cultural affiliation with

### Agriculture

The freshwater stream or moat would have served as a source of irrigation. This makes it plausible that land to the northeast of the settlement (present-day Bras Basah) was used for intensive agriculture, especially as the soil here would have been suitable for rice cultivation. The stream would have also served as a defensive feature.

### The Settlement on the Plain

There would have been a substantial settlement population of 500–2000 people living on the plain on the north bank of the Singapore River and on the river basin. Their houses would have been elevated pole structures typical of dwellings in maritime Southeast Asia. Streets would have been no more than dirt tracks crisscrossing the habitation area, and it is likely that some domestic cultivation of plants for food was carried out in the spaces between buildings.

Freshwater stream

Earth embankment

Metal-working site

### Metal-working Site

Archaeological evidence suggests that different activities were likely concentrated at specific areas of the settlement. The recovery of copper items and iron slag at the New Parliament House site – and nowhere else – suggests that metal-working activities were concentrated here.

Singapore River

**Present-day view of the location of the 14th-century settlement**

**Market square**

**Market**
The range and volume of excavation finds on the north bank of the Singapore River – including thousands of Chinese coins, stoneware jars used for transporting foodstuffs, and fine ceramics from China – provide compelling evidence that this was the site of a thriving marketplace for international and domestic trade.

**Chain boom**

**Singapore Stone**

**Singapore Stone**
A 3-metre-tall sandstone boulder, bearing a lengthy inscription that has hitherto not been translated, stood at the eastern tip of the mouth of the Singapore River. It would have been visible from the sea, greeting all ships passing through Temasek.

**Chain Boom**
A boom stretched across the entrance of the Singapore River served as a toll gate and defensive feature. Chinese and Malay sources indicate that such booms were made of iron chains.

# the Hill

and of which abundant examples are found in Java and Sumatra; while no monuments exist in these countries in their respective vernacular alphabets. The only remains of antiquity at Singapore, besides this stone, and the wall and moat before mentioned, are contained on the hill before alluded to. After being cleared by us of the extensive forest which covered it, it is now clothed with a fine grassy sward, and forms the principal beauty of the new settlement. The greater part of the west and northern [read: north and eastern] side of the mountain is covered with the remains of the foundations of buildings, some composed of baked brick of good quality.

Among these ruins, the most distinguished are those seated on a square terrace, of about forty feet to a side, near the summit of the hill. On the edge of this terrace, we find fourteen large blocks of sand-stone; which from the hole in each, had probably been the pedestals of as many wooden-posts which supported the building. This shows us, at once, that the upper part of the structure was of perishable materials; an observation which, no doubt, applies to the rest of the building as well as to this. Within the square terrace is a circular inclosure, formed of rough sand-stone, in the centre of which is a well, or hollow, which very possibly contained an image; for I look upon the building to have been a place of worship, and from its appearance in all likelihood, a temple of Buddha. I venture further to conjecture, that the other relics of antiquity on the hill, are the remains of monasteries of the priests of this religion. Another terrace, on the north [read: east] declivity of the hill, nearly of the same size, is said to have been the burial place of Iskandar Shah, King of Singapore. This is the prince whom tradition describes as having been driven from his throne by the Javanese, in the year 1252 of the Christian era, and who died at Melaka, not converted to the Mohammedan religion, in 1274; so that the story is probably apocryphal. Over the supposed tomb of Iskandar, a rude structure has been raised, since the formation of the new settlement, to which Mohammedans,

Hindus, and Chinese, equally resort to do homage. It is remarkable, that many of the fruit-trees cultivated by the ancient inhabitants of Singapore are still existing, on the eastern [read: southern] side of the hill, after a supposed lapse of near six hundred years. Here we find the durian, the rambutan, the duku, the shaddock, and other fruit-trees of great size; and all so degenerated, except the two first, that the fruit is scarcely to be recognised.

Among the ruins are found various descriptions of pottery, some of which is Chinese and native. Fragments of this are of great abundance. In the same situation have been found Chinese brass coins of the tenth and eleventh centuries. The earliest is of the Emperor of Ching-chung, of the dynasty of Sung-chao, who died in the year 967. Another is of the reign of Jin-chung, of the same dynasty, who died in 1067; and a third, of that of Shin-chung, his successor, who died in 1085. The discovery of these coins affords some confirmation of the relations which fix the establishment of the Malays at Singapore, in the twelfth century.

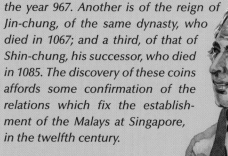

It should be remarked, in reference to this subject, that the coins of China were in circulation among all the nations of the Indian islands before they adopted the Mohammedan religion, or had any intercourse with Europeans. They were dug up in numbers in Java, and are still the only money used by the unconverted natives of Bali.

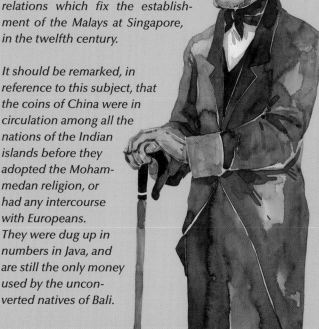

A lead figurine of a horse and rider – with the rider's head missing – recovered during the 1998 Empress Place excavation. This is likely an image of Surya (the Hindu sun god) riding his winged mount. The style of the figurine is reminiscent of temple carvings from East Java in the 14th century.

Java and the social groups' superiority over the other inhabitants of Temasek.

As a final point on the cosmopolitan nature of Temasek, the issue of cultural diversity arising from the presence of ethnic diversity remains an open question. The *Daoyi Zhilue* mentions three groups of people in Temasek – Orang Laut, or sea people; land-based natives; and a group of South Chinese who were resident at the settlement along the Keppel Straits. While the presence of Chinese has often been cited as a sign of ethnic diversity, the mere presence of foreigners does not automatically imply that the local culture was influenced or fundamentally affected and changed.

### Temasek's Economic Sphere

According to economic historian Kenneth R. Hall, there were three indigenous zones of trade in Southeast Asia by the 11th century, one of which was the Sumatra–Lower Malay Peninsula region, into which Temasek would have fallen. These zones, although having characteristic interactions with the Asian trade and economy, consisted of several sub-regional systems of economic exchange, each having a direct or indirect point of access to the Asian trade network.

In the Melaka Straits region, the main characteristic would have been the interaction between hinterland peoples inhabiting the hills and mountains on the one hand, and coastal settlers on the

According to the Chinese traveller Wang Dayuan, very fine hornbill casques were available at Temasek. Only the Rhinoceros Hornbill (*Buceros rhinoceros*) has a solid bony casque made of keratin, the fibrous protein found in human hair and fingernails and rhino horn, which can be carved into belt buckles, figurines, bracelets and other ornaments.

other, with the former supplying the latter with forest and agricultural products in exchange for foreign goods as well as services such as transport. The prosperity of a coastal trading kingdom would have come from two sources – the availability of hinterland produce in demand in the international maritime trade, and a pre-existing intraregional trading network, of which the kingdom's key port would have been the centre.

Temasek appears to have functioned as an export gateway and collection centre for the marine and forest products of the Riau Archipelago and south Johor. These products would have found ready buyers among the Chinese and regional traders that called at Temasek. The inflow and outflow of imported trade goods, foodstuffs and other goods would have created a lively market at the port-settlement.

According to the *Daoyi Zhilue*, Temasek offered three products that distinguished it from other Melaka Straits ports: "top-quality hornbill casques, middle-quality lakawood, and cotton". Cotton appears to have been a re-export product from Java and the Indian subcontinent. Hornbill casques, on the other hand, were found only in the Malay Peninsula, Singapore island, the Riau Archipelago and Borneo. As a substitute for ivory, these casques were highly sought after by China's elite. Apart from Palembang, which likely obtained its supply of casques elsewhere, Temasek was the only known place to have these casques of high quality. Lakawood, whose aromatic properties and wide availability throughout maritime Southeast Asia made it popular as an incense wood in China, was noted by the *Daoyi Zhilue* as being available at 19 ports in Sumatra, the Malay Peninsula and Borneo. However, only five ports offered good-quality lakawood – in the Melaka Straits, these were Lambri and Temasek.

For the population of the Riau Archipelago, Temasek would have been the closest trading port with access to the wider Asian maritime economy. Archaeological surface surveys in the early 1990s at several Riau islands uncovered substantial quantities of 14th-century Chinese ceramics and glassware, pointing to the likelihood of some form of economic arrangement between the Riau islands and Temasek. The Chinese ceramics exhibit similar decorative styles and techniques as those imported by Temasek, while the glassware items are of similar forms, albeit with simpler decorations, to those excavated from Fort Canning Hill. In addition, the glass beads found in the Riau Archipelago and at Temasek have similar chemical compositions, suggesting that they came from the same source. It would appear that the coastal settlements of the Riau Archipelago were intimately linked to Temasek through the exchange of indigenous produce and foreign goods.

Although similar economic linkages between Temasek and south Johor are yet to be supported by archaeological data from the south Johor coastline, it is more likely than not that there were linkages, given the geographical proximity of the two areas. There

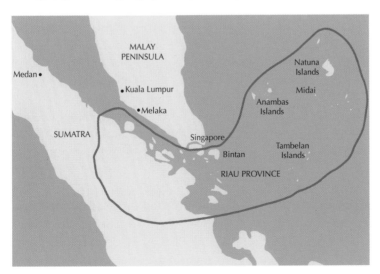

A map of the Riau-Lingga Archipelago and Natuna Islands, where ceramic and glass artefacts similar to those recovered in Singapore have been found. It is likely that this archipelagic area was part of Temasek's economic sphere.

is an interesting reference in the *Yuanshi* to Mongol envoys being despatched by the Yuan court to Temasek to acquire elephants. Although it is not recorded whether the request was fulfilled, such elephants, if made available by Temasek, would have most likely been obtained from the Malay Peninsula.

### Temasek's Decline: A Tale of Two Histories

Within a relatively short span of about 50 years from the point of its founding, Temasek appears to have established itself, by the middle of the 14th century, as a prosperous port-settlement. However, its prosperity may have drawn negative attention from nearby regional powers, including Sukothai, Ayutthaya and Majapahit. Early modern European and Southeast Asian textual sources indicate that both powers sought to bring Temasek into their sphere of influence. According to the Portuguese text *Suma Oriental* by Tomé Pires (c. 1513), by the beginning of the 15th century, Temasek had been brought under the influence of Ayutthaya, with the revenue from its maritime trade being forwarded to the Ayutthaya court.

### Blow, Winds, and Crack Your Cheeks!

King Lear's raging Shakespearean soliloquy might well describe the climate scheme of monsoon winds and sudden squalls that buffeted Singapore and the region.

Weather patterns and climate change are an often overlooked driving force of historical change. The monsoon winds, which generations of Arab mariners navigating the Indian Ocean assumed to be regular, are far more complex and variable when studied within the long timescale of the recent Holocene, when extended droughts and anomalous wet episodes generated by variable and chaotic monsoons profoundly shaped the course of Asian history.

Recent advances in paleoclimatology have revealed the variability of the monsoons in the past millennium, drawing on a variety of sources, including deep sea cores, coral growth, ice cores from the Himalayas, peat bogs, cave formations, especially from Dandak Cave in India, and more recently, tree-ring records.

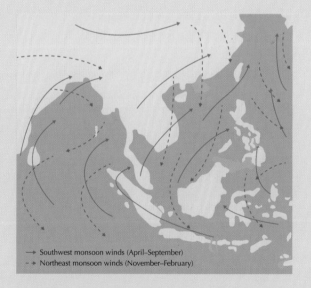

→ Southwest monsoon winds (April–September)
- → Northeast monsoon winds (November–February)

The Asian monsoon system is now conceptualised as comprising at least three components, which are not explicitly correlated: an Indian summer monsoon over the Indian subcontinent and the Bay

By the end of the 14th century, the Asian maritime economic context that enabled Temasek to rise and thrive had also begun to change. Direct Chinese participation in the trade in Southeast Asia during the Song and Yuan dynasties gave way, following the establishment of Ming rule in China in 1368, to the overturning of the maritime policies of the previous four centuries. The Chinese state became proactively engaged with the states of Southeast Asia and the Indian Ocean littoral both economically and politically, with Chinese private trade prohibited from operating abroad. These changes culminated in the Ming imperial voyages of the early 15th century.

These changes in the geopolitics of East Asia did not occur at random. Yuan China, upon which Temasek depended for much of its trade, was hit by several natural disasters that progressively weakened its economy. Chinese texts record a series of floods that were believed to have been brought on by "dragons". These were followed by droughts and famines accompanied by extremely cold winters. Finally, a plague occurred, forcing the Emperor Huizong

of Bengal; a distinct East Asian summer monsoon over the Chinese mainland, the East China Sea and Japan; and a western North Pacific summer monsoon stretching over much of the South China Sea, the Philippines and the western North Pacific Ocean. Much of Southeast Asia is sandwiched between these three systems, making for a chaotic distribution of rainfall, and giving rise to cycles of monsoon failure and droughts.

Edward Cook and his colleagues at the Tree-Ring Laboratory, Lamont-Doherty Earth Observatory of Columbia University, have produced a Monsoon Asia Drought Atlas, which maps the seasonal and centennial variations in Asia's monsoons and the recurrences of extended dry and wet extremes. They identify four cycles of mega-droughts in the past millennium: the Ming dynasty drought from 1638 to 1641; a "Strange Parallels" drought from 1756 to 1768; the East India drought from 1792 to 1796; and the Great Drought of 1876 to 1878. There was also a major famine drought in Bengal from 1769 to 1773. The Strange Parallels drought of the mid-18th century

takes its name from historian Victor Lieberman's description of the persistent mega-drought in large parts of India and Southeast Asia that coincided with the failure of the region's kingdoms. Singapore's fortunes as a trading centre would have been eclipsed by these mega-droughts that drove the demography, agriculture and trade of the world around it.

More specifically, these variations in Asia's monsoons appear to have created rapidly changing winds and shifting currents in the waters around Singapore, making navigation and anchoring around it difficult if not dangerous. The Portuguese complained of the intense winds that could suddenly arise and destroy ships anchored in and around Singapore. The Dutch admiral Cornelis Matelieff noted in his journals and letters that the currents and winds at the southern end of the Straits of Melaka and around Singapore limited the times when it was possible to sail through these waters, and so recommended Jayakarta (Jakarta today) and Banten over Melaka and the Johor River as locations for the rising Dutch East India Company to base itself.

(Toghon Temur), during the Zhizheng era (1341–70), to abandon the capital city of Beijing and return to the Mongolian steppes.

This was the onset of the Little Ice Age, which came on the heels of three centuries of warm and mild weather conditions that had enabled economic growth around the world. In Asia, this climate change had produced a La Niña-like effect that enhanced the monsoons, supporting the expansion of agriculture and economies in Chola South India, Southeast Asia and Song China, and facilitating the Asian maritime trade boom of the 10th to 13th centuries. The onset of a period of dramatic global cooling created an economic, demographic and political crisis of global proportions, leading to the decline of Yuan China and the rise of the Ming dynasty, with its very different political and economic imperatives.

Ports that had previously depended on diffuse and active Chinese economic participation in Southeast Asia had to drastically change their economic and political strategies in order to survive. In 1405, a renegade prince from Palembang, who had recently established a new port-settlement at the mouth of the Melaka River on the west coast of the Malay Peninsula, saw an opportunity offered by the proactive Ming maritime policy and declared allegiance to the Ming court. Overnight, Melaka became the key port of call in the Melaka Straits for the Chinese imperial navy, and in the process became China's primary conduit in its trade with Southeast Asia and the Indian Ocean littoral for the next hundred years.

Within this wider maritime Asian context, there exist two historical accounts of the eventual decline of Temasek. According to the *Malay Annals*, the last ruler of Temasek – Iskandar Shah – had publicly humiliated the daughter of one of his ministers. Acting out of vengeance, the minister – Sang Ranjuna Tapa – betrayed Iskandar Shah by advising the ruler of Majapahit to invade the settlement. During the subsequent invasion and siege, Sang Ranjuna Tapa did not release the store of rice to the populace, and opened the city gates to the invading force, resulting in the fall of the city. Iskandar Shah, after being escorted through inland Singapore, fled northwards to Muar, eventually settling at the mouth of the Melaka River and establishing a new port-city there.

A different account of Temasek's decline is recorded in the *Suma Oriental*. Tomé Pires noted that, according to the oral accounts of Melaka's inhabitants, Melaka's founding and subsequent rise as the key Chinese port of call and trading conduit in the early 15th century led to the merchants who were previously based at Temasek relocating to Melaka, resulting in Temasek's maritime economy being hollowed out. The King of Siam (possibly Ayutthaya), who had been concerned over the loss of revenue due to the decline in trade receipts at Temasek, entered into an agreement with the ruler of Melaka to address the financial situation. Temasek was eventually ceded to Melaka in return for an annual payment of gold. With that, Temasek's existence as an autonomous port-settlement came to an end.

## IN A NUTSHELL

Chapter One traces the emergence and development of Temasek (or Singapura), Singapore's first recorded settlement, dated to the late 13th to early 15th century. The port-city had economic relations with its immediate neighbours in the region, such as the Sriwijaya and Majapahit empires, as well as with those farther afield, including China and India. These economic connections brought along cultural influences, which the people of Temasek adopted and assimilated, as reflected in their material culture, agriculture and religious practices. Details about life in Temasek have been reconstructed from four main sources: archaeological remains; written records of the time, including the *Malay Annals*, one of the key bases of social memory for the Malay world; early colonial accounts; and maps.

In summary, Singapura was a prosperous, albeit modest, collection centre of the Riau Archipelago and south Johor hinterland, with several of the products marketed primarily to China, and a redistribution point for Chinese and other international products. However, by the early 15th century, this role would be taken over by Melaka, with Singapura relegated to a feeder port.

In Chapter Two, we will explore the circumstances leading to the changing role and position of Singapura between the 15th and early 16th centuries, within the context of political relations and ideologies in traditional Malay polities.

Most of the statues recovered
or found at the pre-15th-century
port-cities of the Melaka Straits
are Buddhist. The Bodhisattva
Avalokitesvara, in his Amoghapasa
form, distinguished by the tiger
skin he wears, was a popular
figure. Amoghapasa was also the
central deity in the Majapahit
temple of Candi Jago. This silver
gilded figure of Amoghapasa is
reported to have come out of
Palembang and, as such, reflects
the religious beliefs of Sriwijaya,
which found their way into the
mythology of the early chapters
of the *Malay Annals*.

# CHAPTER TWO

# The 15th Century
## Feeder Port and Homeland
## of Melaka's Naval Forces

*A*nd as the king, who was hunting, stood under a tree, one of his hounds was kicked by a white mouse-deer. And Sultan Iskandar Shah said, "This is a good place, when even its mouse-deer are full of fight! We shall do well to make a city here." And the chiefs replied, "It is indeed as your Highness says." Thereupon Sultan Iskandar Shah ordered that a city be made, and he asked, "What is the name of the tree under which I am standing?" And they all answered, "It is called Malaka, your Highness," to which he rejoined, "Then Malaka shall be the name of this city."

The *Malay Annals*

### Outpost of Melaka

Melaka, according to its court chronicle, the *Sulalat'us-Salatin*, the "Genealogy of the Kings", was founded by the last ruler of 14th-century Singapura, Iskandar Shah, when he was forced to abandon the city to invading Majapahit forces. He fled by way of Seletar to Muar, on the west coast of the Malay Peninsula, before moving again to a river called Bertam. The chronicle continues with a series of loosely linked episodes and anecdotes about the Melaka court and its continuation in the Johor court. Singapura is recalled in the first six episodes as the beginnings of Melaka.

The *Sulalat'us-Salatin*, better known as the *Sejarah Melayu* or *Malay Annals*, is known to us today through some 30 variant texts. The earliest, which carries an Islamic year of 1021 (1612 AD), was copied for Stamford Raffles on paper with an 1816 watermark. Central to all these versions is the assertion that Singapura was founded by a Palembang prince named Sang Nila Utama or Sri Tri Buana. With his two brothers, he descended from heaven onto the sacred hill of Bukit Seguntang Mahameru in Palembang, the spiritual centre of

Sriwijaya, which was the dominant trading power in the Straits of Melaka from the 7th to the 11th centuries.

Making sense of these first six chapters of the *Malay Annals* has been problematic. Most historians have tried to read the *Malay Annals* as a historical text in which they search for nuggets of "factual" information that can be corroborated by other evidence, and on finding no such information, have dismissed the entire text as folklore and myth.

A more useful exercise is to examine the *Malay Annals* through the lens of literature – an imaginative composition that can be subjected to literary criticism – and to consider how it creatively represents the world of Melaka and also Johor. This chapter attempts a literary reading of the *Malay Annals* and examines how Malay social memories of their past were deeply influenced by their reading of their origins recollected in the *Sulalat'us-Salatin*, which shaped their perceptions of their present and future. The chapter reconstructs Melaka's rise as the pre-eminent emporium in 15th-century Southeast Asia and Singapura's role within Melaka's world.

**Singapura in the *Malay Annals*: Sri Tri Buana and a Sacred Pact**
The *Malay Annals* relates how Sang Nila Utama and his two brothers transformed the rice fields on Bukit Seguntang into gold and silver as they descended the hill on their white elephants, claiming to be descendants of Alexander the Great. The eldest brother was invited to become the ruler of Minangkabau in western Sumatra, and the second to rule Tanjong Pura in western Kalimantan. The youngest, Sang Nila Utama, was invited by the ruler of Palembang, Demang Lebar Daun, to take his place. Underpinning Demang Lebar Daun's abdication of rulership to the young prince – who was consecrated on his ascension to the throne as Sri Tri Buana – was a sacred social contract. The *Malay Annals* records it thus:

> *Both of them took a solemn oath to the effect that whoever should depart from the terms of the pact, then let his house be overturned by Almighty God so that its roof be laid on the ground and its pillars be inverted. And that is why it has been granted by Almighty God to Malay rulers that they shall never put their subjects to shame, and that those subjects however gravely they offend shall never be bound or hanged or disgraced with evil word. If any ruler should put a single one of*

*his subjects to shame, that would be a sign that his kingdom would be destroyed by Almighty God. Similarly, it has been granted by Almighty God to their Malay subject that they should never be disloyal or treacherous to their rulers, even if their rulers behaved evilly or unjustly towards them.*

Be that as it may, Sri Tri Buana eventually decided to seek his fortune away from his adopted city. He sailed first to Bentan (Bintan) in the Riaus, where he was adopted by the local queen, Wan Sri Benian. He then set out again from Bentan:

*And Sri Tri Buana came to a very large, high rock. He climbed on to the top of this rock and looking across the water he saw that the land on the other side had sand so white that it looked like a sheet of cloth. And he asked Indra Bopal, "What is that stretch of sand that we see yonder? What land is that?" And Indra Bopal replied, "That, Your Highness, is the land called Temasek." And Sri Tri Buana said, "Let us go thither." And Indra Bopal replied, "I will do whatever Your Highness commands."*

Pages from Abdullah bin Abdul Kadir's c. 1840 publication of the *Sulalat'us-Salatin* under the title *Sejarah Melayu*. As one of Stamford Raffles' Malay-language scribes, Abdullah was aware that Raffles' close friend John Leyden had translated this "Genealogy of Kings" as the "Malay Annals". In following Leyden, Abdullah helped to consolidate and popularise *Sejarah Melayu/Malay Annals* as the preferred title for the *Sulalat'us-Salatin*.

*So Sri Tri Buana embarked and started on the crossing.... And when they reached the shore, the ship was brought close in and Sri Tri Buana went ashore with all the ship's company and they amused themselves with collecting shell-fish. The king then went inland for sport on the open ground at Kuala Temasek.*

*And they all beheld a strange animal. It seemed to move with great speed; it had a red body and a black head; its breast was white; it was strong and active in build, and in size was rather bigger than a he-goat. When it saw the party, it moved away and then disappeared. And Sri Tri Buana inquired of all those who were with him, "What beast is that?" But no one knew. Then said Demang Lebar Daun, "Your Highness, I have heard it said that in ancient times it was a lion that had that appearance." And Sri Tri Buana said to Indra Bopal, "Go back to Bentan and tell the queen that now we shall not be returning, but that if she wishes to shew her affection for us, will she furnish us with men, elephants and horses, as we propose to establish a city here at Temasek." And Indra Bopal set forth to return to Bentan: and when he arrived there, he presented himself before Wan Sri Benian to whom he related what Sri Tri Buana had said. "Very well," said Wan Sri Benian, "we will never oppose any wish of our son." And she sent men, elephants and horses without number. Sri Tri Buana then established a city at Temasek, giving it the name Singapura.*

The image of Singapura that emerges from the first six chapters of the *Malay Annals* is of "a great city, to which foreigners resorted in great numbers so that the fame of the city and its greatness spread throughout the world". Under its second ruler, Sri Pikrama Wira, the son of Sri Tri Buana, Singapura was evidently strong enough to challenge Majapahit Java, the major power in the archipelago, in a display of diplomatic theatrics. This escalated into a major Majapahit invasion of Singapura, which was successfully repulsed.

The ensuing story of Sri Pikrama Wira's marriage to the daughter of the Tamil ruler of Kalinga is essentially an illustration of Singapura's wealth and stature among Indian kingdoms. The story of the Raja of Kalinga pitting his strongman against Singapura's reigning champion, Badang, can be interpreted as an unstated competition for power between the two states. The Raja's despatch of a gravestone for Badang upon his death can, arguably, be read as a show of respect for, if not deference to, Sri Pikrama

An artistic rendition of the story of Badang the strongman, as described in the *Malay Annals*. This scene – a detail from Jimmy Ong's drawing, "Offering at Temasek Stone" (2011) – shows Badang surrounded by an audience of characters from different eras of history.

Wira. Likewise, in another story, the Raja of Perlak's desire to pit his Goliath against Badang can also be seen as an unstated contest of power, in which Sri Pikrama Wira emerged the victor.

Singapura could presumably have gone on to greater achievements if it had not been betrayed by one of its officials. According to the *Malay Annals*, the fourth-generation descendant of Sri Tri Buana, who had the Muslim name Sultan Iskandar Shah, alienated one of his officials, Sang Ranjuna Tapa, when he executed, on a false accusation, one of his concubines, who happened to be Sang Ranjuna Tapa's daughter. Sang Ranjuna Tapa decided to betray his sultan by "opening the gate of the fort" to invading Javanese forces. For his crime of treason, Sang Ranjuna Tapa and his wife were transformed into rocks. According to the author of the *Malay Annals*, the two rocks could still be seen in his day, that is, in the 17th century.

Sri Tri Buana's dreams of establishing a "great city" were critical to the Melaka and Johor sultans' visions of their future. What happened in Singapura between Sri Tri Buana's arrival and Iskandar Shah's flight prefigured the island's present and shaped its future. The underlying mythology of this period of history was that Singapura was emerging as a great city on its way to re-establishing the glory of Sriwijaya. But its historical destiny was undermined by Iskandar Shah's wrongful execution of Sang Ranjuna Tapa's daughter, and Sang Ranjuna Tapa's subsequent betrayal. What happened in Singapura was in effect the consequence of this breach of the sacred contract between a ruler and his subjects sworn to at Palembang. It was a dream, or nightmare, of a chain of events that would culminate in the fall of Melaka to the Portuguese.

This anxiety over the Malay people's loyalty to their sultans and the latter's justice towards their subjects was to haunt the sultans of Melaka and Johor. Six of the seven deathbed testaments of sultans recorded in the *Malay Annals* are not so much instructions for the disposition of properties and succession, but ethical admonitions to their successors to be just to their subjects and injunctions to their subjects to be loyal to their sultans.

This theme of reciprocal obligations formed an underlying template for the history of Melaka and Johor. Melaka's fall in 1511 followed Sultan Mahmud's wrongful execution of his Bendahara (prime minister). Mahmud abdicated in penitence, leaving Melaka to his son, Ahmad. Sultan Ahmad, according to the *Malay Annals*, "had no great liking for the chiefs", preferring instead the company of a group of youthful favourites. The social memories of this "figural interpretation" of the loss of Melaka and, before that, the loss of Singapura, must have weighed heavily on the Johor sultans, especially after the murder of the reigning sultan in 1699, thus ending the genealogy of Johor sultans who could trace their ancestry to Sri Tri Buana.

### Between Myth and Historicity

Interpreting the Singapura stories in the *Malay Annals* has its challenges. Richard Winstedt, one of the foremost scholars of Malay history and literature, dismissed the account of Singapura's founding in the *Malay Annals* as a "hotchpotch of Chola and Palembang folklore [out of which] little can be made". But the mythologising of the creature that Sri Tri Buana saw continued nevertheless, taking the form of the "Merlion" today and used as part of the branding of Singapore as a tourist destination.

Most other historians concur with Winstedt's reading. Oliver W. Wolters, a retired Malayan Civil Service officer who went on to a distinguished career as a historian of early Southeast Asia at Cornell University, wrote a critical study of the *Malay Annals* as the link between the fall of Sriwijaya and Melaka's founding. Wolters joins other historians in preferring Portuguese versions and histories of the founding of the city over the narrative of the *Malay Annals*, assessing these to be more rational. Moreover, as

Wolters demonstrates, Portuguese accounts could be corroborated by Ming dynasty records. Wolters centres the issue on how the *Malay Annals* represents the historical reality archived in Portuguese reports.

For Wolters, the Portuguese accounts were compiled by the officials and scribes sent to administer the city they had captured. Their impressions of Melaka's founding contrasted sharply with the *Malay Annals*. These differences stemmed from different sources of information. Without access to the sultan and his court, the Portuguese turned to the sultan's former subjects in the marketplace. The Portuguese accounts suggest that the circumstances of Melaka's founding a century earlier were still vivid in the social memories of the city's residents.

The thrust of these Portuguese reports was that Melaka's founder was a prince from Palembang who had been forced to flee Majapahit forces that were despatched to crush a coup he fomented. This renegade prince, named Parameswara (a Javanese court title awarded to men who married women of higher royal status or became prince consorts), arrived in Temasek, where he was welcomed by its ruler. In return, Parameswara assassinated his host and usurped his kingdom, for which act he had to flee from a Tai expeditionary force sent to avenge their vassal's murder. Withdrawing through the jungles of Johor, he emerged at Muar on the west coast of the peninsula. Travelling farther up the coast, he founded a new settlement he named Melaka.

Wolters' close reading of Ming dynasty records in tandem with the *Malay Annals* and Portuguese accounts leads him to the conclusion that Iskandar Shah, the last Raja of Singapura and the founder of Melaka, is in fact identical to the Parameswara of the Portuguese accounts. His reconstruction of the chronology of Iskandar's reign is as follows:

| | |
|---|---|
| 1389/1390–1391/1392 | Three years in Palembang |
| 1392/1393–1397/1398 | Six years in Temasek/Singapura |
| 1398/1399–1399/1400 | Flight from Temasek/Singapura |
| 1400/1401–1413/1414 | 14 years' reign in Melaka |

Central to Wolters' study of Iskandar's reign is the *Malay Annals'* attribution of a divine genealogy to Iskandar/Parameswara, transmitted down to him through four generations. Wolters' argument

Portuguese Macau postage stamp of Tomé Pires, whose *Suma Oriental* is the oldest and most extensive account of the Portuguese East at the beginning of the 16th century. Pires included in his account information on the history, geography, ethnography and, especially, the commerce and trade of not only Melaka, but other countries and port-cities in India, China and the East Indies that he visited.

*Dapunta Hyang: Transmission of Knowledge*, an installation by artist Zai Kuning at the 2017 Venice Biennale. Zai created a 17-metre-long skeleton of a ship of the legendary 7th-century Sriwijayan king Jayanasa, rising from the sea with a cargo of books sealed in beeswax. The work symbolises the forgotten histories and disappearing traditions of the Malays, which the artist was seeking to recollect. In doing so, Zai made himself a fluid extension of that lost knowledge.

is that if we were to read the *Malay Annals* from the perspective of its author, then the chronicle is less a record of the *past as it was*, from which we can attempt to reconstruct some events constituting Melaka's past, but more a narrative of *what the past should have been* – one that demonstrates the moral authority and legitimacy of the Melaka sultans. Parameswara's violent and rebellious past became mythologised into Sri Tri Buana and his successors by a genealogist of the Melaka court around 1436 in order to establish a cosmic origin for his sultan and his moral right to rulership as the divinely descended successor of Sriwijayan rulers.

Be that as it may, this poetic rendering of the myths, metaphors and tropes employed by the Melaka court genealogist to legitimise his sultan's lineage also offers a deeper understanding of the *Malay Annals*. The difference between the *Malay Annals* and the Portuguese accounts of Singapura's founding may not, however, be as conclusive as Winstedt and Wolters claim. Both accounts of Melaka's beginnings stem from social memories. The *Malay Annals* records the social memories of the Melaka court, while the Portuguese accounts rely on the social memories of their new Melaka subjects.

Seen this way, the two accounts display a similar underlying narrative structure. Both begin with a departure from Palembang. For Sri Tri Buana, it was a journey to a new future; for Parameswara, it was a flight from danger. Both continue with a dramatic arrival in Temasek, with the sighting of a mythical lion for Sri Tri Buana, and the murder of his host for Parameswara. Singapura under Sri Tri Buana/Parameswara was emerging as a major emporium. However, both the *Malay Annals* and the Portuguese accounts end with a tragic departure from Singapura. The descendants of Sri Tri Buana lost Singapura because they were betrayed by a disloyal subject, while Parameswara had to abandon Singapura to a Siamese overlord avenging his vassal's assassination.

The issue is not to have to select one account as the more "historical" but to try to understand why they have come to be interpreted and written in their respective ways.

### Realism in the Malay Worldview

For Winstedt, the *Malay Annals* was a retelling of folklore and myth. But in the early 17th century, the text's Johor compilers, Tun Bambang, and later, Tun Sri Lanang, believed otherwise. In their minds, they were documenting reality. Tun Bambang was convinced that the social memories he was recounting were true because the places and objects the *Malay Annals* described could still be seen in his time. He assured his audience that the black stone fort of the city of Gelanggui which Raja Chulan overran "still exists to this day", with its name mispronounced as "Linggiu". In 2005, an independent scholar of Malay literature, Raimy Che-Ross, led a well-publicised search for this fort, which, he argued, was located in the upper reaches of the Linggiu reservoir in Johor.

Tun Bambang further confirmed that the story of the strongman Badang was true, because the rock he was said to have hurled across the Singapore River "is there to this day on the extremity of Tanjong Singapura". Could it be that the fragment of the Singapore Stone is all that remains of this rock? Similarly, according to Tun Bambang, the boom that Badang laid across the river "still exists at Singapura", as did the stone that the Raja of Kalinga sent to mark the grave of Badang at Buru.

Bukit Merah, the "red hill" of the *Malay Annals*, is remembered up to the present day as the spot where the young boy who saved Singapura from a swordfish attack was executed by the Dam Raja, who felt threatened by the boy's intelligence. The red-orange lateritic soil of the hill was believed to be the "guilt of this young boy's blood laid on Singapura". Likewise, the stone that emerged from Tun Jana Khatib's blood clot after he was wrongly executed for displaying his magico-mystical powers was also still standing.

Tun Bambang believed the *Malay Annals* he was compiling was a true and verifiable account of the past.

For Tun Bambang, it was not only Sultan Iskandar Shah, but also his predecessors, who were historical personages. The credit for the emergence of Singapura as a great city – respected by others like Kalinga and able to challenge the regional power, Majapahit – belonged to Sri Tri Buana and his successors. Their achievements were largely a consequence of their divine prowess.

To the Iskandar/Sri Tri Buana persona was attributed a genealogy that could be traced back to the Macedonian world conqueror Alexander, or Raja Iskandar Zulqarnain, who, according to another text, the *Hikayat Iskandar Zulkarnain*, spread the faith of Ibrahim to its farthest limits in India. In Tun Bambang's world of 16th- and 17th-century Johor, it made eminent sense to claim this descent because it would have enhanced one's credentials in the Persianised trading world of the Indian Ocean and subcontinent between the 15th and 18th centuries. This was a time when Persian elites played a significant role in the region, helping local rulers install the administrative structures for governing their kingdoms, and facilitating trade across the Indian Ocean.

### Precarious Powers of a Raja

The problem in the *Malay Annals* is that this Alexandrian legend sits uneasily with a series of narratives and myths from an earlier era of Malay history, when, in the words of the *Ceritera asal Raja-raja Melayu* ("Genealogy of the Malay Kings"), which pre-dates the *Malay Annals*, "the Malays had not yet embraced Islam". The saga of the rajas of Pasai (in north Sumatra) and their conversion to Islam, leading to the story of the Islamic preacher and mystic Tun Jana Khatib and his execution, suggest that Islam was a strange and foreign force in 14th-century Singapura. The prevailing political-religious culture in much of maritime Southeast Asia remained a strain of esoteric Vajrayana Buddhism that had taken root in the region from the 7th century onwards. Sriwijaya, whose legacy Parameswara/Iskandar carried to Temasek in the name of Sri Tri Buana, and on to Melaka, was Vajrayana Buddhist to its core.

In a political world swathed in Buddhist lore, a claim to sultanship would be judged on the impeccability of the claimant's genealogy and evidenced by his mystical-spiritual prowess. The 14th-century

Majapahit king, Hayam Wuruk, for example, whose reign is glorified as Majapahit's golden age in the classic Javanese text, the *Desawarnana*, is described in its opening stanzas as an incarnation of Shiva and Buddha.

Other Majapahit and earlier Singhasari kings also claimed to be embodiments of Hindu and Buddhist deities. The art history of the monumental Bhirawa statue recovered from Padang Roco (Sungei Langsat) in west Sumatra tells of its patron Adityawarman's mid-14th-century embodiment as a demonic deity ruling the west Sumatran highlands. Earlier, Adityawarman claimed consecration as the all-seeing Buddhist "merciful Lord", the Bodhisattva Avalokitesvara in his Amoghapasa form. Mahayana theology recognises up to 108 forms of the Avalokitesvara, of which Amoghapasa, with his noose or *pasa*, which is used to snag sentient beings and lead them to salvation, is one form.

In this environment, Sri Tri Buana/Parameswara as an aspirant to rulership had to demonstrate a similar strain of spiritual prowess. He is thus portrayed in the *Malay Annals* as descending from the sacred hill of Bukit Seguntang, symbol of the mountain abode of the Bodhisattva Avalokitesvara at the centre of the old Sriwijayan realm, exuding all the symbolism of not only a regal, but more importantly, a sacred person. That was when the ruler of Palembang, Demang Lebar Daun, recognised Sri Tri Buana's prowess and abdicated in his favour. On behalf of his subjects, Demang Lebar Daun concluded a sacred social contract with Sri Tri Buana which provided that, in return for the undivided loyalty of his subjects, Sri Tri Buana and his descendants would be fair and just in their rule.

Following the conclusion of the sacred covenant and Sri Tri Buana's successful marriage to the daughter of Demang Lebar Daun, the latter then initiated a ceremony for the ritual lustration (*memandikan*) of Sri Tri Buana. This corresponds to instructions for the performance of the rituals of *abhiseka* – a purificatory sprinkling of water to wash away ignorance and initiate an acolyte into the deep knowledge of *prajna* (wisdom) – as described in the *Hevajra Tantra*, a central text of esoteric Buddhism that was widely circulated in Southeast Asia. The 40-day consecration rituals that Sri Tri Buana underwent were to commemorate his embodiment as Avalokitesvara, the Lord of the Three Worlds in Buddhist cosmology.

At the temple of Candi Jago in east Java, the Singhasari King Wisnuwardhana – who is credited with reunifying the realm of Java – was consecrated as Amoghapasa around the end of the 13th century. Adityawarman's Amoghapasa statue was a close copy of the Candi Jago statue. Sri Tri Buana/ Parameswara would have been familiar with such worship and was probably consecrated as an incarnation of the Bodhisattva with the unfailing *pasa*.

Singapore probably received its epithet of "Lion City" because the lion was an auspicious symbol of Buddhism practised in 14-century Southeast Asia. The *Malay Annals* descriptions of Sri Tri Buana suggest he was consecrated as an incarnation of a Bodhisattva, probably the Amoghapasa form of Avalokitesvara, so justifying his claim to rulership over the Malays, who had yet to convert to Islam. As an incarnation of Avalokitesvara, he would have been seated on a lion throne or *singhasana*, as depicted in this 13th–14th-century Chinese figure, in gilt bronze with silver inlay, of Guanyin, the Chinese form of Avalokitesvara.

Portuguese apothecary Tomé Pires, a spice trade supervisor in Melaka (1512–15), learnt from local residents that Parameswara/ Iskandar Shah imbued himself with this Buddhist aura in order to challenge Majapahit overlordship of Palembang and re-establish Sriwijaya's control over the ports of trade in the Straits of Melaka. The Majapahit ruler, who was wise to the challenge, consequently despatched an expeditionary force to quash Parameswara, forcing him to flee to Temasek around 1392.

The myths, metaphors and tropes of the *Malay Annals* must be understood from the viewpoints of its author and its intended audience. Seen in this light, it explains Sri Tri Buana's renaming of the island he landed on as Singapura ("Lion City"). Rather than indicating an actual sighting of a specimen of *Panthera leo*, this renaming was more likely an exercise in asserting where he intended to re-establish the "lion throne" – that is, the seat of Avalokitesvara and an earthly variation of that which he and his consort had sat on for his consecration rituals in Palembang.

Bukit Larangan, or the Forbidden Hill, as the 19th-century Malays dubbed today's Fort Canning, would have been the ideal symbolic representation of the Mount Potala of Avalokitesvara for Sri Tri Buana to relocate his "lion throne". Singapura therefore played a pivotal role in the transmission of this foundation myth of divine genealogy and historic ancestry from Palembang to Melaka and subsequently Johor.

Ultimately, Singapura loomed large in the social memories of 16th- and 17th-century Malays because it was here that the Raja's divine origins and his right to rule the Malay people originated. All claimants to the throne of Melaka and Johor had to be able to demonstrate their descent from Sri Tri Buana at Singapura for their right to rule the Malays. In the 18th century, Raja Kecik would create an elaborate myth to justify his claim to Malay power. The Bugis would rewrite Malay history to justify themselves as the legitimate successors of Sri Tri Buana. It was these social memories that were probably filtering through Tengku Husain's mind when he accompanied the Orang Laut, Batin Sapi, to Singapura to meet Raffles.

### Melaka: "A City That Was Made for Merchandise"
It was this divine genealogy and historic ancestry that Iskandar Shah/Parameswara carried with him to the new port-city he established. Melaka rose rapidly to become the premier emporium for the South China Sea and Bay of Bengal trade and the preferred hub – together with Ryukyu (present-day Okinawa) – of the emerging Ming tribute trade network. The West Asia terminus of Melaka's trade networks was recovering from the Black Death, the devastating 14th-century plague pandemic, and the Mamluke rulers at Cairo were consolidating their position as the leading emporium for Europe's trade with the Indian Ocean and beyond. Southeast Asia entered an "Age of Commerce", which historian Anthony Reid has reconstructed as an era of unprecedented prosperity from 1460 to 1680.

The Ming dynasty, more than the Yuan and perhaps even the Song, was locked into the Nanhai (South China Sea) trade. It became increasingly dependent upon this trade to meet the demand for exotic goods as status symbols. In order to re-establish the prestige and cosmological centrality of China, the Yongle Emperor (r. 1403–24) launched seven naval expeditions, led by the eunuch Admiral Zheng He, into the "Western Ocean" – covering

The symbolism of Avalokitesvara or Guanyin seated on a lion continued into the 17th century, as seen in this Dehua enamelled figurine decorated with black, green, brown and red paints.

A replica of Zheng He's *bao-chuan*, or "treasure ship", at the site of the original shipyard in Nanjing where the ships were built. Depending on how classical Chinese units of measurement are interpreted, Zheng He's *baochuan* may have been around 130 metres long (as in this replica), or, more likely, 60–75 metres long. Building and sailing a 130-metre-long timber ship would challenge the limits of nautical technology even today.

Southeast Asia, South Asia, West Asia and East Africa – to encourage the "barbarian kings" to resume the sending of tribute to the Middle Kingdom. In this respect, Zheng He's voyages were eminently successful.

Parameswara/Iskandar Shah, among other rulers in the Nanhai, responded eagerly, sending missions to the Ming court in 1405 and 1407. In 1411, he personally travelled to the Ming capital at Nanjing, and his successors continued the practice of sending tribute. Like his Sriwijayan forebears in the 7th century, Parameswara/Iskandar Shah had to contend with challenges and threats to his new *negara* from rival emporiums in the Straits of Melaka, notably Samudera-Pasai and Aru in north Sumatra, and especially the Tai, who apparently still remembered his assassination of their Temasek vassal. Ming patronage of Melaka evidently enabled Parameswara and his successors to fend off these threats.

The Ming, in contrast to the Mongol Yuan dynasty, re-emphasised the Confucian rhetoric of a Sinocentric world with its state monopoly of trade and consequent conduct of trade as tribute. Tribute trade climbed to new heights. Ayutthaya led the Southeast Asian kingdoms in sending some 50 tribute missions to the Ming court in the period 1371–1420. The lure of the Nanhai trade, however, led Chinese traders to circumvent the bureaucratic restrictions on trade and venture forth in greater numbers, even after the Ming emperors banned private trade and terminated state-led trade altogether in 1433. Fujian and Ryukyu merchants linked up with Melaka, Ayutthaya and Pasai to supply the insatiable Chinese market until the 16th century. Melaka, more than Sriwijaya, also depended upon the West Asian and early modern European markets for its prosperity.

Melaka benefited from the growing prosperity in China, Europe and the Indo-Islamic world. Parameswara's successor then took the major step of converting to Islam, thereby locating the new trading *negara* firmly within the moral universe of an Indo-Islamic world networked by a Persian diaspora. Melaka's official adoption of Islam was probably done to maintain its comparative advantage vis-à-vis its competitors, especially Samudera-Pasai, which had earlier converted to Islam. Conversion to Islam meant that the negotiation of trade, adjudication of conflicts and formation of diplomatic alliances could be made within an Islamic framework. This appears to have helped make Melaka a more attractive port of call for Muslim traders.

Among the more significant Portuguese reports on Melaka is the one by Tomé Pires. He spent much time recording local traditions and collecting accounts from Malay residents on the history and socioeconomic conditions of Melaka and its neighbours, which he summarised in a report titled *The Suma Oriental of Tomé Pires: An Account of the East from the Red Sea to Japan, written in*

Engraving in Johan Nieuhof's *Travels to the East-Indies* depicting women actively engaged in barter trade with other Asian traders at Melaka. Other European travellers also commented on the active involvement of women in trade, which they found unusual.

Indian textiles were a major trade commodity across the Arabian Sea, West Asia, the Bay of Bengal and Southeast Asia. The Portuguese and the Dutch were major traders of Indian textiles, making very specific orders for designs they wanted on consignment to meet demand back in Europe and in Southeast Asia. This Gujarati double *ikat* (*patola*) textile was specifically made for the Indonesian market for ceremonial use. Indian textiles in the early modern era "clothed the world".

*Malacca and India in 1512–1515.* The Portuguese considered the record so valuable that, in line with the prevailing official policy, its readership was kept very restricted, and it was not until around the middle of the 20th century that a full copy was transcribed and published.

According to Pires, Melaka was "a city that was made for merchandise", where some 84 different languages could be heard on the streets among its estimated 4,000 foreign merchants. Indeed, Pires claimed that "Whoever is lord of Malacca has his hand on the throat of Venice". Besides the Gujarati, who made up a quarter of the foreign merchants calling at Melaka, there were also other Indian merchants from the Coromandel Coast and Bengal. Together with their West Asian counterparts from Cairo and the Persian Gulf, they sailed for Melaka annually in March, aided by the southwest monsoon, bringing with them their merchandise, the bulk of which were textiles.

At Melaka, they met merchants from Sumatra, Pegu (Bago), Java, Kalimantan, Maluku and Mindanao. These merchants had sailed with the southwest monsoon to bring their products – primarily the spices so much valued in West Asian and European markets – to exchange for textiles and other merchandise from the West and China. Products from Cham ports and China arrived with the northeast monsoon. Although the *Suma Oriental* does not mention a distinct Chinese merchant community in Melaka, Chinese products – principally silks, brocades and other items, including ceramics – were brought to the port in Melakan *jong* and other Southeast Asian vessels on the back of the northeast monsoon.

Pires reported that China was "an important, good and very wealthy country", reached in 20 days' sailing from Melaka. Pepper, according to him, was "the chief export from Melaka, which they could buy up to ten junk-loads a year". Other exports to China included "a great deal of incense, elephants' tusks, tin, apothecary's lignaloes, … a great deal of Borneo camphor, red beads, white sandalwood, brazil, infinite quantities of the black wood that grows in Singapore…. Pepper apart, they make little account of all the rest."

This reference to Singapore as the source of a type of black wood indicates that the island may not have been abandoned at the end of the 14th century as both the *Malay Annals* and the Portuguese

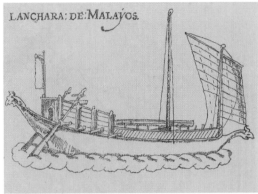

LANCHARA: DE: MALAYOS.

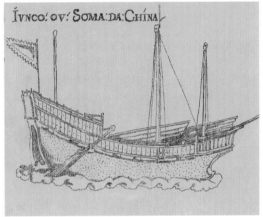

ÍVNCO: OV: SOMA:DA:CHÍNA

reports indicate, but continued to function as a feeder port for various forest products to Melaka. The wood in question may have been ebony or a species of lakawood (probably *Dalbergia parviflora*, which, as John Crawfurd reported in 1820, the Malay Peninsula and Sumatra were major sources of).

The 14th-century traveller Wang Dayuan noted that one of Singapore's exports was *jiangzhen*, a dark timber with a scent that reminded the Chinese of lakawood incense. Throughout the 15th century, Singapura was a feeder port to Melaka for this "black wood" and other jungle products from its Johor and Riau hinterland. Some two centuries later, the country trader Alexander Hamilton may have been referring to this black wood or *jiangzhen* when he recorded in his *New Account of the East Indies* that on Singapura "the soil is black and fat: And the Woods abound in good masts for Shipping, and Timber for building".

Melaka's claim to fame was that it was the emporium at which three different networks of merchants – from the South China Sea

(*Above left*) Printed engraving of a Javanese merchant found in Johan Nieuhof's *Embassy from the East India Company*, printed in 1669.

(*Above*) Sketches of a Malay *lancaran* and a Chinese junk in Manuel Godinho de Erédia's *Description of Melaka*.

A scale model of a 15th-century Chinese vessel wrecked off Bakau island in the Karimata Straits. Similar Chinese vessels would have called at Melaka. (Model built by Nick Burningham.)

littoral, from South Asia and West Asia, and from the "lands below the winds" – met to trade. These merchants needed a port where those sailing on the southwest monsoons from the Indian Ocean could meet their counterparts coming from the archipelago on the same monsoon and on the northeast monsoon.

Melaka's wealth was, however, not only dependent upon its function as an emporium where traders from different networks could congregate to trade. It was also a port where a variety of forest products collected by the aboriginal, or *orang asli*, communities from the jungles of the peninsula could be sourced. These would have included much-valued incense woods (especially gaharu wood, lakawood and "red sandalwood") and resins (such as camphor, benzoin and dammar), gums and oils.

Some seven centuries earlier, Melaka's forebears, a group of Malay chieftains living along Sumatra's Musi River, at its confluence with the Ogan River, had realised the value of the forest products found upstream of where they lived. Oliver Wolters, whose reading of the *Malay Annals* was discussed earlier in this chapter, argued in a benchmark study of early Indonesian commerce that these Malay chieftains sensed an opening up of China's markets under the Tang emperors. They realised there was a growing demand for incense woods, resins, gums and oils for use in worship in an increasingly Buddhist China as well as in Chinese pharmacology. Wolters deduced that Chinese references to these valued resins were not necessarily to genuine Persian products, but to Sumatran resins that had been foisted on them. By the time of the Song dynasty, these goods, along with rare and exotic commodities such as hornbill casques and turtle shells, as well as hard woods for furniture, were major commodities in the Straits of Melaka trade with China.

Several maps by the Portuguese-Malayan adventurer, cartographer and mathematician Manuel Godinho de Erédia (1563–1623) depicting the territory around Melaka are significant in this context. One of them shows a network of rivers behind the city, and also more interestingly, a network of trails that extend beyond the boundaries of Melaka's territories into the hills and jungles of the Malay Peninsula. It would have been along these trails and rivers that the forest products collected by the aboriginal communities of the jungle were brought to Melaka for export. The marine products, on the other hand, such as turtle shells and especially

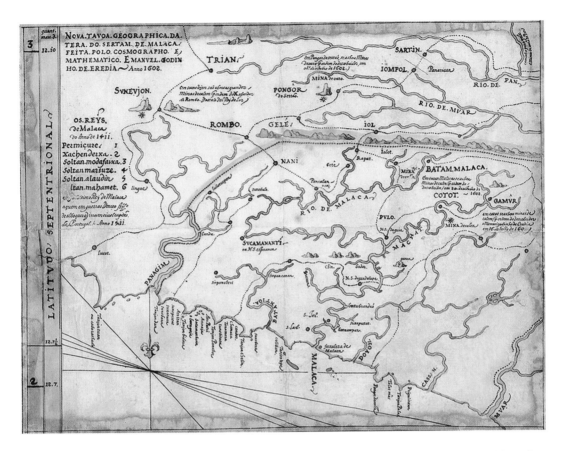

sea cucumbers, were collected by the Orang Laut, the indigenous sea peoples.

### The Orang Laut – Sultan's Warriors

Melaka, like Sriwijaya and Temasek before it, and Johor-Riau after it, was an estuary-riverine society hemmed in by jungles unsuitable for agriculture, and was therefore dependent upon the import of food and other essentials. It also never had the manpower to support the port-city. Central to the *Malay Annals'* narrative of Melaka is the role of a group of communities referred to as the Orang Laut. The Portuguese reports confirm the vital role that these sea peoples played in the establishment and functioning of Melaka during the time of the sultanate and beyond. Tomé Pires is explicit on this point:

> These Çelates [or Bajau] – men who lived near Singapore and also near Palembang – when Paramjçura fled from Palembang they followed his company and thirty of them went along together protecting his life. While Paramjçura was

This 1602 map of Melaka and its surrounding region by Erédia marks the area "claimed" or "controlled" by the Portuguese. It is significant for its depiction of the riverine networks and overland trails linking Melaka to its hinterland, especially the *penarikan* (portage) route linking the Muar River (which Melaka sits just to the north of) with the Pahang River (which flows out into the South China Sea on the east coast of the peninsula). It also indicates the year 1411 as the founding of the Melaka dynasty and lists six rulers to 1511, starting with Parameswara.

*in Palembang they served as fishermen; after they came to Singapore they lived in Carjmam [Karimun], an island near the channel; and at the time when the said Paramjçura came to Muar these thirty came to live in the place which is now called Malacca, and it must be five leagues from Muar to Malacca.... The said fishermen, having been made mandarins by the hand of the said Paramjçura, always accompanied the said king, and as he advanced them in rank they too recognized the favour which had been granted to them. They accompanied the king zealously and served him with great faith and loyalty, their friendship [being] whole-hearted; and in the same way the king's love for them always corresponded to the true service and zeal of the said new mandarins, and they strove to please him, and their honour always lasted right down to the coming of Diogo Lopes de Sequeira to Malacca, when their fifth grandson was the Lasamana and the Bemdara.*

Parameswara's flights from Palembang and Singapura were both managed by Orang Laut, who also advised him to establish his new port at Melaka. These Orang Laut served as the sultan's personal staff, delivering royal missives and other messages, transporting the sultan and his entourage, as well as manning the royal kitchens. But most importantly, as Pires and other Portuguese chroniclers observed, the Orang Laut were the sultan's naval force, sailing forth to war for their sultan and patrolling the seas to enforce his will, including the collecting of taxes.

Anthropological fieldwork today corroborates the Portuguese and Dutch ethno-historical reports about these sea nomads. They were a diverse group of communities who made their home in the labyrinth of tidal channels and waterways in the mangrove swamps of the Riau islands and the southeast coast of Sumatra. Another group of sea peoples, the Moken, made their home on the islands off peninsular Myanmar and Thailand, while a third, the Sama-Bajau, occupied the Sulu zone and seas of Sulawesi.

The Portuguese explorer Pedro Teixeira observed:

*These seletes when they give a daughter in marriage, give her as a dowry one of those little boats, with two oars and a gaff; and the bride and bridegroom being placed therein, they commit them to the current of the tide, by which they let themselves be carried until they come to land; and there where they*

A Melayă Captain.

Printed engraving of a "Melaya captain" leading a group of armed Orang Laut, in Johan Nieuhof's *Embassy from the East India Company*, printed in 1669.

*touch is the place of their habitation when they are on land; that is, if it be not occupied by others, which if it is, they continue to follow the waves until they pitch upon a free spot.*

As nomadic foragers, they sailed the seas of the Riaus and southeast Sumatra in their dugout canoes (which also served as their homes) and were intimately familiar with the currents, tides and sea landscape of their maritime world. They became indispensable pilots to the sailors and traders navigating the maze of channels of the Musi River up to the port-city of Sriwijaya. In later centuries, they were engaged by the Portuguese and Dutch to pilot them through the treacherous waters and passageways around Singapore.

It was a group of chieftains (*datu*) from these sea nomad communities who, in the 7th century, made themselves lords of the realm of the sea and transformed their local trade networks centred on their home base along the Musi River into an emporium serving the emerging Chinese trade. Sriwijaya, as its inscriptions announce, emerged to become the major emporium from the 7th to at least the 11th century, where Arab, Persian and Indian traders met the sea nomads to trade in local products that were sought after in the Chinese market.

It appears that these fragmented and dispersed sea nomad groups were brought together when the *datu* reached out and appropriated Mahayana Buddhism, or more probably, esoteric-tantric Buddhism, with its theology of devotion and loyalty to a spiritual master, to unite their people around themselves as men of spiritual prowess. A series of inscriptions – the Sabukingking or Telaga Batu inscription from Palembang, the Kota Kapur inscription from Bangka, and the Karang Berahi inscription at Jambi – bear testimony to the oaths of loyalty which local chieftains had to offer to the *datu* of Sriwijaya, and the dire consequences of disloyalty.

Seven centuries later, the *Malay Annals* and the Portuguese would report that Demang Lebar Daun, on behalf of his followers, and Parameswara/Sri Tri Buana swore an oath of loyalty to each other. The Portuguese reports attribute the absolute loyalty of the Orang Laut warriors to these deep social memories of the sacred covenant that their forefathers had concluded with Parameswara/Sri Tri Buana. It was these social memories that led a group of Bajau sea nomads to accompany Parameswara on his flight from Palembang to Temasek and later brought him to Muar and helped him to establish Melaka. And it was these same Orang Laut who, according to the *Malay Annals*, responded to the calls of the Melaka sultans to defend the realm from threats and challenges and who carried the last sultan of Melaka to safety and away from his burning city in 1511.

### Temasek-Singapura: Home of the Sultan's Warriors
These aforementioned Portuguese and Dutch reports identify several different groups and tribes of Orang Laut who resided in the estuaries of the Kallang, Singapore and Seletar rivers and around

Some of the sea nomad communities continue to maintain an autonomous nomadic lifestyle today. But they face an uncertain future as their world shrinks in a developing Singapore-Johor-Riau "Growth Triangle".

Pulau Brani in the 16th through the 17th centuries. Until the early 20th century, groups of Orang Laut continued to reside in the river estuaries of Singapore. The Kallang River estuary was home to groups of Orang Kallang. Some of their social memories recalled their descent from the Orang Biduanda Kallang, who followed the Temenggong to Singapore at the beginning of the 19th century. On the north shore of Singapore, around Punggol and the Seletar River, could be found small groups of Orang Johor and Orang Selat. Larger Orang Laut communities resided along the coasts of the Riau islands, and these communities were the ones who in earlier centuries responded to the rallying call of the sultans.

As sea nomads familiar with the waters of the Riaus, these Orang Laut warriors were the rapid response force of the sultan whether he was at Melaka or, during the Johor Sultanate, up the Johor River. When confronted by superior forces, they could equally rapidly withdraw. As the Portuguese and Acehnese would find, destroying the harbour-capital at Johor Lama or elsewhere on the Johor River did not break the sultanate. The sultan and his entourage were able to very quickly re-establish themselves at a new location to challenge the invading forces. This, then, was the significance of Singapura to the Melaka and Johor sultans: it was the home base of their Orang Laut warriors.

The *Malay Annals* cites Singapura as the fiefdom of the Sri Bija Diraja, who was one of the four Great Lords in the Melaka court in the reign of the first four sultans. Together with the sultan, the four Great Lords were the effective rulers of the kingdom. The most senior of the Great Lords was the Bendahara, who performed the functions similar to a modern-day prime minister.

The first Bendahara of Melaka was the sultan's younger brother; later versions of the *Malay Annals* describe the Bendahara as an elder statesman whose daughter the sultan would marry. Two Bendaharas were said to have come from Singapura. Ranking below the Bendahara was the Penghulu Bendahari, the equivalent of a modern-day minister of finance. He controlled the other Bendaharis and Shahbandars, who were the port officials supervising trade for the sultan. Next in the power line-up was the Temenggong, who was responsible for law and order.

The fourth of the Great Lords was the Sri Bija Diraja, who was the Hulubalang Besar, or commander of the military commanders. He shared command of the Orang Laut forces of the Melaka Sultanate with the Laksamana, although in protocol the latter was one of the Eight Lords, the layer of power just below the four Great Lords. During the reign of the fourth sultan, Mansur Shah, the great warrior Hang Tuah was elevated to the rank of Laksamana, to become one of the Great Lords on par with the Sri Bija Diraja.

Both the *Malay Annals* and the Portuguese records indicate that the Sri Bija Diraja and Laksamana were resident in Singapura. One incident recounted in the *Malay Annals* illustrates the pivotal status of Singapura as a fief of the Sri Bija Diraja:

> And Bendahara Puteh said to the Sri Bija 'diraja (who had just arrived from Singapore), "It was Sultan Ala'u'din's dying wish that the Ruler we have now should succeed him on the throne." And the Sri Bija 'diraja replied, "I did not hear his dying wish." When Sultan Mahmud Shah came to hear of what the Sri Bija 'diraja had said, he made no comment but in his heart he bore a grudge against the Sri Bija 'diraja....

> It happened once that the Sri Bija 'diraja did not appear at Melaka (on the eve of the Festival). He only arrived on the Festival day itself. And Sultan Mahmud Shah reprimanded the Sri Bija 'diraja saying, "Why were you not here in time Sri Bija 'diraja? Do you not know the custom?" And the Sri Bija 'diraja answered, "I was late in starting. I did not expect the new moon would have been seen last night. But I realise that I was negligent and I can only ask Your Highness to forgive me." And

*Sultan Mahmud Shah said, "No, I know what is in your mind, Sri Bija 'diraja, you do not like my being Raja." He thereupon gave orders for the Sri Bija 'diraja to be put to death. And when the men who were to put him to death came, the Sri Bija 'diraja said to them, "What is my offence against the Ruler? Can it be that for the trifling offence I have committed I am to be put to death?" When Sultan Mahmud Shah was informed of what the Sri Bija 'diraja had said, he replied, "If the Sri Bija 'diraja does not know what his offence is, shew him this writing." The writing set out four or five offences on the part of the Sri Bija 'diraja, and when he had looked at it he was silent. And he was put to death. It was to his son Sang Stia Bentayan that the fief of Singapura was given.*

This episode is significant for what it says about how delicate and central the issue of absolute loyalty to the sultan was for Melaka's governance. Without the rudiments of a bureaucracy to govern the realm, the sultans of Melaka and Johor had to rely – like their ancestors, the *datu* of 7th-century Sriwijaya – upon their moral prowess and suasion expressed in the oaths of loyalty that their functionaries were expected to take.

The sultans of Melaka and Johor could never be sure how many warriors were loyal to the Sri Bija Diraja and could be counted on to defend the realm when it was threatened. In the 17th-century alliance between Johor and the Dutch, Admiral Cornelis Matelieff de Jonge (who is discussed more extensively in Chapter Four) spent much time trying to estimate the forces the Johor sultan could mobilise to join him in a combined attack on Portuguese Melaka. In 1714, the Dutch Governor in Melaka assessed that the sultan was capable of mustering up to 6,500 soldiers, of whom 2,000 were Orang Laut from the Riaus, a further 500 Orang Laut from Lingga, 400 from Bengkalis and the Siak River, and 700 from the islands off the coast of Pahang. What these numbers suggest is that the Orang Laut from the Riaus and the Melaka Straits consti-tuted about half of the sultan's estimated military might.

The issue of the loyalty of the Orang Laut to the sultan was largely a consequence of the nomadic nature of these communities and their lifestyle in the mangroves and waterways feeding into the Melaka and Singapore straits. Their environment and social struc-ture gave them the mobility to form multiple relationships with competing sultans and centres of authority. An implicit theme of

The complex relationships that the various sea nomad communities and tribes had established with competing Malay kingdoms over the centuries were undermined by the increasingly dominant colonial states in the 19th century. They became confined to fishing-based subsistence, supplemented by the collecting of mangrove and sea products for trade with outsiders. John Thomson's 1848 watercolour captures the marginalised status of these sea nomads under colonial rule.

the *Malay Annals* is that the sultans could never take for granted the loyalty and support of their sea peoples, who could easily switch their allegiance to rulers of rival port-harbours who offered more rewards and better prices for their sea produce. The sultans of Melaka and Johor had to work hard to retain the loyalty of their sea nomad warriors.

The role of these Orang Laut communities as not only the warriors but also the messengers and tax-collectors of the sultans continued until 1699, when the murder of Sultan Mahmud created a dynastic crisis in which the Orang Laut as warriors of the sultan were replaced by Bugis mercenaries. With the Bugis in charge, the Orang Laut were marginalised and reduced to outsiders.

In the first half of the 19th century, Munshi Abdullah, Stamford Raffles' Malay-language scribe and tutor, observed:

> They behaved like animals. Whenever they saw a crowd of people coming, if there was time they made off quickly in their boats; if there was not time they leapt into the sea and swam underwater like fish.… Both men and women behaved like this.

That such timid people could once have been warriors of the sultan was inconceivable to W.H. Read, who in 1883 commented that "the idea of a Batin [chief] being sent on such a mission [to bring Tengku Husain to Stamford Raffles] will make Malays, or those acquainted with their manners and customs, smile". Nevertheless, it was precisely an Orang Laut named Batin Sapi who went to Bintan in January 1819 to fetch Tengku Husain to Singapura to be recognised as sultan.

## IN A NUTSHELL

Continuing from the story of Temasek or Singapura, Chapter Two examines the relationship between the fall of Singapura and the rise of Melaka in the 15th century through narratives and tropes found in the *Malay Annals*. Central to this continuity of relations between the two port-polities was the figure of Singapura's last ruler, Parameswara/ Iskandar Shah, who decamped to establish a new and more successful emporium in Melaka.

Even though Melaka's prominence overshadowed that of Singapura, the island continued to be a crucial harbour for the sultanate, collecting forest products from Johor and the Riau islands for export through Melaka. More significantly, the waters around Singapore were home to sea nomads who served as warriors of the Melaka sultans, with the island itself serving as a strategically significant naval base. Their commander, holding the title of Sri Bija Diraja, resided in Singapore and was one of the four Great Lords of the Melaka court.

As we will see in Chapter Three, the alliance between the Malay sultans and the Orang Laut based in Singapura would continue to be significant even in the next cycle at Johor, after the fall of Melaka in 1511. Singapura served as the gateway port to the realm up the Johor River and continued its strategic involvement as the sultanate's naval base.

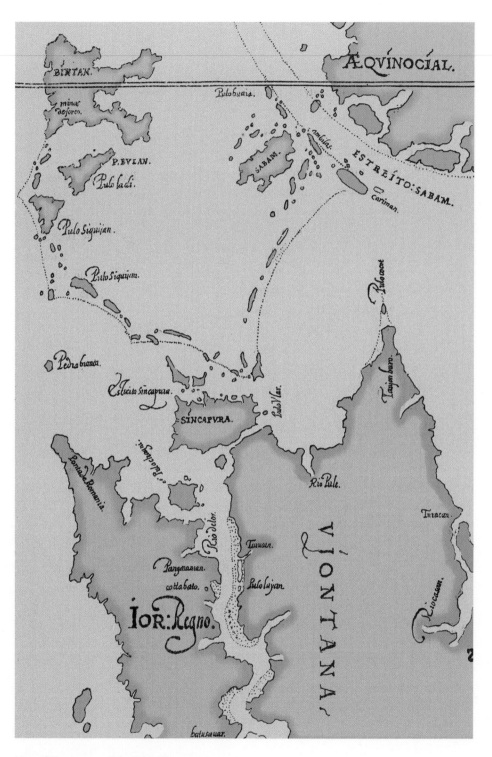

Map of Singapore and the Johor River up to
Batu Sawar by Manuel Godinho de Erédia,
c. 1613. Singapore is disproportionately reduced
in size in relation to the Johor coastline, but
the map gives an insight into Erédia's sensing
of Singapore as the gateway to the Kingdom of
Johor, marked "Jor Regno" on the map.

# CHAPTER THREE

# The 16th Century
## Shahbandaria of the Johor Sultanate

*And the Franks [Portuguese] engaged the men of Malaka in battle, and they fired their cannons from the ships so that the cannon balls came like rain. And the noise of the cannon was as the noise of thunder in the heavens and the flashes of the fire of their guns were like flashes of lightning in the sky; and the noise of their matchlocks was like that of ground-nuts popping in the frying pan. So heavy was the gun-fire that the men of Malaka could no longer maintain their position on the shore. The Franks then bore down upon the bridge with their galleys and foysts. Thereupon Sultan Ahmad came forth, mounted on his elephant Jituji. The Sri Awadana was on the elephant's head, and to balance him on the packsaddle Sultan Ahmad took with him Makhdum Sadar Jahan because he was studying the doctrine of the Unity of God with him. On the elephant's croup was Tun Ali Hati. And the King went forth on to the bridge and stood there amid a hail of bullets… the King fought with the Franks pike to pike, and he was wounded in the palm of the hand…. [But] Malaka fell. The Franks advanced on the King's audience hall, and the men of Malaka fled. Sultan Ahmad then withdrew to Hulu Muar and thence to Pagoh. Sultan Mahmud Shah had taken up his abode at Batu Hampar… the Franks occupied Malaka where they turned the royal palace into a fort; which fort is there to this day [1621, when this version of the Malay Annals was written].*

Account in the *Malay Annals* of Melaka's fall to the Portuguese in 1511

### Port-city Singapore Rises Once More

The military campaign that dislodged Sultan Mahmud from Melaka was a hard-won victory for the Portuguese. While Portuguese chronicles celebrate the glory and heroism, Italian John of Empoli, who worked in the entourage of the Melaka conqueror Alfonso de Albuquerque, offered a more critical view – and arguably a more accurate one, coming as it did from first-hand experience of the campaign and its immediate aftermath.

Alfonso de Albuquerque, the Governor of Portuguese India and conqueror of Melaka in 1511.

In a letter to his father, Empoli explained that Sultan Mahmud fled to a "neighbouring town to seek help to attack our ships because few were left to man them". The desperate Portuguese raced against time to construct a fortification – A Famosa or "The Famous" – with "great haste by day and the use of torches by night", using timber and stone wrenched from private homes and public buildings. "We erected it with great hardship bearing the stones on our backs; and each of us was a day labourer, mason and stone-cutter."

The fortress was built with "weapons about us", for the Sultan and his forces harried them relentlessly: "And while about this work, we heard a great din from the enemy: almost every day they attacked, now from one side and now from another, now by sea and now by land." After the fall, food was scarce, and "we had nothing to eat save rice, so that all our people began to fall sick," Empoli reported. Provisions were strictly rationed and within a month, 700 people – both Portuguese and prisoners – died of malnutrition and starvation. The bodies piled up faster than they could be buried and "there was not a man who did not fall sick of a devilish fever, wherefore the dead lay in the captain's quarters two or three days, for no one to bury them could be found". Empoli himself, "half-dead as… [he] was" after almost two months of illness, barely survived.

The six chapters of the *Malay Annals* following the fall of Melaka record the trials and tribulations of Mahmud Shah in his efforts to regain the city after deposing his son and successor, Sultan Ahmad, to resume the throne. These chapters relate how the Portuguese harried Mahmud and finally drove him from Bintan, where he had based himself, and he was dragged by the Sri Nara di Raja to re-establish the sultanate elsewhere. Ultimately, though, Sultan Mahmud was denied the chance to reclaim Melaka's glory. That opportunity fell to his successor and son, Alauddin Shah, who founded a new *negara* (kingdom) on the upper reaches of the Johor River in 1528.

The Portuguese captured only the empty shell of the great emporium that was Melaka. The networks of loyalties, alliances and trade that had underpinned Melaka's prosperity did not pass to the Portuguese, but were carried by Sultan Mahmud wherever he went. The loyalty of the Orang Laut warriors who were based in Singapore waters was especially important to Mahmud and

Alauddin Shah and their successors as they established themselves up the Johor River. Singapore almost certainly acquired additional significance as the gateway to the Johor River realm of its sultans. The Orang Laut warriors would have served as sentries guarding the entrance to the river, providing early warning of approaching hostile Portuguese or Acehnese forces.

After Melaka's fall to the Portuguese in 1511, the Laksamana (admiral and commander) of the Orang Laut forces returned to his base on the island of Singapore. Portuguese chronicles describe him as a man of about 80 years old at the time. His return to Singapore (where he was at one point briefly joined by the fugitive Sultan Mahmud) gave Singapore a new significance. When the Portuguese apothecary and chronicler Tomé Pires wrote his *Suma Oriental* around 1513–15, he dismissed the commercial importance of Singapore and the surrounding villages. But after 1511, and especially following 1528, Singapore experienced a revitalisation. By the end of the 16th century, the Melaka-based merchant Jacques de Coutre recorded that Singapore was one of the "best ports" in the East Indies.

### Sightings and Testimonials

Several written European and West Asian testimonies mention a port on Singapore in the 16th century. John of Empoli recorded his last will and testament while his ship was anchored at Singapore en route to China, but, understandably, given the document's legal nature, offered no description of Singapore. The Jesuit missionary Francis Xavier, who travelled to and from Japan between 1546 and 1552, offered another testimony. Five of his letters were despatched from the "Strait of Symquapura" or "Cincapura". His first letter, written in Singapore, albeit without places and dates, offers reasonable clues:

> *Thirty-nine days ago I sailed from Japan, where the faith of Jesus our Lord is in very great increase…. If there is [in Malacca] a ship ready to sail [for Goa] speak to the senior captain and ask him to wait for one more day, since I hope that I shall arrive in Malacca some time Sunday….*

The letter suggests the existence of a postal or express courier service between Singapore and Melaka. Could this also be evidence of Singapore's port facilities? A few years later, the Ottoman admiral and navigator Seydi Ali Reis, alias Sidi Ali ben Hossein,

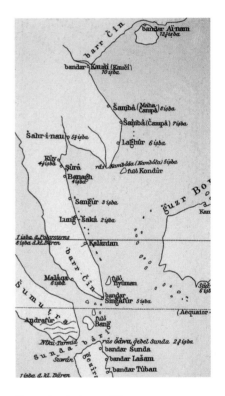

Reconstructed map of the Malay Peninsula based on the information contained in the 16th-century Ottoman-Turkish rutter *Muhit*. The map is taken from the 1897 edition of *Die Topographischen Capitel des Indischen Seespiegels Mohit*. Note that the coastal areas around the South China Sea littoral on the Malay Peninsula and along the present-day coast of Vietnam are marked as "Barr-Čin", the "coast of China".

provided the latitude of "Bandar Singafûr" in his *Muhit*, a rutter, or mariner's handbook, featuring navigational instructions and information on ports around the Indian Ocean rim and the western Pacific. Again, there are no further details.

The important contextual point is that there are several sources attesting to the presence of a settlement and port on Singapore, though they furnish no specifics on how large this settlement or how busy this port was. But Singapore must have been significant enough to attract the attention of the Portuguese in their continuing war against their neighbours, including Johor. The naval forces based at Melaka, and later Johor, would doubtlessly also have been seen as a threat. So, it should come as no surprise that the Portuguese decided to despatch an expeditionary force against Singapore in the first quarter of the 16th century to take out the port and the Orang Laut armada.

Portuguese information on this campaign is fragmentary at best. We are informed only cursorily about the Portuguese strike and the destruction of the Singapore settlement. This is confirmed by the rutter ascribed to John of Lisbon dating from the early 16th century, as well as by another very similar document (c. mid-1500s) by André Pires. The episode is also mentioned by Luís de Matos in a 2015 dissertation in which he concedes that the circumstances leading to Singapore's destruction are uncertain. He suggests that the blow inflicted on the settlement might have happened during Pero de Mascarenhas' campaign against Bintan (1526) or during Francisco da Gama's attack against Johor in 1535. Singapore arguably became a "strategic location" in the continuing Portuguese-Melaka/Johor conflict.

### The Johor Sultanate and Its Riverine Economy
When Sultan Mahmud died, the task and challenge of reclaiming Melaka's glory devolved to two of his sons. Sultan Alauddin, the eldest, established a new *istana* at Sayong Pinang in 1528, which would serve as the first of at least five Johor capitals over the next 200 years. Over time, Acehnese and Portuguese attacks would force the Johor sultans to move their court to different locations along the Johor River.

In selecting Sayong Pinang, Alauddin was not retreating to a backwater divorced from the thriving trade of the Singapore and Melaka straits. A map by Portuguese explorer and cartographer

Portrait of Portuguese mathematician and explorer Manuel Godinho de Erédia. The original is found in the manuscript of his *Description of Melaka*, c. 1613.

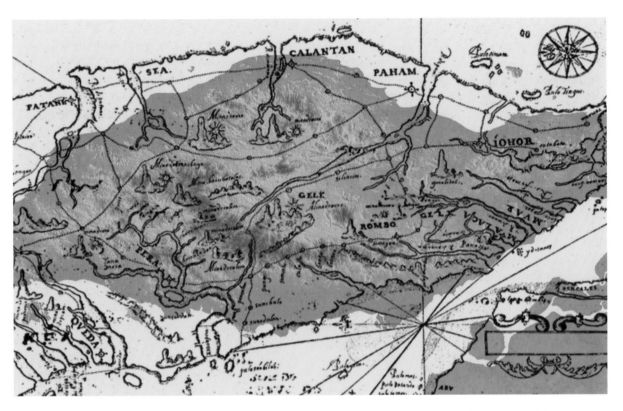

Manuel Godinho de Erédia (*Atlas Miscelânea*, c. 1616–22) depicts a series of trails running largely along the east coast of the Malay Peninsula, stretching from the Kra Isthmus near southern Thailand to Johor.

At several junctions, the trails branch out into the highlands of the peninsula or connect with riverine networks and other trails. The annotations around these junctions suggest that these were locations where specific commodities, such as gold, copper, tin, and perhaps also tree resins and fragrant woods were sourced. In seeking to control the southern terminals of these inland trails and trade routes, the Johor sultans may have been no different from their Sriwijayan forebears, who had located themselves up the Musi River to control the sourcing and export of aromatics and other valued forest products from the Sumatran highlands to regional markets.

Archaeological evidence further establishes the Johor River as a trade node in the Singapore and Melaka straits well before the Johor sultans established their capitals there. Surface archaeological surveys of the sites of former Johor capitals were conducted

Copy of a map of the Malay Peninsula ascribed to Erédia in his *Atlas Miscelânea* (now lost), showing a series of overland trails running the length of the peninsula. Erédia's map broadly matches with a modern topographic map, as this overlay shows. Patani, Kelantan and the Johor River were major nodes in this network of trails.

by Raffles Museum curators and archaeologists in the 1950s and 1960s. They found these sites heavily littered with earthenware and Chinese blue-and-white porcelain sherds, similar to the situation at the sites of other Southeast Asian maritime emporia. The earthenware sherds probably came from large jars used for the storage and transportation of trade goods such as porcelains, grains, spices and preserved foods.

Several boxes of the recovered sherds found their way to the Raffles Museum (precursor of today's National Museum), and are now housed at the Heritage Conservation Centre of the National Heritage Board of Singapore. The blue-and-white export wares have been dated, based on the reign marks stamped on some of them, to the mid-15th century, around the reign of the Xianzong Emperor (1464–87). If authenticated, these sherds suggest that active commerce existed at Johor Lama, and possibly other Johor River sites as well, before they were occupied by the dispossessed Melaka Sultanate.

Other categories of archaeological evidence, including tombstones and a wide assemblage of trade beads spanning some 2,000 years, from Roman times to the early modern European period, collectively suggest that the Johor River was part of a regional trade network from the mid-15th century.

Jacques de Coutre witnessed Johor's flourishing riverine economy in the last decade of the 16th century when he visited the later

Blue-and-white porcelain sherds dated to the 16th–17th centuries recovered from Johor Lama and other sites along the Johor River and now deposited in the Heritage Conservation Centre of the National Heritage Board.

capital of Batu Sawar several times to trade. He was well aware of the Portuguese destruction of Johor Lama in 1587 and the move upstream to Batu Sawar. He wrote:

> *The king of the city of Johor Lama fled and went to live on the island of Bintan, and later returned and built another city 14 leguas upstream, which is called Batur Sawar [but which] the Portuguese call "New Johor".... It is a port frequented by many carracks from diverse nations.... It has a beautiful river and a port with many large and small ships, and it is a land where the merchants do vast volumes of trade and there are abundant provisions.*

Elsewhere, he elaborated: "In the aforementioned city [Batu Sawar], there are many people who make a living only from merchandise and [from] sailing from one land to another." Apart from being a base and regional meeting place for merchants, Johor evidently generated enough wealth through commerce that its material prosperity came to be reflected in the fashionable attire worn by its inhabitants. De Coutre, a textile trader, described Johoreans thus:

> *The native people dress in the same manner as the inhabitants of the kingdom of Pahang. They are Malays by blood and very smartly dressed.*

Which begs the question: what about the fashion sense of the people of Pahang? De Coutre's autobiography offers this gem:

> *The natives are Muslims, however they are very tactful in their dealings and in their manner of dress. [The men] wear shirts made of cassa or beatilha [muslin] dyed in various colours – they call them baju – and as shorts they wear dyed half-beatilha which are made for this purpose along the Coromandel Coast, and they wrap it around between their legs in such a way that they look like shorts. They wear another white or coloured scarf as a turban, twisted like a shawl, and they carry a keris in their belt as a dagger. Some of them have a keris with a golden hilt, and others have a wooden hilt, according to what each individual can afford.*

> *The women also wear a long and narrow blouse which allows a glimpse of their flesh. Some textiles are coloured, others*

Sketch of a Malay woman in John Crawfurd's *Journal of an Embassy from the Governor-General of India to the Courts of Siam and Cochin-China* (1828).

*are blue, and you find them in all colours. [They wear] a short tight jacket, which is tailored from very thin material often with elaborate designs and colours. They also tie back their hair in a very curious fashion with multi-coloured ribbons. As they walk barefoot they wear rings on both their fingers and their toes and are very beautiful in their overall appearance.*

It was not only traders from the Indonesian Archipelago, India and China who came to Batu Sawar, but ironically, the Portuguese from Melaka too, according to De Coutre:

*When the Javanese come to know that in Melaka there is some captain who mistreats them – as sometimes has been the case – though their course is through the Strait of Kundur to Melaka, they go from inside and around the islands in search of the island of Bintan, and then they go to Johor. These vessels come laden with nutmeg, mace, cloves and other merchandise. The Portuguese then go from Melaka to Johor, with cloth to sell, and buy spices and other commodities and return to Melaka.*

To add to the irony, the Portuguese helped Johor to flourish. De Coutre's glowing comments about Johor's wealth via robust trade are echoed by Pedro Barreto de Resende, whose 17th-century account observes:

*The port of Johor is located inside Romania Point [the south-eastern tip of the Malay Peninsula], where many vessels are built. It has many provisions, eaglewood and pitch. The city of Bintan is [located] on the opposite shore of that coast, well-fortified as compared to Aceh…. [Batu Sawar] does a great deal of trade.*

Several other accounts touch on the significance and prosperity of Johor's riverine towns, dating chiefly from the turn of the 16th and 17th centuries. A brief report by Dutchman Stalpaert van der Wiele (*Information Concerning Diverse Lands and Islands Situated in the East Indies*) offers details of Johor and the goods traded there:

*Johor is a famous trading city and is situated on the southern-most tip of the mainland of Melaka [the Malay Peninsula] at 2 degrees north of the equator where there is also a lot of*

An early 19th-century drawing of the clove plant. Cloves are the aromatic flower buds of the clove tree (*Syzygium aromaticum*), which is native to the Maluku Islands.

*pepper. It asserts its rights in war against the Portuguese, but the Portuguese do not have a fortress here. I think one can obtain here many diverse cotton cloth pieces. This is the land where the proper Malay language has its origin. Melaka rightly belongs to Johor's king. He is a very magnanimous king and is greatly respected by the foreigners. [Van der Wiele was referring to Sultan Ali Jalla bin Abdul Jalil Shah, who died in 1597.]*

Other Europeans would later make similar observations about the significance of Johor and the Johor River towns within the context of trade, not least the Dutch, who emerged as the most formidable European competitors to the Portuguese. Referring to the Dutch East India Company, Dutch historian and lawyer Pieter van Dam wrote around the close of the 17th century:

*From the beginning, the Company maintained a factory in Johor, which borders the land of Melaka; not that [Johor] is a land that has, or can deliver, much of itself, but in that it is well-situated for trade, and it always had a lot of maritime traffic.*

In sum, it is clear that the Johor River towns and the royal capitals established there in the 16th and 17th centuries were renowned centres of commerce, and Singapore formed part of this picture.

Johor's commercial success and prosperity was to arouse the jealousy of the Portuguese, prompting them to contain or even break

Bird's-eye view of Aceh viewed from the sea. Taken from the Vingboons Atlas, c. 1665.

Johor's success. This helps explain why the two were bound to clash eventually, which they did by the 1580s. But Johor was also being pressed by a regional power, Aceh. Based around Sumatra's northern tip, Aceh had expanded rapidly and aggressively from the first half of the 16th century onwards, and within a few decades was vying directly with Johor for trade, prosperity and, crucially, cultural primacy in the Malay world. Aceh fought Johor in 1564 in the first of a series of battles in and around Singapore and the Johor River estuary which would culminate in Aceh making a destructive strike in 1613.

Singapore's status as a Johor naval base as well as its role as the gatekeeper of Johor's capital and upstream towns lent it a special significance. It served not only as a strategic nodal point at the intersection of maritime and riverine trade, but also as a gateway to the South China Sea for those sailing from the Straits of Melaka and the Bay of Bengal. The port was significant and busy enough to warrant the presence of a Shahbandar, a high-ranking Malay official often translated as "harbour master" or "port master", but who, in fact, wielded considerable power and responsibilities.

**"Lord of the Haven, Father and Mother of Foreign Merchants"**

The title "Shahbandar" is of Persian origin, meaning "Lord of the Haven", which offers a more complete reflection of his scope and authority than the more prosaic English translation of "harbour master". The Persian meaning was adopted by Sriwijaya and other emporia of the Melaka Straits to designate the officer in charge of administering trade in their ports and harbours. From the Straits of Melaka, this office spread across the archipelago. By the early modern period, the Shahbandar had become an officer who not only administered and taxed trade on behalf of the ruler, but also fulfilled several other administrative functions. The scope of his responsibilities was outlined in the *Undang-undang Melaka*, or *Laws of Melaka*, which probably originated around the second half of the 15th century. After Melaka's fall in 1511, the laws served as a template for organising Malay polities.

The *Laws of Melaka* describe the Shahbandar as the "father and mother of foreign merchants", an analogy that testifies to his key role as a mediator between the foreign merchants and the royals. In the Melakan tradition, the Shahbandar was given jurisdiction over all matters concerning foreign merchants, orphans and persons who had suffered injustice, as well as regulations pertaining to junks, cargo boats and other vessels. Tomé Pires added that the Shahbandar had "charge of the guard" and had "many people under his jurisdiction". Moreover, "all prison cases go first to him and from him to the [Bendahara], and this office always falls to persons of great esteem".

Additionally, the Shahbandar was an investment manager for the ruler, merchant-officials, and their families. He supervised foreign imports – whether by foreign merchants or those on the trading vessels belonging to the royal family – and collected the dues levied on imports and exports. As the supervisor of the royal warehouses, he oversaw a virtual monopoly in essential exports as foreign merchants could only procure key export goods from these warehouses. For this reason, the rulers were often described by Europeans as the largest merchants in their own realms. The rulers usually paid promptly, either in bartered goods or, less frequently, in cash or specie.

Singapore's significance as a 16th-century trading centre should thus be seen against the backdrop of the Shahbandar's vital multi-tasking roles and responsibilities. Its port was important enough

Gold coins were minted and used in the Malay states of Johor, Kelantan, Terengganu and Kedah from the 15th to the 18th centuries. Earlier, the Melaka sultans issued a series of tin currencies in the shape of animals such as crocodiles, roosters, fish and pyramid-shaped blocks known as "tin hats". Probably, as in north Sumatra, where gold coins first circulated in the 14th century, the Malay sultans used these gold coins with Islamic inscriptions to declare their religious affiliation and right to rule.

to warrant the presence of a Shahbandar, and presumably the infrastructure that went along with it, from port to storage facilities. Moreover, he is likely to have played a role in managing the trading and bartering networks that sourced for produce, such as metals, pepper, tree resins and aromatics, from the peninsular hinterland.

There are testimonies to the existence of both the Shahbandar as well as this commercial infrastructure. The most important independent European one comes from the Dutch admiral and VOC fleet commander Cornelis Matelieff de Jonge (Cornelis Matelieff the Younger, also known as Cornelis Corneliszoon Matelief). When his ships arrived off the western coast of the peninsula in late April 1606, the Shahbandar of Singapore was despatched by the ruler to visit the fleet, ascertain its strength, and report back to the court at Batu Sawar. Matelieff's journal contains this account:

> Toward the evening [of 30 April 1606], two perahus from Johor joined the fleet. … The commander was the Shahbandar of Singapore, called Sri Raja Negara. Admiral [Matelieff] welcomed them as they were coming from the king of Johor, our ally, and let them navigate through the fleet and view the ships. They told [the Admiral] that the king had sent them to see if there were ships from Holland, because he had received a message from Perak that some ships had sailed to Melaka which were thought to be Dutch.

This testimony is important on at least two counts. First, it points to the existence of a Shahbandar in Singapore, whom Matelieff confirms meeting. Second, the admiral explains that the Shahbandar held another title concurrently – Sri Raja Negara (or Nugara, according to Matelieff's journal notes). The question then arises: what do we know about the responsibilities associated with this honorific? The title Sri Raja Negara refers to a proxy or representative of the ruler, but significantly also a military commander; so in addition to exercising the functions of a Shahbandar as outlined earlier, Singapore's Shahbandar, according to Matelieff, also had a defence portfolio. This is not surprising given that he was in a line of succession that reached back to at least the time of Melaka's Laksamana, and also given Singapore's function as a naval base of the Melaka and Johor sultanates. These responsibilities in Johor's maritime defence also explain why the Johor ruler despatched him to inspect the Dutch fleet in April 1606.

There is more. The Malay-Bugis chronicle *Tuhfat al-Nafis* (The Precious Gift) notes that the Raja Negara was also known as the Raja Negara Selat or Ketua Orang Laut. This is an important association as it brings the office of the Shahbandar of Singapore, via his other honorific as Raja Negara, to be associated with the leader or chief (*ketua*) of the Orang Laut communities living in and around the straits. It connects with yet another honorific, Raja Selat (Prince of the Strait), i.e., commander of the sultan's naval forces. This may be the reason why European accounts of the 16th and 17th centuries bothered to identify and name these Orang Laut communities in and around Singapore and the adjacent waterways: these sea tribes were the rowers aboard the naval vessels (some of which were stationed at Singapore) for the sultans of Melaka and Johor until the early 1700s.

The third honorific, Raja Selat, brings us back to Admiral Matelieff. Gerritsz Pieter Rouffaer, the Director of the Dutch research institute KITLV, drew attention in a seminal 1921 article to a passage in Matelieff's journal that identifies and briefly describes the four surviving sons of Sultan Ali Jalla bin Abdul Jalil Shah of Johor, who died around 1597. The four were the Yang di Pertuan Agong Ala'uddin Ri'ayat Shah III of Johor; his half-brother, Raja Siak; another half-brother, Raja Bongsu; and a fourth, named Raja Laut. The honorific Raja Laut echoes the Raja Selat who is mentioned in the *Tuhfat al-Nafis*. Were they identical, and, if they were, could it also mean that the Shahbandar of Singapore, the Sri Raja Negara, and the Raja Laut were one and the same person at the turn of the 16th and 17th centuries?

Moreover, this would also imply that the Singapore Shahbandar was a royal prince and a son of the late Ali Jalla bin Abdul Jalil, a half-brother of the next two sultans of Johor, a key figure in maritime defence, the head of the Orang Laut community in the straits, and yes, the titular Shahbandar of Singapore. Given this lineage and possibly that of the Melaka Laksamana in the early 16th century, Singapore would hardly have been a forgotten and neglected backwater, at least since the Portuguese capture of Melaka in 1511. This is a crucial observation to bear in mind and has consequences for our understanding of Singapore in the 16th century.

There is evidence to underscore this important conclusion in European texts and maps of this period. Jacques de Coutre noted in his autobiography that as he exited the Old Strait of Singapore from the west, there was a settlement known as Sabandaria, which was inhabited by Malays loyal to the Johor ruler. The passage reads: "We anchored in front of a place which is called Sabandaria, which is inhabited by Malays, subjects of the king of Johor to whom the saletes [*selates* or Orang Laut], who sail in the straits, pay tribute." He does not mention the size of the settlement, but describes it as "one of the best [ports] that serves the [East] Indies". Thus, there was a functioning port and a settlement that evidently took its name, Shahbandaria ("Shahbandar's town"), from the presence of the Shahbandar, his compound of warehouses and his resident dependents.

The name "Xabandaria" – spelt the Portuguese way – features prominently on maps of the Singapore Straits by the aforementioned Portuguese cartographer Erédia. One map appears in his report entitled *Declaraçam de Malaca e India Meridional com o Cathay*, or *Description of Melaka, Meridional India and Cathay*, which chronicles his travels in the region at the beginning of the 17th century. It is unclear whether Erédia visited Singapore; he probably sailed past it, and his map was drawn according to information he collected during a naval expedition in 1604.

The map, entitled "Chorographic Description of the Straits of Sincapura and Sabbam in the year 1604", is oriented with Johor at the bottom and Sumatra at the top. It identifies a number of features on the east coast of Sincapura; the northernmost feature is Tanjong Rusa, south of which are Tanah Merah, Sungei Bedok, Tanjong Rhu and a "Xabandaria". Tanjong Rusa refers to Changi Point today, and may have taken its name from the shoals off its coast that were once known as Beting Kusah or Tanion Ruça, as Erédia marked it in his map.

Tanah Merah refers to the reddish-orange weathered lateritic cliffs along the coast (since levelled) that were a prominent landmark for navigators and pilots up to the 19th century; they are marked as "Red Cliffs" in James Horsburgh's 1806 chart of Singapore and Melaka. Later sea charts distinguish between the "Red Cliffs" of Tanah Merah and Bedok. Other early maps of Singapore transcribe this old Malay place name as "Badok", in the vicinity of a "small red cliff". On the other hand, Tanjong Rhu takes its name from the Malay *ru* (also *eru* or *aru*), a reference to the casuarina trees (*Casuarina equisetifolia*) that proliferated on its sandy shores.

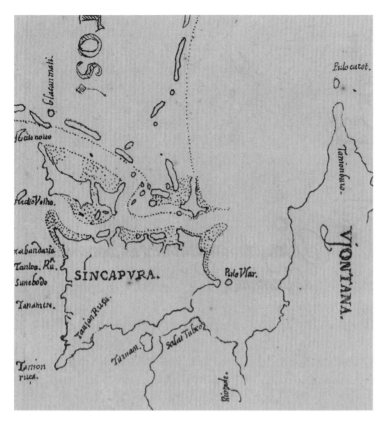

Detail from Erédia's "Chorographic Description of the Straits of Sincapura and Sabbam". The map is oriented with Johor at the bottom. A number of features are marked on the east coast of Singapore island. The northern-most feature identified is Tanjong Rusa (possibly Changi Point), south of which are Tanah Merah, Sungei Bedok, Tanjong Rhu and Xabandaria (harbour master's town). This indicates that there was a thriving port at the Kallang River estuary that needed a harbour master to administer it.

The area was known as Sandy Point to the early 19th-century British settlers.

The significance of Erédia's map, however, lies in the siting of Xabandaria in the vicinity of Tanjong Rhu. The former Puisne Judge of the Straits Settlements, J.V. Mills, who was also a scholar, translated and edited part of Erédia's report in 1930. But he failed to note this reference to Xabandaria in his extensive comments. The last British Director of the Raffles Museum, the polymath Dr Carl Alexander Gibson-Hill, in his detailed but underappreciated 1955 study of the charts and maps of the waters around Singapore, verified Erédia's four place names on the east coast of the island but similarly failed to comment on the reference to or the significance of Xabandaria.

A second crucial testimony is found in a chart of the Singapore and Melaka straits by André Pereira dos Reis dating from 1654, of which there are two hand-drawn specimens: one found in the palace library of the Dukes of Braganza at Vila Viçosa in Portugal, and the other among the maps of the W.A. Engelbrecht collection

Detail from André Pereira dos Reis' 1654 chart, showing a "Xebandaria" on the island of Singapore. Additional entries on the island include references to "red barriers" (or "red hills"), and "Tanjung Tahit" (for Changi Point).

at the Maritime Museum in Rotterdam in the Netherlands. Only the latter specimen features the place name "Xebandaria" on the island of Singapore. Nevertheless, the problem with these texts and maps is that they offer insufficiently clear evidence as to where this Shahbandar's settlement was located, which, in turn, prompts more questions.

### Shahbandaria and the Kallang Sherds

Where was Shahbandaria, or the settlement with the Shahbandar's compound in Singapore? A definite location cannot be inferred from the maps by Erédia and Pereira dos Reis. However, the dredging of the Kallang River estuary in the late 1960s for the construction of the Benjamin Sheares Bridge brought up, entirely by chance, evidence of 17th-century trading activity in the estuary. The British dredge operator, Geoffrey Ovens, noticed unusual objects being dredged from the river bed. He stopped the work, picked up a sackful of blue-and-white porcelain sherds from the mud and contacted the National Museum, asking for help in investigating the finds. But alas, the museum's curators passed on his offer. The sherds were distributed among Ovens' Singaporean friends, and what was not taken up was thrown away. Only nine sherds were kept by one of the friends. On leaving Singapore, Ovens took with him a fairly intact pear-shaped vase and a large dish. He later willed them to the National Museum, where they are housed today.

The sherds, plate and vase can be fairly precisely dated to the reign of the Ming Wanli Emperor (1573–1620). They display

landscape and narrative motifs from classic Chinese novels such as *Xixiang Ji* (Romance of the Western Chamber) and *Sanguo Yanyi* (Romance of the Three Kingdoms), with earlier landscapes being more Daoist in inspiration. Such landscape drawings on porcelain in the style of woodblock prints first appeared at the beginning of the 15th century. They were produced in the kilns of Jingdezhen, in Jiangxi province, for a domestic market of literati-gentry and the rich merchants emulating their lifestyle.

However, declining imperial patronage in the final two reigns of the Ming dynasty forced the kilns to explore overseas markets; they found a ready one in the South Seas and, farther afield, in West Asia. Shah Abbas of Persia amassed a huge collection, which he donated to the dynastic shrine at Ardebil in 1611. J.A. Pope, in his catalogue of porcelains from the Ardebil Shrine, listed dishes with landscapes similar to the Kallang sherds. Like the latter, the Ardebil dishes also have wheel marks and radial chatter on their unglazed bases, with sand adhering to their foot rims. Pope dated them to the late 16th century. The Kallang sherds would have a similar dating, suggesting that the Shahbandar's compound was likely located somewhere in the Kallang estuary.

The Kallang sherds are also similar to those found in large quantities around Johor Lama and other Johor royal capitals. Within this larger Johor River context, the Kallang sherds were thus not an isolated find, but part of a larger Johor River trade dominated by the Johor sultans. How these Wanli export wares came to be found in the Kallang River estuary can only be conjectured for now.

(*Above and top*) Underglazed blue-and-white porcelain sherds accidentally recovered during the dredging of the Kallang River estuary in the late 1960s and early 1970s. They can be dated to the reign of the Ming Wanli Emperor (1573–1620). These sherds are evidence of trading activity in the Kallang River estuary during the late 16th and early 17th centuries.

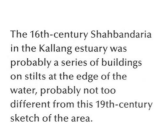

The 16th-century Shahbandaria in the Kallang estuary was probably a series of buildings on stilts at the edge of the water, probably not too different from this 19th-century sketch of the area.

Could the fragments have come from dishes that broke during the journey from China and were then dumped overboard when the vessel anchored at the estuary for a refill of fresh water and other supplies?

The excavation of some five shipwrecks along the east coast of the Malay Peninsula in the past 15 years has recovered heavy cargoes of Ming ceramics destined for the Southeast Asian and West Asian markets. Fishermen found one in 2001 – the Binh Thuan wreck – a classic Chinese junk dated to 1608, which was excavated by marine archaeologist Michael Flecker a year later. The wreck was located in 39 metres of water, some 40 nautical miles east of the fishing port of Phan Thiet, in Vietnam's Binh Thuan province. The holds of the junk were loaded with cast-iron pans. Above these were stacked some 100,000 pieces of Zhangzhou porcelain, the first dedicated shipment ever found. From historical documentations, the wreck appears to have been a junk of the Chinese merchant I Sin Ho, which was on its way to Johor with silks and other Chinese goods.

The routes taken by the Binh Thuan junk and other Chinese vessels on their voyages to the South Seas would have been among those recorded in the late 15th-century rutter titled *Shunfeng Xiangsong* (Favourable Winds in Escort). This mariner's guide provided instructions for 100 sailing routes, of which seven were for voyages from China to Southeast Asia and 19 for voyages within Southeast Asia. J.V. Mills, who in 1932 first examined references

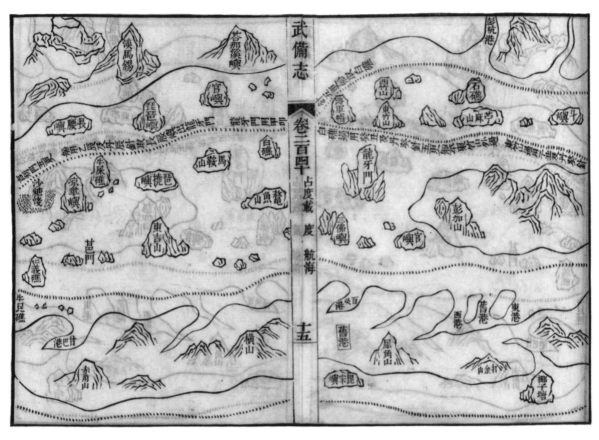

to the Malay Peninsula in Zheng He's voyages as archived in the iconic Mao Kun map, provided translations of some of these voyages. The ports and routes connecting them parallel those in an early 17th-century Chinese map that was rediscovered in 2008. This map had been acquired by the 17th-century English jurist and orientalist John Selden, who willed it as part of his library to Oxford University's Bodleian Library in 1659.

Johor's significance is clearly indicated in this singular cartographic specimen. Measuring 1.5 metres by 0.96 metres, the Selden map is centred on the South China Sea. It is drawn according to early modern European cartographic standards, but uses Chinese landscape painting techniques to outline mountain ranges, rivers and ocean waves, rendering the map a landscape painting of sorts.

The key features of the map are the 60 ports that the map identifies and connects by sailing routes to Quanzhou in Fujian province. One principal route goes northeast from Quanzhou towards

Section of the Mao Kun map plotting the passage of Zheng He's fleet past Longyamen ("Dragon's Teeth Strait"). Danmaxi (Temasek) is shown on the top left of the map. The navigational instructions can be read as referring to sailing past the Old Straits or, alternatively, the wider Singapore Straits of today. Longyamen would then refer not to the twin rocks at the western entrance to Keppel Harbour, but more probably, the twin peaks on Bintan island. It is doubtful Zheng He could have navigated his large fleet through the narrow western entrance to Keppel Harbour, the hazards of which were vividly recorded by Western travellers and sailors.

Nagasaki, while another goes southwest towards the Vietnamese port of Hoi An, and then on to the Malay Peninsula. What is significant is the route leading to Johor, where it branches out into sub-routes – one of which traverses up the Melaka Straits, proceeds southwards along the Sumatran coast to the Sunda Straits, then continues eastwards along the Java coast. Another sub-route leads northeast to Borneo and on to Manila, while yet another extends into eastern Indonesia. Historians are still in the early stages of making sense of the map as a depiction of the Fujian maritime trading world in the late Ming dynasty.

Cartographer Mok Ly Yng has interfaced the Selden map with contemporaneous Erédia maps of the inland trails and trade routes of the Malay Peninsula and Sumatra with interesting results. The terminal points of the inland trails on the east coast of Malaya coincide with the landfalls of the sailing routes marked on the Selden map. The Erédia trails terminate along the Johor River and south Johor, where the Selden map marks the Straits of Singapore as an especially busy junction. The Shahbandaria on Singapore may have been near the juncture where the maritime routes made contact with riverine and land routes.

(*Opposite*) The Selden map of the South China Sea. Maritime routes have been marked out but are barely visible. The map below highlights these routes.

(*Below*) Two systems of routes projected on a contemporary map: overland trails from Erédia's maps of Sumatra and the Malay Peninsula from the early 17th century, and the maritime routes from the contemporaneous Selden map.

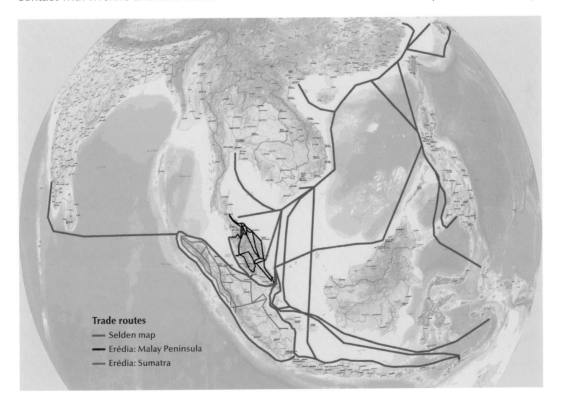

**Trade routes**
— Selden map
— Erédia: Malay Peninsula
— Erédia: Sumatra

### A Historic Rock and the Pitfalls of Sailing Past Singapore

While information about the precise location of the Shahbandaria is sparse, there is far more information on some of Singapore's main landmarks, features and surroundings found in 16th-century European travel literature. These charts, rutters and notices of sailing past Singapore indicate that there was growing interest in the waters around the island.

Singapore's most recognisable landmark in this period – and in the Age of Sail generally – was a rock formation that stood in what is today Labrador Park. This pillar-shaped formation, located across from the northwestern tip of present-day Sentosa, marked the western entrance to the Old and New Straits of Singapore. It was known by a variety of names in different languages. Some believe it to have been the 14th-century Longyamen mentioned in Chinese texts, while in Malay it was known as Batu Berlayar (Sail Rock, which was corrupted into Batu Blair in English) or Batu Cina (Chinese Rock). In Portuguese and Italian, it was known as Varela or Varella respectively, while English sailors sometimes referred to it as Lot's Wife or Sail Rock. The original rock formation was destroyed by the British in 1848 to broaden the access to the New Harbour. Its shape and relative size, however, have been captured in more or less detail in sketches as well as

Sketch of Batu Berlayar, Sail Rock, Lot's Wife, etc., by Lt. Jackson, 1823. This rock formation was arguably Singapore's most iconic landmark in the pre-colonial period and marked the western entrance to the Old and New Straits of Singapore. Part of the area around present-day Fort Siloso on Sentosa can be seen in the background.

A watercolour painting from the Charles Dyce Collection, depicting Keppel Straits and Batu Berlayar. Several scholars believe that the stone formation was probably referred to by Chinese sailors as Longyamen, or "Dragon's Teeth Straits" because it would have lined up visually with the frontal pegs on the bow of a Chinese junk, between which the anchor rope ran. These two pegs were known as *longya*, "dragon's teeth".

watercolours belonging to the Charles Dyce Collection preserved in the National University of Singapore Museum.

Before the middle of the 16th century, skippers plying the waters around Singapore followed one of two paths. The more frequently used one, the Old Strait of Singapore, brought ships from Pulau Pisang or the northern coast of Karimun to Pulau Merambong (formerly Pulau Ular, or Ilha das Cobras in Portuguese), off the western tip of Singapore island. This route led to a passage between what is now Jurong Island and the Singapore mainland and then continued along the coast at Pasir Panjang to the rock outcrop at Labrador Park. After waiting for the right tidal and wind conditions to set in, the ships would proceed through the strait between present-day Harbourfront and Sentosa before exiting at Pulau Brani. The voyage continued by hugging the eastern coast of Singapore and the Johor mainland before exiting into the South China Sea between Tanjung Ramunia and Pedra Branca.

The second and far less frequently used path brought ships along the northern coast of Singapore island, from Pulau Merambong through the Tebrau or Johor Straits toward Pulau Ubin and the Johor River. This passage was narrow and time-consuming. Because of strong water flows during the change of tides, the Tebrau Strait was generally seen as a second arm of the Johor River. Comprehended this way, Singapore island was situated entirely in the Johor River estuary, bounded by two branches of the river, which ran along Singapore's northern and eastern shores. Several cartographic specimens by Erédia confirm such an understanding of Singapore's location in the greater Johor River estuary.

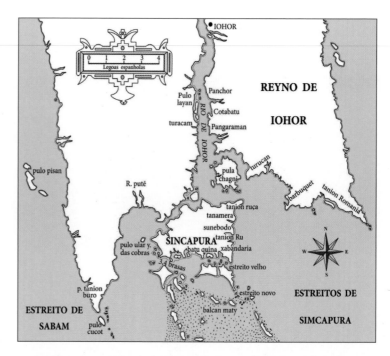

Redrawn map of Singapore and the Johor River based on an original by Manuel Godinho de Erédia, c. 1616–22. Singapore is depicted here as an island in a larger Johor River estuary.

Another understanding confuses the Tebrau Strait for the Old Strait of Singapore. This error, which arose in the second half of the 17th century, traces its origins to Dutch mapmaking. The hand-drawn charts often did not have much space to feature place names. Rather than naming Singapore island, the mapmakers wrote "Old Strait of Singapore" across the island. However, as the Old Strait was discarded after the 1620s, its location was forgotten, and subsequent mapmakers using such specimens as a guide mistook the Tebrau Strait for the Old Strait.

So, why would captains expose their ships to unwelcome danger by hugging the Singapore coastline instead of steering in the safer open waters of the main straits farther to the south like ships do today? The reason is the speed of water flows in the Singapore Straits during tidal changes, and also at different times of the year. Similar to a flowing river, the swiftest flow is in the middle of the straits, and slower toward the edges. In the Age of Sail, safe shipping depended on winds and currents. While the tidal speeds along the edges of the straits were manageable, the flow in the middle was very swift, and the waters deep. A ship could quickly lose control and smash into rocks or cliffs. Moreover, the deep waters of the mid-straits hindered ships from dropping anchor if they were to suddenly became caught in fast-moving currents and tides.

But hug-the-shoreline sailing had its own dangers. High tide often masked rocks, shoals and coral reefs known only to experienced pilots. According to European reports of this period, the shores of Singapore featured large trees with sprawling crowns that were so extensive that they ripped the sails of passing vessels, entangled the ropes and scratched the ships' wooden hulls. Europeans traversing the straits described the confusing landscape from the deck of the ship and the many dangers lurking on water and below. Italian merchant Francesco Carletti described sailing through the Old Strait in 1599 thus:

> *In this voyage [between Macau and Melaka] nothing occurred worth relating…. Except that after passing the Strait of Sincapura… between the main land and a variety of islands… with so narrow a channel that from the ship you could jump ashore or touch the branches of the trees on either side, our vessel struck on a shoal.*

Fortunately, Carletti added, his cargo was undamaged. The drama of navigating the Old Strait is further brought to light in the writings of the Dutch merchant and historian Jan Huyghen van Linschoten, specifically his landmark collection of navigational instructions known as the *Itinerario* and *Reysgeschrift*, published in Amsterdam (1595–96). Linschoten himself never ventured as far east as the Malay Peninsula or the Singapore Straits, but when he lived in Goa and in the Azores, he gained access to privileged materials about routes and markets in the Indies. His detailed instructions for sailing the Singapore Straits were almost certainly taken from a Portuguese original.

Linschoten's instructions are worth reproducing here. After passing Pulau Merambong and sailing along the western coast of Singapore, ships arrived at the Batu Berlayar rock formation. Linschoten's text then explains:

> *The mouth, or entrance, of this Strait lies between two high mountains, about one stone's throw in breadth, and extends towards the east with the length of about one shot of a 12-pounder. The channel of this strait measures at the time of the lowest tide about 4.5 vadem [7.7 metres] in depth. Next to the entrance, at the foot of the mountain on the northern side, is a stone cliff which in its appearance resembles a pillar. This is generally named by all nations who sail this passage the*

Hand-coloured portrait etching of Jan Huyghen van Linschoten taken from the first edition of his *Itinerario* published in Amsterdam in 1595. Linschoten's publication of navigational instructions from Portuguese and Spanish sources lifted the secrecy on the maritime trade routes and opened them up for usage by competitors from Northern Europe.

*Varella of the Chinese; and from the southern side, which is a bit inward from the entrance of the strait, the [channel] forms an inlet. In the middle of this inlet there is a submerged cliff that has a bank running off it towards the middle of the channel. A bit farther ahead, on the same side, [about] the length of a pipe shot, there is an opening that runs into the sea and extends over to the other side, [thus] creating an island. This opening is full of shallow waters, and [it] can only be used by small foists. In the middle of the bay where this stands, there is a rock or stone plate, submerged under two vadem [about 3.4 metres] of water. This stone plate extends as far into the bay as the land extends into the water, and somewhat more, reaching into the middle of the channel. After passing this inlet, the land forms a promontory or a point [featuring] a steep, broken-off hill, where the channel [also] ends. After sailing around this, one reaches a red hill, where one finds deep and clean ground; and when one has passed this, the land then extends farther in a south-easterly direction.*

*On the shore to the north of this strait – to wit, from the beginning to the end – there are three inlets, of which the first two are small and the third large. [The third inlet] is situated on the right, opposite the [aforementioned] promontory or point [with] the red hill, where the strait ends. This third inlet features a stone bank, which is exposed with a spring tide at low water, and [it] extends from the one point to the other. One has to be careful not to run into it. All of this is located on the northern side, the bank being outside the bay, across the entire channel from one point to the other, clean and nice.*

*Towards the exit of the strait, after having passed this [bay], there are two reefs, the first situated directly opposite the exit of the strait, one shot of a lepel to the east. This [first reef] extends from the land on the north [side] and extends towards the south. The other [reef] is situated [on] the south [side], about one shot of a 12-pounder away from the shore; from the strait, [it extends out] towards the east. Together, the two pass through each other like a cross. Between the two reefs there is the channel, and the two reefs can be seen exposed at the low water of a spring tide. This channel that runs between the two [reefs] barely measures 4 vadem [6.8 metres] in depth; the ground within the channel is muddy, and outside the channel it is sandy. I wanted to explain this all in detail for the service and convenience of those who henceforth desire to pass through [the strait], for older descriptions of the route, or navigational [instructions] prepared for it, are very short and not easily understood by those who have never [before] passed through. For this reason many ships have run aground, or scraped the hull and experienced great danger, indeed, even lost [both ship and cargo].*

A few years later, the Portuguese explorer Pedro Teixeira delved into the twists and turns of navigating the Old Strait, describing it as V-shaped (resembling the Roman numeral for 5) and then "for a half a league so narrow that the ships, bound either for India or China, cannot tack therein. Therefore they anchor at either entrance, awaiting a good tide, with which, and a boat sent ahead to help the helm, to pass the strait." The waiting points mentioned here by Teixeira were located off Batu Berlayar on the western end of the strait, and off Pulau Brani on the eastern end.

While the ships were anchored there, mariners would fetch water from Sentosa island. The freshwater source in question would

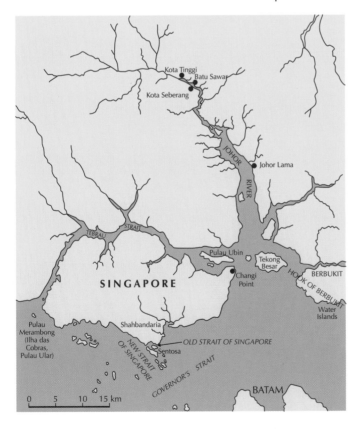

Map of the southern portion of the Malay Peninsula, showing the various straits around Singapore and the historic upstream towns of the Johor River region.

Map of Southeast Asia by Cornelis Claesz, 1595, found in the first edition of Jan Huyghen van Linschoten's *Itinerario* and *Reysgeschrift*. This map was particularly influential in shaping Northern European minds at the turn of the 16th and 17th centuries about the geography of Southeast Asia – the source of valuable spices, aromatics and resins.

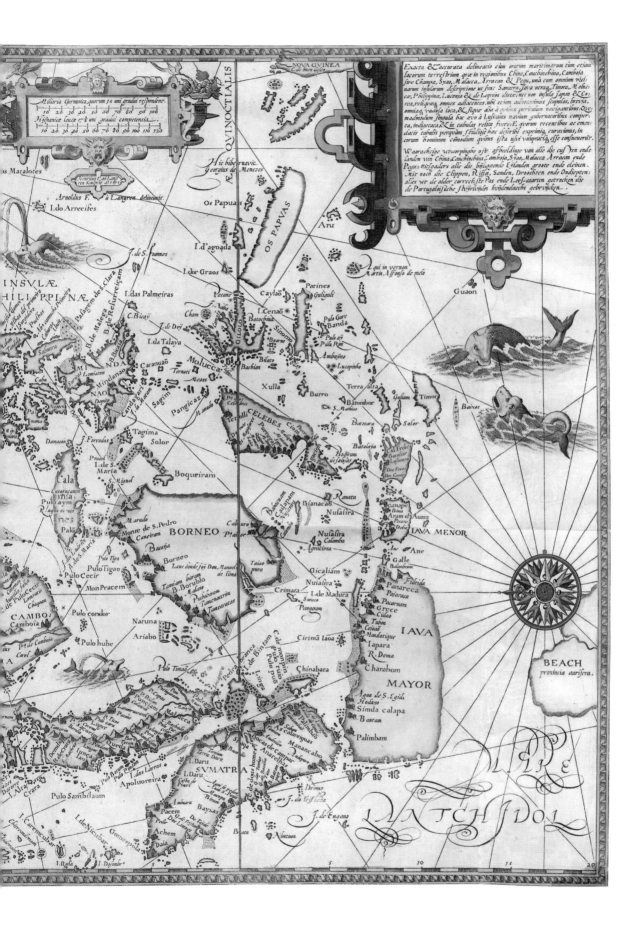

almost certainly have been Siloso Spring, which still exists today. But gaining access to fresh water on Sentosa was not without its dangers, and mariners had to keep a hand on their weapons as well as ensure that the strong currents and tides in the strait did not carry their vessels off to another location altogether, as Jacques de Coutre observed from personal experience:

> We reached the Strait of Singapore, and they threw the batel [boat] into the water. The friar [Friar Jorge] tried to coerce me to go in this batel with three companions to fetch fresh water on an island that was called Isla de Arena [present-day Sentosa]. We approached it, I got the water. By the time we returned night had fallen. I could not see the junk, they did not light either a lamp nor did they fire any shots, even though I made many signals.

The English merchant Peter Mundy in his journal entry for 1 June 1637 also described the strong currents:

> From Pulo Carimaon to Piedra Branca, all the sea over in a Manner is strowed with smalle Ilands, rockes and shoalds, causing straunge variable and strong currentts, sometymes keeping itts Dew course ebbing and Flowing every 6 and 6 howers; sometymes running For 2 or 3 Daies together all one way (by relation) according to the windes that rule.

### The Orang Laut of the Old Strait

After describing his Sentosa escape, De Coutre continues with an account of how some Orang Laut vessels attacked and attempted to capture him and his two companions. Early modern European sources of this period are replete with stories of the *saletes*, *selates* or Orang Laut, a collective name for various tribes who lived and moved around the *selat*, or straits. Most of the accounts of the Orang Laut from this period highlight their disposition toward violence, but not exclusively. To be sure, De Coutre always kept a wary eye on them. Describing them as "treacherous… by nature", he elaborated:

> For this reason we deal with them very carefully and with weapons in our hands, because it has happened that they were allowed to come aboard our ships in such numbers, ostensibly to sell fresh fish, and in the blink of an eye they attacked and killed everybody aboard the ship. They are armed with

*poisoned daggers, which they call kerisses, and spears made of wild palm without any iron. These are called seligis, and [the Orang Laut] throw them so hard they can even penetrate an iron breastplate and any shield, no matter how sturdy they are.*

The Orang Laut would have performed the functions of guides and pilots, similar to the boat people of Tondano (on Sulawesi), captured in this 1677 sketch by Robert Padtbrugge, the Dutch Governor of Ternate.

Yet, De Coutre and authors like Domingo de Navarrete, Francesco Careri and William Dampier also described the Orang Laut as petty but honest merchants. Some descriptions suggest that they were the pushcart vendors of the sea who pulled up alongside passing vessels in their small boats and offered provisions of fish, poultry, fruit picked in the hills of Singapore, and basic handicraft (like parasols made of palm leaf). They usually bartered these, according to De Coutre, for blankets, rice and even rusty nails. Iron in any form, after all, was a scarce metal in the region of the Malay Peninsula and therefore highly prized.

The Orang Laut also acted as guides and pilots to vessels passing through the straits, and when tidal conditions were right at night, they put out little lights to mark danger spots to passing ships. They were also a source of information for the Portuguese and subsequently the Dutch. "If one accompanies and pays them," De Coutre underscored, "they will serve that person well." He also admired the Orang Laut for their healthy lifestyle (compared to Europeans at the time), which gave them longevity. Their small boats were their homes, in which they also kept their dogs, cats, hens and chicks – De Coutre was openly amazed at how they all crammed into such tiny spaces. As for their fishing techniques, he noted: "When they go fishing, the man sits on the perahu with a harpoon and the wife and children paddle very fast and very skilfully."

De Coutre's first-hand account of the Orang Laut is supported by a slightly later one, dating from the early 17th century, by Pedro Barreto de Resende. His little-known account reads:

> The Strait of Singapore… has many channels so narrow that in places the branches of the trees on shore touch the ships, and the currents are very strong. The water, though deep, is so clear that the fishes can be seen swimming about in it. Fish is brought by the merchants of the ships from the saletes, or inhabitants of the Straits, who live in very swift baloons (boats) with their families. They catch the fish by spearing them in the water, and then sell them.

Edward Hall, who sailed through the Old Strait aboard the *Planter* a few decades later, saw a similar situation with regard to the Orang Laut and their sale of fresh produce to passing ships. His diary entry for 1 June 1637 notes:

> The First of this Month wee went through the old straightt which May bee about a good league in length and not above ¼ Mile broade att the Coming in and going outt, butt within wider, with many little baies, Creeks, Ilands, etts., Where wee saw sundry companies of small boates covered over with Mattes, which is the Ordinary habitation of those thatt live among these Ilands, Where they have their wives, children and Household goods…. Here they [the Orang Laut] broughtt us More Fish, Fresh and Dried, which I conceave is their Cheifest Mayntenaunce, Killing them with Fishgaes [harpoons or spears] in which they are very Dextrous and pretty sport it is to see them pursue the Fish with their little boates, who scudd before them as porpoises Doe before the stemme of a shippe in a gale of wynde untill they are strucke. They use allsoe nets, hookes and lynes.

In 1669, Spanish friar Domingo de Navarrete passed through the Singapore Strait and met an Orang Laut who served as a pilot: "There was a great number of fishermen call'd Saletes, who always live upon the water, and in their boats carry their wife, children, cats, dogs, hens, etc.... One of the boats made to us, the master of it came aboard and carried us thro' very safe...." But the vessel's pilot subsequently ran the ship aground. An astute Navarrete noted that the Orang Laut were poised to plunder the wares aboard the vessel if it had to be abandoned: "Our obstinate pilot would needs keep close under the shore; he lost the channel, and the ship struck upon the sand; being it sprung no leak, we were not much troubled. As soon as this happen'd, abundance of the Saletes took their posts to observe us, to take their advantage in case the ship were cast away."

Writing a century after De Coutre, Italian traveller and adventurer Dr Francesco Gemelli Careri's testimony suggests that the Orang Laut's lifestyle had not changed much, nor had fears about their piratical violence lessened among skippers and sailors:

*Malays known as Saletes live along this channel in numerous floating and portable homes. They live on the water, in boats covered with wicker and woven canes in the middle, to sleep: in them they endure their harsh conditions, the brutal solitude, the bad air and the horrors of the nearby woods. They ingeniously engage in fishing (which serves as their sole form of sustenance) with hooks and spears made of bamboo, with which they dextrously spike any small fish. Some of them came up alongside our vessel, with their wives and children, in their floating houses, to obtain jars, iron, knives, tobacco and other trifles, in exchange for fish; since they are unfamiliar with money. On the other hand, they are not content to receive even one hundred pieces of eight in exchange [for fish]; they are extremely suspicious, treacherous and shrewd; in fact they stab people for even the slightest reason with their spears and small knives, known as krises, which they carry beside them. They are subjects of the King of Johor, who for this reason maintains the customs house for fish in the middle of the channel. We cast anchor yonder in that area, due to the calm which had fallen.*

### The Singapore Straits, Johor and the Portuguese

In brief, the Portuguese captured Melaka in 1511 and succeeded in stabilising their presence by constructing a fortification to protect the city and by forging agreements for trade and food deliveries with neighbouring rulers. The Portuguese and the Malay rulers were wary of each other, and keen to exploit signs of

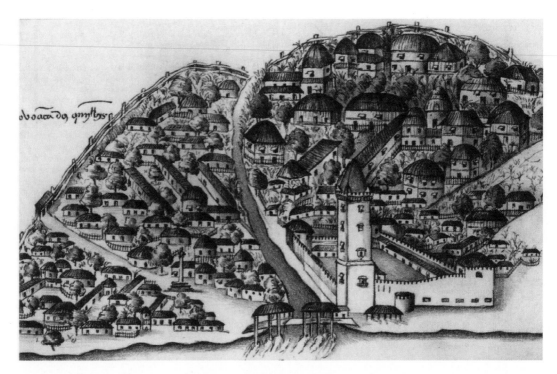

Artist's impression of Melaka shortly after the conquest in 1511. The original is found in Gaspar Correia's *Lendas da India* of c. 1550.

friction or military weakness. Up until the founding of Perak and Johor in 1528, the Portuguese fought their regional neighbours in Sumatra and the Malay Peninsula in a series of naval skirmishes off Muar (1512 and 1523), Siak and Kampar (1515), Pegu (1520), Pasai (1520 and 1522), Pahang (1523), Bintan (1524–26), Lingga (1525) and Aceh (1527). Other skirmishes took place off the coast of Melaka in 1513, 1519, 1521, 1523 and 1525. In 1513, the Portuguese fended off an attack by Jepara.

By far the most troublesome pair were the Melaka Laksamana and the ruler of Bintan, where the violence climaxed in the 1520s and 1530s. Several naval campaigns also took place along the Johor River, in the lower reaches around the eastern coast of Singapore and farther upstream. The information gathered during these military campaigns found its way into the maps of the period, with the first Portuguese chart depicting Singapore – as an unnamed but discernible island – penned by Gaspar Viegas in 1530.

Portuguese-Johor relations during this period, especially around and after the middle of the 16th century, oscillated between trading partners and hostile neighbours. When they were friendly, the Melaka merchants arguably contributed towards the growth of Johor's overseas trade and wealth. When they quarrelled, military campaigns ensued. These included attempted Portuguese blockades of the Johor River and upstream sallies against Johor's royal capitals, of which the most emblematic was the destruction of Johor Lama in 1587. The Johoreans also imposed blockades – famously choking the Old Strait with sunken ships, logs and debris.

With the Old Strait suddenly unviable as a shipping route, vessels were forced to seek alternative passages through the islands off Singapore. This may have led to the discovery of the New Strait, which the Portuguese chronicler João de Barros named the Channel of Santa Barbara. The logs and debris in the Old Strait must have remained for some time, for De Coutre, who passed through it around the mid-1590s, noted with some relief that the strong currents and tides had naturally cleared the debris away.

Historically, the maritime arteries that crossed from the southern Melaka Strait to the South China Sea – and collectively known as the Singapore Straits – cut right through the heart of the sprawling Johor-Riau empire and straddled the southern reaches of the Malay Peninsula and the Riau Archipelago. Mariners considered them dangerous waters in which their cargo-laden ships were exposed to passing galleys of the Johor sultan as well as rapacious maritime tribes. Portuguese trade in Melaka depended on maritime commerce with destinations in the east. Periodic conflict with Johor and other regional enemies led the Portuguese to seek greater protection of their mercantile shipping in the straits.

Official Portuguese documents raised security issues and, more importantly, discussed ways to solve them. One of the options was to identify key locations around the straits to build fixed fortifications. But these were costly and complicated (involving pacts with local rulers) to build and maintain. Given the nature of the monsoon winds, moreover, and with it the different sailing seasons for commercial vessels, the prospect of maintaining a garrison and equipment in these forts even during the lull season when few or no ships passed by was too costly a prospect.

Instead, the Portuguese decided to deploy naval squadrons at key locations in the straits at different times of the year. During the northeast monsoon from October to February, a squadron would be deployed in or around the Johor River estuary to escort trading ships arriving from China and Japan on their journey to Melaka. An agent on Tioman island, a victualling station for ships arriving from or departing for Pulau Condor (off the southern coast of present-day Vietnam), was tasked with warning inbound ships to Melaka of dangers that might be lurking along the main sailing route and especially along the Singapore Straits. When there were problems in the straits, the Portuguese merchant ships could be rerouted to the port of Pahang, and their cargo despatched overland via the riverine route to Muar. During the April-to-August southwest monsoon, the squadron would be redeployed to the northern entrance of the Melaka Strait, to deter attacks by Aceh and Kedah.

The composition of the Portuguese naval squadron reflected the different types of waters that had to be navigated as part of the patrols and featured a series of smaller craft that could be sailed or oared. Smaller, locally built craft were ideal for sallying forth swiftly to hunt down native enemies – the galleys of the Malay rulers and the fast, oared boats of the Orang Laut – while the shallow draught of the vessels facilitated riverine pursuits around mangrove swamp hideouts. Correspondingly, the vessels were equipped with light arms and well-manned with soldiers or mercenaries. By the late 16th century, the Portuguese recrafted their naval patrols and fighting style to match the guerrilla-style warfare of the Malays, whose principal tactic, as Erédia informs in his *Description of Melaka*, was the ambush – on land and evidently also on water.

While the Portuguese squadron of smaller, well-manned vessels may have been suitable against native enemies, it was a different story by the close of the 16th century, with the arrival of Portugal's Northern European competitors and enemies in Southeast Asian waters. In particular, Dutch ships of the blue-water mercantile fleet were fortified with heavy artillery, and with these the Portuguese in Asia were confronted with a very different kind of enemy. The Dutch were about to export their ongoing war against the dynastically united empires of Spain and Portugal globally, not least to Southeast Asia.

Hand-coloured etching of a junk, from the first edition of Linschoten's *Itinerario*. The rolled-up sail appears to be made of reeds, a common sight in this period.

## IN A NUTSHELL

If in Chapter Two we saw the ascent of the Melaka Sultanate, in Chapter Three we explore how the Portuguese conquest of Melaka in 1511 precipitated the revitalisation of other parts of the Malay Peninsula under the sultanate's reach: Perak and Johor as new seats of power, and Singapura as the latter's Shahbandaria.

Archaeological evidence, such as 15th-century Ming blue-and-white porcelain sherds, although scant, suggests trading activity along the Johor River. Meanwhile, Singapore persistently appears in European cartographical documents and personal letters of the 16th century. Despite the sultanate relocating and establishing a court in the Johor River region, Singapore continued to act as the sultanate's gateway to the emerging and prosperous riverine economy and also reprised its role as the sultanate's naval outpost, helmed by the Laksamana. Singapore's strategic importance was strongly alluded to in Portuguese notices, which record that the settlement was not spared from attacks by the Portuguese on settlements around the Singapore Straits and the Johor River during the first quarter of the 16th century.

Singapore's importance as a strategic Shahbandaria would continue well into the 17th century, its fate waxing and waning with that of the Johor Sultanate – a story that will be fleshed out in Chapter Four.

Etching depicting the arrival of
Raja Bongsu of Johor in his galley
at the flagship of Jacob Pietersz van
Enkhuysen after the battles against
the Portuguese in the Johor River and
Singapore Straits in October 1603.
The sketch has been taken from the
illustrations supporting the journal of
the eighth Dutch voyage to the East
Indies, published by Johann Theodor
and Johann Israel de Bry in Frankfurt
am Main, 1607.

# CHAPTER FOUR

# The 17th Century
## Contested Waterways

By his second wife, the king of Johor had Raja Bongsu who is now called Raja
Seberang, meaning "king of the other side" because he lives on the opposite side
of the [Johor] River from the city of Batu Sawar where he has a fortress as well, and
part of his subjects; but he is a vassal of the Yang di Pertuan. He is about 35 years old,
almost white, not very tall, but wise, forgiving, not choleric, and very prudent; an enemy
of the Portuguese, industrious in his business, which he would also conduct diligently if
he held power. In short, worthy of being king of Johor and Melaka.

Records of Dutch Admiral Cornelis Matelieff de Jonge,
assessing Johor's most promising princeling

### Legitimising Royalty Through Singapore: The *Malay Annals*

It is to Stamford Raffles that we owe our acquaintance with the
earliest verifiable dated copy of the *Malay Annals*, which he studied
in Penang with the poet and brilliant linguist John Leyden, whose
translation of the work Raffles published in 1821. The circumstances leading to the writing of the *Malay Annals* are stated fairly
clearly in the preface, translated by C.C. Brown thus:

> In the name of God, the Merciful, the Compassionate. Praise be
> to Allah, the Lord of both worlds and peace be on the Apostle
> of Allah and his four companions: Allah have compassion on
> them, Be it known. In AH 1021, a dal awal year, on the 12th of the
> month Rabi-al-awwal [13 May 1612] on a Sunday, at the hour of
> the morning prayer, in the reign of Sultan Alauddin Riyat Shah,
> shadow of Allah upon earth, while he had a settlement at Pasir
> Raja, came Sri Narawangsa, whose name was Tun Bambang,
> a son of Sri Akar, a Patani raja, bearing a command from His
> Highness Downstream…. The command of His Highness was:
> "I ask for a history to be compiled on all the Malay Rajas and

*their customs, for the information of my descendants who come after me, that they may be conversant with the history and derive profit therefrom."*

The recipient of this instruction from this "Downstream Highness" was the Bendahara (prime minister) of the Johor Sultanate, Tun Sri Lanang. He wrote that his head and his limbs were bowed beneath the weight of this command as he was conscious of his weakness and ignorance. Who was this "Downstream Highness" with the power and authority to command the Bendahara to compile this genealogy of the Malay rajas? Also known as Raja Seberang ("prince of the other side"), this Raja di Ilir ("prince from downstream") is perhaps better known as Raja Bongsu ("youngest prince").

Raja Bongsu was a dynamic and proactive ruler who very early on tried to capitalise on the presence of the Dutch to drive the

## A Renaissance Raja in a New Malay World

He was, observed Johannes Verken, a German-born member of the Dutch East India Company fleet, immaculately dressed, fair, handsome and articulate. His bejewelled accoutrements included a hat trick of gem-studded gold chains draped around his neck, and by his side hung a custom-crafted kris, or Malay dagger, worth some 50,000 Dutch guilders (S$1 million by today's reckoning). The personage in question was Raja Bongsu, a princeling of the region's pre-eminent native power, the Johor Sultanate.

Raja Bongsu defined and personified the cosmopolitan, informed Malay aristocrat-ruler-politician of the 17th century in a new Southeast Asian age of acute global contestation for power and wealth. Politically astute, he nimbly navigated the crowded, complicated web of regional and European interests to advance Johor's – and his own – position by luring the Dutch into their first regional alliance. He capped his career by being crowned Sultan (1615–23), not a minor feat in a faction-riddled court for a princely runt of the royal litter in a succession scheme predicated on primogeniture. Like a Renaissance politician, he was a canny public relations and

literary strategist, under whom the most important Malay treatise, the *Sulalat'us-Salatin* (Genealogy of Kings), was commissioned in 1612. Better known as the *Sejarah Melayu* or *Malay Annals*, its first half-a-dozen chapters remain the sole recorded source of Singapore's royal founding by the Sriwijayan prince Sang Nila Utama (Sri Tri Buana).

The book resonates today as a collective social memory of the Malays. Its literary heft is admired for imaginatively wrapping actual events around fables and tales of the fantastical. But its heart was – as Raja Bongsu and his "editor" Bendahara Tun Sri Lanang intended – political, and politically two-fold: an affirmation of Johor's link to its royal predecessors Melaka and Sriwijaya through Sang Nila Utama's Singapura; and a manual for ruling justly. The lasting impact of Raja Bongsu's statecraft remains relevant today through the treatise's iteration of the sacred compact between righteous rulership and the subjects' absolute loyalty to it. Perhaps the clearest homage to Raja Bongsu's recrafting of Malay royalty and loyalty is that both ideals have become accepted, for better or not, as traditional Malay political and cultural benchmarks today.

Portuguese out of Melaka. A shrewd diplomat, he was greatly admired by the Europeans. Dutch Admiral Matelieff de Jonge perceived him as "wise, forgiving, not choleric, and very prudent; an enemy of the Portuguese". Raja Bongsu was well aware of his status as a descendant of a long line of rulers and he was conscious of the mandate to revive the Melaka Sultanate – in communications with the Dutch, he referred to himself as the legitimate successor of Melaka's prestige and its "lands".

Given Raja Bongsu's shifting fortunes among Johor's high-ranking courtiers and the deepening divisions among his siblings and their respective followers, his motives for commissioning the revision of the *Malay Annals* become clearer. The rewriting yielded a legitimising text that situated Singapore not only at the centre of Malay myths and social memories, but also ensured its importance in the Melaka-Johor legacy and argued for the continuity of Malay rule in an increasingly uncertain world following the arrival of the Dutch.

### Arrival of the Dutch and Its Impact on Singapore

The Dutch arrived in Southeast Asia in 1596. Their first trading expedition called at Banten in northwestern Java to buy spices. Massive profits arising from imported spices spurred the start of a series of highly leveraged trading ventures in Europe focused on East Indies trade. Within years, however, the Dutch ventures began withering and in March 1602 they were merged at the behest of the Dutch government into the Vereenigde Oostindische Compagnie, or VOC (United Netherlands East India Company).

From the start, the VOC was designed as a joint-stock company which included international shareholders beyond Dutch borders. In terms of paid-up capital it dwarfed its English counterpart, the English East India Company (EIC), founded in 1600 and known then as "The Company of Merchants of London Trading into the East Indies". The EIC only became a temporary joint-stock company in 1612 and a permanent joint-stock company in 1657.

While the two companies represented integrated trading enterprises, there were vital differences. The VOC's charter endowed the firm with substantial quasi-state powers, including the right to sign international agreements and treaties, appoint and dismiss officials, levy troops, wage war, conclude peace, mint coins, acquire colonies and adjudicate crimes. Importantly, neither firm was allowed to pass legislation, and for the period under review

(*Top*) Corporate logo of the VOC, the Dutch East India Company.

(*Above*) The English East India Company's original coat of arms, granted in 1600, featuring a pair of "sea-lions".

Printed engraving of the market at Banten in 1596, taken from the travelogue of Cornelis de Houtman's voyage to the East Indies.

in this chapter, the VOC acted as the private arm in an ongoing global war against Spain, whose king was also the crowned head of Portugal.

Both companies focused on trade with Asia, but the differences in their charter territories were also important. The VOC was restricted to activities in the Indian and Pacific oceans, between the Cape of Good Hope at the tip of Africa and Cape Horn at the tip of South America. By contrast, the EIC could develop the Americas, specifically the British colonies in North America, as a key market for its colonial produce and wares. A revolt against the English and the EIC at the infamous Boston Tea Party triggered American independence and the birth of the United States of America in 1776.

The drive for profits and market share in Europe would pit the Portuguese, Dutch and English in a deadly contest in lands and waters far away and take European rivalry to Southeast Asia. Sometimes described as the Century of Conflict, the 17th century saw European kingdoms, both substantial as well as small, fighting for political eminence, religious ascendancy and territory in Europe as well as globally. This competition created a patchwork of colonies in an increasingly Europeanising, polyglot world. One long-running conflict was between the Dutch and the Portuguese, the Luso-Dutch conflict ("Luso" refers to the old Roman province of Lusitania, which approximates today's Portugal).

By the late 16th century, Singapore had turned from being a feeder port in the Melakan empire into the gatekeeper of the Johor River. With the royal court located just up the Johor River, Singapore acted as a natural gateway to the Sultanate's riverine economy. Cartographic evidence suggests that for at least the first half of the 17th century, Singapore played a role in this riverine trade as the base of the Johor navy and the gatekeeper of the upstream towns. It continued, as before, to be administered by a Shahbandar appointed by the Johor sultan. Being part of this riverine economy, it was natural that the waters around Singapore would become a zone of contestation. Regional powers, including Aceh and Patani, were hovering for a bigger slice of the commercial pie. An equally muscular Johor made strategic alliances with the Europeans in its wars against these regional rivals.

### Plunder of the *Santa Catarina*

While the Portuguese tried to maintain their European monopoly of the East-West trade, the Dutch wanted to end the Portuguese-Spanish colonial trade monopolies globally. They were prepared to use any means necessary, including violence, to achieve their aim in the Straits of Melaka and the waters around Singapore. Thus in 1603, they resorted to plundering the Portuguese merchant ship, the *Santa Catarina*, off the eastern coast of Singapore, near present-day Changi Point – an act that had far-reaching consequences.

Dutch activities in Southeast Asia were not limited to trade. There was also piracy and privateering. Privateering was simply a legalised form of piracy that required a commission and licence known as a letter of marque issued by a sovereign lord or state. Privateers had to abide by the laws of war, bring seized cargo to the home port, and pay taxes on its value. Privateering began in the 16th century as a way to lure private agents into aiding war efforts. To the victims, it was piracy all the same. Walter Raleigh and Francis Drake, who plundered the Spanish during the reign of Queen Elizabeth I, were technically privateers but were – and still are – decried as pirates in Spanish accounts. Southeast Asia, the Caribbean, and the Azores in the North Atlantic were notorious hunting grounds for privateers, corsairs, buccaneers and pirates, whose heyday lasted until around the middle of the 1700s.

In February 1603, the Dutch seized the Melaka-bound *Santa Catarina*, brimming with goods from Japan and China, as the 1,400-ton carrack entered Singapore waters. Admiral Jacob van

Jacob van Heemskerk led the capture of the *Santa Catarina* in 1603 and was later killed in combat off the coast of Gibraltar in 1607. This etching is found in the 1637 edition of Emmanuel van Meteren's *Commentarien ofte Memorien van den Nederlandschen Staet, Handel en Oorlogen* (Commentaries or Memories Concerning the Dutch State, Trade and Wars).

Heemskerk, the supreme commander of a Dutch commercial fleet to the East Indies, plundered the Portuguese ship, but the instigator (so we are told) was Raja Bongsu. He had approached the Dutch at Patani and showed them the ideal spot to ambush the richly laden Portuguese ships sailing back from China and Japan.

The sale of the plundered cargo was groundbreaking. It revealed to Northern European merchants the range of goods the Portuguese were trading in Asia over and above spices, convincing them of the potential wealth in the Sino-Japanese trade. The plundering of the *Santa Catarina* also marked the beginning of Luso-Dutch conflict in the waters around Singapore and the Straits littoral. The conflict shaped the course of the region's history for the next 40 years by turning the Singapore Straits into a favourite hunting ground for Dutch captains bent on waylaying Portuguese vessels from eastern ports en route to Melaka and India.

The taking of the *Santa Catarina* is important in three other ways. First, the close-knit bond between Raja Bongsu and Admiral Heemskerk stemming from the seizure is a historical marker for the opening of formal diplomatic relations between Johor and the Dutch. In 1603–5, Johor became the second of only three Southeast Asian powers (besides Aceh in 1601 and Siam in 1608–9) to successfully despatch a group of emissaries to the Dutch Republic.

Maurice of Nassau, the Prince of Orange and Stadtholder of Holland and Zeeland, receiving the Acehnese ambassador on his arrival in the Netherlands in 1601. This is a 19th-century artist's impression.

Led by a courtier known in Dutch sources as Megat Mansur, the embassy left in 1603 for the Netherlands with Heemskerk's fleet. Although the principal envoy died en route, the surviving diplomats were hosted in Europe at the VOC's expense and later returned to Johor with the fleet of Admiral Cornelis Matelieff de Jonge, who dropped anchor off the western coast of the Malay Peninsula in May 1606.

Second, the *Santa Catarina* booty exposed Portuguese secrecy about the wanton wealth accruing from their intra-Asian trade. It removed any lingering doubt over the fantastic profitability of privateering as a relatively predictable source of revenue. This new-found conviction would prompt the Dutch into building their naval and artillery might, elevating them as a top-tier global power for almost 200 years. The VOC's maritime presence turned safe passage through Southeast Asian waters into a grave concern for the Portuguese, especially in the decades leading up to the capture of Melaka by a joint VOC-Johor force in January 1641. Portuguese Pedro Barreto de Resende, who blamed heavy Portuguese losses on Orang Laut connivance with the Dutch as spies and informants, lamented:

> These Saletes are a wicked people and especially so to the Portuguese. They are evil-hearted and treacherous and the best spies the Dutch possess. Wherever, of the many places in this vicinity, our ships may be, they immediately inform the Dutch and lead them there; so that most of our losses are due to them. This is because the Dutch give a great share of all thus seized, and thus it is very necessary that our fleets of jaleas [armed galleys] and ships that go to these straits to wait for the said fleets should make war as much as possible on these Saletes and drive them from these parts.

Third, no account of the *Santa Catarina* incident is complete without explaining its implications on maritime law. Was the plunder legal? Heemskerk had attacked the ship without authorisation, which raised the question of whether he had committed piracy. The VOC's central board, comprising directors who were known collectively as the Gentlemen Seventeen, commissioned a young and talented Huig de Groot, better known today by his Latinised name Hugo Grotius, to justify the taking of the *Santa Catarina*. It is assumed that what the directors had in mind was a short pamphlet

Pamphlet entitled *Corte ende sekere Beschrijvinge* (Short and Accurate Description) announcing the seizure of the *Santa Catarina* in February 1603. The printed etching depicts the three ships of Admiral Jacob van Heemskerk engaging the *Santa Catarina* with cannon fire. Troops and some oared vessels of the Johor ruler arrive at the scene of action. The landscape, city and background embellishing the picture do not represent Singapore.

*ROIT          HORA.*

Portrait of the mature Hugo Grotius (Huig de Groot) taken from the 1658 Latin edition of his *Annales et Historiae de Rebus Belgicis* (Annals and Histories of the Low Countries).

(*Opposite*) Schematic printed map of the 1603 naval battle between Jacob Pietersz van Enkhuysen and Estevão Teixeira de Matos in the Johor River, off the eastern coast of Singapore, in the waters around Pedra Branca, and along the northern coast of Batam. The Johor River is called "Rio de Batusavar", but it is unclear whether the entry "Tanse Pora" represents a corruption of the Malay toponym Tanjong Pagar.

attacking the Iberians' policies of obstruction in Asia, thereby justifying Heemskerk's deed as morally justifiable and legally permissible.

Instead, Grotius produced an expansive treatise in Latin in which he laid out and systematised ideas on the just war and natural law. This was Grotius' first major engagement with the laws of war and peace and formed the foundation of his landmark publication, *Three Books on the Laws of War and Peace*, published in 1625. This oft-published and translated legal tome is the work for which Grotius is best remembered today as one of the pathbreakers of modern international law.

The loss of the *Santa Catarina* prompted a swift Portuguese vendetta against Johor. Portuguese Melaka's Governor, André Furtado de Mendonça, sent a galleon accompanied by several smaller craft to the Johor River, where Portuguese soldiers harassed coastal settlements and imposed a blockade on the river to block supplies and trade to upstream settlements. They captured and occupied the sultanate's former capital, Johor Lama.

Against this backdrop, Dutch Vice-Admiral Jacob Pietersz van Enkhuysen sailed into the waters off Singapore with four ships. While searching for the entrance to the Old Strait of Singapore between Sentosa and present-day Harbourfront, he was told of the Portuguese blockade by Johor fishermen. He decided to help Johor lift the blockade, engaging the Portuguese ships in three separate incidents between 6 and 11 October in the Johor River and the Singapore Straits.

The main battle took place off Changi Point on 10 October 1603. The Portuguese fleet at Johor Lama comprised some 40 vessels – mostly smaller craft, and the galleon *Todos os Santos* (All Saints) serving as the flagship. The smaller craft were locally built *prahu* or galleys that the Portuguese used to enter shallow waters and to chase after pirates. While useful in such contexts, they could only carry light arms and were not suited for battle with blue-water ships armed with heavy artillery.

On 10 October, the Dutch ships sailed up the river to Johor Lama, where they spotted the Portuguese vessels at anchor.

The Dutch shot into the sails of the Portuguese flagship to compromise its manoeuvrability. As the Dutch followed up with an artillery barrage, the Portuguese flagship took in water, forcing its crew to transfer to the smaller vessels around it. Remnants of the Portuguese naval squadron fled toward Pedra Branca and the open waters of the South China Sea. They later regrouped in shallow waters off the northeastern coast of Batam, most likely in the vicinity of today's Nongsa islets and nearby Tering Bay.

The successful lifting of the Portuguese blockade had a bracing effect on the ties between Johor and the Dutch. The members of the Johor royal family witnessed the naval drama, either from their galleys stationed around present-day Tanah Merah, or from aboard Vice-Admiral Enkhuysen's ship, *Zierikzee*. Period literature credits the strengthening of cooperation between Johor and the Dutch in the early 17th century to this specific naval confrontation.

### The Johor Court and the European Rivals
Another Dutch fleet commander to pass through the region, a few years later, was Admiral Matelieff, who had been appointed supreme commander of the second VOC fleet that set sail from Europe for the East Indies. The voyage to the East brought Matelieff's ships around the Cape of Good Hope in Africa and across the Indian Ocean to Johor, Melaka, Banten, the Maluku Islands, Mindanao, the Fujian coast of China, Champa on the coast of present-day Vietnam, and back to Java.

Matelieff's voyage is mostly remembered for his maritime siege against Melaka with the help of Johor troops between May and August 1606. He also engaged with the armada of the Portuguese Viceroy in the Melaka Straits, where he substantially destroyed the Portuguese fleet. Johor's support for the attacks against Melaka was the result of a treaty that Matelieff had struck with Raja Bongsu in May 1606.

From the perspective of Singapore's history, Matelieff's role is significant as he personally encountered the Shahbandar of Singapore. Matelieff's journal explains that the Shahbandar also held the Malay title of Sri Raja Negara, that is, the head of the Orang Laut community around the Straits. It would appear that Singapore was more than a port – it was also a base, if not the principal base, of Johor's own war armada, such as it was. A later

Spanish testimony informs that this Johor armada based in the Singapore Straits consisted of 18 galleys that probably carried light artillery.

Matelieff's account of his negotiations with Raja Bongsu for the division of the spoils of their planned allied campaign to take Melaka reveals the Johor prince as a tough and astute negotiator. Raja Bongsu's desire to retake Melaka, which his forebears had lost to the Portuguese, clashed with the admiral's demands to acquire the settlement for the Dutch as war booty and as a reward for abetting Johor. Why, Raja Bongsu wondered aloud, would he consent to a situation where the Dutch simply replaced the Portuguese in the city and its surroundings? Matelieff promised the surrounding lands to Johor, but Raja Bongsu made it clear that he was interested in people, trade and the city, and not in more territory – he had already 20 times more land than he could fill with people.

Printed etching of the landing of VOC troops at Melaka in 1606. Under the command of Admiral Cornelis Matelieff, the Dutch would launch a joint attack with Johor against Melaka, but failed to wrest the colonial settlement from Portuguese control. The sketch comes from Johan Isaksz Pontanus, *Historia urbis et rerum Amstelodamensium* (History of the City and Affairs of Amsterdam), first published in 1611.

Cornelis Matelieff de Jonge
was a director of the Rotterdam
Chamber of the VOC and
served as one of the Gentlemen
Seventeen on the VOC's central
board of directors. Appointed
commander of a VOC fleet in
1605–8, he attacked Portuguese
Melaka with the assistance
of Johor, founded a fort on
Ternate in the Maluku Islands,
and made an unsuccessful
attempt at opening China to
direct Dutch trade.

On his return to Europe, Matelieff penned a series of memorials seeking fundamental changes in how the VOC conducted its business in Asia, with the aim of expanding Dutch political and commercial influence across the East Indies. Key proposals included the establishment of a permanent VOC base in the East Indies, the appointment of a resident Governor-General for Asia, and the monopolisation of cloves, nutmeg and mace at source. He also recommended farming out parts of the VOC's monopoly, but this was not taken up. This would have enabled private citizens to engage in commerce at their own risk and trade in commodities that stood little chance of generating a substantial or regular profit for the Dutch company.

Although VOC ships called periodically at Johor from 1602 to 1609, there were long gaps between such arrivals. These gaps were exploited by the Portuguese, who, at this time, made diplomatic overtures to the Johor rulers. Prior to the arrival of the Dutch in its waters, Johor's relations with the Portuguese were fluid – an oscillating relationship typical of Southeast Asian politics. These relations remained in a state of flux during the first half of the 17th century. At the Johor court, Raja Siak and the *orang kaya* (local elites), and possibly Raja Laut as well, were generally well-disposed towards the Portuguese, not least on account of the trading opportunities that they hoped their friendly relations might yield. The Portuguese had also been generous in their gifts to court officials; their strategy was to exploit the fractious court at Batu Sawar and wean Johor off its support for the Dutch.

Batu Sawar probably maintained more active and deeper commercial links with Portuguese Melaka than Dutch sources concede. This serves to underscore the view that while goods and money continued to flow despite volatile relations between the Portuguese and Johor, the Johor rulers skilfully used the VOC primarily as a political tool, and only secondarily as a commercial partner. The Portuguese backed up their diplomatic manoeuvres at the court with military pressure, using their locally based fleet to harass coastal settlements and impose blockades on riverine traffic. Johor paid a high price during these blockades because the population in the upstream towns found themselves cut off from external supplies of food, especially rice, most of which was imported from as far away as Java, Sulawesi, Siam, Burma and the eastern coast of India.

Towards this end, the Portuguese sent an emissary, João Lopes de Morero (also spelt as d'Amoreira), to the Johor court. Lopes de Morero was the Temenggong of Portuguese Melaka and reportedly spoke Malay fluently. He had extensive experience dealing with Muslims and was familiar with their customs and culture. Some sources also describe him as a personal friend of the late Sultan Ali Jalla bin Abdul Jalil. According to Jacques Obelaar, a senior official at the Dutch factory at Batu Sawar, Lopes de Morero met with the Johor Sultan and finalised a peace treaty. This treaty was ratified by the Sultan on 16 October 1610, and subsequently endorsed on 22 October by the Captain of Melaka, Dom Francisco Henriques, in the presence of two Johor ambassadors and the Bishop of Melaka, Dom Frei Cristóvão de Sá e Lisboa. Unfortunately, neither the draft nor the actual treaty has been found so far.

There is some confusion, moreover, as to whether the October 1610 treaty ever took effect, because some clauses were reportedly rejected by the vice-regal authorities in Portuguese Goa. Was peace between Johor and the Portuguese in fact the outcome of a later agreement, struck after the 1613 Acehnese invasion of Johor? One source claims that the Johor ruler was negotiating with the Portuguese in the closing weeks of 1614, and that peace arrived in 1618, though Johor likely only accepted it under duress.

Whatever the case may be, a single, or more likely, several peace agreements of varying formality, scope and duration were forged during the second decade of the 17th century. Their existence is said to have been widely known across the archipelago. Commercial relations between Portuguese Melaka and Johor may have been strained at times, but they were occasionally also close. The implications of this flourishing relationship on the Dutch-Portuguese war disturbed the VOC greatly.

Obelaar is interesting not least because he defected to the Portuguese subsequently and may have been working or spying for them throughout his tenure at the VOC factory at Batu Sawar. He was present at the 1610 treaty negotiations, and may very well have acted against the interests of his Dutch employers. He was also there when Raja Bongsu paid an unusual nocturnal visit to the Dutch factory after the peace agreement had been proclaimed. On this occasion, Raja Bongsu reportedly apologised profusely to the Dutch for the Portuguese pact and revealed that Johor had inked it under duress. This pressure came from various sides, including from among the rank and file at the Johor court, in other words from those Malay merchant-officials and *orang kaya* who were carrying on a brisk trade with the Portuguese. Rumours were also swirling about a potential popular uprising. Raja Bongsu, so one is informed, found himself with no other option but to cave in and sign off the agreement with the Portuguese.

### Aceh Strikes, 1613

Portugal's peace with Johor after 1610 would have led to a resurgence of Portuguese maritime trade through the Singapore Straits from the South China Sea and the revival of Melaka as a port. Following Admiral Matelieff's unsuccessful joint attack with Johor on Portuguese Melaka in 1606, trade had slowed to a trickle for more than a year. The situation was reportedly so dire that merchants, fearful of going out to sea, resorted to making a living by farming, while Dutch patrols scoured the Singapore and Melaka straits for Portuguese vessels to plunder.

But the 1610 peace deal had two consequences that were arguably unforeseen. The first concerned Raja Bongsu's position at the Johor court. His standing among the fluid hierarchy of his three siblings and the intrigues of the *orang kaya* was not particularly strong at the time – a point that Admiral Matelieff made when he noted that the *orang kaya* would lose power if they had Raja Bongsu as their king. Johor's peace with the Portuguese only served to further weaken and ultimately marginalise Raja Bongsu, and with him, the pro-Dutch faction at the Johor court.

The second consequence concerns the bigger picture: Johor's relations with Aceh were patchy at best, but the Acehnese had a long record of hostile relations with the Portuguese. Unsurprisingly then, the peace deal of 1610 was seen to have tipped power relations in the Straits, and was mentioned as one reason that prompted Sultan Iskandar Muda of Aceh to attack Johor on 4 May 1613.

Aceh arrived with dozens of war galleys manned by an estimated force of between 20,000 and 40,000 men. According to the journal of Ralph Standish and Ralph Croft recording the 1612–16 voyage of EIC captain Thomas Best, "[Aceh's] army was 100 small frigotts and gallies, some haveing ordinance, some none; the number of souldiers 20,000."

A Dutch ship, the journal further informs, had been caught in the attack while it lay at anchor at the "isle of Johor" (presumably around the eastern coast of Singapore near Pulau Tekong):

> *A Flemish shipp att this tyme happened to be att [the] ille of Joar, tradeing there; which did, in the King of Joars behalf, resist and shott att the army of this Kinge of Achen and Sumatra.*

The crew were taken prisoner and brought to Aceh, as reported by Thomas Best. The attack was newsworthy enough to be reported in an updated edition of Sebastian Münster's widely read and richly illustrated *Cosmographia oder Beschreibung der gantzen Welt* (Cosmographia or Description of the Whole World) printed in Basel, Switzerland, in 1628. According to this account, the Acehnese Laksamana arrived with 200 galleys and frigates, overwhelmed Johor and Siak, and brought their rulers back to Aceh as prisoners. As they came from the west, the Acehnese fleet would have had to pass Singapore, where the Johor armada was based. Before running up the Johor River, the Acehnese would have destroyed the Johor war galleys based at Singapore, and may have set the Singapore settlement ablaze. But this is by no means certain.

Aceh's strike on Johor was reported in Sebastian Münster's *Cosmographia*, one of the most widely read books on geography in the early modern period. This title page comes from the third edition, printed in Basel in 1628, well after the death of its author.

A different explanation was provided by Carl Alexander Gibson-Hill. In an unsubstantiated footnote buried in his 1957 study of the Singapore straits, Gibson-Hill claimed that Ian Macgregor, a history lecturer at the University of Singapore then, had made an interesting discovery. While trawling the Portuguese sources, Macgregor had found a reference to a Portuguese attack in August 1613 against a Johor garrison at Singapore. Gibson-Hill surmised that in the course of their attack on the garrison, the Portuguese may very well have also burnt down Singapore's entire settlement with it.

Unfortunately, no additional details were provided, and Macgregor's letter to Gibson-Hill remains undiscovered as yet. It is unclear, currently, whether the target in question was located in Singapore, and whether the damage inflicted by the Portuguese was as substantial as Gibson-Hill and Macgregor believed. The

Portuguese source in question has also not been retrieved, so the claim that the Portuguese gutted Singapore in 1613 is little more than a legend originating from an incomplete footnote.

It also makes little sense since Johor and Portugal were at peace then, unless of course – and here is where exact dates become important – the target in question was not manned by soldiers from Johor, but by the Acehnese. Surely that would have been the case following the Acehnese invasion of Johor a few weeks earlier. In other words, assuming Macgregor was right to place the attack at Singapore in the first place, the Portuguese were not attacking a target held by their (former) ally Johor, but by their long-standing enemy and rival Aceh.

Dutch documents recount that Batu Sawar was destroyed by fire, including the VOC factory that was located along the banks of the Johor River. The account by Standish and Croft in the journal entry for 28 June 1613 explains that the fire at the Dutch factory had been deliberately set by the fleeing employees: "But the Capttain of the Flemings and his merchants ashoare burned their housse and fleed…." The losses to the company were substantial, as a short report on the damages testifies. It provides a useful snapshot of the range of goods, as well as their volume and value, traded by the Dutch in the Johor capital at the time:

> 200 *bahar* of pepper at 14 reals-of-eight per *bahar*
> 31 *pikul* and 65 *kati* of benzoin at 26 ¾ reals-of-eight per *pikul*
> About 4,000 guilders worth of cotton cloth at cost
> 40,000 reals-of-eight in cash
> 44 *tael* of gold
> A few items that had been pawned for money
> 2 gold krisses

As Johor was principally known as a pepper port, the large stocks of pepper were unsurprising. Benzoin, a tree resin, served a number of functions, for instance as incense and medicine. The cotton cloth almost certainly originated from India and was routinely used by the Dutch company to barter for other goods – here at Batu Sawar probably for pepper or benzoin. The 44 *tael* of gold were of unspecified form or purity, but the gold in question was probably unminted gold dust panned in the river beds of the peninsula. The two gold krisses had probably been pawned by members of the Johor nobility. The aggregate loss was estimated

Drawing of the pepper plant from the William Farquhar Collection. The black or white fruit of the vine *Piper nigrum* was traded in Rome and China from the time of the Tang dynasty, becoming a major commodity of trade from the time of the Southern Song, and a century later in Europe. Trade documents from Cairo indicate that after the 12th century, there was a growing consumer demand for pepper owing to its ability to improve the flavour of poor-quality meats.

at 45,000 guilders (about €665,000 or slightly over S$1 million today)*, a sum that seems to have been pegged rather low going by the items mentioned in the list above.

Members of the court, including Raja Bongsu, and about two dozen Europeans were taken prisoner and brought to Aceh. There are mixed reports about the fate of Sultan Alauddin. Some sources claim he was brought to Aceh as well, but a far more credible account, given by Pieter Floris, is that the Sultan fled to Bintan, where he passed away around 1615. Raja Bongsu, meanwhile, wed one of Iskandar Muda's sisters. He was returned to Johor, where he ruled as Sultan Abdallah Ma'ayat Shah until his death around 1623.

Once returned to Johor as the new ruler, Sultan Abdallah sought almost immediately to mend fences with the VOC. In Europe, political tensions over religion, commercial rivalries and dynastic changes were rising. The Thirty Years' War, described as one of the bloodiest conflicts in European history, would erupt in 1618

---

* Source: International Institute of Social History. Calculation based on purchasing power parity (PPP).

and only end with the Peace of Westphalia in 1648. Important changes had also taken place in the regional balance of power. Melaka, and the Portuguese at large, were from the perspective of the new Johor ruler no longer the principal threat. The power to fend against was now evidently Aceh, which was continuing to expand rapidly not just in Sumatra but also on the Malay Peninsula.

### Singapore's Strategic Importance to Early European Powers
The early colonial powers in the region recognised Singapore's strategic location and potential. They drafted various plans to construct fortifications on and around the island and even considered founding a colonial settlement. Locations to the east and west of the island were used as regular cruising grounds by VOC ships to choke the flow of trade through the Singapore and Melaka straits as well as their tributaries.

The Portuguese were already toying with the idea of establishing a fort in the waters around Singapore in 1584. The Bishop of Melaka, Dom João Ribeiro Gaio, suggested building one in the Straits of Singapore. The main aim was to provide better security cover for Portuguese merchant shipping coming from East Asia. Melaka was too far from the southeast coast of the Malay Peninsula to effectively serve as a base from which to send naval forces to escort Portuguese mercantile shipping coming from the South China Sea and guide them onwards to Melaka. But these suggestions died as the Viceroy of Goa, Dom Francisco da Gama, thought that an armada positioned in the waters around Singapore would be a more effective deterrent against attacks.

A subsequent proposal for Portuguese fortifications came from Jacques de Coutre, who sailed the waters of the Singapore Straits and called a number of times at Batu Sawar to trade between 1596 and 1602–3. De Coutre's proposed site was on Ysla de Arenas (present-day Sentosa), which lay "in the middle of the Straits of Singapore" – a reference to Sentosa's location between the Old and New Straits of Singapore.

The island, he argued, had many trees suitable for making ships' masts, stones that could be used in construction, coral that could be pounded up and used as mortar, and a freshwater source (Siloso Spring today). He also proposed a second fort at the mouth of the Johor River, opposite the extreme eastern end of Ysla de la Sabandaria Vieja (Island of the Old Harbour Master's Office; that is, Singapore island). De Coutre believed that fortifications at these two locations – along with a naval squadron stationed permanently at Sentosa – would ensure the security of Portuguese shipping traversing the waters around Singapore.

After the *Santa Catarina*'s seizure, the Dutch increased patrols and privateering in the waters around Singapore, between Karimun in the west and Pedra Branca in the east, focusing particularly on two locations: the northern coast of Karimun and the Hook of Berbukit (Tanjung Pengerang). From Karimun, it was possible to monitor maritime traffic arriving through the Melaka, Kundur (or Sabam) and Durian straits – important for ships heading to or coming from Palembang, Jambi, Java, Sulawesi (Makassar), the Malukus, Bandas and Timor. This location also enabled the monitoring of ships taking the Singapore and Tebrau straits. The Hook of Berbukit, on the Johor mainland roughly across from Changi, had a sandy beach suited for careening vessels during repair, and was protected by hills from full exposure to the northeast monsoon winds.

Coloured sketch of Palembang in south Sumatra, dating from the second half of the 17th century.

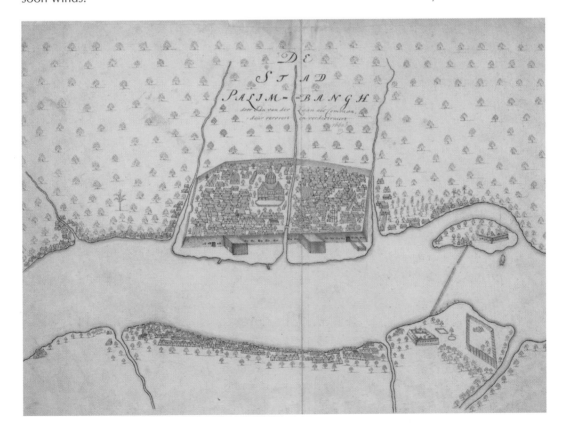

To elude Dutch naval patrols, Portuguese skippers resorted to a range of tactics, often with the open or clandestine support of local chiefs and rulers, including Johor. There were, of course, always those who used the cover of night and shallow waters to conduct their business and spread their risk over several smaller craft. Some of the strategies pursued, however, were quite elaborate.

One was to re-route cargo overland along the Pahang and Muar rivers and their tributaries. This option required the cooperation of the ruler of Pahang and later, of Johor. A second was to explore and open up new routes between the islands of Riau and eastern Sumatra. Friendly relations between the Dutch and Johor, however, made this increasingly difficult. The third way was to re-route long-distance vessels through the Sunda or Bali straits. This, too, became increasingly difficult with the growing Dutch presence around Java and the King of Mataram's wars against the princes of eastern Java. Finally, the Portuguese also resorted to the use of Asian or European proxies to conduct their trade between India, Melaka and China. Among the Europeans, the English and the Danes were particularly favoured.

The Dutch had similar ideas as the Portuguese about building fortifications to secure their merchant shipping very early on. At one time, Matelieff and the directors of the VOC considered establishing the VOC's main Asian base at a location around the Singapore Straits that would include Singapore, the Johor River estuary, Karimun and the northern coast of Bintan.

In various petitions addressed to the VOC directors and leading members of the Dutch government, Matelieff weighed the merits of six geographically suitable sites across Southeast Asia: Aceh, Melaka, the Johor River estuary-Singapore region, Palembang, Banten and Jayakarta (Jakarta). Ultimately, he rejected the Singapore-Johor River region because it could not be easily reached year-round and relied substantially on imported food supplies. He then cast his attention southwards, and, together with other leading VOC officials in Europe, opted for a location nearer the Sunda Straits. This, Matelieff underscored, could be sailed all year round, unlike the Melaka Straits.

Matelieff's travelogue, memorials and letters written in the first two decades of the 17th century answer one of the most puzzling questions about the history of early modern Singapore: why was Singapore's strategic location along key maritime arteries supposedly only discovered in the early 19th century with the arrival of the British in these waters? Matelieff's writings reveal that Singapore's potential – as a strategic point, as a port, and as a possible site for a colonial settlement – was well-recognised long before that. This insight significantly challenges and changes the British colonial narrative.

Admiral Pieter Willemszoon Verhoeff succeeded Matelieff and arrived in the first days of 1609 with instructions from the VOC directorate to build on Dutch relations with Johor. One task was to consider the construction of a fort in the region through the offices of the Johor ruler. This was the first time that the VOC directors had issued concrete instructions to erect a fort in the region of the Singapore Straits.

Pieter Willemszoon Verhoeff led a VOC fleet to Southeast Asia and called at Johor during the opening weeks of 1609. He was murdered later that year in the Banda Islands.

The Sultan, however, was unconvinced by Verhoeff's suggestion that a fort would have security benefits for Johor's riverine economy. The Portuguese, he remarked, did not detest him as much as his esteemed visitors assumed. In the event that Portuguese forces should impose another naval blockade and cut off the riverine trade centred at Batu Sawar – or indeed, should they launch an attack on the royal capital – he could flee farther upstream.

Moreover, the Sultan was unwilling to give the Dutch the "keys to his river". The construction of a fort on his territory would inevitably mean that the Dutch would live among his subjects, creating unwelcome social repercussions, as the Dutch men, like the Portuguese, were likely to fraternise with the local women. So, the Sultan bargained for cash and arms instead. Realising that further discussion would be fruitless, Verhoeff broke off the negotiations.

The breakdown marked the beginning of a new low for Johor-Dutch relations. If the Johor rulers were riled by Verhoeff's request for permission to build a fort in the Johor River estuary, news of a truce between the Dutch Republic and the Iberian powers in April aggravated the situation. Raja Bongsu felt that as a Dutch ally, he should have been consulted about the truce, which the Dutch were, in fact, obliged to do under the terms of the 1606 treaty signed between them.

The Dutch continued to pursue the idea of a fort in the region, including one at the very same spot in Singapore as proposed by De Coutre a decade earlier. After his defection to the Portuguese, Jacques Obelaar revealed to the authorities in Goa in 1612 that the Dutch had plans to "erect a fortress on an island that divides the Straits and where the vessels heading off to China pass through". This location, Obelaar added, was at a distance of about 5 *legoas* (31 kilometres) from "the Johor kingdom". If this distance was estimated as the crow flies, then the "Johor" in question here was most probably around Johor Lama and not the royal capital Batu Sawar.

As a senior official at the Dutch factory in Johor, Obelaar would have been privy to VOC plans. If Matelieff, and Verhoeff after him, had been vague about the exact location of any new Dutch fortification around the Johor River estuary and the Straits, the men-on-the-spot evidently had much clearer ideas. Obelaar's testimony is unambiguous about the intended location: an island that separates two straits some 30 kilometres from Johor Lama – in other words, present-day Sentosa.

It was not until after Aceh's attack on Johor in 1613 that Raja Bongsu, having become Sultan, revived the conversation with the Dutch where it had ended at the time of Verhoeff's visit. In 1614, the VOC despatched Jan Gommerszoon Cocq and Adriaen van der Dusschen to negotiate with Sultan Abdallah and examine possible sites for the proposed fortification. Cocq died shortly after arriving at Batu Sawar, leaving Van der Dusschen to negotiate alone. After inspecting several sites, including Singapore and the northern coast of Bintan, he settled for the northeastern tip of Karimun Besar (Great Carimon) as an ideal strategic location for monitoring shipping entering and leaving the Singapore and Melaka straits, as well as ships sailing along the eastern coast of Sumatra in the direction of Java and the Spice Islands.

But the plans were scuttled as the Dutch began developing a strategy away from the Melaka Straits littoral. Like Matelieff before him, Jan Pieterszoon Coen, who became the Dutch Governor-General, firmly preferred a Javanese location near the Sunda Straits. The Acehnese strike and Portuguese blockades had exposed the Johor River's vulnerability. A Dutch fort on Singapore or Karimun Besar would not have guaranteed the safety of the waters around Johor, thereby scuttling prospects for attracting trade. Push came

BATAVIA OPT EYLANDT IAVA.

to shove when Coen presented a fait accompli by conquering Batavia (Jakarta today) in 1619 while Amsterdam was still mulling over possible sites for a Dutch base in Asia.

In the final analysis, there was always a lack of money to build a fort on Singapore or nearby. The VOC, as a shareholder corporation, had to consider the bottom line, and in this period it was struggling to contain runaway spending on commercial and military infrastructure. Some VOC factories, including Batu Sawar, were running at a loss, but for now, at least, they could not be closed for political reasons. Maintaining a fort and deploying manpower to garrison it was costly.

For this reason, the company found it more cost-effective to seasonally deploy naval squadrons in and around the Singapore and Melaka straits instead. Even after finally taking Melaka from the Portuguese in 1641, Dutch naval squadrons continued to patrol the waters, though by this time their function had changed. Apart from keeping a close eye on pirates and rapacious maritime tribes,

Hand-coloured print (mid-17th century) depicting a bird's-eye view of the entrance to the port of Batavia (now Jakarta) on Java.

they were to ensure that Asian shipping was discouraged from calling at local ports and redirected to Dutch Batavia instead.

### The Spanish Armada in Singapore and Governor's Strait

The arrival of a Spanish armada off the coast of Singapore in February 1616 marked an important turning point for the Dutch-Portuguese conflict in the Straits region. Although no major fighting took place, the tide began to turn against the Iberians in Southeast Asia from this point. The armada's failure was the result of a confluence of factors, but the single most important one was without doubt Juan de Silva, the Governor of the Spanish Philippines at the time.

The start of De Silva's governorship in 1609 coincided with the signing of the Twelve Years' Truce that halted the conflict between the Dutch Republic and Spain, and between the Dutch and the Portuguese. The truce was meant to be enforced around the globe, but local conditions in the empires' far-flung network of colonies and settlements made this a difficult task. In Southeast Asia, the Maluku Islands proved to be the most significant flashpoint in the continued rivalry between the Dutch and the Iberians. The Malukus had become heavily contested after the Dutch wrested the island of Ambon from the Portuguese in 1605. In response,

Ternate was one of the clove-producing volcanic islands of the Maluku group and home to the court of the Ternatan sultan.

the Spanish had stepped up their presence, maintaining forts and garrisons on the islands of Tidore and Ternate.

When De Silva succeeded as governor, he managed to score initial successes against the Dutch. His defeat of François Wittert near Manila in 1610 fuelled optimism in Madrid, Lisbon, Portuguese Goa and Spanish Mexico City that the Dutch could be dealt a decisive military blow. To this end, the Spanish Viceroy of Mexico helped finance the construction of an armada that would be built in the Philippines, comprising 10 heavily armed galleons, four oared galleys, one *patache* (a type of warship), three frigates and additional support vessels.

Aboard these ships were some 5,000 men, including soldiers from Europe, Mexico and the Philippine Islands, as well as 500 Japanese mercenaries. The Portuguese were equipped with four large warships built in India. After years of preparation, the Spanish and the Portuguese were ready to unite at Singapore in the closing weeks of 1615 and jointly proceed to the Malukus to take on the Dutch. However, in September 1615, the Portuguese warships were destroyed in two separate naval attacks – by the Acehnese in the Melaka Straits, and then by the Dutch while the remaining ships lay at anchor off Melaka.

De Silva, who knew nothing of the fate of the Portuguese ships, set sail from Manila in late January or early February 1616 and dropped anchor off Singapore on 25 February. He penned a menacing letter in Spanish addressed to Sultan Abdallah, exhorting him to stand by his peace treaty with Portugal, and also stating that a trading vessel had earlier been captured by Johor forces off Changi. When the Portuguese warships failed to show, De Silva decided to proceed to Melaka to ascertain their circumstances, leaving the rest of the armada that had arrived from Manila anchored off Singapore. On arrival in Melaka, he was greeted with pomp and ceremony but died mysteriously soon after.

Meanwhile, the soldiers and crew aboard the Spanish ships anchored off Singapore were being decimated by disease, with the bodies of the dead thrown into the sea. The Dutch, who were monitoring these developments from their network of factories around the region, cited rumours that the freshwater supplies taken on by the Spanish had been poisoned by the Orang Laut. With news of the death of De Silva, the armada set sail for Manila on 4 May, after its commanding officers decided to abort their disastrous campaign.

One legacy stemming from the arrival of the Spanish armada in Singapore waters was the name given to a new maritime artery – Governor's Strait, or sometimes the Strait of John de Silva, as it is known in pre-1800 maps and maritime charts. This strait, running south of St John's Island, is equivalent to the main fairway used by international shipping today.

After the opening up of Governor's Strait, ships began increasingly to sail farther south and no longer in view of Singapore's coastline. One example is the 1637 account by Portuguese missionary Fray Sebastien Manrique. In Melaka, he boarded a vessel bound for Cochinchina and set sail on 15 August, heading south to the Karimuns. Here, on 21 August, they spotted two VOC cruisers, described as "Dutch pirates", who began to give chase. The captain "took no notice of them and they maintained their course under favourable winds which far more resembled that of spring rather than winter". Three days later, they passed through the Singapore Straits, headed out to Romania Shoal and from there set course for Pulau Condor, a group of islands off the southern coast of present-day Vietnam. There are no further details on Singapore to be found in Manrique's diary.

Another example touching on the ascendancy of the new sailing route was written by the Spanish friar Domingo de Navarrete, whose travelogue published in 1669 describes a passage through the Governor's Strait. Navarrete claims that "most people now go that way", in other words, the Governor's Strait was by then the preferred maritime route, albeit not the only option. Unsurprisingly, after the opening up of the Governor's Strait, written records of passage close by the shores of Singapore also began to diminish.

### The English in Southeast Asia

Raffles' arrival in Singapore waters was not the first time an Englishman had popped up in the waters of Southeast Asia. Francis Drake, who became the second person to circumnavigate the globe between 1577 and 1580, had visited the Maluku Islands (sailing from Europe westwards via the Americas and the Pacific) during his historic voyage and eventually returned to England with a cargo of spices and treasure plundered from Spanish galleons carrying gold and silver from the Americas to Spain.

Portrait sketch of Sir Francis Drake, taken from William Cullan Bryant and Sydney Howard Gay's *Popular History of the United States*.

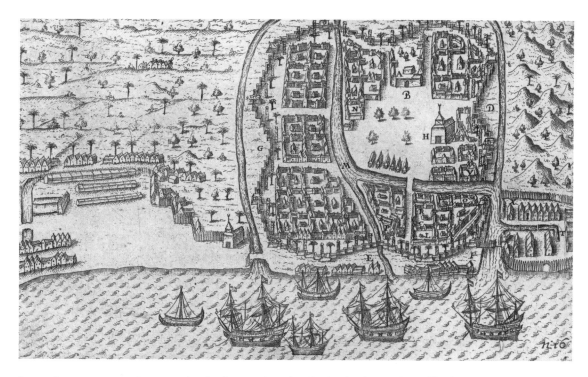

James Lancaster, a privateer who had served under Drake in the English fleet that defeated the Spanish Armada in 1588, sailed to Southeast Asia in 1601, representing the newly founded EIC and bearing letters from its patron, Queen Elizabeth I. The generic letter he presented to local rulers sought trading privileges. The Sultan of Aceh was the first recipient, after which Lancaster sailed to the Maluku and Banda islands, better known as the Spice Islands.

Although the Spice Islands were relatively tiny in size, nutmeg and cloves grew exclusively there, in the fertile volcanic soil. In 1603, Lancaster set up a factory to trade in spices at Banten, the first English trading post in Southeast Asia. Besides Banten, the EIC would maintain factories in several other places, such as at Jambi and Makassar as well as in the Malukus.

Initially, the Dutch did not react aggressively, but tightened their grip on the spice trade. Dutch policy called for driving out its European trading rivals by extending control over the sources and production of spices, destroying spice-producing trees such as on Pulau Run in the Malukus, deporting native populations, and handing parcels of controlled spice-producing plantations to new planters. As part of their strategy, the VOC representatives entered

Printed bird's-eye view of the city of Banten on Java in 1596, taken from the printed travelogue of Cornelis de Houtman's voyage to the East Indies.

Had the fort on Sentosa been built, would it have looked something like this? Hand-drawn sketch (17th century) of the Dutch Fort Concordia at Kupang on the island of Timor.

into negotiations with local leaders to gain control of the sources of spices and to attempt to build fortifications to protect Dutch trade, and inevitably also to supervise the local population.

In 1615, the English, who had fortified factories on Pulau Ai and Pulau Run, found themselves under attack from the Dutch. The following year, the inhabitants of the islands swore allegiance to King James I by presenting EIC representatives there with a precious nutmeg seedling as a token of fealty. This allegiance allowed James I to call himself "King of England, Scotland, Ireland, France, Puloway [Pulau Ai] and Puloroon [Pulau Run]".

Swearing allegiance to James I did not win the Pulau Run inhabitants any favours. The Dutch struck anyway, destroyed the nutmeg trees that were their source of wealth, and killed or evicted the inhabitants. In 1621, the Dutch occupied the Banda Islands, massacred the non-Dutch European factors there as well as the islanders, essentially depopulating the islands and gaining control of the nutmeg trees. Many trees in the Bandas as well as the Malukus were destroyed to create artificial shortages and sustain spice prices in Europe. In 1623, the Dutch executed 20

English and Portuguese and one Japanese on Ambon on charges of treason.

Despite Dutch hostility, the EIC maintained its presence in Southeast Asia, even toying at one stage with the idea of constructing a fortification on Karimun. However, as tensions between the Dutch and English mounted and the VOC tightened its hold on the spice trade, the English had, by 1624, closed their factories on Borneo, at Patani, Ayutthaya and Japan, leaving a presence only at Batavia, Jambi, Jepara and Makassar. They were subsequently evicted from Makassar in 1667 and Jambi in 1679.

The English also officially "lost" Pulau Run and Pulau Ai with the signing of the Treaty of Breda in 1667; in exchange, they gained Manhattan Island and its port of New Amsterdam (now New York City). Once Banten was taken by the Dutch in 1682, the English were confined to the west Sumatran port of Bengkulu (Bencoolen) for the next hundred years. From 1652, when the First Anglo-Dutch War broke out, until a landmark peace settlement was reached with the Anglo-Dutch Treaty of 1824, the two sides fought numerous naval battles for supremacy. Concerns over Dutch hostility would influence the choice of Singapore as an EIC trading post in the 19th century.

## IN A NUTSHELL

While Chapter Three introduced us to the presence of a Shahbandaria in Singapore during the 16th century, Chapter Four elaborates on the centrality of Singapore's strategic location across the 17th century, including how its position as a Shahbandaria of the Johor Sultanate shaped intense conflict and competition in its waters. This competition took place between the naval powers of Europe, as well as between regional rivals such as Aceh and Patani.

On one hand, Singapore's strategic location prompted the European powers to consider fortifying it into a naval bastion to protect their trading interests. On the other, Singapore's significance as a settlement was closely tied to the fortunes of the Johor Sultanate: it thrived as Johor prospered during its "golden age", but started to decline as Johor experienced social, political and economic convulsions at the close of the 17th century.

In Chapter Five, we will explore how the regicide of Sultan Mahmud in 1699 plunged Johor into a protracted civil war, with various figures claiming to be the rightful heir of the sultanate. Singapore was evidently marginalised by the conflict that ensued.

Detail from a 1755 navigation chart by French hydrographer Jacques Nicolas Bellin of the Singapore and Melaka straits that clearly marks out the different passages for sailing past Singapore. The chart warns mariners of the numerous unknown small islands south of Singapore, which is marked as "Pulo ou Isle Panjang", or "Long Island".

# CHAPTER FIVE

# The 18th Century
## From Malay Entrepôt to Colonial Port-City

> A nd the time for Friday prayers arrived. And the Royal Sedan chair was ready. Then His Highness mounted the chair and was carried to Friday prayers. At the gate to the mosque the Bendahara and the noblemen were waiting. Then Megat Seri Rama arrived, bowed and said, "Your slave is committing treason, My Lord," and with his parang [cleaver] hit the head of His Highness. White blood flowed, like the cream of coconut milk....
>
> *Hikayat Siak* (Chronicle of the Kingdom of Siak)

### A Royal Assassination

News reached the Dutch in Melaka in October 1699 that Sultan Mahmud II of Johor had been assassinated by his noblemen, the *orang kaya*. The Sultan's naked corpse was apparently dragged around the town and left exposed until the afternoon when the conspirators would proclaim the Bendahara (prime minister) as the new Sultan; only then could Mahmud be buried.

The *orang kaya* were driven to dispose of Mahmud because of his increasingly erratic and intolerable behaviour, culminating in his order to disembowel the pregnant wife of an *orang kaya*, Megat Sri Rama, after she partook of a slice of jackfruit stolen from the royal compound. The *Hikayat Siak* – the court chronicle of the Kingdom of Siak on the east coast of Sumatra – claims that Mahmud had her belly carved open, wanting to see her unborn child sucking on the jackfruit.

A distraught Megat Sri Rama led the regicide and struck when Mahmud was being carried to the mosque for Friday prayers. In the popular history of Johor, Mahmud is referred to as the "Sultan who passed away on the royal sedan chair" (Marhum Mangkat di

The mausoleum in Kota Tinggi where the grave of Sultan Mahmud Shah is today housed with other royal graves.

Julang). His grave – with a mausoleum erected over it – as well as that of Megat Sri Rama are venerated sites in Kota Tinggi, Johor, today. The death of Mahmud would lead to a profound and unfortunate turn of history for Johor and Singapore as well as a shift in regional and global trade patterns.

The British country trader Alexander Hamilton, who visited Johor and may have witnessed these events, provided a different account from that conveyed to the Dutch at Melaka or documented in the later Malay histories. It would appear that Mahmud, who had been installed in 1685 as the 10th Sultan of Johor at the age of 10, apart from his youth and incompetence as a ruler, favoured the intimate company of men. Hamilton's account of the regicide is a riveting story of a brutal tyrant, a concerned mother, a rejected beauty, and a father seeking revenge:

> *Their King was a Youth of twenty Years of Age, and being vitiously inclined, was so corrupted by Adulation and Flagitious Company, that he became intolerable. I went to Johore Lami at that Time, to traffick with his Subjects, and some China Men…. He continued his insupportable Tyranny and Brutality for a Year or two after I was gone, and his Mother, to try if he could be broke off that unnatural Custom of Converse with Males, perswaded a beautiful young Woman to visit him, when he was a Bed, which she did, and allured him with her Embraces, but he was so far from being pleased with her Conversation, that he called his black Guard, and made them break both her Arms, for offering to embrace his royal Person. She cried, and said it was by his Mother's Order she came, but that was no Excuse. Next Morning he sent a Guard to bring her Father's Head, but he being an Orankay did not care to part with it, so the Tyrant*

*took a Lance in his Hand, and sware he would have it; but,
as he was entring at the Door, the Orankay past a long Lance
through his Heart, and so made an End of the Beast.*

The killing of Mahmud plunged Johor into a succession crisis. The
Bendahara Paduka Raja, who was elevated to succeed as Sultan
Abdul Jalil Shah IV, inherited a fragmented kingdom, of which the
Shahbandaria of Singapura was a part. Malay histories claim that
the new Bendahara-Sultan did not have in his veins the supposedly "white blood" that Sultan Mahmud Shah II had as a direct
descendant of Sri Tri Buana, and was thus unable to command the
same loyalty from the Orang Laut and the Malay populace.

Without the moral authority of sacred lineage, Abdul Jalil could
only rule Johor with the continued support of the *orang kaya*.
However, Hamilton believed that while Abdul Jalil was a sin-
cere ruler accepted by his subjects and trade flourished during
his reign, he was also manipulated by his younger brother, Tun
Mahmud, who exercised the real political power.

Hand-drawn and coloured
chart of the southern portion
of the Malay Peninsula and the
Singapore Straits together with
part of the Riau Archipelago by
Thomas Bowrey, c. 1690.

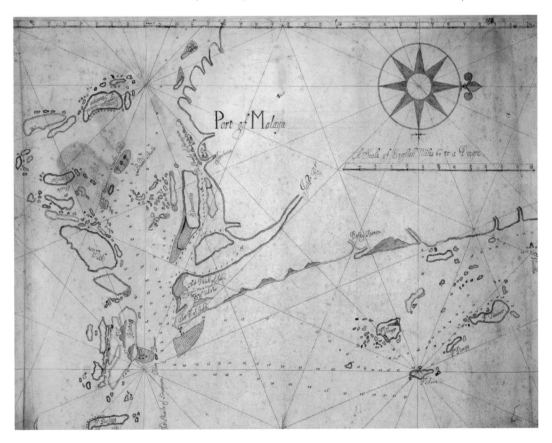

Printed map found in Alexander Hamilton's *A New Account of the East Indies*, published in 1727. The Singapore Strait is marked here as "Straits of Governdore", a variant of Governor's Strait, named after the Spanish Governor of the Philippines, Juan de Silva, who had arrived with his armada off Singapore in 1616.

By 1716, Tun Mahmud was facing serious challenges, and two years later, he would face an adversary in the form of Raja Kecik. Raja Kecik (sometimes Raja Kecil) appeared off the coast of Sumatra near Bengkalis in 1718, claiming to be the posthumous son of Sultan Mahmud Shah II – with the "white blood" of Mahmud and his Melaka ancestors coursing through his veins – and hence the bearer of the mystical right to rule Johor-Riau.

According to the *Hikayat Siak*, Raja Kecik was born to a slave woman attending to the Sultan on the eve of the regicide. The text recounts that Mahmud was dallying with a young man, whom he preferred to his concubines. When Mahmud spilt his royal seed, he ordered the slave woman to swallow it; which she did, and thereby became impregnated. Thus did Raja Kecik issue forth into the world, infused with the royal "white blood" of Sri Tri Buana in his veins. Raja Kecik succeeded in convincing the people who mattered – the Orang Laut warriors – as well as other groups disenchanted with the new dynasty, of this fantastical tale of his bloodline.

In 1719, Raja Kecik attacked the Johor capital, and in another act of regicide, the Bendahara-Sultan Abdul Jalil Shah was assassinated while fleeing to Pahang. His son and heir, Raja Sulaiman, recruited Bugis settlers in Selangor and Linggi to help repel Raja Kecik. The war-like Bugis were part of a diaspora who had fled Sulawesi in the wake of the Makassar War of 1666–69. In return for successfully battling Raja Kecik, the Bugis demanded and received a permanent position at the Johor-Riau court through the office of the Raja Muda and through marriage into the royal family. The new Bugis Raja Muda, Daeng Merewah, came to wield most of the political – and arguably economic – power.

The enmity between Raja Kecik's kingdom of Siak in eastern Sumatra, which he established in 1723, and the Bugis at Riau continued for much of the 18th century, during which time, according to the *Hikayat Siak*, sporadic naval battles took place between them in and around Singapore waters. One naval battle in 1767 reportedly took place at the entrance to the Singapore River.

Underlying these conflicts was a deeper ideological battle for hearts and minds in the Malay world. The *Hikayat Siak* contends that Raja Kecik was the rightful heir to Singapura's legacy established by Sri Tri Buana. Like the latter, Raja Kecik crossed the seas to Sumatra to establish a new kingdom at Siak, which was Singapura's true successor, not the Bugis at Bintan.

Both men were "strangers" who appeared among a host society claiming to be an immigrant warrior prince whose father was a god or former king of the land, and further claiming the political legitimacy to rulership. Singapura was then the spiritual base of Raja Kecik's claim to his right to rule. What is important to understand here is that the succession crisis caused by the regicide of 1699 resulted in a rift between the Johor-Riau Sultanate and the Kingdom of Siak, one that would eventually have consequences on the fate of Singapore in 1819.

With the benefit of hindsight, and given the ascendancy of the Bugis in the Melaka Straits in the first half of the 18th century, the major losers of the regicide were the Orang Laut communities. As the Bugis appropriated concessions and leading positions, the Orang Laut, who had occupied key economic, political and military roles since the Melaka Sultanate, became increasingly marginalised.

### Strangers Who Would Be Kings

Opting for the title of Raja Muda rather than that of the conventional Bendahara, Tun Mahmud had reasserted Johor's supremacy over its historic dependencies on the Malay Peninsula and along the eastern coast of Sumatra between 1708 and 1718. In so doing, he and the Sultan steered Johor-Riau to a new era of commercial prosperity. This was achieved by adopting the old Malay strategy of undercutting lesser regional rivals by forcing them to export through Bintan, which had now become the Sultanate's main port.

Tun Mahmud's decision to transfer Johor's port from Kota Tinggi to Bintan island in the Riaus, where the Johor sultans had occasionally located themselves, would have rendered irrelevant the Shahbandar's position on Singapore island. There was now no need for a Shahbandar to oversee the first port of call for traders proceeding up the Johor River to Kota Tinggi once the port had shifted to Bintan and nearby Pulau Penyengat. Furthermore, the Singapore-based Orang Laut warriors were split in their loyalties to the new Bendahara-Sultan. Singapore's harbour would have been significantly scaled down, and the Shahbandar, despite the absence of documented evidence, would have likely relocated to Bintan.

Hamilton, in his book *A New Account of the East Indies*, recalled that in 1703 Sultan Abdul Jalil Shah had offered him the island of Singapore as a gift, which he turned down:

> *In Anno 1703. I called at Johore in my Way to China, and he treated me very kindly, and made me a Present of the Island of Sincapure, but I told him it could be of no Use to a private Person, tho' a proper Place for a Company to settle a Colony on, lying in the Center of Trade, and being accommodated with good Rivers and safe Harbours, so conveniently situated, that all Winds served Shipping both to go out and come into those Rivers. The Soil is black and fat: And the Woods abound in good Masts for Shipping, and Timber for building. I have seen large Beans growing wild in the Woods, not inferior to the best in Europe for Taste and Beauty; and Sugar-cane five or six Inches round growing wild also.*

It is unclear why the Sultan would offer Singapore to Hamilton, but Hamilton's comments about Singapore confirm earlier views

Printed engraving capturing the reputation of Bugis warriors, taken from Johan Nieuhof's *Embassy from the East India Company*, printed in 1669.

expressed by Portuguese and Dutch agents about the island being situated at the crossroads of trade, and worthy of being colonised. Significantly, Hamilton mentions no settlement, suggesting perhaps that by 1703, Singapore's role as a gatekeeper of the Johor River was already being transformed.

## Rise and Fall of Independent Riau (1758–84)

In 1722, Raja Sulaiman became Sultan of Johor-Riau, but Daeng Merewah, who became the first Yang Dipertuan Muda, held the real power. The Bugis transferred the royal court from the Johor River region to Bintan, turning it into a significant trading emporium by the second half of the 18th century. Over the next few decades, the Bugis would rebuild the networks connecting the port of Riau to local and transregional trade.

Several vital developments underscored the success of the Bugis. Daeng Kemboja's accession as the third Raja Muda (or Yang Dipertuan Muda, 1745–77) brought political stability to Johor-Riau. He expanded the Malay Straits trading networks, linking them to Bugis networks that spanned the Indonesian Archipelago and extended eastwards as far as China. The port attracted business from Borneo, China, Siam and Cochinchina (now part of Vietnam), as well as from India, including European country traders – the British, the French, the Portuguese and the Danes – based in Bengal and the Coromandel Coast.

The Bugis also did a thriving trade in tin. As one of Riau's largest exports, tin was procured through Bugis trading networks from Bangka and Palembang in Sumatra, and from Kedah and Selangor on the Malay Peninsula. Turnover was high, and the main buyers included the Europeans and the Chinese. Of such importance was

| Reigns of the Sultans of Johor | | |
|---|---|---|
| **Melaka-Johor Dynasty** | **Bendahara Dynasty**<br>(Based in Muar after the regicide of the Melaka-Johor dynasty) | **Bugis-Riau Dynasty**<br>(Related to the Bendahara dynasty through marriage with the house of Sultan Sulaiman) |
| • Mahmud Shah II, 1685–99 (assassinated)<br><br>• (Claimed legitimacy of descent) Abdul Jalil Rahmat Shah I (Raja Kecik), 1718–22 | • Abdul Jalil Shah IV (Bendahara Abdul Jalil), 1699–1720<br><br>• Sulaiman Badrul Alam Shah, 1722–60<br><br>• Abdul Jalil Muazzam Shah, 1760–61<br><br>• Ahmad Riayat Shah, 1761<br><br>• Mahmud Shah III, 1761–1812<br><br>• Abdul Rahman Muazzam Shah I, 1812–19<br><br>• Ahmad Husain Muazzam Shah (Tengku Long), 1819–35 | • Daeng Parani bin Daing Rilaga (m. Tengku Tengah Fatimah, daughter of Abdul Jalil Shah IV)<br><br>• Daeng Merewah bin Daing Rilaga (first Yang Dipertuan Muda), 1722–28<br><br>• Daeng Pali (Raja Chelak) bin Daing Rilaga (second Yang Dipertuan Muda), 1728–45<br><br>• Daeng Kemboja bin Daeng Parani (third Yang Dipertuan Muda), 1745–77<br><br>• Raja Haji bin Raja Chelak (fourth Yang Dipertuan Muda), 1777–84 |

the tin trade that the Dutch and Riau Bugis fought a fierce battle for its control between 1756 and 1758.

Instigated by a Dutch alliance with Raja Sulaiman to topple the Bugis hold over the Johor-Riau Sultanate, the Bugis led a contingent to lay siege on Dutch Melaka, which the Dutch only managed to put down with the arrival of naval reinforcements from Batavia in July 1757. The turn of fortunes saw the Dutch, supported by Raja Sulaiman, sacking Daeng Kemboja's stronghold in Linggi. Daeng Kemboja came to terms with the Dutch, and by 1 January 1758 a peace treaty was signed. In exchange for retaining their positions, Daeng Kemboja and other local ruling chiefs were to cease all trade with other European nations, and all the tin of Linggi, Rembau and Klang were to be sold to the Dutch at a preferential price.

While the treaty of 1758 saw a momentary return of prestige to Raja Sulaiman's base at Johor, Daeng Kemboja continued to develop the trade and influence of the Bugis at Riau, and cultivated friendship with the Dutch (leading to a new treaty signed on 11 November 1759). At the same time, unlike earlier rulers of Malay entrepôts, he did not try to suppress or destroy potential competitors, nor did he seek to assert a hegemonic regime. This, and the VOC's policy of non-intervention in Malay-Bugis conflict, implemented after the earlier Bugis siege of Melaka, preserved stable trade relations in the region. The two decades between the end of the siege of Melaka and the death of Daeng Kemboja marked Riau's golden age as an independent port and entrepôt.

### Snared by Shifts in Global Trade and Power

The fact that Daeng Kemboja, and before him, Tun Mahmud, could turn Riau into the region's port of choice was also due to shifts in the interconnectedness of 18th-century global commerce. The shifts arose from a long-term consumer revolution and disruptions to global supply and demand that were caused by a series of wars – from the Peace of Westphalia (1648), the Spanish Wars of Succession (1699–1714), the Seven Years' War (1756–63), to the beginning of the French Revolution and the Napoleonic Wars (1789–1814).

These conflicts were fought in Europe as well as in the colonies, from the Americas to Africa and Asia, and they affected demand patterns as well as international trade flows. The consumer revolution, in particular, together with protectionist government regulations, impacted the range and volume of spices, medicinal substances, stimulants, textiles and consumer goods that the East India Companies would trade in.

The first half of the 18th century saw the birth of several short-lived companies. In Britain, the English Company Trading in the East Indies (established in 1698), competed with the more established East India Company for a decade before they merged in 1708 to form a new, united EIC. Despite the disastrous speculation and collapse of the South Sea Company (entering the annals of history as the South Sea Bubble), chartered companies of varying sizes and financial strength continued to be founded in France, the Austrian Netherlands (now Belgium and Luxembourg), Brandenburg (Germany), Denmark, Sweden, Austria and Spain. The fate of these later commercial East India Company ventures – whether ending in merger or demise – is evidence that the EIC and VOC should be treated as exceptions rather than the norm in the burgeoning commerce of Europe and the Americas with Asia.

In the meantime, Bugis-Riau rose with a dynamism brought about by the country traders. These were private merchants who were permitted to trade alongside the East India Companies, or Company officials who were allowed to trade on their own accounts, sourcing for products from ports that the EIC and VOC did not trade at.

As mentioned, the diversion of trade to Bugis-Riau and the success of its port would have rendered the Shahbandaria at Singapura redundant. Daeng Kemboja and his predecessors might have noticed that the skippers plying the waters of the Melaka and Singapore straits no longer saw themselves confined to using the Old and New Straits that bordered Sentosa. Since the arrival of the Spanish armada off the coast of Singapore in the early 17th century, European ships increasingly also used the Governor's Strait farther south. As a consequence, they no longer passed within sight of the Singapore coastline or any settlement on it, which would have been in any case enclosed by sprawling greenery.

Not surprisingly, there are fewer written testimonies after the 1620s that mention Singapore and its immediately surrounding islets and waters. Nonetheless, there are several documented passages

(*Opposite*) Hand-drawn and coloured map of the Riau Straits with the port of Bintan, dating from the second half of the 18th century.

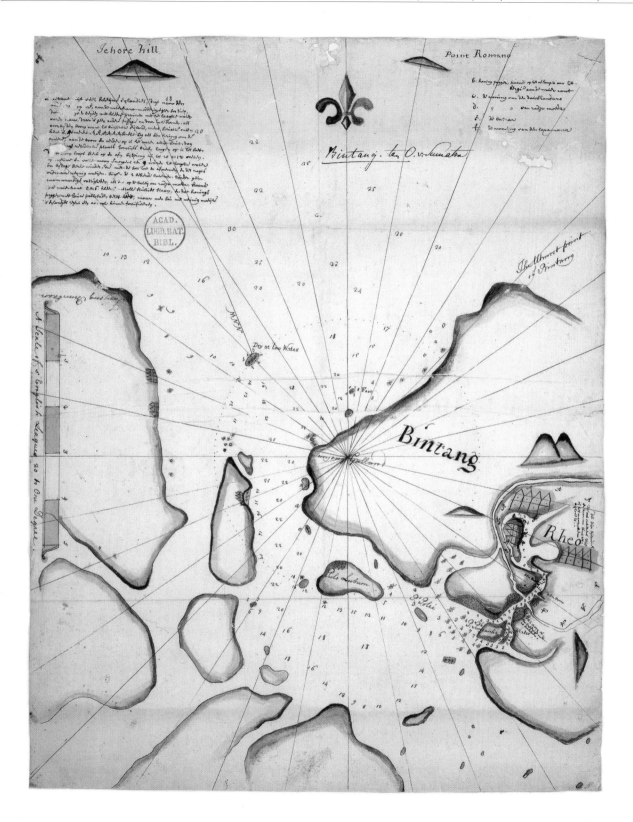

through the Old Strait, as well as various cartographic specimens, that collectively point to a Singapore that was well known and charted, quite at odds with the conventional view that the island was a forgotten, scarcely recognised backwater at the close of the 17th century and into the 18th.

### Singapore Drops Out of Sight, but Not Out of Mind

The most substantive testimony of this period in Singapore's history comes from the Italian adventurer and traveller Francesco Gemelli Careri. His 1699 travelogue *Giro del Mondo* (Voyage Around the World) describes his passage through the Singapore Straits in 1695 and contains accounts of the region's geography, geopolitics and economy. Careri's ship passed Pulau Pisang (Banana Island) and anchored in the channel between the two Karimun islands. He observed that some of the islands in the region "belong to the king of Jambi and the king of Palembang (islands contiguous to Sumatra on the coast across from Melaka, where the Dutch have a factory) and some of them [belong] to the king of Riau to the right of the Strait of Singapore. All three monarchs are Mohammadans and Malays."

Careri's ship sailed through the Singapore Straits on 12 July 1695. Given the approximate distances he cites, it is clear that his passage took him past the islands off Jurong, down the western coast, through the Old Strait, before emerging at Pulau Brani. Careri's account reflects the understanding depicted on an anonymous

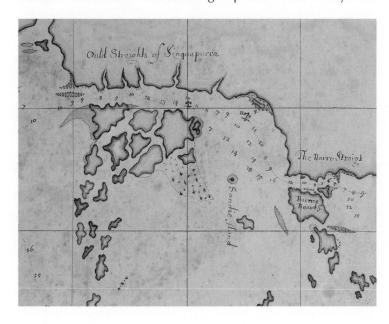

Detail from an anonymous hand-drawn, coloured map from 1680. Unusually, the map uses the term "Old Streights" to refer to the passage between the mainland and the cluster of islands that is now Jurong Island, while the passage traditionally known as the Old Strait is featured here as the "Narro Straigt". Present-day Sentosa is labelled "Burne Beard I[sland]".

chart of the Singapore Straits dating from 1680 that is housed in the British Library. The entire passage from the entrance of the Singapore Straits to Pedra Branca took three days.

Careri noted that the Straits of Singapore was "surrounded by so many islets, which form an intricate labyrinth for vessels… it seems to those who are passing through it for the first time that it is impossible to find a way out", and that at certain narrow points the rapid waters made for dangerous sailing. At the exit around Pulau Brani on 13 July, Careri passed "ten thatched houses built on wooden stilts on our left", but that is as far as he goes in describing any settlement at Singapore.

William Dampier, an English pirate and adventurer, passed through the Singapore Straits in 1688. His account makes reference to a "Pulo Nuttee" belonging to the Kingdom of Johor, which he encountered as he arrived from the east en route to Melaka, sailing through "a narrow passage called the Streights of Sincapore". Here, while taking on fresh water, he noticed some "Indian inhabitants", who are clearly the Orang Laut; but the exact location of the island is not completely certain.

Carl Alexander Gibson-Hill is of the opinion that 17th-century London cartographer Herman Moll's map illustrating Dampier's account is mistaken in his placement of Pulo Nuttee where Bintan is located since Dampier "clearly says that they kept near the Melaka shore and passed Kuala Johor after leaving the island". Gibson-Hill proposed that present-day Sentosa (or Pulau Blakang Mati, as it was known then) was Dampier's Pulo Nuttee. Blakang Mati was also called Nyiur, meaning coconut in Malay. "Nuttee" would then be understood as "Nutty Island", a place where nuts or coconuts grow. Such an understanding is echoed by several map specimens on which Sentosa is named as Niry (Hacke and Eberard), or Toly (Thornton and Jeffreys), before becoming Tooly on the early maps by James Horsburgh.

A third key source is the French warship *l'Oiseau*, which sailed through the Straits in 1687. The route of this passage provided the plotting for a printed chart of the southern Malay Peninsula and the Singapore Straits drawn by the French royal cartographer Jacques Nicolas Bellin and published in 1755, one of the most sophisticated and detailed maps of this region dating from the early to mid-18th century.

(*Following pages*) Coloured, printed chart by Jacques Nicolas Bellin of the Singapore and Melaka straits, 1755. The map is noteworthy for its reference to Singapore as Pulau Panjang, as well as the route taken by the French warship *l'Oiseau* on its way from Siam to Pondicherry during the northeast monsoon of 1687.

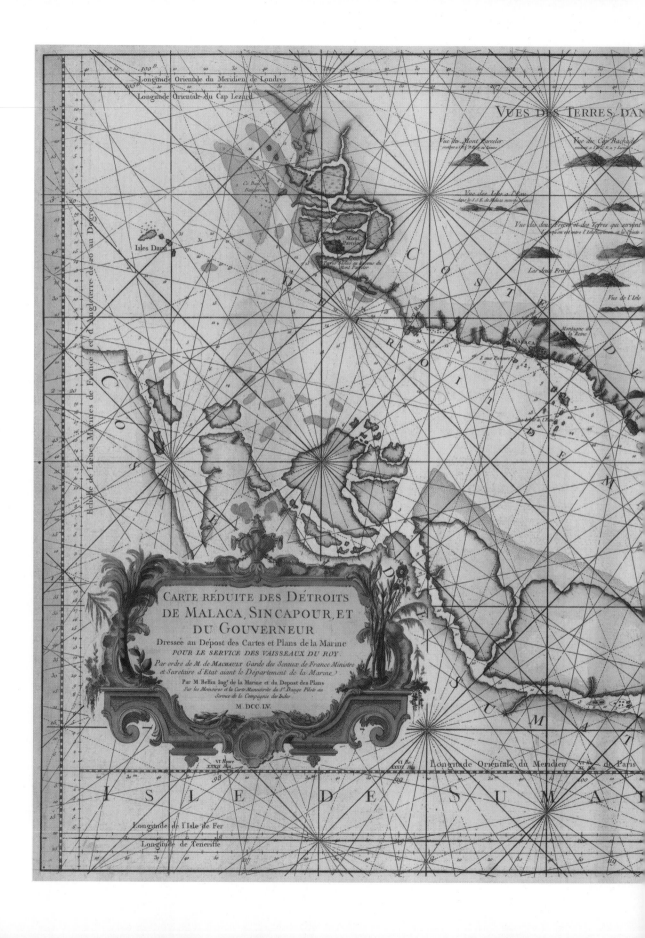

VUES DES TERRES, DAN

Vue du Mont Parcelor

Vue du Cap Rachade

Vue des Isles en Eau

Vue des deux Freres et des Terres qui servent

Les deux Freres

Vue de l'Isle

COSTE

Montagne de la Reine

MALACA

DROIT DE

Mont Parcelor

Isles Dam

COSTE DE SUMAT

DE FE

CARTE RÉDUITE DES DÉTROITS
DE MALACA, SINCAPOUR, ET
DU GOUVERNEUR
Dressée au Dépost des Cartes et Plans de la Marine
POUR LE SERVICE DES VAISSEAUX DU ROY.
Par ordre de M. de MACHAULT Garde des Sceaux de France Ministre
et Secretaire d'Etat aiant le Departement de la Marine.
Par M. Bellin Ing.ʳ de la Marine et du Depost des Plans
Sur les Memoires et la Carte Manuscrite du S.ᵗ Dauge Pilote au
Service de la Compagnie des Indes
M. DCC. LV.

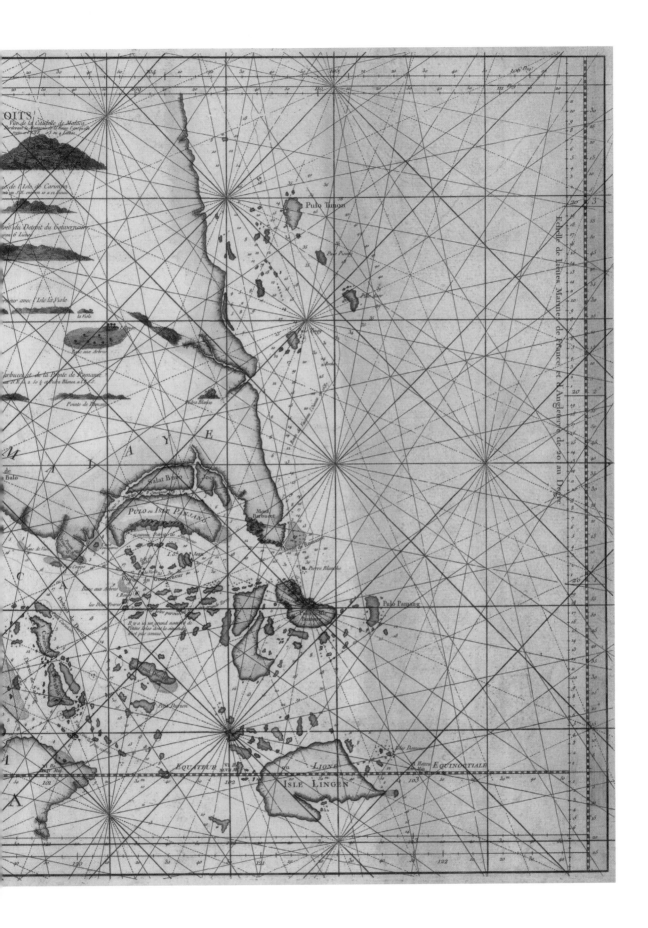

The *l'Oiseau* made more than one voyage, but the travelogue of the Abbé de Choisy, who accompanied the embassy of Chevalier de Chaumont, the Jesuit Guy Tachard and Father Bégnine Vachet of the French Missionary Society to Siam on this ship, does not describe a passage through the Singapore Straits. On its second home voyage, the *l'Oiseau* passed through the Singapore Straits around December 1687 en route from Siam to the French colony of Pondicherry in southeastern India.

### Singapore by Many Other Names

In addition to travel accounts, another indication that Singapore continued to be remembered, despite the trading centre being located in Bugis Riau, can be found in the contemporaneous referencing of the island in maps and other materials.

Map of Singapore and the Straits by Dupré Eberard, 1700. The reference on the main island reads "Isles De Sincapoure" (Islands of Singapore).

The aforementioned Bellin map of 1755 indicates the main island of Singapore as "Pulo ou Isle Panjang" (Pulau Panjang, or Long Island). This naming was retained on later specimens of French cartography, and influenced Dutch and early English maps printed until the first two decades of the 19th century, appearing as 't Lange Eylandt in Dutch, or Long Island in English. Guillaume Dheulland's printed chart of 1770 features the hybrid toponym

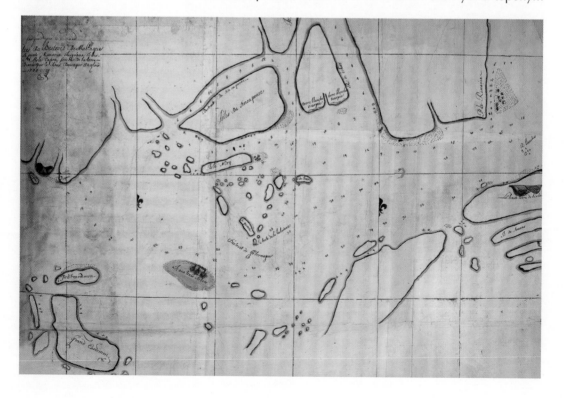

| | |
|---|---|
| 1502 | 1558 bandar Singâfûr |
| 1504 | 1569 |
| 1507 | 1570 |
| 1508 | 1625 |
| 1513 | 1675 |
| 1516 | 1680 |
| 1522 | 1710 |
| 1525 | 1755 |
| 1529 | 1770 |
| 1541 | 1785 |
| 1547 | 1803 |
| 1548 | 1823 |
| 1554 | 1826 |

The confusion over Singapore's identity in charts and maps is mirrored in written texts. It is not always clear what a given name refers to, or where exactly it is located. Over time, different names and locations were given for the settlement/island.

"Isle Panjang", with Captain Milner and William Heather still naming Singapore as Pulo Panjang in 1803.

Yet another 18th-century name for Singapore island was given by the Austrian Jesuit Gottfried Xavier von Laimbeckhoven (who would later serve as Nanjing's Catholic Bishop). When he passed through the Singapore Straits in 1738 on his outbound journey to Macau and China, he named the island Insel Gubernator, or "Governor's Island", after Governor's Strait.

In fact, few maps name the island Singapore (or one of its many variant spellings) during the long 18th century. The name "Sincapour" begins to reappear on maps and charts only in the

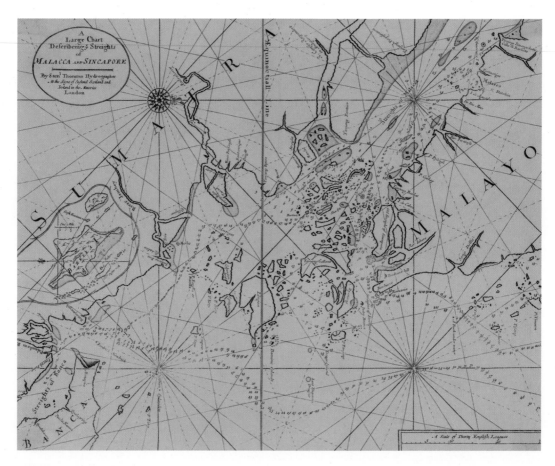

Printed chart entitled *A Large Chart Describeing the Streights of Malacca and Sincapore* by Sam Thornton, 1703. Singapore island has no name, but features the entry over the island: "Old Streight of Sincapore". Entries like this confused readers, who began to identify the Tebrau or Johor Strait as the Old Strait of Singapore.

last quarter of the century – such as on the two charts by A.E. van Braam Houckgeest dating from 1795 and preserved at Leiden University. The name "Sincapour" – or spelt with a "k" in Dutch – remained well after the founding of the British settlement in 1819, with James Horsburgh, the Scottish hydrographer who worked for the EIC, naming the island Sincapour in 1823, and spelling it "Singapore" on his maps only three years later.

A different category of evidence can be found in five entries relating to Singapore in Johann Heinrich Zedler's *Universal-Lexicon*, a German encyclopedia published in Leipzig between 1731 and 1755. These entries are not eyewitness reports but a short summary of what a literate, resourceful and informed person proficient in Portuguese, Italian, Spanish, French, Dutch, German or Latin would have been able to retrieve about Singapore in the first decades of the 18th century.

The Zedler record was almost certainly not current, however, and therefore may not have been an accurate reflection of actual conditions at the time of publication. The presence of five separate entries for Singapore – *Sincapor(e), Sincapur, Sincapura, Sincapurum Promontorium* and *Singapour* – reveal the different ways the location was thought of: as a promontory, a strait, a ridge, an island, as well as a settlement, together with the confusion surrounding the what and where of all of these. Zedler's entries drew on earlier materials, ranging from texts to cartography. What the entries confirm is that the memory of a city named Singapore was still very much alive in Europe at the time. More difficult to ascertain is how big the settlement might have been, especially in the absence of concrete and reliable eyewitness accounts.

Given the number of written and cartographical references that have been documented, it would appear that the Europeans showed considerable interest in Singapore and its adjacent waters, especially during the final two decades of the 17th century.

### The Context of Riau's Maritime Trade

One reason for Singapore continuing to be remembered is linked to what eventually contributed to the demise of Riau as a trading port: the rise of the China trade.

The 18th century witnessed the revival of Chinese chic in Europe, ushering in an era of chinoiserie – an infatuation with Chinese luxury goods, aesthetics and, naturally, tea. Contrary to earlier historians' view of an insular Qing, the dynasty's first Emperor, Kangxi, reversed the Ming's closed-door policy and opened China to international maritime trade in 1684. The China trade rebounded after China finally shook off the debilitating consequences of prolonged drought and famine, which had helped the Qing dynasty topple the Ming in 1644.

Prior to the Kangxi Emperor's move to accept international trade, Chinese traders were defying the official ban, venturing abroad to travel, trade and settle in the South Seas. These merchants, mostly from Fujian, linked up to form tight, extensive networks, interfacing with Bugis, Malay and other traders, and in so doing came to dominate China's South Seas trade. The early 17th-century Selden map, discussed in the previous chapter, is one of many documents that demonstrates the extent of the junk trade that constituted the Fujian trading world.

This Chinese trading network was an essential resource and lifeline for the Malay sultans from Sulu through the Straits of Melaka

"Singapore" or one of its variants could refer variously to (*from top*) a gateway or promontory, a cape, or a city on the mainland.

to Terengganu and Patani. Meanwhile, the East India Companies developed an ambivalent relationship with these overseas Chinese trading communities, whom they depended on for access into local Malay markets but at the same time did not trust. Kangxi's opening of the Chinese port meant that European and international traders were no longer obliged to go through the middlemen of the South Seas, but could trade directly in China.

Daeng Kemboja and his predecessors could neither have anticipated this growing shift in global interconnectivity nor foreseen the fallout from the Fourth Anglo-Dutch War (1780–84), as well as the French Revolution and the Napoleonic Wars (1789–1814). What they should have noticed were the increasing number of ships sailing through the waters of Singapore en route to China, beyond the Riaus. At the same time, it is because of the China trade that Singapore continued to be noticed.

### Raja Haji and the Bugis Tragedy of 1784

Daeng Kemboja had been a stabilising force for the Malay-Bugis trade networks. As the Dutch had anticipated, his death in 1777 reignited and escalated tensions between the Bugis and Malay communities in Johor-Riau, allowing the Dutch to take advantage of the ensuing confusion to enforce the terms of the 1758 treaty. In practice, that meant cutting off much of the external lifeline of the port in Riau, including visits by British country traders and other Europeans, as well as direct trade with China. The Fourth Anglo-Dutch War, pitting a Dutch-French compact against the British, worsened Riau's fortunes. Initially the region remained unaffected, until a French privateer attacked and seized the *Betsy*, a British trading vessel, in the port of Riau in 1782.

The *Betsy* incident and its ensuing repercussions put Johor-Riau on a direct collision course with Dutch Melaka. The Dutch were worried that their refusal to give in to the Bugis Raja Muda, Raja Haji Fisabilillah, who was demanding compensation over the *Betsy*, could find them facing a tripartite alliance comprising Johor-Riau, Bugis and British forces. Raja Haji assembled a force at Muar, threatening to attack Melaka. The Dutch in turn responded with a blockade of Riau, which Raja Haji resisted despite the economic trauma it wrought on the port.

When the Dutch forces returned to Melaka, they found it under siege by the Bugis from Selangor. A few weeks later, Raja Haji and his supporters arrived and joined the assault. Dutch Melaka's fate looked uncertain until Admiral Jacob Pieter van Braam arrived with a dozen heavily armed ships from the Dutch navy, helping to lift the siege of Melaka after Raja Haji was killed by gunfire on 18 June 1784. The siege of Melaka may have ended with the heroic death of Raja Haji in the battlefield, but not the Dutch conflict with the Bugis. Van Braam separately attacked and defeated Selangor and Riau four months later.

The defeat of Johôr-Riau and its Bugis allies was sealed in two treaties, dated 1 and 10 November 1784, which additionally staked out the power arrangements between the Dutch and Johor-Riau. It was stipulated that Johor, Pahang, Riau and all of the dependent islands (including Singapore) would comprise a single kingdom, "in lawful and perpetual fief from the Dutch which shall [continue to be ruled as a vassal state by Paduka Sri Sultan Mahmud] and his legal heirs".

Johor-Riau's defeat, and its new status as a hereditary Dutch dependency, was a key turning point in the long and eventful 18th century. It would leave a deep imprint on relations between the

View of Tanjung Pinang on Bintan from the sea, by Charles Dyce (1845), with the Dutch fort in the background.

Dutch and Johor for at least the next 40 years. The 1784 treaty, together with the renewal of its terms on 23 November 1818 via a treaty sealed by Vice-Admiral Constantijn Johan Wolterbeek, formed the legal basis on which the Dutch would later contest the legality of Raffles' trading post on Singapore. The issue persisted until the Dutch formally withdrew their objections (and implicitly, their claims to Singapore) in the 1824 Anglo-Dutch Treaty.

The treaty also curtailed the influence of the Riau Bugis at the court. A Dutch garrison, followed by a Dutch Resident at Riau, kept the Bugis in check and denied port access to all other Europeans. The treaty also disrupted the Bugis-nurtured trading networks that underpinned Riau's prosperity, making Riau significantly less attractive to the Chinese and European traders, especially the British, who had benefited greatly from trading there. This was one of the factors that led the British to begin exploring alternative locations from which they could trade.

The concurrent end of the Anglo-Dutch War in 1784 dashed Bugis hopes of British assistance. The only way forward, as Sultan Mahmud saw it, was to expel the Dutch from Riau, and to this end he wrote with the support of some of his highest-ranking nobles to the Sultan of Sulu, requesting his assistance. That help arrived in May 1787. A fleet carrying over 2,000 Iranun from Tempassuk in Sulu made a "distress call" at Riau. They claimed to have been caught in a storm on their way to Borneo and blown off course, and thus needed to repair their vessels and replenish their food supplies.

The Iranun (or Ilanun) were a Moro ethnic group from southern Mindanao who had migrated to the coast of Ialan Bay, where they allied themselves with the emerging Sulu Sultanate in the 18th century. (In British colonial times they were called Illanun, from which the Malay word *lanun*, referring to a pirate, is derived.) The Iranun were reputed as pirates and coastal raiders who depopulated regional villages for profit in the Sulu slave markets; they may even have raided settlements in and around Singapore, Riau and the Johor River region.

Promised a bounty by Sultan Mahmud, the Iranun plundered Riau and drove the Dutch garrison and Resident out. Going beyond the bidding of Sultan Mahmud, however, they took everything they could, including weapons and ammunition from the

A heavily armed Iranun warship known as a *lanon*. These outriggered ships could reach up to 30 metres in length and had two shear masts which could be lowered when needed to function as ladders to board other ships or to land Iranun warriors ashore. The *lanon* had three banks of oars rowed by slaves inside the ship, leaving the top deck clear for the Iranun warriors to fight from.

An Iranun warrior armed with a *kampilan* (scimitar-like sword) decorated with human hair, a kris tucked into his waistband, and a spear. He wears a rattan helmet and a quilted red vest which would have afforded minimal protection against sword cuts.

now-abandoned Dutch fort. This left Sultan Mahmud defence-less against any Dutch bid to retake Riau. He fled Bintan with his supporters for Lingga. When the Dutch returned to Riau in December, they found that the Malays and Bugis had left, leaving behind a community of several thousand Chinese farmers growing gambier and pepper, a number of whom crossed the straits to Singapore.

### The VOC Fades and the EIC Rises as the Century Closes
By the close of the 18th century, the VOC had become a depleted force. Mired in debt and plagued by internal corruption, it had hardly turned a profit in decades. The Dutch defeat in the Fourth Anglo-Dutch War heralded the VOC's gradual demise after almost 200 years of operation.

As part of the peace agreement signed with the British in Paris in 1784, the Dutch had to make several important concessions. Although they retained their prized monopoly in nutmeg, mace and cloves in the eastern Indonesian Archipelago, the active preservation of this monopoly and the suppression of interlopers was a costly burden.

The most significant concession of all was having to grant the British the freedom of navigation in the Southern Seas. The EIC lost no time in despatching its ships, and the country traders were just as swift in following suit, sailing unhindered through the straits of Melaka and Singapore. This concession effectively broke Dutch maritime hegemony in parts of the Indonesian Archipelago.

The free navigation clause also addressed Britain's shifting needs in navigating between India and China. In the 1780s, and particularly in the wake of Britain's victory over the French and the Dutch in India and the Dutch defeat of Johor-Riau, an increasingly bustling British seaborne trade emerged between the eastern coast of India and China. Growing in lockstep with this was Britain's interest in the Straits region, and it became imperative to have a strategic base to entrench British presence there.

Since the early 1770s, the Kedah Sultan had been sounding out British interest in setting up a trading post on Penang, mainly as a way of co-opting British assistance in his war against Selangor. Country trader Sir Francis Light was worried that if the EIC hesitated, the Sultan would turn to the VOC instead. If this came to pass, mused Light, the Dutch "would possess the entire command of the whole streights, for on the coast of Kedah is a river capable of receiving their largest ships".

The 1784 Dutch defeat of Johor-Riau tightened the Dutch commercial grip on the lands surrounding the southern Melaka and Singapore Straits – an area that had now become vital as a shipping artery for British ships sailing between India and China. This added to the urgency of preventing Penang from potentially falling into Dutch hands. Light was right in concluding that the Dutch were consolidating their power in the Melaka Straits littoral in the 18th century while the British were distracted by warring against the French in India. But Penang was not the only potential EIC base in the Straits. While the Dutch defeat of Johor-Riau created a new set of political and economic realities for the EIC,

the Company continued to regard the port of Riau as a commercial prize and strategic priority (specifically with the mission under Thomas Forrest from 1783 to 1784). Aceh, and fleetingly, Ujung Salang (Phuket today), were also considered as potential bases.

Detail of watercoloured sketch of Dutch Melaka seen from the sea, by Jan Keldermans, 1764.

In March 1786, the EIC asked Light to secure Penang after EIC Governor-General John Macpherson pronounced that Penang lay along the sailing route between India and China, and that the Dutch should be prevented from dominating the route. But shortly after British-ruled Penang – then known as Prince of Wales Island – took hold, it became clear that the island was not ideally located along the main shipping route between India and China. It was also inadequate for serving Britain's evolving geostrategic and economic needs in the Straits. A growing number of British ships were avoiding Penang altogether and, ironically, calling at Dutch Melaka for supplies. As such, the British still hoped to find a place for a new post in the southern Melaka Straits region.

In 1787, the British changed tack and opened negotiations with the Dutch "in an effort to control Riau". But five years of negotiations still got them nowhere. They even toyed with the idea of seizing Dutch colonies by force, with Melaka representing an

Portrait of Baron Godert van der Capellen, Governor-General of the Dutch East Indies.

obvious target. The British also never entirely lost sight of the port of Riau as a desirable spot on the map: Raffles himself would consider it – albeit briefly – in 1813, and William Farquhar in 1818. Had the British succeeded in prying Riau from Dutch hands in the final decades of the 18th century, the founding of Singapore would arguably not have materialised.

### A Letter, a Rumour and Raffles' Gambit

The French Revolution and the Napoleonic Wars threw Europe into chaos between the end of the 18th century and the start of the 19th. The Dutch Republic was not spared. In 1795, the French invaded the Netherlands and helped set up the Batavian Republic, a French proxy that ended the federal structure of the old Dutch Republic. In 1806, the Netherlands became a kingdom, and was subsequently annexed as part of the First French Empire (1810–13). When the London Convention was drawn up in 1814, Britain was keen to give the Dutch a chance at reconstruction. But the Dutch coffers were empty.

What is of direct significance to Singapore's history is the way in which the British took over Dutch Melaka in 1795 and exercised their role as its trustees. Since 1784, Johor-Riau had been under the aegis of Melaka's Dutch Governor. Questions have been raised about what transpired during the 1795 handover to the British, in particular the alleged deeds of Abraham Couperus, the last Dutch Governor of Melaka in the 18th century.

Speculation in British circles – notably repeated by Farquhar in a letter to Governor Timmermann-Thijssen dated 31 October 1818 – claimed that Couperus had formally restored sovereignty to Johor-Riau at the time of the handover to the British, or in Farquhar's words, "giving entire and complete effect to the absolute independence of Sultan Mohammed at Riouw, Lingen, etc". (The underlying assumption was that the Dutch wanted the British to have minimum control as Melaka trustees.) The Dutch dismissed the rumours, further arguing that even if Couperus had done as alleged, his act was invalid as it was not sanctioned by his superiors.

The rumours may well be traced to a letter written by Couperus to Sultan Mahmud on 23 August 1795. According to Elias Netscher, who reproduced this letter in his book *De Nederlanders in Djohor en Siak* (The Dutch in Johor and Siak), Couperus' letter, which was countersigned by the new British agents H. Newcome and A. Brown, noted that the Dutch Governor-General and Council at Batavia wished to "restore" Johor-Riau to the Sultan, and urged the ruler to act quickly and garrison the forts because a ship was on its way to evacuate Dutch troops and personnel. Significantly, there is no mention of the words "sovereignty" or "suzerainty", which would be expected of a letter formally returning full sovereignty to a ruler.

The confusion may thus have arisen from the word "restore". What did it mean? Current evidence suggests that Sultan Mahmud himself did not take Couperus' letter to imply a restoration of full sovereignty. He arranged for a note of thanks to be sent to the Governor-General in Batavia, sometime before 2 May 1796, to which Batavia issued a formal reply. In late December 1797, in his annual report to the authorities in Europe, the Dutch Governor-General advised that the Asian princes, and especially the ruler of Johor-Riau, should continue to maintain close links with Batavia. In return, Batavia sustained goodwill by supplying rice and other necessities. These exchanges suggest a continued relationship of dependence between Johor Riau and the Dutch. According to Netscher, the close relations between Mahmud and the VOC continued perhaps until the Sultan's death on 12 January 1812.

After being appointed Governor-General of the Dutch East Indies, Baron Godert van der Capellen also weighed in on the issue. In a letter dated 25 February 1819 and addressed in French to the British Governor-General, the Marquess of Hastings, Van der Capellen explained Couperus' actions, insisting that the Governor had discharged his duties with the countersignature of the new British authorities at the time, represented by Newcome and Brown. According to Van der Capellen, the letter issued specific instructions for the Dutch to withdraw the garrison and functionaries from Riau without requiring the Sultan to further comply with certain conditions imposed upon him by the 1784 treaty.

In another letter, dated 16 December 1818, Van der Capellen explained that during Britain's trusteeship of Melaka (1795–1818), the issue of Dutch Melaka's earlier relations with Johor-Riau never arose with the British authorities, certainly none that would have demanded a detailed explanation. Like Johor-Riau, other territories

Portrait of the Marquess of Hastings, to whom Raffles reported.

in the region such as notably Sambas and Pontianak were argued to have retained their connections to the Dutch during the period of the Napoleonic Wars. The British authorities in Melaka at the time had not questioned this understanding.

Judging by a letter dated 25 January 1820, even the secret committee at East India House in London broadly concurred with Van der Capellen's take on these matters. The committee noted: "[A]lthough we are not prepared, immediately upon the perusal of it, to express an unqualified concurrence in all these details of the reasoning which it contains, we have no hesitation in saying we believe it to be generally correct."

The question now arises as to what bearing the 1784 treaty and Couperus' alleged deeds had on Singapore's history. When Raffles founded the trading post on Singapore in 1819, the Dutch protested immediately on two grounds: the first was that the trading post violated not only the rights of the Sultan of Johor-Riau but also the terms of the 1784 treaty and its reaffirmation in the Wolterbeek treaty of November 1818.

The second concerned the scope and longevity of the 1784 treaty. The British argued that the alleged restoration of full sovereignty to Sultan Mahmud effectively nullified the validity of that treaty in 1795. As Charles Assey, Raffles' former secretary in Java, wrote in his book, *On the Trade with China and the Indian Archipelago* (1819), the "native chiefs of Bintang and Rhio may consequently be considered independent of the control of any European power, and free to select that connexion which is most agreeable to themselves".

The British resorted to yet another argument by questioning the political structure and integrity of the Johor-Riau empire. Hastings, Raffles and Assey adopted the view that Johor-Riau was a very loose political entity in which the constituent parts were virtually independent of the political centre as well as the persons of the Raja Muda and the Sultan. This was similar to the tack taken by Francis Light in acquiring Penang, mainly as a way of overcoming objections that Kedah was a vassal of Siam.

The Dutch, for their part, were also aware of how the authority and prestige of the Raja Muda had waned over time. They noted that some of the Johor-Riau chiefs like the Temenggong and the

Bendahara were exercising power that was close, if not equal, to that of Raja Ja'afar, the incumbent Raja Muda. To entice Raja Ja'afar, they promised him military backing should he decide to subdue his rivals and reassert his authority. Arguably, it was this Dutch pledge that served to nudge the Temenggong into an agreement with the British.

Couperus would play another important role in Singapore's history, namely in his proposal to found a new Dutch colony around the Singapore Straits. After leaving Melaka, he served as a member of the Raad van Indië, or Council of the Indies, a body that advised and assisted Batavia's Governor-General. In an 1809 report addressed to Marshal Herman Willem Daendels, Couperus speculated on future trading relations in the region, arguing that it might be better to let the British keep the underperforming Melaka after the war was over. He recommended that the Netherlands should instead establish a greenfield colony – a new settlement built up from scratch.

And where would this new colony or trading emporium be founded? For Couperus, two locations came to mind: one was Bangka, an island located off the southeastern coast of Sumatra that was subject to Palembang. Bangka and neighbouring Belitung were important centres of tin production and trade. The other was at the Singapore Straits, around the southern tip of the Malay Peninsula. Was Couperus eyeing Singapore for this proposed greenfield colony? He likely did, and in any case, he found either of these locations – Bangka or Singapore – far preferable to Melaka.

This episode reveals two interesting perspectives. First, the Dutch and the British were thinking along surprisingly similar lines as to how to reposition their trade flows and networks in the early 19th century – so similar, in fact, that one wonders whether there might also be a direct connection.

Raffles, after all, acquired Bangka and Belitung for Britain just a few years later but ultimately chose Singapore as his trading post. Was that just sheer coincidence? The Dutch clearly had an informed grasp of the commercially advantageous position that Singapore and its surrounding waters would have in the post-war trading order. This contextualises and relativises the significance of Raffles' choice of Singapore in 1819.

### 1814–19: From Convention to Trading Post

The French Revolution and the Napoleonic Wars created a set of circumstances that reduced the urgency for the British to establish a forward post. Moreover, Melaka was in British hands – in practical if not formal terms – and served British ships sailing between India and China as a provisioning station. Arguments were of course advanced to keep the colony after the war, but that was not what the politicians in Europe decided – at least not at first.

The need to found a new forward post resurfaced with the London Convention of 13 August 1814. The British Foreign Secretary, Robert Stewart, Viscount Castlereagh, and the Dutch ambassador in London, Baron Hendrik Fagel, assumed a leading role in hammering out this agreement. It stipulated the return of the colonies to the Dutch which they had held on or before 1 January 1803, aside from certain named exceptions. It also required the British to surrender Bangka Island. Both parties pledged to cooperate in abolishing the African slave trade and to reach an agreement that supported peaceful commercial interaction.

But the devil was in the implementation, and the Convention came under fire and was contested on numerous counts following its ratification. Some British agents took a narrow view of the restoration clause and in so doing acted against the spirit of the agreement. They wanted to return as little as possible to Dutch rule.

Melaka was under British administration in 1814, and so the question naturally arose as to whether or not this settlement and colony would have to be restored to Dutch rule in the spirit and under the terms of the London Convention. Was this even desirable, given its newfound significance to British shipping?

The British country traders loudly opposed Melaka's return to Dutch rule. Doing so, they argued, would help the Dutch reimpose a chokehold on trade as well as navigation across the Straits region and the archipelago, thus adversely affecting Britain's trade between India and China. Raffles added his support, openly worrying for the future of free trade, which, in Raffles' mind applied only to British and native trade, but not to that of its European competitors. But, as seen, the 1784 Treaty of Paris had granted the British freedom of navigation across the Southern Seas, and so the question arises: Was there really a danger that the Dutch could close the Straits to British maritime traffic?

Just how thriving this region was when the London Convention was sealed transpires from an account by John Crawfurd, who would later become Singapore's second British Resident. In his book review of William Thorn's 1815 *Memoir of the Conquest of Java*, Crawfurd offered an extensive discussion of trading conditions across Southeast Asia. The review appeared in the *Edinburgh Review* of 1817, just two years before Raffles' arrival in Singapore. Crawfurd singled out the Chinese and the Bugis as the drivers of commerce – especially seaborne commerce – across the region:

> *The navigators, or maritime tribes, comprehend all the nations which speak the Malay language, and the greater portion of the spirited and enterprising population of Celebes. The foreign settlers are a few Europeans, emigrants from the maritime ports of continental India – some adventurous Arabs; but, above all, the Chinese – the industrious and indefatigable Chinese – in a tropical climate at least, the most productive class of subjects which any state can possess. … The carrying trade, in all these commodities, is principally conducted by the enterprising navigators of Celebes, and especially by the Bugis of Wajo, who, by their skill and activity, may be said to form the very life of the native commerce of the Archipelago. … There is no country, from New Guinea to Mergui, to which their enterprise does*

The Malay *prahu* was a mainstay of trade in the region. The larger *prahu mayang*, measuring 15–20 metres long, was used to carry heavy cargoes of Straits produce between the ports of the archipelago.

*not extend. ... Their original outward cargoes are chiefly composed of the excellent durable cloths of their native country, manufactured from the cotton of Bali and Lombok. The greater number of the traders direct their course towards the fertile and extensive countries to the westward. One body takes the direction of Java, where they exchange their cloths, and gold and silver specie, for the highly prized tobacco of that island, which supplies the extensive consumption of the Indian islanders throughout with that drug, – for the opium of Bengal – the cotton fabrics of Europe and India – and the iron, broadcloth, and steel of Europe.*

*The most considerable body, however, performs a trading voyage along the coasts of Celebes, Borneo, Sumatra, the eastern shores of the Gulf of Siam, the islands in the mouth of the Straits of Malacca, and the western shores of the Peninsula, until it terminates in Malacca or Penang, where they give the gold and bullion, collected in their voyage, for the same commodities obtained by their brother traders in Java.*

This was the bustling maritime trading world that Raffles sought to tap into. An avowed enemy of past Dutch monopolies and an alleged spokesman of free trade, Raffles had actively sought to prevent Melaka's return to the Dutch, insisting in a letter to his friend Colonel Addenbrooke, that "it is not our interests alone that have suffered by this unexpected return [of the colonies to the Dutch]; those of humanity and civilization suffer more deeply". In his view, the Dutch were not entitled to any places "where their flag did not fly on the 1st of January 1803", the critical date laid down by the London Convention.

A rift opened up between the particularistic interests of the country traders and their supporters like Raffles on the one hand, and on the other, among the leading politicians in London, who had to keep their sights on the big picture and engage in a careful and vigilant reconstruction of Europe after the Napoleonic Wars.

The Convention and its gradual implementation over the next few years created for the British Governor-General, Lord Hastings, as well as Raffles and his likeminded associates a sense of urgency to found a new British post between India and China. Raffles' choice after Melaka – which was slated for return to Dutch rule – was Semangka Bay (sometimes Simanka or Keyser's Bay), located on

Sumatra near the Sunda Strait. Dutch protests, and objections from higher British authority in Bengal, however, thwarted this proposal.

Over time, Raffles would consider other options, including Bintan, Karimun, the coast of Borneo, the Johor River and, of course, Singapore. The point that bears remembering here is that Singapore was not Raffles' first choice, but rather became his preferred choice from among a dwindling range of options. In 1819, Raffles took a calculated risk in the face of likely Dutch opposition to establish a British trading post on Singapore.

With the benefit of hindsight, taking this risk was Raffles' real achievement. As expected, the Dutch lodged vigorous protests right from the start. Fortunately for the young trading post, the Dutch did not opt to resolve the matter with armed intervention, though admittedly the option to evict the British by force had been briefly contemplated at a very early stage. Instead, over the next five years, the Dutch relied on diplomacy with Calcutta and London to arrive at a peaceful settlement. These negotiations have entered the annals of history as the "Singapore Paper War".

## IN A NUTSHELL

In Chapter Five, we see how in the aftermath of Sultan Mahmud's regicide in 1699, Singapore, otherwise the site of social memories of Malay ancestry, became increasingly marginalised as the contest over the rewriting of the norms for moral authority shifted to the Bugis centre at Bintan and to its rival, Siak. As the Minangkabau and the Bugis diaspora started expanding into the Malay Peninsula and Riau, the old Malay political order of the *Malay Annals* was dissolved. This had seen a covenant between the white-blooded royals and the Orang Laut.

While Singapore faded from importance, it continued to draw the occasional attention of Europeans passing through the region, evidenced by the different names they gave to Singapore in their maps and charts. Towards the end of the 18th century, the British began to make greater inroads into the region's waters. A contest with the Dutch for supremacy in the Straits region shaped the final years of the century. The British and the Dutch sought to align themselves with Johor-Riau's Malay sultans and their Bugis under-kings.

As Chapter Six will demonstrate, such Anglo-Dutch competition would pique European interest in acquiring Singapore as a trading post by the early 19th century.

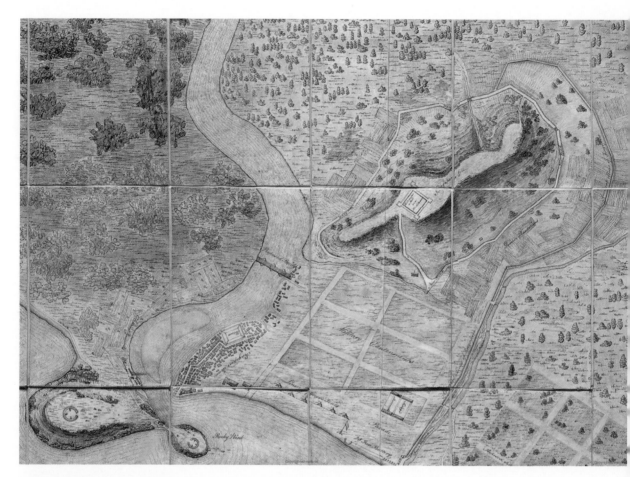

Map of Singapore around 1819–20,
from the Bute Collection. This is one
of the earliest maps of Singapore
after the establishment of the British
station on the island. The ancient
embankment is clearly marked,
running alongside what is today
Stamford Canal and then around
the north side of Bukit Larangan, the
"Forbidden Hill", as Fort Canning Hill
was known then. The map also marks
a proposed bridge across the river, as
well as a gun battery on the hill, which
was never constructed. Raffles on his
last visit in January 1823 built himself
a bungalow on the hill.

# CHAPTER SIX

# The 19th Century
## Port-City of the British Empire

> I have now the satisfaction to report, for the information of the Most Noble the Governor General in Council... that a British Station commanding the Southern entrance of the straits of Malacca, and combining extraordinary local advantage with a peculiarly admirable Geographical position, has been established at Singapore the ancient Capital of the Kings of Johor, on terms and conditions, which I trust will meet the approbation and confirmation of His Lordship in Council.
>
> Formal report by Stamford Raffles to the office
> of the Marquess of Hastings, Governor-General
> of India, on 13 February 1819

### Hunt for a British Foothold

The search by the British East India Company (EIC) for a station at the southern entrance of the Straits of Melaka arose from several factors, one of which was the Napoleonic Wars in Europe, in which the Netherlands allied with Britain in the latter's war against France. During the war, Dutch colonies in the East Indies came under EIC administration (1811–16). Thomas Stamford Raffles was appointed Governor-General of Java, and Major William Farquhar the Resident of Melaka.

With the region under EIC administration, the private trade conducted by British country traders grew. For 200 years, these traders had been privately financed individuals, but by the 19th century, they comprised mainly retired Company officials trading outside the EIC's trade monopoly. These traders had long challenged the regional monopoly by the Dutch and, despite being unwelcome, they continued to trade at ports in the Malay Peninsula and in the

Dutch heartland of eastern Indonesia. They were always on the lookout for a Dutch-free trading base. Bugis-controlled Riau had been a welcome trading base until 1784, when the Dutch defeated both the Bugis and Johor-Riau and as part of the peace agreement made the latter a hereditary fief of the Netherlands.

In 1786, persuaded by the concerns of country traders, the EIC accepted the Sultan of Kedah's offer of Penang to country trader Francis Light. It was not a Malay ruler's first bid to seek an alternative to the Dutch. As seen in the preceding chapter, the Johor Sultan had offered Singapore to another country trader, Alexander Hamilton, in 1703. When the Napoleonic Wars ended in 1814, the Dutch were promised the return of their former colonies (with certain exceptions) with the ratification of the so-called London Convention (1814). Calcutta, the EIC's Asian headquarters, began considering the interests of the country traders only belatedly in 1818 as the Dutch were reasserting control over the ports that had been returned to them.

Raffles joined the EIC as a 14-year-old clerk in 1795. Within a decade, he was appointed Assistant Secretary to the newly formed Penang Presidency. Southeast Asia gave Raffles a different perspective from his India colleagues. For him, the main challenge for the EIC was Dutch competition in the Eastern Seas. Raffles' five-year stint as Governor-General of Java gave him the opportunity to develop plans to counter the Dutch. Recalled from this post, in part because of maladministration, Raffles returned to London, wrote *The History of Java* to substantiate his case for the British retention of Java, and earned a knighthood in 1817. The following year, he returned to the East as Lieutenant-Governor of Bengkulu in Sumatra and discovered that the Dutch had tightened their grip on the East Indies and were expanding farther into Sumatra. Alarmed, he alerted London:

> *The Dutch possess the only passes through which ships must sail into the Archipelago, the Straits of Sunda and Malacca; and the British have now not an inch of ground to stand upon between the Cape of Good Hope and China, nor a single friendly port at which they can water and obtain refreshment.*

Penang, in Raffles' view, was an isolated British outpost surrounded by Dutch-controlled territory – although this was not actually the case. He wanted to counter Dutch influence and make

Britain the leading trading nation, but his superiors dismissed his attempts after the Dutch protested. Holland, after all, was Britain's European ally in spite of their rivalry in Asia. In September 1818, Raffles visited Calcutta to lobby the Governor-General of India, Lord Hastings. The latter proved receptive and authorised him to reach an agreement with Aceh in northern Sumatra. The Aceh plan, aimed at protecting the British trade route through the Straits of Melaka, also allowed Raffles to establish an EIC trading post at the southern end of the Melaka Straits – provided he did not antagonise the Dutch.

Raffles arrived in Penang in January 1819, where he met Farquhar, who was preparing to return to England. The two men had met earlier in Melaka and shared a distrust of the Dutch. Like Raffles, Farquhar had urged the EIC to set up a British post at a similar location. Before ending his Melaka Residency, Farquhar had negotiated a treaty with the Riau court to secure the southern end of the Melaka Straits against a Dutch monopoly. In Penang, Raffles learnt that the Dutch had returned to Riau, reinstalled a Dutch Resident, and strong-armed the Riau Sultan into voiding his treaty with Farquhar. The Dutch also aimed to lay claim to the territory

A portion of James Horsburgh's chart of the Melaka Straits, capturing the southern end of the Malay Peninsula, Singapore, Batam and Bintan. Raffles would have used an earlier edition of this chart to navigate around the Straits of Singapore.

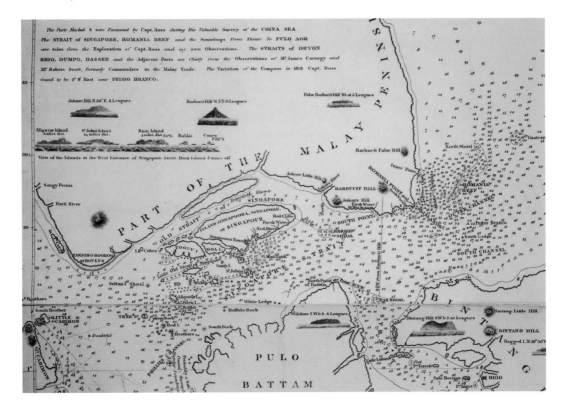

belonging to the Johor-Riau Sultanate, including Johor and the islands south of it.

To quickly stake a claim ahead of the Dutch, Raffles despatched Farquhar south on the brig *Ganges* to link up with hydrographer Captain Daniel Ross, whose *Discovery* was moored at the Karimun islands. Raffles himself would sail to Aceh to negotiate a treaty with the Sultan there. However, Colonel John Bannerman, the Penang Governor, stymied Raffles' plan, insisting that Aceh was under Penang's – and therefore his – purview. He ordered Raffles to remain in Penang until Calcutta issued a clarification, but Raffles ignored the injunction and slipped away to join Farquhar.

Raffles was interested in the Karimun islands because they were situated in such a way that ships could not bypass the key islands – Greater and Lesser Karimun – when they sailed through the Melaka Straits and turned east for the South China Sea past Pulau Satumu, where Raffles Lighthouse stands today. The Karimuns could also control access into the Kampar River, which led to the Minangkabau highlands of central Sumatra. However, after several days of surveying, Raffles and his expedition found no suitable anchorage.

### Nine Days That Changed Singapore's World

Persuaded by Captain Ross, Raffles then stopped at Singapore en route to the Johor River. On the morning of 28 January 1819, he brought his fleet of eight ships to anchor off St John's Island. At 4 pm, he landed at the Singapore River mouth. He was greeted by the Orang Laut, who told him that the Temenggong of Johor lived on the island and – even better news – that there was no Dutch presence.

It would appear that Raffles was aware of Singapore but thought that the Dutch might object, so his first choice was the more strategically positioned Karimun islands. The stopover at Singapore was purely incidental as he was travelling en route to the estuary of the Johor River, capital of the former Johor Sultans. However, once in Singapore, Raffles realised that there were several factors which made the island attractive. Apart from the absence of the Dutch, he was encouraged by the presence of Temenggong Abdur Rahman, who knew Farquhar from Melaka. It was not difficult to convince the Temenggong of the material advantages of setting up a British factory in Singapore, and he soon signed a provisional

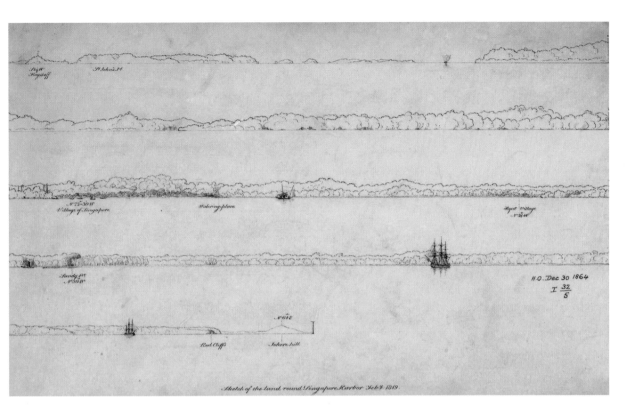

Drawings of the coastline at Singapore harbour, dated 7 February 1819. The date suggests that the sketch was made by a member of one of the Bombay Marine's survey ships – the *Discovery*, under the command of Captain Daniel Ross, or the *Investigator*, under Captain John Garritt Fisher Crawford. These two survey ships were accompanying the armed ship *Indiana*, with Sir Thomas Stamford Raffles onboard.

agreement with Raffles, pending the arrival of Tengku Husain (also known as Tengku Long) from Riau. A third factor Raffles considered was the split in the Riau-Lingga court that made it possible for him to legitimise Singapore as a British settlement in the Malay world.

According to Wak Hakim, an Orang Laut who witnessed Raffles' arrival, the Orang Laut chief Batin Sapi was sent to Riau to fetch Tengku Husain to Singapore to be recognised as the Sultan by Raffles. Batin Sapi's role continued the Orang Laut's long tradition of escorting the 15th-century prince Parameswara and successive Melaka and Johor sultans on their expeditions to establish new realms.

Tengku Husain and the Temenggong became the central rationale for Raffles' choice of Singapore. In a letter to his former secretary Charles Assey in England, Raffles argued:

> *Mynheer [i.e., the Dutch] will probably enter into a paper war on the subject; but we may, I think, combat their arguments without any difficulty. They had established themselves at Rhio*

*[Riau/Bintan], and by virtue of a Treaty, which they had forced the Raja of that place to sign, they assume a right of excluding us from all the Islands and declaring the people their vassals. The legitimate successor to the empire of Johor is with us, and, on the ruins of the ancient capital, has signed a Treaty with us which place Singapore and the neighbouring islands under our protection. We do not meddle with the Dutch at Rhio.*

The "legitimate successor to the empire of Johor" was Tengku Husain, the elder son of Sultan Mahmud Shah of Johor, who had died unexpectedly in 1811 while Husain was in Pahang for his wedding nuptials. The powerful Bugis faction in the Riau-Lingga court exploited his absence and the Malay custom of mandating the declaration of the new Sultan before the dead Sultan could be buried. They proclaimed Husain's devout and compliant younger brother, Tengku Abdur Rahman, as the new Sultan. Husain, being thus excluded, would have welcomed the news from Batin Sapi that the British in Singapore were eager to recognise him as the Johor Sultan if he agreed to the setting up of a British factory in Singapore.

To Husain, Raffles' offer was no different from the Dutch collusion with the Johor sultans to expel the Portuguese from Melaka in the 17th century. Moreover, there were several precedents within Husain's social memory for seeking or accepting external help in resolving the sultanate's succession disputes. In 1722, the Malay heir to the Johor throne, Raja Sulaiman, had sought Bugis aid to expel the Minangkabau usurper Raja Kecik. The rise of the Bugis in the Malay court, and the political divisions they created, could be traced to this event. Husain probably regarded Raffles' invitation to Singapore as a chance to counter Dutch support for the Bugis and his younger brother, and perhaps to build for himself a new trading *kerajaan* (realm), replicating the strategy of Malay princes going back to the time of Sri Tri Buana and earlier.

Husain met Raffles aboard Raffles' ship, the *Indiana*. Bugis historian Raja Ali Haji described this meeting some decades later in his *Tuhfat al-Nafis*, the Bugis version of Johor-Riau history:

*Tengku Temenggung… then sent Raja Ambung to Riau to fetch Tengku Lung [Husain], and when Raja Ambung met Tengku Lung he informed him of all the secret plans of Mr Raffles,*

*Colonel Farquhar, and the Temenggung. Tengku Lung was amenable and when night fell he set sail with Raja Ambung for Singapore. When he arrived, the Temenggung and Mr Farquhar took him aboard the warship to meet Mr Raffles, who honoured Tengku Lung in the way kings are honoured, by firing cannon, beating drums, and so forth. Afterwards he was taken below and given a chair sitting beside Mr Raffles and Mr Farquhar. Mr Raffles told him everything, using courteous words, advising him, and paying him delicate compliments. And Tengku Lung agreed to whatever Mr Raffles proposed, and so the affair was settled, and the discussions and agreements were put into effect.*

On the evening of Raffles' arrival on 28 January 1819, it was over dinner onboard the *Indiana* that he agreed to explore the potential of Singapore island.

The treaty signed on 6 February 1819 gave the British the right to set up a factory in Singapore in exchange for paying 5,000 Spanish dollars (about US$95,000 or S$130,000 today) a year to the Sultan and 3,000 Spanish dollars (about US$57,000 or S$78,000 today) a year to the Temenggong.

Tengku Husain never referred to himself as Sultan of Singapore. In his correspondence with the Riau-Lingga court, he referred to himself as the Yang di-Pertuan of Singapore. The *Tuhfat al-Nafis* refers to Husain as the Yang di-Pertuan Selat (Lord of the Straits), never as Sultan Husain. In the Malay worldview, Husain was not laying claim to the Johor throne, and, as such, the Riau court styled him as "Sultan Husain Syah, son of the late Sultan Mahmud Syah in the state of Singapore and all its subject territories". The kingdom's moral authority continued to be vested in Sultan Abdur Rahman at Bintan. What Husain had done was to create the equivalent of a "satellite" *kerajaan* on Singapore.

If communications then were as immediate as they are today, Singapore as a British settlement might never have happened. The EIC in London had ordered Calcutta on the day before Raffles dropped anchor at St John's Island to rescind his mission because the British Foreign Office was not keen to upset the Dutch government. But by the time Raffles received this countermand, the British trading post in Singapore had already become a reality. It would embroil the British and the Dutch in a paper war` that was only settled by the 1824 Anglo-Dutch Treaty.

The Dutch were enraged when their allied Malay chiefs informed them of Raffles' treaty. In their view, Singapore was part of Riau, whose chief had just renewed a treaty with them in November 1818, reaffirming the arrangements laid down in 1784. The Dutch Governor of Melaka protested to Penang, and contemplated military action to oust the British from Singapore. A worried Farquhar sought reinforcements from Penang, only to be told by an unsympathetic Bannerman to evacuate Singapore.

### 1824: Complete British Ownership

The Dutch fully expected the British to repudiate Raffles' venture, accept Holland's jurisdiction over Singapore and withdraw. However, they underestimated the passionate support for Raffles' actions by Calcutta's British merchants, which, in turn, persuaded Hastings to agree provisionally to the Singapore treaty. Thereafter, the question of Singapore's fate was turned over to London, whose reception was initially unenthusiastic.

British politicians were concerned with keeping Holland strong in Europe against France and, as such, were sympathetic to Dutch protests over Singapore. However, the EIC in Calcutta, including

### The Tengku and the Temenggong

It is likely that Tengku Husain and Temenggong Abdur Rahman thought of the offer made by the British in 1819 as an opportunity to rebalance the scales within the Johor-Riau Sultanate following the death of Sultan Mahmud in 1811, which was marked by a newly intensified rivalry between the Malay and Bugis factions.

In a surprising turn of events, the Bugis Viceroy Raja Ja'afar and his lieges in Riau entered into an agreement with their old enemies, the Dutch, to install Tengku Husain's younger half-brother, Abdur Rahman, as the new Sultan of Johor, in exchange for Dutch trading privileges in Riau. The Malay nobles, including the Temenggong, were dismayed by this development – the late Sultan Mahmud had previously sought an alliance with the Dutch to fend off Bugis ambitions for the throne. Hence, the offer extended by the British to intercede by siding with the Temenggong, Tengku Husain and by extension, the Malay faction, might have been regarded as a possible solution to keep the Bugis faction in check. Here was another European power who, very importantly, was a key rival of the Dutch. The Bugis and Malay factions could be evenly matched.

For Tengku Husain, establishing a new seat of power in Singapore that, like the court in Riau, had equal claim as heir to the Johor-Riau Sultanate also presented a chance to bring the family dispute to a close. Despite being crowned as Sultan Husain Shah of Johor, he was careful in correspondences not to address himself as the Sultan of Johor, but always as Yang di-Pertuan Selat, or Lord of the Straits. His younger brother, too, preferred to use the more modest title of Sultan of Lingga. Thus, Singapore was to be another Malay polity or a satellite court within the constellation of the old Johor-Riau Sultanate, rather than a rival to Riau.

The Temenggong, however, might have seen the 1819 agreement differently: as a chance to restore his family's influence within the sultanate, which had been sidelined in favour of the Bugis faction since the mid-18th century. According to the *Hikayat Kerajaan*, his uncle and predecessor, Engku Muda, had supposedly reminded him that "we ought to own the country because we are co-inheritors with the Sultan... we've got to look after ourselves or be worsted". When the Temenggong retreated to Singapore in 1811, he continued the practice of the merchant and shipping communities and British manufacturers, wanted to expand trade in the East and pressured London politicians to keep Singapore. Raffles, Husain and the country traders were actors in a larger drama, in the scripting of which none had a real say.

Ultimately, the justification for retaining Singapore was the defence of the empire in India against the French. In June 1824, Foreign Affairs Secretary Lord Canning announced to the House of Commons that retaining Singapore was "the *unum necessarium* for making the British Empire in India complete". Explained former Raffles Professor of History Wong Lin Ken:

> *Raffles' acquisition of Singapore was the unforeseen long-term result of Anglo-French rivalry in the Indian subcontinent, the consequent rise of the British Raj, and the need to defend its interests in the Bay of Bengal and the transoceanic route to the Archipelago and China.*

leasing out land to the Chinese to cultivate gambier, with hopes of turning Singapore into a port that could rival the one in Bulang, Riau. The key difference was that it would be under his firm control, not shared with or ceded to the Bugis.

Hence, the initial arrangement with Raffles in 1819 was seemingly to the benefit of both the Tengku and the Temenggong: on top of a regular salary, they would have a 50 percent stake in the profits made by the EIC at Singapore. Above all, they could continue to exercise de jure rule over the island. All they needed to do was lease out a small portion of the island to the British.

Both Tengku Husain and Temenggong Abdur Rahman believed they would remain the key players in the region – the British were partners they could influence at will. But it would not take long for them to realise that the reins of power had slipped from their hands, and into those of the British and the Dutch.

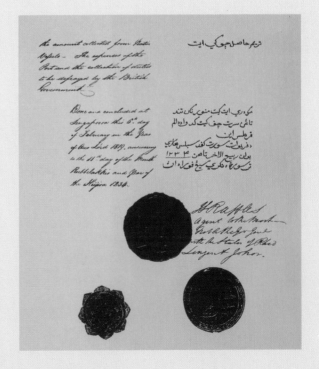

The 1819 Treaty

The 1824 Anglo-Dutch Treaty settled the Singapore imbroglio, with the region divided into British and Dutch spheres of influence. The Dutch withdrew from the Malay Peninsula, leaving Melaka and Singapore to the British, while the British left Bengkulu and Belitung to the Dutch. In turn the Dutch formally withdrew their objections to the British occupation of Singapore.

Other legal issues remained, however. The British in Singapore were unhappy with the uncertain title on which the settlement was based. The second Resident, Dr John Crawfurd, recognised that the 1819 treaty "amounted to little more than a permission for the formation of a British factory and establishment along two miles of the northern shore, and inland to the extent of point-blank range of a cannon shot". There was in reality no land grant. The only law was the Malay code. The native chief was considered the lord of the land, even within the confines of the British factory,

An 1861 lithograph showing the variety of ships calling at Singapore. European square-rigged vessels are the most numerous, with Chinese junks in the lower right corner of the picture. In the centre, some Bugis vessels can be seen.

and entitled, in perpetuity, to half of such duties or customs as might thereafter be levied at the port.

As there was no longer a threat of a Dutch military intervention to evict the British from Singapore, Crawfurd strategised to make the island a British sovereign possession. With Calcutta's permission, he parleyed successfully with Husain and the Temenggong. On 2 August 1824, both men were driven up to Government Hill (now Fort Canning) to sign a new treaty with Crawfurd. Raffles' scribe, Abdullah bin Abdul Kadir (also known as Munshi Abdullah), who probably heard enough about what transpired that morning to reconstruct the meeting, reported in his *Hikayat Abdullah*:

*On arrival they were greeted by Mr Crawfurd and invited into his house where they sat down. After they had been seated for a few moments, Mr Crawfurd said, "Is it true that Your Highness*

## Eye of the Pen

Some of the most illustrative descriptions of Stamford Raffles, William Farquhar and John Crawfurd come not through their letters and despatches, but through the reflections in a work by a certain polyglot: *Hikayat Abdullah* by Abdullah bin Abdul Kadir, better known as Munshi Abdullah (1797–1854). The Melaka-born writer composed the *Hikayat* throughout the 1840s, and published it in 1849 in Singapore, partly as an experiment in autobiography, a genre not yet existent in Malay literature at the time. Over the centuries, however, *Hikayat Abdullah* has come to be appraised differently. More than just a literary text, it is also an alternative entry point to imagining the Singapore of the first half of the 19th century.

Of particular interest are Munshi Abdullah's relations with Raffles, Farquhar and Crawfurd. He worked closely with all three of them (albeit at different points in time) as scribe, translator and Malay-language teacher. He was already acquainted with Farquhar and Raffles at Melaka, and he worked with Crawfurd when the latter arrived as the second Resident of Singapore in 1824. Where Abdullah's account differs from others is his nuanced attention to their temperaments – something not easily discernible through other historical sources.

The following descriptions are extracted from A.H. Hills' translation of *Hikayat Abdullah* in 1955, published in the *Journal of the Malayan Branch of the Royal Asiatic Society*.

### On Farquhar

*From the time he became Resident in Malacca right up to the time of Singapore he had never hurt people's feelings or done the smallest disservice to anyone of any race whatever. He was very fond of his people and showed them much consideration and kindness. So all the people were fond of him, and yet they respected him for the fairness of his rulings. If there was one feature of his character which was commendable above all others, it was that in all his actions and decisions he made no distinction between rich and poor, treating everyone alike. Most other people in high positions paid more attention to the rich than to the poor, treating the poor harshly and the rich with favour.*

### On Raffles

*As to Mr Raffles's physical features I noticed that he was of medium build, neither tall nor short, neither fat nor thin. He was broad of brow, a sign of his care and thoroughness; round-headed with a projecting forehead, showing his intelligence. He had light brown hair, indicative of bravery; large ears, the*

*is ready to accede to the wishes of the Governor-General?" The Sultan said, "It is true." Then Mr Crawfurd asked the Temenggong who also gave his assent. After that Mr Crawfurd took two pieces of parchment out of his writing-box saying, "This is a copy of the agreement for Your Highness and this one for the Temenggong. May Your Highness be pleased to listen while I explain its provisions to you in Malay. This document is to certify that I, Sultan Husain Shah ibn Al-Marhum Sultan Mahmud Shah, ruler of the Kingdoms of Johor and Pahang,*

*mark of a ready listener. He had thick eye-brows, his left eye watered slightly from a cast; his nose was straight and his cheeks slightly hollow. His lips were thin, denoting his skill in speech, his tongue gentle and his mouth wide; his neck tapering; his complexion not very clear; his chest was full and his waist slender. He walked with a slight stoop.*

*I noticed that he always looked thoughtful. He was very good at paying due respect to people in a friendly manner. He treated everyone with proper deference, giving to each his proper title when he spoke. Moreover, he was extremely tactful in ending a difficult conversation. He was solicitous of the feelings of others, and open-handed with the poor. He spoke in smiles. He took the most active interest in historical research. Whatever he found to do he adopted no half-measures, but saw it through to the finish. When he had no work to do other than reading and writing he liked to retire to a quiet place.*

**On Crawfurd**

*I noticed that Colonel Crawfurd was by nature inclined to impatience and outbursts of temper. He did all his work slowly, without hurrying. He was conscientious as well as capable, and he was also a man of education. Yet in spite of this he was fond of material wealth. He was tight-fisted and gave himself airs. His temperament made him intolerant of listening to long-winded complaints. Neither had he the ability to fully enquire into peoples' affairs. He preferred short, abbreviated statements of fact. Malays and other races which live in the East enjoy long dissertations and repetition. For this reason I heard many Malays and Chinese grumbling because they felt aggrieved in that their course of action had not been arrived at with their own consent but had been dictated to them.*

(*Opposite*) Munshi Abdullah
(*Above, left to right*) Farquhar, Raffles and Crawfurd

*whose sovereignty extends over the settlement of Singapore, do sincerely declare in this Treaty of my own free will I have ceded this Settlement of Singapore and all authority over it to the East India Company."*

With this treaty, Crawfurd secured Singapore's cession "in full sovereignty and property to the East India Company, its heirs and successors". Husain and the Temenggong had signed away Singapore in return for 33,200 Spanish dollars (about US$820,000

The Singapore River rapidly developed into a centre of trade after 1819. This view of the Singapore River from what is Elgin Bridge today looks out to the sea. The sketch shows cargo being manually loaded onto small crafts, which were then paddled out to the large vessels anchored outside the mouth of the Singapore River. The group of Orang Laut *prahu* in the left middle ground of the sketch were moved out of the Singapore River in the 1840s.

or S$1.12 million today) and a monthly stipend of 1,300 Spanish dollars for life for the Sultan, and for the Temenggong, 26,800 Spanish dollars (about US$663,000 or S$907,000 today) and a monthly stipend of 700 Spanish dollars.

The stipends were a slight increase on the sums agreed to in the 1819 treaty. In the months preceding the signing, Husain and the Temenggong had bargained unsuccessfully with Crawfurd for more money. Earlier, Crawfurd had complained to Calcutta that the two Malay leaders were earning more from port duties, gifts and profits on monopolies and revenue farms than they were contributing to the settlement's development. He wanted to rectify this situation upon taking office but could only act after the Dutch and the British had come to an arrangement over Singapore in the Anglo-Dutch Treaty of 17 March 1824. The two Malay leaders were rendered irrelevant by larger global forces they did not anticipate, and certainly could not influence.

### Towards a Crown Colony: Singapore Takes Off
As Singapore swiftly prospered, the locally based European merchant community grew increasingly dissatisfied with Calcutta's imperious and inefficient bureaucracy. The businessmen wanted a say in administrative decisions governing Singapore and, with growth, sought more port amenities than the EIC administrators were willing to finance. In 1855, *The Straits Times* proposed a "Reform League" to demand administrative change for the colony. Frustrations with Indian rule included the perceived failure to eliminate piracy, the transfer of Indian convicts to Singapore and plans

to implement port fees. In a public meeting, the motion to upend Calcutta's rule was raised but rejected by the majority. A group of men began hatching a plan to eventually break free.

In 1857, matters came to a head. Tighter police regulations in February provoked the Chinese to strike and the Indians to riot in Singapore, and disturbances erupted among the Chinese in Penang over new municipal laws. Reports of the sepoy revolt in India arrived in May, and rumours of an impending uprising among the Indian convicts in Singapore caused a general panic. A subsequent public meeting produced a petition by Singapore's European merchants to the British Parliament requesting that the three British settlements be separated from India and ruled directly as a Crown Colony. The petitioners' grievances included Calcutta's disregard for local wishes, the exclusion of Straits representation from the Indian Legislative Council, and the bid to impose port and tonnage dues on the ostensibly free port. But the petition was largely driven by Singapore: an overwhelming majority at a public meeting in Penang voted against supporting the petition.

This photo taken from the ramparts of Fort Canning shows the cannons pointed at Chinatown rather than out to sea to defend the port, suggesting a threat from Chinatown. In hindsight, that threat was the triad rivalry breaking out into riots and fights, which threatened the European community. Fort Canning was built as a refuge they could withdraw into in the event of further riots.

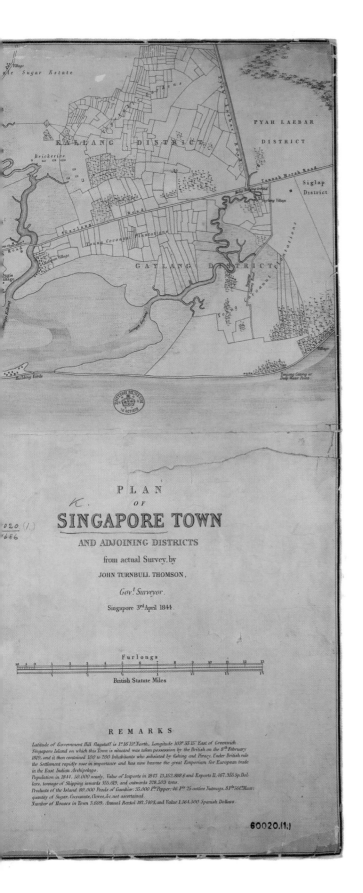

PLAN
OF
SINGAPORE TOWN
AND ADJOINING DISTRICTS

from actual Survey, by

JOHN TURNBULL THOMSON,

Gov.ʳ Surveyor.

Singapore 3ʳᵈ April 1844.

Furlongs

British Statute Miles

REMARKS

Latitude of Government Hill flagstaff is 1° 16' 15" North, Longitude 103° 55' 15" East of Greenwich.
Singapore Island on which this Town is situated was taken possession by the British on the 8ᵗʰ February
1819, and it then contained 100 to 200 Inhabitants who subsisted by fishing and Piracy. Under British rule
the Settlement rapidly rose in importance and has now become the great Emporium for European trade
in the East Indian Archipelago.
Population in 1844, 50,000 nearly. Value of Imports in 1843 13,152,888 $ and Exports 11,467,355 Sp.Dol-
lars. tonnage of Shipping inwards 355,619, and outwards 328,503 tons.
Products of the Island. 80,000 Peculs of Gambier: 35,000 Pʰ Pepper: 46 Pʰ 25 catties Nutmegs. 81ᵖʰ 56Cᵗ Mace:
quantity of Sugar, Cocoanuts, Cloves, &c not ascertained.
Number of Houses in Town 3,609. Annual Rental 187,740$ and Value 1,564,500 Spanish Dollars.

60020.(1.)

From 1841 to 1853, John Turnbull Thomson served in Singapore not only as a surveyor, but also as an architect and engineer. Thomson was a prolific map-maker who created several of the most important maps of early colonial Singapore. This map, Plan of Singapore Town and Adjoining Districts (1846 edition), is regarded as the most detailed map of Singapore town of the time.

London was primarily concerned about the costs of additional colonial holdings. The 1857 Indian Mutiny had culminated in the transfer of EIC's India acquisitions to the Colonial Office in 1858, which created the British Raj. But Calcutta continued making administrative decisions for Singapore, Penang and Melaka. In 1863, the British government tasked Hong Kong Governor Hercules Robinson to report on the state of Singapore, and he recommended a transfer to direct colonial rule from London. Change finally came when the War Office sought an alternative base to Hong Kong in Asia and picked Singapore as a strategic option. A bill was pushed through Parliament, reluctant senior officials were hastily retired, and on 1 April 1867, Penang, Melaka and Singapore, now collectively called the Straits Settlements, became a Crown Colony governed from London, with Singapore as the administrative centre.

As had happened in India, expanding trade opportunities brought the British Crown more territory, this time in the Malay Peninsula. In 1848, huge tin deposits were discovered in Perak's Larut Valley; tin mining, however, proved to be a double-edged sword. Rival Chinese secret societies came to dominate the industry, sparking violence that the Malay rulers could not contain. The violence disrupted the supply of tin, which in turn affected British businesses in Penang and Singapore. A royal succession dispute in Perak starting in 1871 and an appeal for help from one of the claimants ended the British policy of non-intervention in domestic issues.

The newly appointed Governor of the Straits Settlements, Andrew Clarke, who arrived in 1873, was more open to securing the safety of the tin industry and protecting Singapore's commercial interests than London's Colonial Office. The Pangkor Treaty, signed in 1874, marked the start of the eventual creation of the Federated and Unfederated Malay States and the formation of British Malaya. The Malay Peninsula would thereafter focus on becoming a major producer of primary commodities – tin, rubber, copra, sugar – that would turn Malaya into Singapore's hinterland and Keppel Harbour into a significant global economic player.

### Singapore's Winning Combination
The lucrative India-China trade was the motivation for establishing a British port of call along this trade route. Before the EIC lost its China trade monopoly in 1833, Singapore was useful to country traders who were eyeing a share of the China trade. These

traders met Chinese junks at Singapore to trade and circumvent the EIC monopoly. During the First Opium War (1839–42), when Guangdong was closed to trade, Singapore enjoyed a temporary boom. But after the 1842 Treaty of Nanjing opened five Chinese ports and ceded Hong Kong to Britain, Singapore's China trade links faded.

Yet, Singapore was more than a China trade station. It had established itself as a centre for the local trade networks once focused on Bintan. Bugis traders and country traders who had been trading in Riau before the 1784 Dutch attack now flocked to Singapore. Within six weeks, there were more than 100 native craft in the harbour, which, at the time, was located at the mouth of the Singapore River. It had no regional rivals to contend with, Penang being too far north and attracting mainly traders from its immediate neighbourhood. Contributing to Singapore's growth was the stability afforded by the 1824 Anglo-Dutch Treaty, making the island an effective substitute for Bintan. At the same time, British presence in the waters around Singapore helped curtail piracy, with maritime laws allowing ships to destroy pirates. By this stage, European privateering was no longer a security issue, with attention turned to regional piracy instead.

Another draw was Singapore's free port status, which was initially meant to be a temporary measure. Singapore's rapid rise as a commercial centre was due in no small part to its free port policy, which, although often attributed to Raffles' foresight, may have been accidental. The original intention of declaring a free port was to encourage ships to call at the nascent port. Exempting

Singapore's maritime trade legacy is preserved in this 1980 postage stamp issue. (*From smallest denomination*) Hainan junk; clipper; Fujian junk; *golekkan*; *palari*; East Indiaman; galleon; caravel; Jiangsu trader.

ships from stamp duties, import and export taxes, tonnage and port clearance fees, and other ancillary charges resulted in large savings for Singapore-based commercial enterprises. The concept of a free port within Southeast Asian intraregional trade was not a new phenomenon. Fifteenth-century Melaka became a great port because of its open-door policy, as did Riau until the Dutch tightened control at the end of the 18th century.

Singapore's two main trading seasons were governed by the trade winds. The junk season was regulated by the northeast monsoon winds, starting in November, that brought junks from China, Cochinchina and Siam. The junks would return home at the beginning of April, when the southwest monsoon winds arrived. The same winds would usher Bugis traders from the Celebes (Sulawesi), Bali and southern Borneo to Singapore between September and October. The traders would then leave in November at the onset of the northeast monsoon. "The chief function of the Bugis merchants," noted Wong Lin Ken, "was to bring the products of the eastern half of the Archipelago to the western ports, especially the ports under European controls, where these commodities were in demand, and to take back in exchange European and Indian piece goods and other manufactures."

The Bugis formed the other essential end of the trade network with China, with the Melakan Chinese in Singapore acting as middlemen for the European agency houses. In Singapore, the Straits produce brought by the Bugis *prahu* and Chinese and Siamese

This lithograph of Siamese junks moored in Singapore speaks to Singapore's growing importance as a trade hub in the 19th century. By the 1820s, Singapore had become the most important port of call for Siamese junks trading within the Malay Archipelago, with items such as sugar, sapanwood and elephant tusks from Siam finding their way to Europe by way of Singapore.

A Chinese junk moored in Singapore. These ships sailed from China laden not only with goods such as porcelain, tea, silk and sugar, but human cargo as well. Thousands of labourers arrived each year to work in tin mines and plantations across the Malay Archipelago.

junks were exchanged for textiles, opium and firearms and, increasingly, manufactured goods from an industrialising Britain.

The British traders also brought raw opium from India to Singapore, where it was processed and packaged and used by the Chinese middlemen to barter for Straits produce with the Bugis traders. Not surprisingly, Singapore also did considerable trade with its sibling settlements of Penang and Melaka, most of which was dominated by Chinese merchants. Not long after its establishment, Singapore superseded Penang as the primary port among the three. By the 1850s, it was claiming the major share in both imports and exports.

In 1825, nearly half (48 percent) of the total commerce in Singapore was conducted with Southeast Asia. By 1826, Singapore had overtaken Batavia (Jakarta) as the main entrepôt port for Siamese trade with the region. Singapore's successful free port model did not escape the notice of the Dutch, who copied it for their regional ports – Riau (1829), Pontianak and Sambas (1834), Makassar (1847), Menado and Kema (1848), and Amboyna (Ambon), Banda and Ternate (1852). After Makassar became a free port in 1847, Bugis trade in Singapore declined considerably.

However, Singapore had another edge: its free port status was complemented by a laissez-faire trade policy that allowed traders of all nationalities to compete freely. At the Dutch ports, not only did Dutch ships have priority over other ships, but non-Dutch traders were not allowed to enter the market until the Dutch-owned import and export agency, Nederlandse Handelmaatschappij (NHM), had met its needs first. The free port policy and laissez-faire trade proved to be a central plank of Singapore's growth in the early years, as Crawfurd noted:

> There is no Asiatic and few European ports of which the trade is so diversified as that of Singapore. The following are branches into which it may be naturally divided: The trade with Great Britain and the continent of Europe, with the British and other European possessions on the continent of India, with Malacca and the Prince of Wales's Island, with New South Wales, with the Mauritius, with the Dutch possessions in the Archipelago, with the Spanish possessions in the same or Philippines, with South America, with China in European vessels and Chinese junks, with Cochin China and Kamboja, with Siam, with the Bugis nation, with Borneo, and with Sumatra and the Malay Peninsula.

### Glory Days for Country Traders and Chinese Middlemen

Singapore was an instant success with the country traders, many of whom set up agency houses, buying and selling the goods of others on commission. This business model was one based on trust and required little capital: goods were sent to the agency house, which then remitted the money when the goods were sold. The first agency house was set up in 1820 by Alexander Laurie Johnston, a former EIC servant. Others soon followed, with warehouses mushrooming along both banks of the Singapore River; by the mid-19th century, there were 43 agency houses.

Much of the trade in the 19th century and earlier involved transshipment – the transfer of goods from one trading vessel to another while in transit at the port – as well as the repackaging and redistribution of imported manufactured goods and regional produce. This latter function was known as entrepôt trade. The reliance on regional and entrepôt trade meant that Singapore was part of a fluid trading environment – its economic, social and cultural space was defined by the flow of its maritime activities and the networks organically developed as a result of its commercial functions.

Many European firms involved in the Asian trade operated through Chinese middlemen who had little experience of trading

Alexander Guthrie arrived in Singapore in 1821 as a "country" or "private" trader licensed by the EIC. He initially traded in British manufactured household items such as knives, axes, nails and textiles with the European and Chinese communities through Chinese middlemen. He then expanded to trade in rice, coconut oil, spices and other local products. The company he established continued to grow and diversify after his retirement in 1847. It was one of the early companies to invest in rubber in the Malay Peninsula, in 1896. Today it continues as a global investment company.

with Europeans. In 1820, Crawfurd suggested that the problem could be solved through "an intermediate class in whom both can repose confidence". These intermediaries were mainly Peranakan or Melakan Straits Chinese who moved to Singapore with the arrival of the British, as did Chinese from Penang. Conversant in English and Malay, they became the ideal conduits between the Malay-speaking traders with their Straits produce and the European firms.

Agency houses gradually expanded their scope of activity, trading on their own account as well as providing services such as banking, shipping, freighting and insurance. Some agency houses expanded into agriculture when the cultivation of cash crops such as pepper and nutmeg took off. Eventually, however, the plantation economy moved into Malaya, where tin and rubber became key export commodities and the bedrock of the Malayan – and Singapore's – economy.

The first rubber trees were brought from Kew Gardens and planted in the Singapore Botanic Gardens in 1877. Botanic Gardens Director Henry Ridley, who invented the herringbone cut for tapping rubber latex, which effectively extended the trees' productivity, began promoting rubber at a time when the rubber tyre for motor cars had just been invented. The demand for rubber also coincided with the collapse of coffee plantations, nudging planters towards a new cash crop.

(*Below*) Henry Ridley was known as "Mad Ridley" for his incessant attempts to interest both European and Chinese businessmen in cultivating rubber trees as a cash crop. His efforts paid off when, during World War I, rubber became a strategic commodity and prices skyrocketed, sparking off a frenzy among the business community in Singapore to open large tracts of rubber plantations (*below left*). The Malay Peninsula quickly became the world's second largest producer of rubber, and by the 1930s, Singapore had become the home of the international rubber exchange.

Malayan rubber and tin gave Singapore's agency houses fresh business opportunities. Some became representatives of the foreign owners of rubber plantations or managed them. In turn, these links improved their profits in shipping and insurance. After 1900, the profits of agency houses in Singapore came increasingly from the rubber industry. Singapore's European agency houses also started dominating tin mining after dredge mining technology was introduced in 1912. Although tin mining started as a Chinese venture, the Chinese did not have the capital to import the new technology to raise the productivity of the increasingly exhausted mines. Greater European involvement offered agency houses a more profitable role in tin mining, as it did for rubber. After World War I, Singapore firms dominated these two most vital sectors of the Malayan economy.

### Cradle of the Port-city – Keppel Harbour
Until the 1840s, the Singapore River was the economic lifeline where shipping congregated. However, the river port was too small to handle the increasing volume of shipping as Singapore became a major British port of call alongside Aden (in present-day Yemen) and Karachi in India. The waters at the river mouth were

Following the advent of steam shipping in Southeast Asia from the 1840s, Singapore managed to capitalise on its position as a regional trading centre to develop itself as a coaling station, and therefore a nodal port of call in the Southeast Asian steam shipping network as well. The additional port function allowed Singapore to become an international port of call from the 1860s onwards.

too shallow for larger ships, silting was chronic, and space for wharves and coaling depots limited. The arrival of steamships and the development of the port as a coaling station diminished the lighterage business along the river. In the era of sailing ships, vessels would anchor at the river mouth, sending their goods to the warehouses via lighters plying the river.

The growing demand for wharfing facilities was largely met by private enterprise. The port shifted from the Singapore River to New Harbour – renamed Keppel Harbour in the late 1850s – where major agency houses began developing wharves and coal depots. The biggest port development company was Tanjong Pagar Dock Company, the forerunner of Singapore Harbour Board and today's Maritime and Port Authority of Singapore and PSA International. Established by private investors, the company constructed a large dry dock for ship repairs. Victoria Dock, located on the west side of Tanjong Pagar, was opened in 1868, just in time to take advantage of the Suez Canal's opening in 1869. A second dock, Albert Dock, was opened in 1879.

View of Battery Road, which linked Raffles Place to Fullerton Square, in the early 1900s. The fountain was built in 1882 to commemorate Tan Kim Seng, whose philanthropy was instrumental in improving the town's waterworks. In 1925, it was relocated to its present site at Queen Elizabeth Walk.

The growth of Raffles Place, Chinatown and Tanjong Pagar as Singapore's commercial heart arose from the development of port facilities at Keppel Harbour. Trade growth strengthened the sinews of commerce in tandem with the port's infrastructural expansion. Private commercial facilities and financial institutions blossomed. The earliest bank in Singapore, the Oriental Bank, was established in 1846. Others followed: the Mercantile Bank of India (1855) and the Chartered Bank of India, Australia and China (1859). By the time Singapore was transferred to direct colonial rule, it was among the busiest ports in the British Empire.

### Melting Pot of Migrants

In the 19th century, Singapore's existence depended entirely on the economic viability of the trading networks that criss-crossed its waters; overland trade with mainland Southeast Asia to its north was insignificant (less than 5 percent). These economic networks were sustained by a sea-linked foreland covering much of the Indian Ocean and the South China Sea. Before the development of a plantation economy in Malaya, Singapore had no clearly defined hinterland. What it had was a significant foreland of precolonial intraregional trading networks. The revival of these old trading networks sparked the emergence of a mosaic of diverse migrant communities drawn to the thriving settlement.

When Raffles arrived in 1819, Singapore was populated by a handful of followers of Temenggong Abdur Rahman, who had a large house beside the Singapore River. There were also several Orang Laut communities in coastal villages, and Chinese planters who cultivated gambier and pepper. With the shift of the regional trading networks to Singapore from the Riaus, the Malay-Muslim community grew rapidly. By 1901, there were 23,060 peninsular Malays, 12,335 from various parts of the Indonesian Archipelago (including Acehnese, Javanese, Boyanese, Dayaks and Filipinos), approximately 1,000 Arabs, and 600 Jawi Peranakan (the offspring of intermarriages between South Indian Muslims and Melaka Malays) residing in Singapore.

Singapore became the centre of the Malay world in the 19th and 20th centuries. One attraction was its position as the seat of British colonial government after the extension of British protection to various parts of the Malay Peninsula. Malay chiefs and their followers frequently visited Singapore to seek legal, official and financial assistance. Singapore also became a convenient sanctuary from Malay rulers or rival chiefs, akin to an enforced place of exile, and a land of employment opportunities for the Malays in the Straits region. In the process, the Malay community in Singapore also became something of a hotbed of rivalries.

Kampong Glam, alongside the Kallang estuary, where Sultan Husain chose to live, was the heart of the Malay-Muslim trading communities, reprising the role of the Kallang River estuary as the Shahbandar's base between the late 16th and 17th centuries. A sketch of the waterfront by hydrographers accompanying Raffles shows the "Village of Singapore" at the Singapore River and a "Ryat Village" (a corruption of the Malay word *rakyat*, or ordinary people) at the mouth of the Kallang River, indicating a settlement in the estuary.

From his *istana* (palace) at Kampong Glam, Sultan Husain commanded the Kallang estuary and its trade through the custom of trading ships calling at the port to give the Malay rulers "presents" (*hantar-hantaran*). Wealth oiled political power and this indirect toll bankrolled the Sultan's ability to dispense patronage, attract loyalty and form the essential alliances and allegiances that in turn supported his royal status.

On each of his three visits to Singapore, Raffles tried to put the government of Singapore on what he considered a "proper footing". The temporary compromise was to limit the *hantar-hantaran* to the *nakhoda* (captains) of the native craft when they anchored in the Kallang estuary, which was under Husain's jurisdiction from his palace at Kampong Glam. The captains of British and other European vessels were exempted and only required to pay a courtesy call on the Sultan and the Temenggong.

The Rochor River and Kallang estuary was the alternative harbour to the Singapore River. It was where the Bugis and other Southeast Asian traders converged.

It was in the Kallang estuary that the Bugis who arrived after 1819 as traders were encouraged to congregate. The second largest group of regional migrants were the Javanese, who came as traders and craftsmen specialising in metal and leather crafts. In 1891, there were 8,541 registered Javanese migrants residing

Office staff of Alkaff and Company. One of several successful Arab trading companies in Singapore, Alkaff and Co. was established by two brothers, Ahmad and Abdul Alkaff, who had arrived in Singapore in the 1860s. The Alkaff family was one of the wealthiest in colonial Singapore and owned a string of warehouses along the Singapore River, in the vicinity of present-day Robertson Quay.

in Singapore, a number that grew subsequently owing to harsh economic conditions in central Java and the active recruitment of Javanese as contract labourers for the Malayan plantation and tin mining sectors. During the Japanese Occupation (1942–45), the Javanese population rose by some 10,000 when the Japanese conscripted labour from Java. Many did not survive the war and abuse; some of those who did eventually settled in Singapore.

Among the most prestigious Muslim migrants were the Arabs. An extensive Arab-Persian trading network stretching from the Persian Gulf to the South China Sea existed long before the Europeans reached Asia. The first Arabs who arrived in Singapore soon after the establishment of the British settlement were two wealthy merchants from Palembang. Mohammed bin Harun Al-Junied and his nephew, Syed Omar bin Ali Al-Junied, hailed from a community that originated from the Hadhramaut region in southern Arabia. The Al-Junieds were believed to be direct descendants of Prophet Mohammad. Raffles encouraged them to settle in Singapore in the belief that Arab trade and ships would enrich his settlement. His hopes were not misplaced.

In 1824, the pioneer of another prominent Arab family in Singapore, Abdul Rahman Alsagoff, moved his trading business from Arabia to Singapore. His son, Syed Ahmad Alsagoff, set up Alsagoff and Company in 1848 and married into a Bugis family who owned a fleet of *prahu* engaged in a thriving trade, particularly in spices.

Pilgrims on the Hajj onboard a ship. By the mid-19th century, Singapore was a major port where Muslim pilgrims from the surrounding region converged and waited – sometimes for months – for an onward ship to Jeddah.

The marriage strengthened Alsagoff's commercial networks. The Alsagoff family business comprised the export of all kinds of produce and woods to Arabia and Europe – including rubber, sago, coconuts, coffee, cocoa and pineapples – as well as the pilgrimage trade, as many Arabs were active in the shipping business.

In the 1870s, the opening of the Suez Canal and the convenience of steam travel encouraged more Arabs to settle in Southeast Asia. Records show that in the 1880s, as many as 800 Arabs concentrated in the area bounded by Arab, Baghdad, Bussorah, Jeddah and Muscat streets. In the late 19th century, Singapore was regarded as home to the most flourishing Arab colony in the region, with its numbers rising to some 2,500 in the 1940s.

The Al-Junieds were among the first to shift their focus from trade to real estate, with other Arab families following suit. By the 1930s, the Arabs, together with the Jews, were Singapore's largest property owners, with an impressive portfolio of houses, hotels and entire streets of shops. It was estimated that the primary income of about 80 percent of Arabs in Singapore came from house rents. In addition, the Alsagoffs and Alkaffs ran companies that acted as handling agents for overseas Arab investors. By 1885, a quarter of Arab investments in the real estate sector in Southeast Asia were in Singapore.

The Arabs, particularly the earliest migrants – the Al-Junieds, Alsagoffs and Alkaffs – were influential within the Muslim community, and their Arab names invested them with a certain religious authority. Not surprisingly, they originated the pilgrimage brokering business in Singapore, conveying Muslim pilgrims to Mecca to perform the Hajj. By the end of the century, Singapore had developed into the Southeast Asian transit hub for pilgrims, particularly when the Dutch restricted Hajj travel for political reasons.

### Southeast Asia's Indian Links

Through trade with West Asia and contact with Arab traders, the Indians on the Malabar and Coromandel coasts were some of the earliest converts to Islam, with Indian Muslim traders among the earliest Muslims in Southeast Asia. Melaka was home to a substantial community of settled Tamil merchants who had intermarried with Malay women to evolve into the Jawi Peranakan community. Munshi Abdullah, Stamford Raffles' Malay-language scribe and tutor, was a Jawi Peranakan. Many of the members of this community, like the Melakan Chinese, achieved prominent positions in 19th-century society.

There is no record, however, of any Indian community in Singapore before Raffles' arrival in 1819. It was his entourage of some 120 sepoys and lascars (Indian assistants and domestic servants) who formed the beginnings of an Indian community here. Excluding the soldiers, it was recorded that in the first few years after 1819, there were 132 Indians among a total population of nearly 5,000.

The EIC in Calcutta grew the Indian community in Singapore by turning the island into an Indian penal colony. In April 1825, the first batch of convicts was transferred from Bengkulu to Singapore following the 1824 Anglo-Dutch Treaty. Bengkulu had served as an Indian penal colony. The EIC believed that given the scarcity of labourers in Singapore, the convicts could be put to good use in the building and maintenance of public roads. The argument was that it would be harder for convicts to escape into a society where there were so few Indians. By 1860, there were 2,275 Indian convicts serving their jail terms in Singapore, which continued to receive Indian convicts until 1873. This took place despite the protests of Singapore's business community, who made it one of the reasons for wanting Singapore to be out of Calcutta's jurisdiction.

Sri Mariamman Temple, c. 1890. Believed to be the oldest Hindu temple in Singapore, it was established in the early 19th century by Narayan Pillai, a government clerk from Penang who came to Singapore with Raffles. Sri Mariamman Temple was gazetted as a national monument in the 1970s.

But there was also voluntary immigration of Indians to Singapore, with most arriving as indentured workers. In 1849, about one-third of the Indian population was registered as indentured labourers. Many worked in the expanding port, and the Indian labour force soon formed the backbone of the Public Works Department, with practically all of the major early buildings of Singapore built by Indian labour.

Singapore also attracted Indian traders, the first of whom was Narayan Pillai, who arrived with Raffles from Penang on the *Indiana*. He stayed and started a brick kiln just outside the town. Sending for a few carpenters and bricklayers from Penang, he became one of Singapore's first building contractors. Pillai eventually became a leader in the Indian community and played a key role in building the first Hindu temple in Singapore – the Sri Mariamman Temple on South Bridge Road.

Other Indian merchants, particularly from Penang, followed. In 1849, there were 17 Indian merchants of some standing in Singapore and, by the 1860s, there were substantial numbers of Parsee, Bengali, Sindhi and Tamil merchant houses on the island.

By the turn of the 20th century, Singapore's Indian community stood at over 16,000, constituting nearly 9 percent of the population. This was a largely transient community, predominantly male, and a heterogeneous mix of different groups characterised by occupation, religion, education and language in addition to ethnic and sub-ethnic differences based on place of origin.

Of these compartmentalised groups, the most prominent were the South Indian Muslims, who had established themselves early and made enough money to build the first mosque in Singapore. The Chuliahs, as they were called here, were renowned retail traders with a long tradition of trading in Southeast Asia. They mostly originated from the southern districts of Tamil Nadu, primarily Tanjore and Ramnad, where traders of the earlier period had also originated. Other South Indian traders included the Malabar Muslims or Moplahs, a community traditionally engaged in retail trade in India. These Indian commercial communities found a niche operating credit, banking and accounting services through their widespread community networks. Such activities fitted in neatly with the development of the port-city.

In the moneylending business, the Chettiars were particularly successful. Their clientele was not restricted to Indian traders but often included European proprietary planters and Chinese businessmen. Nattukodai Chettiars from the Ramnad and Puttukottai districts in southern Chennai began migrating into the Straits Settlements

(*Below left*) A group of Chettiars in Singapore. The term "Chettiar" followed the original group of Nattukodai Chettiars, who hailed from the Chettinad region of Tamil Nadu, but slowly became synonymous with all South Indians involved in moneylending and financial activities.

(*Below*) Rm. V. Supramanium, a prominent Chettiar money-lender, in a 1920s studio photo.

Postage stamp commemorating P. Govindasamy Pillai (1889–1980), the founder of the successful chain of PGP stores in Singapore, Johor and Melaka. He was also a philanthropist and a leading member of Singapore's South Indian community.

in the early 19th century. In a time when economic enterprises were often hampered by the lack of modern financial services, the Chettiars were an invaluable source of credit for small businesses that needed capital but had no collateral to offer. P. Govindasamy Pillai, a prosperous and prominent provisions and textile retailer in Singapore, was known to have started his business with a loan from the Chettiars.

The Chettiars quickly established themselves as the major sources of finance for agriculturists in Southeast Asia who traded in produce and commodities such as rice, tea and tin with the Madras Presidency. Wherever they functioned, the Chettiars formed an important part of the financial and credit system. By the 1930s, the community was running an extensive and complex financial network that stretched from Rangoon (now Yangon) to Saigon (now Ho Chi Minh City), with bases in Madras (now Chennai), Colombo, Penang and Singapore. The Chettiars remained a moneylending institution until the 1970s, when the growth of banks and financial institutions as well as changing aspirations among the younger generations put an end to their traditional vocation.

### *Sinkheh*, Straits-born and the Chinese Networks

Like the Arabs and Indians, Chinese traders in maritime Southeast Asia (known to them as Nanyang, or the South Seas) go back to pre-European times. Chinese communities could be found along the two legs of the China trade network. One was the southeastward route that took junks round the Philippines to the Malukus (the Spice Islands), northeast Borneo and back to the Philippines. The second, and more lucrative route ran westward to the Straits of Melaka.

After the Dutch capture of Melaka in 1641 and the entrenchment of Dutch power in Southeast Asia, Chinese traders began actively sourcing for a good trans-shipment base in the region. The Dutch-controlled ports were unattractive mainly because of Dutch antagonism and, in some cases, persecution. Nevertheless, by the early 19th century, Batavia had become part of the Chinese junk trade network despite heavy Dutch taxes on Chinese merchandise, and even heavier duties if the Chinese cargo included European goods. To take Straits produce out of Batavia, the Chinese traders had to pay export duties, and Chinese junks were not allowed to fill their holds with Straits produce until the needs of Dutch ships had first been met.

Not surprisingly, when Singapore opened up as a free-port alternative to Batavia, it immediately drew the Chinese junk trade. Just two years after its founding, the Chinese in Singapore numbered some 1,200, up from the 30 who were mostly gambier planters when Raffles first landed. Many of the newcomers were Straits-born Chinese from Riau and Melaka eager to get away from the repressive Dutch regime.

The Chinese trading community settled in Boat Quay – in accordance with the Raffles town plan that divided the new migrants into ethnic enclaves around the Singapore River – and formed one end of the Chinese junk trade. The other end comprised the China-based traders. The first four junks arrived from China in 1821, and thereafter, Singapore grew into the new centre of the Southeast Asia-China trade, replacing Batavia. Paradoxically, the EIC monopoly on the China trade helped to promote Singapore's junk trade.

The Chinese junks in Singapore gave the country traders a slice of the lucrative China trade. The junks brought Chinese silks, brocades and tea to Singapore, which in turn were sold to country traders who brought Indian goods such as cottons and opium to be sold to the junk traders. With the ending of the EIC monopoly in 1833 and the opening of the China trade to private traders, the importance of Singapore as a trans-shipment centre in the lucrative China trade declined. From 1842, Hong Kong became the British hub for the China trade after it was ceded to the British following the First Opium War, a war in which the victors were the drug dealers.

Until the outbreak of World War II, Chinese traders in Singapore continued to be the main force in Singapore's trade with China and Southeast Asia even as European agency houses enjoyed the bigger share of Singapore's total import trade, which included trade with Europe and North America. Chinese companies also competed successfully with European agency houses to develop the import trade with Japan, the first Asian country to adopt European industrial methods to manufacture products. Singapore became Southeast Asia's distribution centre for Japanese goods, which were cheaper than European products. This trade link, however, would have serious consequences for the Chinese in Singapore following Japanese aggression in China in the 20th century.

Postage stamp commemorating Tan Tock Seng, a Melaka-born Chinese who moved to Singapore soon after 1819, where he started out selling vegetables and poultry. His break came when he joined J.H. Whithead of Shaw, Whithead & Company to speculate in land. His tremendous success in this enterprise led him to become an influential member of the Chinese community and a donor to many philanthropic causes.

The development of Singapore as a Chinese trading centre turned the Chinese community into the colony's largest ethnic group, comprising mainly southeastern Chinese from the coastal provinces. By 1867, the Chinese made up 65 percent of Singapore's population, numbering some 55,000. The largest dialect group was the Hokkiens, followed by the Teochews, Cantonese and Hakkas. Many Hakkas and Cantonese would end up working in Malayan tin mines. Most of the Chinese migrants were fleeing the wars, famine and poverty of a China that was in the middle of a dynastic change. The migration was abetted by a lucrative, albeit abusive, trade in Chinese labour in Southeast Asia. Called the "pig" business and funnelled through Singapore, the coolie trade shipped out able-bodied young Chinese men as cheap labour for the expanding region.

In the 19th century, the fresh arrivals saw themselves as sojourners seeking to make their fortunes and then return home. Known also as *sinkheh* (new guests), they were often transient and bound for other destinations. By contrast, the Straits-born or Peranakan Chinese, who formed about 10 percent of the community, regarded themselves as settlers and were the community's early leaders in the 19th and 20th centuries. They were Chinese by social identity but shared a bond with the Malays in language and lifestyle. Being proficient in English and Malay made them a useful interface for the *sinkheh* as well as the Malays and the Europeans, and gave them an early economic advantage. Almost always merchants, Straits-born Chinese filled the crucial role as middlemen for European agency houses. They soon formed the community's wealthy elite, although swelling economic opportunities also made rich men of several China-born migrants like Tan Kah Kee and Tan Lark Sye. Many China-born migrants were also absorbed into Straits Chinese families through marriage.

The Straits-born, who knew no other homeland apart from the Melaka Straits region, kept enough of their Chinese-ness to identify with developments in China. The politics of China suffused Singapore and Malaya, with the contending factions in China manifesting themselves on a smaller scale in Southeast Asia, comprising pro- and anti-Kuomintang groups, or essentially left- and right-wing groups. Although the community ran its own affairs, there was always the possibility of conflict between British policies and Chinese patriotism. The British intervened more than once to suppress Chinese patriotism, one instance being the banning of

the Kuomintang that was sparked by London's recognition of Yuan Shikai as the President of China. Another instance took place in the 1920s, when the British tried to combat rising Chinese nationalism in Singapore by mandating that Chinese schools teach in dialect rather than *guoyu* (the "national language", i.e., Mandarin) if they wanted government aid. In the early 1930s, when Britain was Japan's ally, the Chinese community's anti-Japanese activities were suppressed.

Although it was in the community's interests to cooperate with the colonial government to maintain order and stability to facilitate business, patriotism often got in the way. Working with the British was easier for the Straits Chinese. With exposure to English education and early entry into Singapore's middle class, the more Westernised Straits Chinese developed an identity that made them more acceptable to the colonial establishment but at the same time also set them apart from the larger China-born community.

Singapore's societal structure developed from its physical connections and maritime routes as well as its functional interdependence

Built in the 1820s, Hokien Street was one of Singapore's earliest main streets.

Tan Jiak Kim led the Straits-born Chinese to form a Straits Chinese British Association to promote their interests as loyal subjects of the British Empire while retaining their Chinese identity, as seen in this 1900 photograph of the association's members.

(trade, labour, commodity exchange and capital flows) and community connections. The trade networks provided the resources that sustained the colony and the manpower that eventually constituted Singapore's plural society. As Singapore's success was built on its status a free port and an open emporium, colonial immigration policy was unrestricted. The key element in the development of a trading centre was the free movement of traders and manpower. And so, by the middle of the 19th century, the port-city had become home to a kaleidoscope of communities – divided into defined communal zones but trading alongside one another and intermarrying. The municipal design of Singapore came to reflect the three main concerns of the port-city: enabling business, anchoring the mercantile community, and segregating the different ethnic and occupational groups that had converged on the island.

## A Century of Global Economic Revolution
In the evolution of the global economy, nothing has played a more seminal role than Britain's Industrial Revolution. Beginning in the late 1700s and spreading swiftly to Europe and the United States by the 1800s, the evolution of mass production facilitated by steam- and electric-powered machinery left no aspect of life untouched.

The Industrial Revolution generated geopolitical forces that changed where and how people lived, raised their families, fed and entertained themselves, as well as how they organised their relations with one another. It turned some countries into manufacturers and others into producers of the primary commodities from which manufactured goods were made. The revolution decimated cottage industries worldwide, created the working classes and brought an end to centuries of self-employment, subsistence agriculture and traditional crafts as a livelihood. The development of cash crop economies produced massive movements of people, turning once homogeneous societies into plural and polyglot societies. The revolution opened an avenue for individuals to rise in society through entrepreneurship and ability rather than birth or patronage. Throughout the 19th and 20th centuries, the global spread of technological innovation made a tremendous impact on social, economic and political developments.

Japan was the first Asian country to industrialise, adopting a European model of governance with distinct Japanese features. The 1868 Meiji Restoration, realised by a game-changing revolution two years prior that restored power to the Japanese monarchy, introduced heavy industry to Japan as well as the essential toolbox of modern military might: a well-trained army as well as state-of-the-art weapons and a fleet of warships and airplanes, which by the early 20th century were all Japanese-made.

The era would eventually see the formation and rise of the *zaibatsu* (business conglomerates) such as Mitsubishi and Mitsui, both formed in 1876. Sumitomo, founded in the 17th century, became a *zaibatsu* during the Meiji Restoration. These *zaibatsu* invested in heavy industries such as steel, shipbuilding and the manufacture of arms and planes. Adopting industrialised mass production, Japan became the source of cheap manufactured goods for Asia, competing effectively with Western manufacturers for Asia's mass market.

### Wiring Up the Hardware on Land and Sea...

As a port, Singapore was already affected by the advent of steamships in the 1840s. Unlike in the days of sail, traders no longer depended on the winds, and their voyages could be completed in much less time. Shipping times were further cut when the Suez Canal opened in 1869, bringing rapid socioeconomic changes to

The opening of the Suez Canal in 1869 shortened the sailing time between the Indian Ocean and Europe, giving a boost to maritime traffic in Singapore.

Singapore. State-of-the-art technologies in communication, transportation, lighting and industrial development arrived swiftly from London via steamships.

The telegraph, which was invented in 1816 for military purposes, was adopted by the Colonial Office as a means of exerting finer control over an enormous empire, which peaked at 35.5 million square kilometres in 1920. By 1880, 141,000 kilometres of undersea cable connected Britain with India, Canada, the Straits Settlements and Australia.

Singapore was a thriving entrepôt port by 1850, and a key part of this communication network. The first cross-channel cable between Singapore and Malaya was laid in 1851, while a submarine cable linking Singapore to Batavia was laid in 1859. After 1869, Singapore was linked to Australia via a cable with Java laid by the British Australian Telegraph Company Limited. In 1929, Singapore was finally linked directly to London. The communication time for each telegraphic transmission was radically cut from 10 hours in 1870 to two seconds by 1929, across 16,900 kilometres of cable.

Singapore had its own domestic telegraph network, too, which was installed in key public buildings such as Government House and the main police stations. The Eastern Extension, an associate company of the Eastern Telegraph Company, opened its first office on Prince Street in 1870. Government telegraph lines in the Straits

Settlements quintupled within five years, from 209 kilometres in 1885 to 1,022 kilometres in 1890. Tens of thousands of cable-grams criss-crossed the Settlements annually.

The telephone, another technological innovation, caught on quickly in Singapore. Just three years after its 1876 patent by Alexander Graham Bell, Singapore had a telephone line connecting the port at Tanjong Pagar with the commercial hub at Raffles Square. In 1894, there were 256 telephone lines operating in the city, and by 1931, the British Oriental Telephone & Electric Company was employing 300 staff to operate 5,000 lines. One effect of speedier communications was the elimination of commodity speculation across localities. Now the middlemen could no longer "buy cheap and sell dear".

The cityscape changed with the arrival of new transportation technologies. In 1821, Singapore had only 24 kilometres of poor-quality gravel roads that were prone to damage by bullock cart traffic and heavy monsoon rains. Road construction technology improved with the introduction of the motor car. The number of automobiles leapt from 842 in 1915 to 4,456 in 1925. The rise created a strong demand for better roads. Electric tramways had been introduced in 1886, but they could not compete with much cheaper man-powered rickshaws, a Japanese invention that

The bullock cart was typically used to ferry goods from the river bank and godowns into town, playing a crucial role in the transportation system of early colonial Singapore. Motor cars were introduced to Singapore in 1896 and gradually came to replace animal-drawn carriages.

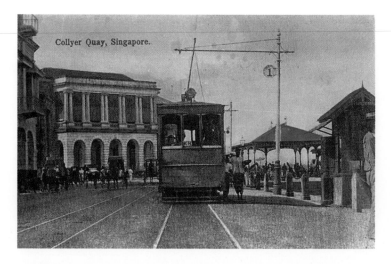

Collyer Quay, Singapore.

An electric tram service was started in 1905 by Singapore Electric Tramways Limited. The company struggled for years before a revamp and fare restructuring exercise helped it finally turn a profit in 1923. Still, the venture was wound up soon after and the trams were replaced in 1925 by electric trolley buses.

flooded Singapore from 1880. The introduction of electric tramways also spurred the introduction of electricity into the homes of the elite.

The electrification of Singapore started as private investment to extend working hours at the wharves to cope with the increase in shipping and to maximise usage of the facilities. Not long after the introduction of power stations in the US, the Tanjong Pagar Dock Company invested in electrification in 1878. George Bogaars in his 1956 book *Tanjong Pagar Dock Company 1864–1905* wrote:

> *The installation served the docks and workshops principally but was extended to the wharves and roadways. The power station was built just outside the eastern dock entrance. A marine boiler supplied the steam which drove three engines of 108 horsepower each, geared to three generators capable of developing 480,000 candle power together.*

The company's power station, completed by 1897, brought electricity to the wharves, extending its hours of operation. The commercial advantages of turning night into day were obvious, but the original impetus for public street lighting had been to enhance residents' safety. Singapore streets were first lit with oil lamps in 1824. Gas lighting was introduced in 1864, and by the 1890s, there were some 1,000 gas street lamps. Gas lighting was also used in homes for those who could afford to pay. Although these lamps would not have been able to generate as much light as a modern 25-watt light bulb, they were still a significant disruption to oil lamp technology. Improved domestic lighting enabled later mealtimes, evening conversations and reading. In 1901, gas-light went mainstream after the Municipality purchased Kallang Gasworks, although the working classes and rural residents still had to make do with oil lamps.

In 1906, electric street lighting was introduced to central Singapore with the construction of the Mackenzie Road Power Station. The St James Power Station (1927) electrified more parts of Singapore. However, many outlying areas remained without electricity supply until enterprising businessmen stepped in to fill the gap.

The modern petroleum industry started in the 19th century in the United States, Russia and Europe. In 1891, an agency house in Singapore, Syme & Co., set up a kerosene depot on Pulau Bukom for M. Samuel & Co. of London – an Asian first. Six years later, under the name Shell Transport and Trading Company, Syme & Co. expanded to Borneo following the discovery of oil there.

In 1907, Shell merged with its Dutch competitor, Royal Dutch Petroleum Company, which had discovered oil in Dutch Indonesia. The two rivals formed Royal Dutch Shell, which would develop into an oil giant in Asia in the 20th century – and in the late 1930s would catch the eye of the militant hawks in the Japanese government. Shell at Pulau Bukom was the company's hub, with its tankers transporting oil from British Borneo and Indonesia to Singapore to be stored, blended and reshipped to Europe. Singapore was the company's storage depot for Asia. The demand for oil in Malaya, British Borneo, Indonesia, Thailand and Indochina was also supplied from Singapore.

### …And Powering the Region's Software

By the end of the 19th century, Singapore was developing into a regional intellectual hub for the various local communities. It was also becoming a regional printing and publishing hub. This development grew out of the availability of printing presses and trained pressmen, introduced by Christian missionaries as early as 1823. The earliest Singapore-printed books bore the imprint of Mission Press or Institution Press. The oldest extant Japanese version of any portion of the Bible was published in Singapore in 1837.

The earliest Malay publications were religious tracts, as were the early Tamil works. Among the early newspapers published and printed in Singapore were *Jawi Peranakan* (1876), the first Malay

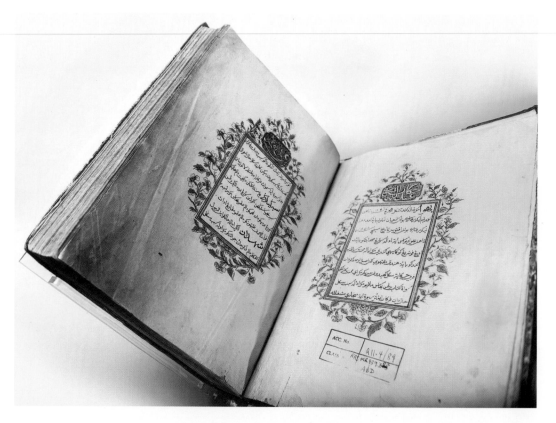

The *Hikayat Abdullah* was among the most impressive Malay works printed in the Straits Settlements. Mid-century developments in lithography allowed calligraphic text to be transcribed directly onto limestone blocks, pressed and transferred onto paper. Intricate illustrated manuscripts could thus be reproduced more rapidly than with the traditional handcopying method.

newspaper, and Chinese papers such as *Tifang Jih Pau* (Local News, 1845), *Jit Sheng* (Rising Sun, 1858) and *Lat Pau* (1881). Among the earliest printed books were Munshi Abdullah's *Hikayat Abdullah* (1849) and the colonial Singapore classic, Charles Burton Buckley's *An Anecdotal History of Old Times in Singapore* (1902).

The demand for Malay reading materials, which were also read by literate Straits Chinese, led to a thriving translation industry of both Chinese and English classics. Munshi Abdullah, who moved from Melaka to Singapore in 1822, noted in his iconic *Hikayat Abdullah*:

> *I am astonished to see how markedly our world is changing. A new world is being created, the old world disappearing. The very jungle becomes a settled district, while elsewhere a settlement reverts to jungle.*

He would have found Singapore unrecognisable half a century after the publication of his tome.

# IN A NUTSHELL

If regional developments eclipsed Singapore's position in Chapter Five, then Chapter Six resituates Singapore at the centre, as it becomes a point of interest for the British East India Company and a point of contestation for the Dutch East India Company, especially after the British set up a trading post on the island in 1819. The 19th century was one of growing trade, enabled by Britain's rise as a global power. Singapore benefited as a port around which a city developed to service the port's trading activities.

While the godowns along the Singapore River were where Chinese and European traders unloaded their goods, the Bugis and other regional traders congregated at the Kallang River. Other than trading activities, the 19th century also saw an influx of migrant labour from the region and beyond, including China and India. The latter half of the century also saw the expansion of steam-powered technology in Singapore, as well as the advent of the telegraph and electricity.

In Chapter Seven, we will see to what extent these developments continue into the 20th century and form the foundations of the nascent nation state of Singapore after 1965, despite interruptions such as the Great Depression, the two World Wars, merger and separation.

Boat Quay at the turn of the
20th century, photographed by
Charles J. Kleingrothe. Boat Quay
flourished with the settlement
of traders and labourers as well
as the construction of trading
facilities in the area. It maintained
its role as a vital trading centre
right up to the late 20th century.

Chang Chin Fai's 1992 watercolour
captures the "Changing
Cityscape" of Singapore with
the iconic Sultan Mosque in the
centre of the painting, surrounded
by the conserved architecture
of Kampong Glam, and high-rise
office blocks in the background.

# CHAPTER SEVEN

# The 20th Century
## Becoming a Global City-State

I t is the role of the cities in Asian countries, established and developed as beach-heads of Western Imperialism, to transform themselves under their independent national governments into beach-heads of a dynamic modernisation process to transform the countryside.

Singapore's economic architect Goh Keng Swee,
in an article written in 1967 when he was
Singapore's first Finance Minister

### Conflict and Nationhood

If the 19th century experienced technological disruption and economic ferment, the 20th was riven by conflict. The global forces that had turned an island at the southern end of the Malay Peninsula into the focus of British imperial power now swept Singapore into war, occupation and political change.

By the beginning of the 20th century, Singapore was integrated economically, financially and politically into the Malay Peninsula. Legally, British Malaya was a combination of the Federated and Unfederated Malay States along with the Straits Settlements of Penang and Melaka. Singapore was technically part of the Straits Settlements but in practice functioned as the administrative centre of this colonial world that also included the British Borneo territories. In many ways, Singapore was its cultural capital as well. The latest ideas and trends flowed into the port and spread through a thriving publishing industry churning out newspapers and magazines in multiple languages.

After the Causeway opened in 1923 – initially as a railway connection to transport primary commodities to the port-city – Singapore

Singapore-Johore Railway Ferryboat Johore Jetty.

*Love from
Mother
10-9-06.*

Prior to the construction of the Causeway, Singapore was linked to the Malay Peninsula by a ferry service that plied between Woodlands and Johor Bahru.

became physically linked with Malaya. The railway terminus in Singapore was located at Tanjong Pagar, in front of Keppel Harbour. While the Malayan hinterland supported Singapore as a port, it was, in turn, sustained by the port's trade activities. Singapore was Malaya's primary port and the conduit through which supplies from Thailand, Burma and Indochina were channelled to Malaya. As the British Empire attained global-power status at the end of the 19th century, Singapore gained symbolic and strategic significance, backed by its standing as the leading entrepôt in Southeast Asia.

Just as Singapore's economy was bound up with that of British Malaya, so too was its defence, going back to the very foundation of colonial Singapore. London's initial indifference to Raffles' acquisition turned to official interest only when the War Office began hunting for an alternative base to Hong Kong after the First Opium War ended in 1842. However, the cost of maintaining a defence base in Singapore turned the proposal into a political football that was kicked back and forth between governments – right up to Britain's 1967 announcement of its troop withdrawal from Singapore, a whole century after Singapore became a Crown Colony.

After World War I, a more coherent Far East defence plan was mooted. Although Japan was still a British ally then, Lord Jellicoe, the British First Sea Lord, saw it as a potential threat and recommended the creation of a powerful Singapore-based Far East fleet to match the growing Japanese naval might. But the war had gutted British appetite for a military build-up; London's focus was on economic recovery and disarmament. At the 1921 Imperial Conference, when representatives from Britain and its colonies met to discuss the empire's defence, it was decided that the "Singapore Strategy" would entail constructing a naval base in Singapore but not a Far East fleet. Instead, the British navy would be despatched to Asia if the Japanese attacked. The colonies would have to hold out on their own for the six weeks the naval forces took to arrive.

The initial blueprint for Sembawang Naval Base was an impressive affair, with 10 docks, a floating dock, an inner basin, over 3 kilometres of wharves, and housing for 2,000 personnel. Cost considerations swiftly shredded the plan, which was redrawn at a far more modest scale. Building it was a ponderous 15-year affair. Construction only began five years after its 1923 announcement, prodded by rising Japanese militarism. The project was delayed

The increasing integration between the economies of Singapore and the Malay Peninsula necessitated the building of a land crossing over the Straits of Johor. When the British eventually completed the construction of the Johor Causeway, rail and road transport links extended directly from the Malay Peninsula to Singapore.

again following the 1929 Wall Street collapse and the Great Depression of the 1930s, which crippled not only the American economy but the world economy too. Singapore suffered because demand for primary commodities like rubber and tin stalled. In addition, the US had supplanted Britain as Singapore's top market by then.

Construction was finally completed in 1938 but the base was little more than an empty shell without a fleet to defend it. Still, the reality did not stop the British from proclaiming Singapore an "impregnable fortress". The propaganda was aimed at deterring the Japanese, but ironically resulted in lulling the Singapore population into a false sense of security.

### Japan and the Events Leading to World War II

Prior to World War I, the cornerstone of British imperial defence in Asia was the Anglo-Japanese Alliance, forged in 1902 and renewed in 1905 and 1911, which saw Russia as the common enemy. Britain's preoccupation with containing the German naval threat in Europe also prompted them to rely on this alliance to safeguard their Asian interests. It became increasingly apparent after 1919 that the balance of power in the East was shifting steadily in Japan's favour.

During the 19th century, Japan had embarked on the Meiji Restoration, a dramatic modernisation programme that by the end of the century had turned her into an Asian power with expansionist ambitions. In 1895, Japan acquired Taiwan (then known as Formosa) as part of the Treaty of Shimonoseki that ended the First Sino-Japanese War (1894–95). The Japanese then trounced Russia in the Russo-Japanese War (1904–5), becoming the first Asian nation to defeat a major Western one, gaining the Liaodong Peninsula, where Port Arthur was located, the South Manchuria Railway and half of Sakhalin island. In 1910, Japan annexed Korea – the final step in a long process of creeping control that had begun in the late 19th century. Five years later, Japan presented China with "21 Demands" that sought to open the China market to Japanese goods and which clearly made Japan a competitor for European economic interests in China.

The 1919 Treaty of Versailles gave Japan a League of Nations mandate over the Mariana, Caroline and Marshall islands in the Pacific. By this time, the Japanese navy was the world's third-strongest maritime power. The West sought to limit Japan's naval build-up and ease the arms race with the 1921 Washington Naval Agreement. The pact, which limited Britain's naval size, sounded the death knell of the Anglo-Japanese Alliance. Britain could no longer undertake simultaneous naval engagements in the European and Asian maritime theatres and had no Asian ally to serve as a custodian of her colonies. Worse, a war with Japan meant confrontations with the Imperial Japanese Navy, which would require the deployment of the Royal Navy from the British Isles.

In 1937, Japan invaded China following the Marco Polo Bridge Incident, triggering the Second Sino-Japanese War. But China was too big for Japan to swallow. Despite being embroiled in a civil war between the People's Liberation Army led by Mao Zedong and the Kuomintang, or Nationalists, led by Chiang Kai-shek, as well as experiencing the horrors of the December 1937 Nanjing Massacre, China held out. Japan was now in a no-win situation. In a bid to end the war in China, in 1938 the US imposed an embargo on the export of manufactured goods to Japan; by 1940 the embargo extended to the export of oil. Japan could withdraw from China and end the embargo, or continue the war to a face-saving negotiated settlement. Once the debate among the Japanese hawks began to focus on the essentials for continuing the war in China, the "Southern Road" strategy, which involved taking the oil fields of the Dutch East Indies and British Borneo, became Tokyo's only option in 1941.

The British anticipated a Japanese attack on Singapore and in the mid-1930s reinforced its coastal defence with machine-gun pillboxes similar to this at Labrador, along the island's southern coast.

General Archibald Wavell (*third from right*), Commander-in-Chief India, inspecting Singapore's fortification and Indian troops in November 1941. Wavell was to return to Singapore in January 1942 as Commander-in-Chief Far East with command over General Percival. It is doubtful that Wavell could have done much to prevent the fall of Singapore in the final five weeks of the battle. But questions remain whether the decisions he took, or did not take, accelerated the surrender of Singapore.

### Defending Singapore and a Clash of Loyalties

The role of the British Indian Army in the defence of Singapore illustrates several issues in Singapore's pre-war society. The principal issue was the conflict of loyalties when ethnicity and nationality became enmeshed. The pre-war migrant communities – the Chinese, including the Straits-born, and the Indians – were politically affiliated with their putative homelands. Disentangling the issue was even harder in the Malay community, which comprised migrants from the regional islands and peninsular Malaya. It was natural that the politics of independence in India and Japanese aggression in China would affect their respective Indian and Chinese communities overseas.

Indian troops were a key component of British imperial might even during the colonisation of India in the 18th century. When Raffles arrived in Singapore, he was accompanied by 120 sepoys

### Mutiny on an Eastern Bounty

From the mid-19th century, Singapore offered the West and the world the image of a bustling, exotic port-city in the far-flung reaches of the Eastern Seas. It was part of the priceless string of maritime hubs that bankrolled Britain in exercising a global imperial outreach unseen and unmatched before. But within 10 days, and four years shy of a glorious century of Pax Britannica on this little Southeast Asian dot, the image of Singapore as a prized commercial pearl was shattered by mutinous troops for reasons that also resonate today.

The main force on Singapore, the 5th Bengal Light Infantry, embarked on a trail of rampage at Alexandra barracks, Tanglin barracks, Keppel Harbour and Pasir Panjang. Europeans were shot on sight. The British were utterly caught off-guard and it required a motley crew of French, Russian and Japanese marines supplementing a ragtag force of police and volunteers to tip the scales against the rebel soldiers.

What provoked this turning against the European community, which, just months prior, had been feted and serenaded during the Christmas Eve dinner and dance at the Sea View Hotel? According to the Court of Enquiry, feelings of dissent were seeded by anti-colonial elements. The first source of misinformation was Kassim Mansoor, a coffee-shop owner who lived near the Alexandra barracks. Another source of propaganda was Nur Alam Shah, a charismatic imam at the Kampong Java mosque. Both were supporters of the Ghadr movement that sought to stage an empire-wide uprising simultaneously on 19 February 1915. The distrust and misinformation effectively corroded the credibility of an already thin and complacent British colonial administration, especially in matters of security. The anti-colonial saboteurs convinced the soldiers that they were being shipped to Europe to fight their Muslim brethren, the Ottomans, who had just joined the Great War in Europe against the British. In reality, the soldiers were being sent to Hong Kong.

After the mutiny was resolved, punishment against the mutineers was swift and fatal. Far more ominous, the British profiled an entire race – resident Indians, most of whom had, ironically, flocked to Singapore because of British rule – for sanction. All Indian residents were required to register themselves with the colonial authorities. Virtually overnight, the British, and everyone else resident from the Bengal Native Infantry. With the threat of Dutch hostility after the signing of the treaty with Sultan Husain, these troops were reinforced by 200 more sepoys from Penang and 485 from Bengkulu. The Indian Army numbered as many as 150,000 men during the Napoleonic Wars, making it one of the world's largest standing armies.

Deploying these troops overseas helped Britain defend its empire and project global influence. Led by British officers, it was an army of mercenaries, most of whom enlisted not out of any love for the British Crown but because they wanted a military career or simply because it was a job that paid the bills. Indian Army regiments were ethnically and religiously diverse, although low-caste Hindus were barred. The Fifth Light Infantry Regiment, which would play a role in the 1915 Singapore Mutiny, comprised Pathans and Rajputs, Hindus as well as Muslims.

in Singapore, had to come to terms with a rapidly changing, riskier world.

The mutiny sparked the Straits Settlements to establish the Special Branch, the forerunner of systematic undercover surveillance, policing and capture of anti-colonial elements deemed dangerous, seditious or trafficking in illegal firearms or manufacturing fake passports. Recognising the integrated and global nature of misinformation and terrorism, the Special Branch also shared political intelligence with other security agencies. The Special Branch learned quickly that underground political organisations could use any association to front their activities. In response, they built up a network of informants that infiltrated all groups.

Public execution of convicted Indian mutineers.

While the 1915 mutiny by the backbone of British colonial security seems like a dimly remembered episode today, its consequences – including administrative complacency, exploiting religious and emotive ethnic sensitivities across boundaries and an excessive racial backlash by the colonial rulers against a largely innocent resident community – echo the concerns of today's era of globally linked security challenges.

The 1915 mutiny highlighted the influence of world events on Singapore, with the mutineers motivated by transnational revolutionary ideas and battle lines based on World War I alliances. On 15 February, a group of soldiers tasked with guarding German prisoners of war from the recently captured *Emden* mutinied. They were agitated by rumours that they were being posted to the Turkish front, where the Ottoman Sultan had allied with the Triple Alliance (Germany, Austria-Hungary and Italy) and urged Muslims to wage *jihad* (holy war) against the Triple Entente (Britain, France and Russia). The mutineers were caught between their divided loyalties to their British officers and to the wider Muslim *ummah* (community) under the Ottoman Caliphate. This conflict of loyalties added to Indian nationalist discourses that had been sparked by the radical Ghadr Party in India.

Anti-British feeling in India was also aroused by an incident that highlighted South Asians' second-class citizenship in the British Empire. On the eve of World War I in 1914, a group of Indians on board the SS *Komagata Maru* trying to migrate to Canada had been refused entry at Vancouver. On their return to Kolkata, 19 of them were killed by British police.

The British eventually suppressed the Singapore Mutiny through an international volunteer force comprising civilians and sailors from allied ships in port – Japanese, French and Russian. Although many Indian Army troops were not involved, and Sikh policemen in

A group photograph of the officers of the Singapore Volunteer Corps at Seletar Camp in 1928.

Singapore even fought against the mutineers, the incident aroused British suspicion of Indian soldiers, and of the wider Indian community. Indian troop deployment to the Straits Settlements was suspended, and a form of compulsory military service was introduced with the formation of the Singapore Volunteer Corps for adult male British citizens. Indian troops would not be deployed to Singapore until the outbreak of World War II.

The British also introduced greater surveillance of Indian residents, who had to register with the colonial authorities. The Seditious Publications (Prohibition) Ordinance (1915) was passed to allow for tighter censorship of Indian Muslim nationalist materials. All Indians – including Chettiars and Sikhs – were no longer regarded as loyal subjects but cast as the mistrusted Other. The Indian community took pains to advertise their loyalty to King and Country, with Indian Muslims organising large-scale rallies and denouncing the mutineers.

If the wider Indian population thus bore the brunt of British suspicion due to the actions of a relatively small section of their fellow countrymen, the Chinese communities in Southeast Asia, too, bore the brunt of Japanese retaliation for the actions of anti-Japanese elements among them. Like the Indians, Southeast Asian Chinese, including the Straits-born, tracked political developments in their homeland. Japanese aggression in China aroused their patriotism, which they expressed through boycotts of Japanese products as well as attacks on Chinese companies handling Japanese goods and buyers of Japanese goods.

Among the more aggressive anti-Japanese activists were members of the Malayan Communist Party (MCP) that was founded in 1930, nine years after the Communist Party of China. MCP members and sympathisers would later form the core of the resistance against the Japanese, aided by the British Special Operations Executive, a predecessor of Britain's intelligence service.

The main Chinese community, led by Tan Kah Kee, formed the China Relief Fund to raise money to help arm the war effort in China. Patriotic young Chinese returned to China to fight the Japanese. As Japan was still an ally of the British then, anti-Japanese actions caused problems for the colonial administration until 1940, when Japan joined the Axis powers.

Tan Kah Kee addressing a gathering of Chinese community leaders at Ee Hoe Hean Club.

When Singapore fell to the Japanese in 1942, one of the first things the Japanese military did was to single out Chinese men in a haphazard inspection process called Sook Ching. This exercise resulted in the deaths of tens of thousands of men, who were taken to remote areas of the island and executed. The actual numbers are unknown. Eurasians were another affected community because of their perceived loyalty to the British; although the men were not selectively killed, they had to wear a label and observe a curfew. Some were interned towards the end of the Japanese Occupation.

### British Collapse, Syonan and the Rise of Political Agendas

Britain's war with Japan was fought with officers and troops cobbled together from its colonies and spared from the war in Europe. From 1935, the Singapore garrison grew to over 3,000 officers and men. A series of defensive installations was quickly built between Sembawang and Changi, including concrete gun emplacements, airfields and hangars. Artillery defences comprising 29 guns were readied. But British and Singapore press reports of the "impregnable fortress" of Singapore were mere bluster. The naval base was empty, the airfields undermanned and ineptly equipped with ageing aircraft. The few Buffaloes and Brewsters were no match for the state-of-the-art Japanese Zeroes. Troop strength rose in the run-up to the end of 1941 but they comprised mostly raw recruits from Australia and New Zealand and Indian Army troops.

Initially, Malaya and Singapore were unaffected by the European war, which, in fact, propelled profitability and prosperity. In 1939, Malaya was supplying almost 40 percent of the world's rubber and nearly 60 percent of its tin. The Singapore economy was booming. The only source of distress among the mercantile community was the introduction of income tax in February 1941 to help fund the war in Europe.

In 1940, after the US oil embargo, the Japanese government began considering its "Southern Road" strategy. To access the Southeast Asian oil fields, it would have to battle American troops in the Philippines, the British in Hong Kong, Malaya and Singapore, and the Dutch in the East Indies. Bombing the US naval base at Pearl Harbor, Hawaii, to reduce American effectiveness was part of the strategy, which, as it turned out, forced an isolationist US to join the war in Europe and in the Pacific.

(*Above*) Japanese tanks rolling past Singapore's Supreme Court.

(*Left*) Artist Liu Kang included this sketch of Japanese soldiers in his compilation *Chop Suey* with the caption: "The Japanese Army entered Singapore on 15 February 1942 as conquerors. The supercilious behaviour of every rank and file was remarkable. They never expected that one day they would have to play the role of the vanquished."

Japan's Malaya Campaign began in the early hours of 8 December 1941, with troop landings in Singora (now Patani) in southern Thailand and Kota Bharu in northern Malaya, the bombing of Singapore, and across the International Date Line on the morning of 7 December, the bombing of Pearl Harbour. The speed and relative ease with which General Yamashita Tomoyuki's 25th Army captured Malaya and marched south to Singapore surpassed even Japanese expectations, with the British surrendering Singapore on 15 February 1942. The Malaya Campaign lasted a mere 70 days,

*The Meeting of General Yama-shita and General Percival* by Saburo Miyamoto, one of a group of Japanese artists commissioned to paint Japan's conquest of Southeast Asia. The artist exercised creativity in including a white flag of surrender with the British flag in front of it, which were not in the cramped room of the Ford factory where the surrender took place.

with British Prime Minister Winston Churchill describing the fall of Singapore as "the worst disaster and largest capitulation in British history".

Singapore was renamed Syonan, meaning "Light of the South", and was plunged into 42 months of oppression and hardship. Just days after Singapore fell, the aforementioned Sook Ching massacres took place, and as the weeks turned into months, the Japanese Occupation wrought devastation and major disruptions to ordinary lives, wrecked the economy, and saddled post-war Singapore with social problems that included crime, corruption, disease, homelessness, crumbling infrastructure, damaged facilities and a ravaged population.

It also left behind a state of political chaos. While the occupation did not plant the seeds of sustained cross-communal nationalist resurgence in Singapore, the trauma of war stimulated a sense of political awakening among locals. Indian nationalism emerged

Subhas Chandra Bose declaring the formation of the provincial government of Azad Hind (Free India) on 21 October 1943 at Cathay Building, Singapore.

with active Japanese support. Led by the charismatically militant Subhas Chandra Bose, the Indian National Army (INA) took root in Syonan. Comprising a coterie of Indian Army prisoners of war and civilians, including women, the INA, abetted by Japanese forces, marched on India to expel the British. The Indian-Japanese force reached only as far as Imphal, in northeast India, where Allied forces repulsed them in early 1945. With Bose's death in August that year, the INA story ended

Directly or indirectly, Japan's war sparked nationalist fervour and anti-colonial attitudes in Asia. The defeat of the Europeans by an Asian power, the growing momentum of the nationalist movement in India, the civil war in China and the emergence of nationalist movements across Southeast Asia all contributed to the sense of an imminent end to colonialism in Asia.

**Out of Chaos Come the Communists**
In Singapore, the prevailing state of social chaos and instability made the island fertile ground for political agitation. The conditions were ripe for developing anti-colonial attitudes and action, and the main political force capable of challenging the legitimacy of continued colonialism was the MCP. The communists who had been the anti-Japanese resistance in Force 136 – or the Malayan People's Anti-Japanese Army (MPAJA) – emerged from the Malayan jungles as the best-organised political group with the clearest agenda. Not only did the MCP have clout as defenders of the Chinese, Britain's recognition of its anti-Japanese efforts had

The returning British Military Administration was initially prepared to acknowledge the contribution made by the emerging MCP in sustaining an underground resistance against the Japanese Occupation of Malaya and Singapore. The MCP reciprocated by having their MPAJA commanders accept British awards. Chin Peng was one of the MPAJA leaders decorated by Admiral Mountbatten in a ceremony at the Padang on 6 January 1946. But thereafter the British started clamping down on the MCP, which retaliated by adopting a strategy of armed struggle led by Chin Peng for the next 12 years.

legitimised the party. Chin Peng, one of its more militant leaders, was decorated by the British. As a legitimate political entity, the MCP was represented in official committees tasked to redress post-war deprivations.

The MCP asserted itself in Singapore and major Malayan towns, forming open front organisations to press for self-rule, infiltrating trade unions to win over the working class, and championing Chinese schools and cultural groups to support Chinese education. Even before the return of the British, MPAJA forces had made their agenda known in Malayan towns by killing Malay policemen seen as Japanese collaborators and flying the MCP flag. These actions polarised the Malay and Chinese communities and also helped reinforce the anti-communist position of the Malays.

Initially, MCP tactics included industrial action, open front political activism and participation in Singapore's first non-communist political party, the Malayan Democratic Union (MDU), inaugurated in December 1945. The MDU's aim was a "self-governing united Malaya (inclusive of Singapore) within the British Commonwealth". However, the MCP's political goal was a communist Malaya, and its open front strategy changed when Chin Peng took over leadership. An advocate of armed revolution, Chin Peng succeeded Lai Teck, who was believed to have been a double agent (for the British and Japanese) and had absconded with party funds.

Under Chin Peng, the MCP grew more strident. Strikes increased and became more violent. Even as the unions pressed for higher wages, workers' rights and protection against dismissals, workers who did not conform to the orders of union leaders were threatened, assaulted and even murdered. At the same time, a core of secret party leaders and guerrillas retreated into the Malayan jungle, arming themselves with hidden caches of wartime arms. The incoming British Military Administration in 1945–46 was only partially successful in disarming these former resistance fighters.

### A 12-year Guerrilla War Disguised as an Emergency

The MCP struck Singapore with anti-colonial agitation, disruptive strikes and Chinese school protests, and mounted an armed terrorist insurgency in Malaya starting in 1948. With the aim of undermining the Malayan economy, the insurgents attacked rubber planters in remote plantations. At the height of the insurgency, the Malayan High Commissioner Sir Henry Gurney was ambushed and killed at Fraser's Hill in 1951. Called the "Emergency" for insurance purposes (Malayan rubber plantation owners did not want it labelled a war as Lloyds of London was unwilling to insure them against war losses), it was in fact a 12-year guerrilla war that only ended officially in 1960.

The British banned the MCP and imposed a series of regulations to combat the insurgency, the most severe of which were the Emergency Regulations applied to Malaya and Singapore. The regulations imposed the following: death penalty for firearms possession; detention without trial for up to one year; searches of persons and premises without warrants; seizures of belongings

The British printed this four-page pamphlet to brief – or warn – the local population of the terms of the Emergency Regulations. The inside pages included sections on assembly, publicity, property, detention, search, arrest, curfew, penalties and arms. As shown, the back page offered rewards for information.

General Gerald Templer (*centre*) is credited with the strategy for defeating the Malayan Communist Party guerrillas during his two years as High Commissioner to Malaya and Director of Operations. He famously declared that "the answer lies not in pouring more troops into the jungles, but in [winning] the hearts and minds of the people".

without warrants; the imposition of curfews; and the closure of open front organisations.

The Special Branch arrested hundreds of people. The mandatory carrying of identity cards arose from these regulations, which called for the registration of all residents above the age of 12 to deter communist infiltration. The identity cards replaced all other forms of identification papers, the first of which had been introduced in 1938, when registration of births and deaths became compulsory. After 1948, failure to show one's identity card could make a person liable to be arrested as a communist terrorist. The Emergency Regulations narrowed public discourse and dissent and stymied the development of civil society. Anti-colonial politics became more easily labelled as pro-communist. The Malayan Democratic Union eventually folded.

### Political Parties and Polls

Singapore could not be excluded from the political changes sweeping through the European colonies in Africa and Asia. The viable route towards replacing colonial rule, however, was a political party that was acceptable to the British. The promise of constitutional devolution of power and electoral reforms gave rise to several new political parties, which contested the first elections for a few seats in the Legislative Council in 1948. Parties like the Singapore Progressive Party comprised conservative elites who did not reflect grassroots anti-colonial sentiments. The electoral politics of 1948 and 1952 were experiments limited to a small group of Western-educated professionals.

Draconian controls did not stop radical political activism from sweeping Singapore by the early 1950s. The now-underground MCP continued its tactics of disruptive industrial agitation and Chinese school activism, perpetrating an ideology that was a mix of Marxism-Leninism, anti-colonialism, Chinese chauvinism and socialism. Stark inequalities coupled with poor socioeconomic conditions among workers and limited economic opportunities for the largely uneducated young stoked anti-colonialist feeling. There was organised action against unpopular colonial policies, a heightened sense of political consciousness and rising student activism among Chinese-educated and English-educated undergraduates.

In February 1953, the University of Malaya Socialist Club was formed by a group of students committed to the anti-colonial cause. The club's publication *Fajar*, with its anti-colonial tone, prompted British colonial authorities to act. In 1954, *Fajar*'s editorial board members were controversially arrested and charged with sedition. Defending the editors in court was Queen's Counsel D.N. Pritt, who was assisted by a young lawyer, Lee Kuan Yew. The editors were acquitted, and the publicity surrounding the case burnished the club's and Lee's anti-colonial credentials.

In May 1954, hundreds of students demonstrated against the National Service Ordinance, and over the following three weeks, thousands of students from several Chinese middle schools protested, demanding National Service exemption. A year later, the Singapore Bus Workers' Union organised a strike and picketed the Hock Lee Bus Company in response to a mass sacking of workers.

By 1955, Singapore had elected prominent criminal lawyer David Marshall as its first Chief Minister. Marshall, who led the Labour Front, promised independence for Singapore through political merger with the Federation of Malaya, which was about to obtain independence in 1957. Charismatic and popular, he had no hope of ending colonial rule if he could not control the situation on the ground. Left-wing forces had generated their own political momentum, and as labour unrest and riots continued unabated, Marshall emplaced a set of security laws, including the Preservation of Public Security Ordinance, promising to rescind the draconian Emergency Regulations after independence. But, unable to advance his Merdeka agenda in constitutional talks in London, he resigned in 1956.

His successor, Lim Yew Hock, was more amenable to cooperating with the British to take tough security measures against the left-wingers. Between September and November 1956, nearly 300 activists were arrested, with several trade unions, cultural organisations and middle school unions dissolved and publications banned. These measures triggered a general strike by Chinese middle school students, followed by three days of rioting, to which the police responded with tear gas attacks and a citywide curfew. The police raided trade union offices and arrested prominent left-wingers, including union leaders Lim Chin Siong, Fong Swee Suan and Devan Nair. In 1956, the adoption of the Rendel Constitution and the proposed introduction of mass-based electoral politics changed the political climate. New citizenship regulations had greatly enlarged the electoral base, and devising

An outstanding barrister, David Marshall shot to fame as the leader of a Labour Front alliance in 1955 and was Chief Minister for 14 tumultuous months of strikes and riots. His resignation, however, was due to his failure to secure from Britain an agreement for self-government for Singapore. He established the Workers' Party in 1957 in an attempt to return to active politics but lost control of the party and, in 1963, withdrew from politics.

Artist Tan Tee Chie captured the mood of Hock Lee Bus Company workers picketing against the sacking of their fellow workers, which escalated into the 1955 Hock Lee Bus riots.

ways to court the electorate would be the next stage of political development in Singapore.

## Cold War, Communal Politics and a Federation Idea

The Allied victory in World War II plunged the world into a new conflict: a covert war of competing political ideologies that weaponised spies and propaganda. The Cold War emerged soon after the German surrender and the disintegration of the uneasy alliance between communist Soviet Union and capitalist US and Britain. By 1948, Europe was divided into Eastern and Western blocs, separated by an ideological Iron Curtain. The Eastern Bloc comprised countries liberated by the Soviet Army and where Soviet Russia had installed communist regimes. The Western Bloc – the democratic bloc – comprised nations liberated by the US Army; in 1949 these nations would form the North Atlantic Treaty Organisation to combat Soviet influence, with their post-war recovery assisted by the US Marshall Plan. As agreed between the Allied powers, Germany was divided into West and East, and its wartime capital, Berlin, was similarly divided and separated by the Berlin Wall.

The Cold War's geopolitical tensions played into the rising tide of Asian anti-colonial nationalism, not least in Singapore. The Korean Peninsula had been divided into the North and South at the 38th Parallel, where the Soviet Army halted its liberation of Japanese-occupied Korea. As in Eastern Europe, Soviet Russia installed a communist regime, headed by Kim Il-sung, creating North Korea.

Kim, who was a captain in the Soviet Army, had enlisted to fight the Japanese. In 1949, China emerged as a communist republic and would serve as an ideological beacon for young overseas Chinese. Chinese chauvinism and communism became easily conflated.

During the post-war Allied occupation of Japan, Cold War strategy influenced General Douglas MacArthur's treatment of Japanese communists and socialists who had formed the only resistance to Japan's wartime government. The decision to leave Emperor Hirohito on the throne was part of his strategy to entrench right-wing conservatism and prevent the rise of the left wing.

In Vietnam, the war for independence led by a left-leaning Ho Chi Minh was shaping into a war fought by US-backed right-wing Vietnamese to staunch communism's advance. After the communist-nationalist Vietnamese army defeated the French at the Battle of Dien Bien Phu in 1954, the US was drawn into the Vietnam War as part of its Cold War strategy. Political unrest in Burma (Myanmar today) and Indonesia, where the PKI (Partai Komunis Indonesia, or Communist Party of Indonesia) was a powerful force, reinforced the belief that Southeast Asia was on the verge of turning Red.

Post-war Asia convulsed with Cold War tension and great power rivalry, which the British feared would jeopardise their interests in the region. They were alarmed by the attempts by the MCP and its covert organisations to control the political narrative and seize power. In coming to terms with its diminished status after World War II and its inability to continue maintaining its vast empire, Britain was motivated by Cold War tensions to divest itself of its colonies in a way that would keep the newly independent nations within the Western Bloc. For Singapore and Malaya, communal politics came to be mixed with Cold War strategy.

Communal politics emerged with the promulgation of the Malayan Union plan in 1946. It was based on Britain's desire to create a stable federation that would ensure the protection of its strategic and economic interests in the region after decolonisation. The plan separated Singapore from Malaya, although, as originally conceived, this was intended as a temporary arrangement. However, political developments on both sides of the Causeway made the reunification of the two territories increasingly unlikely. Not unexpectedly, with its liberal citizenship provisions for

Ho Chi Minh established communist rule over the Democratic Republic of Vietnam in 1945, which defeated French colonial forces at Dien Bien Phu in 1954, before going on to fight in US-backed South Vietnam for the reunification of the country. While Singapore had a policy of non-alignment during the Cold War, there was concern that events in Vietnam might trigger a "domino effect" that would impact Singapore eventually.

Malcolm MacDonald was Britain's Commissioner-General for Southeast Asia from 1948 to 1955, based in Singapore and tasked with implementing long-term British plans to form a confederation of the Federation of Malaya, Singapore, Sarawak, North Borneo and Brunei into a "British Dominion of Southeast Asia". This photograph shows MacDonald greeting the widow of wartime hero Lim Bo Seng at the laying of the foundation stone of the Lim Bo Seng Memorial in 1953.

non-Malays and recommendation to end the sovereignty of the Malay rulers, the plan met with vociferous opposition from Malay nationalists. Perceiving Malay rights and prominence to be at risk, they established Malaya's first Malay political party, the United Malays National Organisation (UMNO).

In 1948, the Malayan Federation plan to ensure Malay dominance addressed the concerns raised by detractors of the Malayan Union. Both plans left Singapore's position unchanged: the port-city with its predominantly Chinese population had no place in a Malay-dominated Federation. However, the issue of a merger between Singapore and Malaya remained alive as the idea that Singapore could survive on its own outside the Federation was never regarded as realistic. The prevailing view in Singapore was that the port-city would eventually return to the fold of its former Malayan hinterland and regain the economic advantages of such a political union.

Throughout the 1950s, Singapore grappled with economic woes caused by rapid population growth and declining entrepôt trade. Its exports to the region were significantly reduced because of protectionist policies by neighbouring countries and the increase in direct trading between them. To create enough jobs for its young, fast-growing population and reduce dependence on entrepôt trade, Singapore had to embark on a course of rapid industrialisation. To create a sufficiently large domestic market for its manufactured goods, integration with the Malayan hinterland was crucial.

During the 1955 and 1959 local government elections in Singapore, the topic of political merger with the Federation of Malaya, newly independent after 1957, featured prominently. Such a move was widely accepted as the only way Singapore could convince the British to grant it independence. Both the Labour Front coalition government, which was formed in 1955, and the People's Action Party (PAP), which came to power in 1959, pledged to achieve independence for Singapore through political merger with Malaya. The leaders of the respective governments – David Marshall and Lim Yew Hock, both of whom served as chief ministers of the Labour Front government, and Lee Kuan Yew, who headed the PAP government – made repeated overtures to Malayan Prime Minister and UMNO leader, Tunku Abdul Rahman, on the issue of merger.

PAP members canvassing for votes ahead of polling day 1959.

The Tunku, however, showed no interest in such a move. A direct merger with Singapore and the addition of 1 million Chinese to the Federation would upset Malaya's racial and political balance and serve as fuel for the right-wing elements in his party to undermine his position. Yet, the Tunku was also acutely aware that Singapore was at risk of being taken over by a radical left wing, a development that would have worried the strongly anti-communist Federation.

## A Tough, Thorny Slog to Merger

The PAP was formed in 1954 as an anti-colonial socialist party with the Tunku himself present at the founding ceremony. From the outset, the PAP was, to quote historians Yeo Kim Wah and

Lim Chin Siong's release from Changi Prison, 1959. The PAP's demand for the release of Lim and other political detainees after winning the 1959 elections created a dilemma for the colonial authorities. Should they concede to the PAP? Or should they stand firm and risk a standoff with the PAP then refusing to take office and possibly voiding the elections?

Albert Lau, "divided between two ideologically diverse factions with incompatible ends and means". Lee Kuan Yew and his band of English-educated democratic socialists – comprising economist and civil servant Dr Goh Keng Swee, university lecturer Dr Toh Chin Chye, civil servant K.M. Byrne and journalist S. Rajaratnam – were committed to achieving independence for Singapore through constitutional negotiations with the British.

However, a faction within the PAP with the same desire for independence believed in achieving it through a different ideology and methods. This latter group, who were also part of the PAP leadership, included largely working class trade unionists like Lim Chin Siong, Fong Swee Suan, Devan Nair and S.T. Bani. The colonial authorities viewed this group as the "radical left" and believed them to be communists or at least sympathetic to the Comintern's ideology of revolutionary anti-colonialism.

A party that did not include a Chinese-educated leadership would not have survived in the post-Rendel Constitution political climate, and the PAP was no exception. The significantly enlarged Chinese vote had to be taken into account. On the other hand, a Chinese-educated left-leaning leadership would have made the party unacceptable to the British. After the emergence of communist China in 1949, British suspicions of a communist agenda in the Chinese-educated community became heightened. This was not helped by the ongoing Emergency in Malaya. The deep divide between the English- and Chinese-educated in the 1950s was partially fuelled by the disaffection of the Chinese-educated in a colonial society where being English-educated was the best means for employment and advancement. This divide was a vote factor that the English-educated leadership of any political party had to take into account.

By 1959, when the PAP took over the reins of self-government, the party's left-wing faction had strengthened, fuelled by the popularity of left-wing politics, economic woes and a more pervasive Chinese chauvinism. Cold War tensions were about to realise Britain's "Grand Design", a strategy to control and influence the handover of power in its colonies to safeguard its strategic and political interests. The Federation of Malaya, with its solid anti-communist credentials after the Emergency, made the perfect counterweight to what looked like an increasingly powerful left-wing party in control in Singapore.

Concurrently, the British wanted to shed their colonial responsibilities in Borneo in a way that did not let the left wing triumph. Resource-rich Sabah (then known as North Borneo) and Sarawak and their non-Chinese populations of Dayaks and Ibans made perfect sweeteners for the incorporation of Chinese Singapore into a Federation of Malaysia. Oil-rich Brunei with its Malay population would have been even more acceptable to Malayan leaders.

In May 1961, the Tunku raised the possibility of linking Singapore, Brunei, Sabah and Sarawak and the Federation of Malaya closer together politically and economically. His reference to the danger of Singapore being a "Little Cuba" made obvious his rationale for this merger: he was afraid of communist contagion from Singapore.

Between 1955 and 1959, given the political and economic imperatives for merger, Lee Kuan Yew had demonstrated his willingness to cooperate with the Federation government by backing

Lee Kuan Yew taking the oath of office as Prime Minister in 1959. As there was no photograph taken of Lee's swearing-in, the National Museum worked with artist Lai Kui Fang in 1994 to reconstruct this visual of the historic event.

measures unpopular with PAP's left-wingers. One such measure was the creation of the Internal Security Council (ISC), comprising British, Malayan and Singapore representatives, to control security in Singapore. The PAP's left wing was deeply suspicious of the retention of extrajudicial powers, regarding it as an affront to genuine freedom from colonial rule. Lee's argument in the Legislative Assembly was that since the PAP's ultimate aim was to effect merger between Singapore and Malaya, "it was logical to recognise that the Federation would have a decisive voice in the affairs of Singapore, including its security".

From 1959, Lee also took steps to encourage a pan-Malayan outlook in Singapore with the hope of creating, in his own words, a "Malayanised Singapore man who would talk, think and act like the exemplary Malayans of the Federation". To facilitate the social integration of Singapore's predominantly Chinese population into the Malayan hinterland, and to impress UMNO-led Kuala Lumpur, Malay was made Singapore's national language and a Malay head of state (Yang di-Pertuan Negara) was installed. A Malay Education Advisory Committee was set up in 1959, and a Malayan school syllabus introduced.

The Tunku's 1961 proposal split the PAP. The crisis had already been brewing within the party. The longer the Tunku held out

The changing political mood of the 1950s was captured by Chua Mia Tee in this painting of a group of Chinese school students learning Malay as the national language of the emerging Singapore nation.

against merger, the weaker Lee's position would have been in several ways. Without merger, there was apparently no fix for Singapore's economic woes. Without fulfilling the PAP's election promise of merger and independence, Lee had no credibility with voters. As long as the possibility of achieving merger seemed remote, the left-wing faction had found it politically expedient to support reunion with Malaya. As anti-colonialists, the left-wingers regarded the split between Singapore and Malaya as a colonial decision that had to be corrected politically. However, once plans of the merger became a distinct possibility, left-leaning opposition to merger emerged. The key reason was the serious threat to the left posed by the Internal Security Council and an anti-communist Malayan government.

In 1961, when the PAP's left-wingers formed the Barisan Sosialis (Socialist Front) and crossed the floor in Parliament to join the opposition, the PAP government was faced with domestic objections to merger as well as tough Malayan negotiators. Lee countered the domestic opposition with a series of pro-merger radio speeches known as the "Battle for Merger" talks. He also called for a referendum that was structured in such a way that all voters were assumed to be in favour of merger and the vote was one about the specific form of merger. When the left called for the casting of blank votes as objection to merger, Lee countered with the argument that all blank votes would be regarded as for merger but its form was to be left to the government. In any event, blank votes played no part in the final outcome, so deep was the belief that Singapore's survival was tied to merger.

The three Borneo territories – Brunei, Sarawak and Sabah – were not exactly ecstatic over merger. Last-minute left-wing agitation had led to a referral to the United Nations to determine the will of the people and a delay in the proclamation of Malaysia Day. Brunei made an eleventh-hour withdrawal but not before political resistance to the Greater Malaysia project culminated in armed rebellion in December 1962, led by A.M. Azahari of the Parti Rakyat Brunei. Although the Brunei Revolt was short-lived, its repercussions were far-reaching. It precipitated a major crackdown on the radical left in Singapore and Malaya, where the left wing's growing influence and electoral base worried Kuala Lumpur. One of the Tunku's conditions for Singapore's entry into the Federation was the arrest of the radical left in Singapore. British historian T.N. Harper has argued that "the detention of the left, and in particular Lim Chin Siong, was the price to pay for Singapore's independence within Malaysia, and played no small part in accelerating its achievement".

Shortly before the Brunei Revolt, Lim had met with Azahari. This meeting, coupled with the Barisan Sosialis' subsequent expression of support for the revolt, was highlighted by the PAP government as an act of "subversion and violence by Communists in aid of alien interventionists" and therefore a threat to Singapore's security. Singapore's Special Branch obtained intelligence reports that Brunei rebels had approached Barisan elements to whip up support for the rebellion beyond Brunei. This raised concerns that the left-wing forces in Singapore were contemplating subversive activities, in concert with external elements, to sabotage the Malaysia plan.

In the early hours of 2 February 1963, a security swoop codenamed Operation Coldstore was launched following orders from the joint Security Council of Singapore, Malaya and Britain. Lim Chin Siong was among the 130 people arrested. Detainees included political leaders, trade unionists and student leaders. Two months earlier, the Malayan Special Branch had launched a similar operation and arrested 50 suspected communists. Operation Coldstore dealt a severe blow to the Barisan Sosialis, which was left rudderless with the arrest of several party leaders. It eased, however, the political tension for Lee Kuan Yew and enabled him to navigate the final stages of merger negotiations with the Federation.

### One Country, Two Citizenships

Negotiations with the Malayans were even harder. Issues over citizenship and voting rights were tough nuts to crack. While the Tunku was prepared to integrate the territories of Malaya and Singapore, he was less inclined towards uniting its people. The Malayan Prime Minister was primarily concerned about the effect on the Federation's racial balance and the impact on Malay political primacy. Preferring the politically safer policy of exclusion through restrictive citizenship arrangements for Singapore, he introduced the distinction between Malaysian "citizens who are Singapore citizens" and Malaysian "citizens who are not Singapore citizens".

The differentiated citizenship and its concomitant voting rights were designed to protect the dominance of the Malay vote. After independence in 1957, Malaya had enforced a strict citizenship policy for non-Malays, a policy that was reinforced during the

Malayan Emergency, which saw significant Chinese involvement and heightened communal tensions between the Chinese and Malays. The Tunku would see to it that the Chinese in Singapore would not upset the Federation's political and racial equation.

When the differences between the citizenship rights in the Borneo territories and those in Singapore became known, it proved to be one of the thorniest issues between the PAP and the Barisan Sosialis as well as with the Tunku, who was determined to refuse Malaysian citizenship to an additional 1.3 million Singaporeans. Unlike the citizenship provisions in the Malayan Federal Constitution, the Singapore Citizenship Ordinance (1957) was more liberal. A person could obtain citizenship in Singapore quite simply by having parents who were already citizens, or by registration if he was born in the Federation or a Commonwealth country or had resided in Singapore for a total of 12 years. He could be a naturalised citizen if he had resided in Singapore for an aggregate of 10 years during the preceding 12 years, and if he had spent three to four years serving the armed forces in Singapore.

Lee Kuan Yew with Tunku Abdul Rahman, with whom he had a close but difficult relationship.

To allay the acrimony, Lee proposed a change in terminology: Singapore citizens were to be called "Federation citizens", "citizens of the new Federation (Singapore)" or a "national of the new Federation". The 1962 London Agreement on Citizenship was a political compromise. The Tunku acceded to Lee's appeal for a change in terminology because the he knew that he was not conceding any significant political ground. Whatever Singapore citizens were called, their right to vote remained restricted to within Singapore, and the politics of the two territories would remain separate. This may have been the Tunku's plan but it was not to be, as post-merger events would prove.

Negotiations over financial controls, revenue sharing and a common market were equally difficult. One issue was a $150 million loan from Singapore to Sabah and Sarawak for development projects, with $100 million being interest-free for five years. On the eve of its signing, the Tunku and Lee agreed and initialled on the back of an envelope that 50 percent of the labour for these developments was to come from Singapore. The loan never materialised, as difficulties arose over the conditions for labour deployment and the interest to be levied at the end of five years. Singapore was unwilling to discuss the terms of such a huge loan without a clearer Malayan commitment to a common market.

Besides demanding a taming of the left wing in Singapore, the Tunku also wanted to reduce Singapore representation in the Federal Parliament to only 15 members, 10 fewer than it was entitled to based on its population size. In return, he was prepared to concede to Singapore the retention of wider local powers than the other Federation member states. Among these wider powers was control over labour and education. Chinese education, a long-standing issue even in colonial times and a major concern of the PAP's Chinese-educated base, had been hijacked by the left to further its political agenda.

The differences were papered over and the Malaysia Agreement was signed in London on 9 July 1963, marking the official formation of the Federation of Malaysia. The creation of Malaysia was an ambitious project that brought together disparate territorial entities at varying stages of political and economic development with different histories and ethnic compositions. The Borneo territories were even in a different time zone. The only common link between them was the experience of British rule.

### Regional Opposition to the Federation

Apart from being difficult, the birth of the Federation of Malaysia stirred regional opposition. The Philippines and Indonesia objected to the merger as both had vested interest in the Borneo Sea littoral. Manila had laid claim to Sabah in 1962 while Indonesia had seized the disputed territory of former Dutch West New Guinea (autonomous provinces within Indonesia today).

Indonesia's President Sukarno in his September 1963 speech declaring Indonesian confrontation against Malaysia.

The most serious opposition came from Indonesia, which was Singapore's southern hinterland and an important trading partner. Spurred by the nationalist PKI, which had influence on President Sukarno, Malaysia was labelled a "neo-colonialist plot", and Indonesia embarked on a militant Konfrontasi (confrontation) in an attempt to unravel the already tenuous Federation. First, Indonesia banned trade with Malaysia. This crippled but did not end Singapore's centuries-old barter trade with the Indonesian islands. Then, saboteurs were sent to perpetrate terrorism in Singapore, Malaya, Sabah and Sarawak. Konfrontasi only ended in 1966 after the Indonesian Army staged a coup to overthrow Sukarno and the PKI, and Suharto, an army general, came to power.

The actual day picked for proclaiming Malaysia Day had been postponed to 16 September 1963, pending the outcome of a

United Nations report on the will of the people of Sabah and Sarawak regarding merger. The delay prompted Lee to take matters into his own hands. On 31 August 1963, the Federation of Malaya's national day, he held a Malaysia Solidarity Day mass rally and march-past on the Padang. There, he made a speech declaring de facto independence for Singapore:

> *We look upon ourselves as trustees for the Federal government in these 15 days. We will exercise these powers [in foreign affairs and finance] in the interests of Malaysia…. This proclamation today is an assertion of our right to freedom.*

The Tunku reprimanded Lee for his audacity, who was reported to have shot back: "If anybody has got to complain, it is we and the British. We run this place." The British representative in Singapore, Lord Selkirk, chose to say nothing. However, the sharp exchange was an ill omen – the first of many to come.

### Singapore Exceptionalism

The PAP government saw Singapore as a special political entity, different from the other member states of Malaysia. For one, it was independently wealthy, with reserves of $100 million, accounting for about 40 percent of the economic power of the new Federation. Attempts by Malaysian Finance Minister Tan Siew Sin

Singapore suffered the wrath of Indonesia's opposition to the Federation when, on 10 March 1965, a bomb planted by two Indonesian commandos inside MacDonald House on Orchard Road exploded, killing three people and injuring 33. The perpetrators were caught, convicted and sentenced to death. The Singapore government's rejection of Indonesia's appeal for the lives of the two commandos led to a chill in relations up to 1973.

to tap this wealth would further sour relations with Singapore (it did not help that Tan was a cousin and rival of Goh Keng Swee, Singapore's Finance Minister).

Right up to the eve of the signing of the Malaysia Agreement, money matters had been difficult to resolve. One sticking point was Tan's insistence on the central government being the collector of Singapore's taxes. This was resolved by Singapore agreeing to do the collection but handing over 40 percent to the central government for services. Defence, internal security and finance came under the central government. Unsettled even when the Malaysia Agreement was signed was the question of a Malaysian common market. In exchange for the institution of a common market, Singapore had to agree to impose a raft of tariffs that Malaya had in place. The common market became hostage to Tan's plans for Singapore. To balance the Federal budget, the Malaysian Finance Minister wanted a revision of Singapore's contribution to the central government – from 40 to 60 percent of its revenue.

For the first Malaysian Budget, Tan, who did not consult Singapore's Finance Ministry, unilaterally raised revenue by introducing a new turnover tax and payroll tax. This would have affected labour-intensive industries in Singapore. Tan's other measures seemed designed to undermine Singapore's industrialisation programme. As Singapore was about to start producing light bulbs at a new factory, Tan's ministry introduced an import tax on light bulbs and

Malaysian Finance Minister Tun Tan Siew Sin (*fourth from left*) visiting Jurong Industrial Estate with his Singapore counterpart, Dr Goh Keng Swee (*fifth from left*), in 1964. Goh's vision of Singapore and Malaysia having a common market was blocked by Tan.

designated Singapore-made light bulbs as imports even though Malaya had no light bulb factory to protect and Singapore was part of Malaysia.

When Britain introduced a textile quota to protect British textile manufacturing, Singapore's share was reduced to less than its pre-Malaysia quota, although the bulk of the Malaysian textile industry was Singapore-based. The drastic quota cut scuttled plans for 50 more garment factories and the potential for 10,000 jobs for Singaporeans. Goh, whose primary concern at this time was to expand employment for the growing population, responded by threatening a boycott of British goods, which upset Kuala Lumpur. Differences over economic strategies and money matters spiked, ratcheting up Kuala Lumpur-Singapore tensions.

More insoluble differences surfaced. During the post-Malaysia Singapore general election in September 1963, the Tunku visited Singapore to campaign for an UMNO Singapore candidate and learnt that South Africa had a consulate in Singapore. Malaya was a key proponent of an international trade boycott of South Africa for its apartheid policy. The Tunku was even more disturbed to discover that the Bank of China and Bank of Indonesia were still active in Singapore. Not only did anti-communist Malaya have no formal relations with communist China, it had long regarded the Bank of China as a conduit for funding subversive communist activities regionally. By ordering the Chinese bank's closure, the Tunku was trying to cut a traditional tie with Beijing that would affect thousands of Chinese businesses in Singapore. Goh refused to close the bank, citing a clause in the Malaysia Agreement that allowed existing institutions in Singapore to carry on after merger. Still, the Malaysian Finance Ministry took over the Chinese bank and began the process of shutting it down.

### Managing Multiracialism as Separation Looms
Political differences were simmering too. Although Singapore and Malaya were superficially alike in having a multiracial society, their politics of managing such a society differed significantly. The vote in Singapore was along non-communal party lines, whereas in Malaya the different communities voted along communal party lines: the minority community parties – the Malayan Chinese Association (MCA) and the Malayan Indian Congress (MIC) – had allied with the majority community party, UMNO, to form the Alliance government.

In Singapore's 1963 general election, parties in Malaya's Alliance government joined hands with the Singapore People's Alliance to contest the polls. Alliance candidates were resoundingly rejected and the PAP won in the three Malay-dominated constituencies despite the Tunku and Kuala Lumpur-based UMNO politicians campaigning for UMNO Singapore candidates. Relations between Singapore and Kuala Lumpur worsened after these election failures.

Communal tensions rose, fanned by Malay extremists decrying the PAP's alleged oppression of Singapore Malays and attempts to undermine Malay special rights. Exchanges grew more racially charged, and UMNO extremists led by Syed Ja'afar Albar, UMNO's strident Secretary-General, whom Lee labelled as "ultras" or "ultranationalists", seized every opportunity to incite communal tensions between Chinese and Malay Singaporeans. The Malay newspaper *Utusan Melayu* kept up a hate campaign against Lee. At a highly publicised convention hosted by UMNO Singapore on 12 July 1964, Syed Ja'afar Albar set the tone with a zealous speech and called for Lee's arrest for alleged pro-communist leanings:

> *I am happy today we Malays and Muslims in Singapore have shown unity and are prepared to live or die together for our race and our future generation. If there is unity no force in this world can trample us down, no force can humiliate us, no force can belittle us. Not one Lee Kuan Yew, a thousand Lee Kuan Yews… we finish them off.*

UMNO Secretary-General Syed Ja'afar Albar vowed to "fix" Lee Kuan Yew for UMNO's electoral loss in the September 1963 Singapore general election.

The PAP held a counter-meeting on 19 July attended by 900 Malays representing 103 organisations in Singapore. Lee addressed the meeting, saying that efforts were being made to help the Malays overcome the problems of education, employment and housing but the Singapore government would not go back on its constitutional provisions and introduce special rights, as in the Federation, for Singapore Malays. Singapore Malays, however, did have one affirmative action privilege that no other community enjoyed, and that was free education up to university level if they qualified. The goal was to advance the Malay community based on the principle of education as the route up the economic ladder.

The inflammatory speeches and extremist press created a febrile atmosphere ripe for the communal riots that erupted during a rally to celebrate Prophet Muhammad's birthday on 21 July 1964. Despite a curfew, the violence continued for a week, leaving 23 dead and 454 injured. More racial violence occurred in September, taking 13 lives and injuring 106, allegedly triggered by Indonesian saboteurs exploiting heightened tensions between the two communities.

While Lee and the Tunku and ministers in Singapore and Kuala Lumpur set up goodwill committees and toured the island to restore calm, the extremist press continued its vitriolic anti-Lee campaign, blaming him for the riots. When race riots erupted in Kuala Lumpur between Malays and Chinese in 1969, the communal tension spread to Singapore. One Chinese and three Malays were killed, and 11 Chinese and 49 Malays injured. This would be the last communal riot in Singapore.

The Tunku was unwilling or unable to control his party's more extreme members, and his bid to separate the politics of Singapore from the politics of Malaya quickly unravelled. When Lee tried a different tack in March 1964 by courting UMNO to displace the MCA from the Alliance, the Tunku stayed loyal to the MCA. Lee's manoeuvre was in tandem with a PAP bid to contest the Malayan general election in March 1964. Technically barred from contesting in Malayan elections, the PAP had navigated around this by establishing the Democratic Action Party (DAP). Part of the motivation in wanting to increase its presence in the Federal Parliament was to have more say in it, and in the process protect Singapore's interests. Even so, with the exception of Devan Nair

A police contingent forming up against rioters in 1964. The scale and nature of the race riots that erupted in July and again on 3 September severely taxed police resources. Military reinforcements had to be called in.

in Bangsar, the DAP lost every seat it contested despite attracting massive crowds at its rallies.

In April 1965, while racial tensions were still unresolved, the Singapore representatives in the Federal Parliament – Malayan-born Toh Chin Chye and S. Rajaratnam, and Lee, who was Singapore-born – set out to form a united front in the Federal Parliament to oppose the Alliance government. The Malaysia Solidarity Convention to promote a "Malaysian Malaysia" was to be a grouping of non-Malay parties that did not subscribe to communal-based politics. Besides the PAP, the Convention included four Malaysian opposition parties, including Sarawak parties. The Convention declared:

> A Malaysian Malaysia means that the nation and state is not identified with the supremacy, well-being and the interests of any one particular community or race. A Malaysian Malaysia is the antithesis of a Malay Malaysia, a Chinese Malaysia, a Dyak Malaysia, an Indian Malaysia or a Kadazan Malaysia. The special and legitimate rights of different communities must be secured and promoted within the framework of the collective rights, interests and responsibilities of all races. The people of Malaysia did not vote for a Malaysia assuring the hegemony to one community. Still less would they be prepared to fight for the preservation of so meaningless a Malaysia.

This proved to be a key turning point. The concept of a Malaysian Malaysia redefined Malaysian nationalism and raised the issue of native and immigrant rights and citizenship. By drawing together a grouping of non-Malay parties, the Convention had the potential to draw attention to non-Malay dissatisfaction with Malay domination and, if it succeeded in building up more non-Malay support, could tip the balance of power in favour of the non-Malays. As the Convention's enormous potential began sinking in, the extremists began calling for Lee's arrest, with rumours circulating of this impending probability. In 1962, the Tunku had said that he firmly believed "in peace and racial harmony, and I will fight any element that aims to destroy them":

> If in merger with Singapore there is likely to be trouble and bloodshed, I would rather leave Singapore alone in spite of the potential danger that an independent Singapore would bring to the Federation.

In March 1965, Lee's high-profile tour of Australia and New Zealand further angered the Tunku when Lee spoke his mind about Singapore-Kuala Lumpur relations. The Tunku wanted Malaysia portrayed as a prosperous country enjoying racial harmony. In May, Lee returned from a tour of Asian countries and on arrival at the airport said: "If we find Malaysia cannot work now, then we can make alternative arrangements." Malaysian Finance Minister Tan Siew Sin reminded Singapore that it could not exist alone, warning: "Even secession from Malaysia cannot eliminate the fact that less than 1.5 million Chinese are surrounded by over 100 million people of the Malay race in this part of the world." In a heated parliamentary exchange on 6 June, Tan said that as long as Lee remained Prime Minister of Singapore, there could be no cooperation with Singapore.

In July, a year after the race riots and with no let-up in the political tension, Goh Keng Swee met privately with Malaysian Deputy Prime Minister Tun Abdul Razak and a coterie of Malayan leaders in Kuala Lumpur to discuss ways to resolve the issues. The decision for Singapore to separate from the Federation was made. Singapore's political merger with Malaya proved to be short-lived and turbulent, lasting just one year and 11 months.

### Separation and the Aftermath

Independence for Singapore came overnight, unexpectedly for all but a tiny few. When the news broke on 9 August 1965, there was shock and disbelief. A strongly worded editorial published in *The Straits Times* on 10 August 1965 declared that "separation was the last thing the public expected". Singapore had joined the Malaysian Federation in September 1963, and the ferocity of the high-stakes contest over the political merger was still fresh in public memory. The editorial continued:

> *The dangers of separation have not vanished. The economic advantages of integration have not grown less. It is a thousand pities that the clock has been thus set back.*

The pre-Malaysia political narrative about Singapore's decline without Malaya had been too effective. The prevailing view was that Singapore's survival depended on staying in the Federation, and the decision to leave was seen as a serious existential threat to Singapore's future. Yet, it had been clear early on that merger was proving to be economically disadvantageous to Singapore.

The Singapore flag was raised at the United Nations for the first time in September 1965. Two years later, the establishment of the Association of Southeast Asian Nations (ASEAN) ushered in a new era of regional stability and cooperation for Singapore and its neighbours.

Although it had served to entrench the PAP's moderate faction in power by wiping out its left-wing opposition, in economic terms merger had been a failure. Dutch economist Dr Albert Winsemius, who served as an economic advisor to the Singapore government between 1961 and 1984, recalled in his 1982 oral history interview with the National Archives of Singapore: "It was practically impossible to launch any project in Singapore during the Malaysia days. Everything was dragged down."

Throughout the 1950s, Singapore was under mounting economic pressure because of explosive population growth and declining entrepôt trade. Its exports were reduced significantly because of the import quotas that many countries, including Britain, imposed to protect their industries. Entrepôt trade, Singapore's lifeblood, was threatened by an increase in direct trading.

Pre-war Singapore had a small industrial sector linked to the processing of primary commodities sent from the Malayan hinterland. Tin smelting was one. The first modern tin smelter in Singapore was financed by European investment and built on Pulau Brani in 1890 by the Straits Trading Company. Before this European investment, Chinese tin smelters were only able to extract 60 percent of tin from its ore. The tin from the Pulau Brani smelting facility was marketed as Straits tin and its quality began attracting tin ore from places as distant as Alaska, Australia and South Africa as well as neighbouring Bangka and Belitung in the Dutch East Indies.

Other pre-war industrial enterprises included pineapple canning, brickmaking, sawmilling, the manufacture of simple rubber goods and various food enterprises, such as the production of soya sauce, fresh noodles and cooking oils. The first Singapore census of industry was conducted only in 1960. In the 1950s there was also a market gardening sector where farmers reared chickens, ducks and pigs, and supplied the island with eggs. None of these economic sectors, however, would have created enough jobs to engage the post-war baby boom.

Tin ingots smelted in Singapore. Singapore functioned as a staple port processing the tin, rubber, timber and other products of the peninsula up to the 1980s.

As early as 1954, a team of World Bank experts invited to examine the economies of Singapore and Malaya identified industrialisation as an avenue for job creation. One proposal was to establish a board to promote industry. A predecessor of the Economic Development Board, the Industrial Promotion Board had a short life – beginning in 1957 and ending the following year. Its chairman,

David Lee, who was the president of the Singapore Manufacturers' Association, resigned in frustration, citing the impossibility of establishing industry and promoting economic development with a measly budget of $1 million and no means to borrow money. He proposed an Industrial Development and Finance Corporation backed by $10 million and given borrowing powers.

In 1960, a second United Nations team visited Singapore to study its industrialisation potential. The team was led by Winsemius, who had been a director of industrial development in the Netherlands' Ministry of Finance and had overseen Dutch post-war recovery. On the team's agenda was a review of the plans for Jurong Industrial Estate, Goh Keng Swee's brainchild. Goh himself had half-joked that the plan might end up being dismissed as "Goh's Folly" because of its audacious premise of creating an industrial park in the wilderness.

The Economic Development Board (EDB) was formed in 1961 with a $100 million budget. Unlike the Industrial Promotion Board, the EDB could borrow and lend money to back viable industrial projects. In 1968, the EDB's industrial financing activities would be taken over by the Development Bank of Singapore (DBS Bank today). Easily available factory space combined with the EDB's slew of incentives drew investors to Jurong. Pioneer certificates, tax breaks and official assistance were accorded to investors to set

The transformation of the mangrove swamps of Jurong into an industrial estate was first proposed by the 1960 UN Survey Mission led by Dr Albert Winsemius. Spearheaded by Dr Goh Keng Swee (*fourth from left, in white shirt and white trousers*), the Economic Development Board started developing Jurong, completing the first phase in 1967. In the 1990s, under the Jurong Town Corporation, Jurong was further developed to become a model for industrial estates in China and India.

up shop in Singapore with minimum fuss. This one-stop take-off approach would eventually turn into the hallmark of the EDB, and of investing in Singapore as a whole.

The early industrialisation programme was based on the model of import substitution, where industries were established to produce for the home market, and tariffs put in place to protect these industries. Given Singapore's tiny domestic market, integration with the Federation's economy and access to its much larger markets was crucial for this model to work. Goh made this clear when he noted, "Major changes in our economy are only possible if Singapore and the Federation are integrated as one economy."

## "Black Swan from the Netherlands"

Dr Albert Winsemius (1910–96) started by suggesting the manufacture of shirts and pyjamas, and more brazenly, that women be employed as factory hands to stitch the garments for export – a revolutionary notion at a time when women, especially Asian women, were conventionally confined to the home. By the time he relinquished his job as chief economic adviser some 23 years later, the Dutch economist turned out to be an economic and sociopolitical seer whose initial five-stage blueprint to lift Singapore out of the doldrums of underdevelopment to a "From-Third-to-First-World" achievement reverberates to this day.

Winsemius played a key role in helping Singapore's founding fathers (Lee Kuan Yew, Goh Keng Swee, Hon Sui Sen, Lim Kim San and Howe Yoon Chong among them) develop a blueprint for the nation's progress. He arrived in 1960, leading a UN task force that answered the fledgling self-governing island's call for expert economic help. A mere eight months later, he delivered a detailed report that helped identify markers that have since become iconic hallmarks of Singapore's exceptionalism.

Winsemius recommended that the government: (1) Make use of the high aptitude of its people. (2) Build homes for everyone, connecting families personally to the nation-building project. (3) Introduce technical education in a world where the rule of technology was still nascent. (4) Turn Singapore into a financial centre. (5) Grow Singapore into a container and air hub (with the expectation that the terminal would be a virtual white elephant initially), stripping from the start any sort of protection via tariffs and landing rights by air.

The idea of a Malaysian common market had been the economic lure of merger with Malaya. Yet, Goh had pessimistically shared with Winsemius that the Malaysians would not go for the common market plan. He anticipated the difficulties that Singapore's development plans could face from Malaysian Finance Minister Tan Siew Sin. In the run-up to merger in 1963, the EDB pushed through as many applications for pioneer industry start-ups as quickly as it could, said S. Dhanabalan, a young EDB officer then:

*We knew that once the Malaysian Finance Ministry was in charge, everything would slow down. In fact, during our two years in Malaysia, only two applications were approved, but*

Winsemius was counter-intuitive, unconventional, and a hard-nosed outlier. Impressive as his blueprint of the brick-and-mortar tools of economic modernisation was, some would argue that his most vital contribution was his sociopolitical astuteness, which hewed to one basic golden rule: to cut Singapore's cloth to fit what worked in order to grow an undeveloped and subsequently orphaned nation which was economically unprepared and sociopolitically unsettled.

His first two vital bits of advice for the government were to muzzle the Communists and to keep colonialism's icon – the statue of Raffles – standing (literally). This was advice that ran against the grain of conventional political and economic belief and practice among most of the newly independent nations then, which favoured protectionism over open trade borders.

And where many new nations believed that the tide of history and the East would inevitably turn Red and that that was a good thing, Winsemius diagnosed an ideology that spelt economic devastation: senseless strikes and stoppages that no nation, particularly a struggling, straggling one, could afford.

So, where many young nations righteously tore down vestiges of their colonial past, Singapore's leaders internalised the Dutchman's advice about the practicality of prominently displaying Raffles' statue as a subliminal marker of a young nation's trustworthiness and credibility to becalm and attract modern, wealthy, largely Western investor nations.

Sensibility rather than sentiment underscored his expert advice. The irony is probably inescapable to Singaporeans with a sense of history: that while the British took the Dutch out of the colonising equation in Singapore, ruling it for almost a century and a half, it was a Dutchman who arrived here to help craft postcolonial Singapore's economic epiphany. He did it without a formal pact and within a spare time-frame: two weeks in every year, he returned to Singapore to help shape the nation's growth.

Winsemius' legacy was that he not only helped craft the hardware that Singapore needed to hardwire its economy, he went further, immersing himself in its "software" – the culture, the politics. He understood the need to navigate the intricate multi-ethnic and multi-religious nuances that could easily derail the best-laid economic plans.

*with unimplementable conditions. Those which we had quickly approved pre-Malaysia were what kept us going during those years.*

Years later, in 1996, Goh revealed in an interview that he was the one who raised the secession of Singapore as a solution to the intractable differences between the two governments. If the political merger was proving impossible, so was economic integration, and no one was more aware of the difficulties than Singapore's Finance Minister. If economic development for Singapore through merger was not possible, the purpose of merger was negated.

### A Counter-intuitive Road to Economic Relevance

After independence, Singapore's survival as a nation depended on its economic relevance. If it could not develop economic relevance, its days would be numbered. The region's earlier great port-cities had all faded when they lost their economic relevance as trading ports, as had happened to Singapore in centuries past.

Goh thought counter-intuitively on the question of hinterlands. Contrary to the traditional perception of cities as the creations of their countryside, he argued the reverse, that cities created their hinterlands and countryside. Pointing to the Malay Peninsula, he wrote in an article in 1967 that as Singapore's hinterland during British colonialism, the peninsula was financed by Singapore capital and nurtured by Singapore management and skills, all the way until 1967, for not only Malaysia, but also Indonesian Kalimantan and Sumatra. Goh explained:

> *It is the role of the cities in Asian countries, established and developed as beach-heads of Western Imperialism, to transform themselves under their independent national governments into beach-heads of dynamic modernisation process to transform the countryside.*

Overnight, the EDB changed its industrialisation strategy from import substitution to export-led industrialisation through multinational corporations (MNCs). In this new strategy, Singapore would manufacture for global markets and make the entire world its hinterland. This step towards a globalised economy was a natural trajectory given Singapore's early history when its relevance had been regional. But in the 1960s, at a time when developed and developing countries were walling up their industries with protective tariffs on the import substitution model, it was a bold move. Singapore's export-led industrialisation may have anticipated the sea change in industrial practices that were in the offing, which would see manufacturers in industrial nations capitalising on cheap labour in developing countries.

The shift to export-led manufacturing and attracting multinationals presented multifaceted challenges. One was the need for skilled manpower at every level of production, thus necessitating the establishing of more polytechnics and training institutes, as well as increasingly sophisticated tertiary education. Singapore Polytechnic had been established in 1954 as soon as an industrialisation plan was mooted.

Another challenge was making products that met international market standards and demands. The Industrial Research Unit was set up in the EDB in 1963 with Colombo Plan aid from New Zealand. Backed by engineers and scientists from Singapore Polytechnic and the University of Singapore, the unit would subsequently evolve into the Singapore Institute of Standards and Industrial Research in 1969. In 1961, the EDB's $100 million budget included not only financial but also technical assistance for local entrepreneurs. It was the ability to keep up with new technology, meet the demands of MNCs and become part of their valuable supply chains that kept Singapore's manufacturing sector humming. This was due in no small part to the engineers and

"The Conventional Way" by Au Yee Pun refers to the pre-container loading and unloading of cargo at the wharves of Keppel Harbour.

scientists brought in to raise manufacturing standards and improve product quality.

Singapore's rapid development on all fronts owed much to its pool of well-trained manpower, in which the Colombo Plan played a big role. Conceived at the 1950 Commonwealth Conference in Colombo, Ceylon (now Sri Lanka), the Colombo Plan provided the framework for the Commonwealth's developed countries to share solutions for development issues – through human resource development, transfer of technology and equipment, training and consultancies – with the newly emerging nations. Once Singapore became self-governing in 1959, it joined the Colombo Plan.

By 1971, more than 1,200 Singaporeans had received their university education and training on Colombo Plan scholarships, with

Singapore's aspirations to global-city status are captured by Thang Kiang How in this dense painting.

"Construction of Sheares Bridge" by Lai Kui Fang documents the beginnings of the development of the reclaimed land at Marina South. Land reclamation started in the 19th century with the reclamation of the coast along Beach Road. Between 1960 and 1990, a systematic reclamation programme added 7.6 percent (or 44 square kilometres) to Singapore's land area. Since then, Singapore has continued to reclaim land, with plans to increase its land area by a further 7 percent by 2030.

many trained as engineers and scientists. Skilled manpower went on to develop a reliable supply of electricity, clean water, good housing, transport facilities and financial structures as the essential facilities for attracting direct foreign investment to Singapore. By 1971, Singapore was contributing to this technology transfer to other developing countries by offering Colombo Plan study and training awards.

Royal Dutch Shell was among the first multinationals to ramp up investments here. Pre-war Singapore, with its excellent shipping facilities, had been the MNC's oil storage facility. In 1961, Shell invested in its first Asian oil refinery, which would lead to the plastics and chemicals industries in Singapore. Another early Singapore investor was Dutch multinational Philips. Winsemius personally

Workers at Sembawang
Shipyard, in a painting by
Lee Boon Wang.

visited Philips' headquarters in Eindhoven to plead Singapore's case. Shipbuilding and ship repair came in the late 1960s with the Japanese multinationals. Singapore's very first heavy industry initiative was National Iron and Steel Mills in 1961. Managed entirely by local businessmen, it was the first major industrial enterprise to be set up at Jurong Industrial Estate, in August 1963.

The focus of the 1960s industrialisation programme was on labour-intensive industries as a way of creating jobs for the baby boomers. The textile industry – from the making of garments to textile manufacturing – was important for generating jobs. Factories making low-tech consumer goods such as mosquito coils and light bulbs sprang up, followed after 1965 by TV assembly and the production of small domestic appliances.

Goh officiated at every factory opening, and these events were always publicised extensively for political capital. The voters had to see that jobs were being created. After 1965, economic development took place at such a fast clip that the 1971 withdrawal of British troops and the closure of its Singapore military base went by with a whimper instead of a bang. When the withdrawal had been announced four years prior, there were fears of a major recession because of the 20 percent stake the British military presence had carved into the Singapore economy. The bases employed some 30,000 civilians, thousands of women worked as domestic helpers for British families, and many shops, bars and restaurants depended on military patronage.

By 1971, Singapore was practically at full employment. If the economic strategy in the 1960s was labour-intensive industries, the 1970s would see the focus shift to skills-intensive industries, and in the 1980s and 1990s, Singapore would pivot towards capital-intensive industries and a knowledge-based economy. In the 21st century, the early investments in agencies promoting science and

The public housing programme undertaken by the Housing and Development Board from 1960 changed not only Singapore's landscape but also Singaporeans' social memories of urbanism as a way of life. Ong Kim Seng's painting captures a typical scene that more than 85 percent of Singaporeans would see on returning home in the evening.

technology as well as education in science and engineering would take the knowledge-based economy to new heights (led by the Agency for Science, Technology and Research) and prompt huge investments in research and development. The industrial sector is today a far cry from the 1960s economy, when the manufacture of mosquito coils was big news.

In 2015, Monetary Authority of Singapore Managing Director Ravi Menon, in a keynote address at the Singapore Economic Review Conference, said:

> In 1965, Singapore's nominal GDP per capita was around US$500. We were at the same level as Mexico and South Africa. In 1990, GDP per capita had risen to about US$13,000, surpassing South Korea, Israel, and Portugal. In 2015, GDP per capita was about US$56,000. We had caught up with Germany and the United States.

The current Port of Singapore encompasses six different sites – Keppel, Brani, Tanjong Pagar, Pasir Panjang, Jurong and Sembawang.

Post-independence economic relevance was no longer an issue. Preserving and developing this relevance is the challenge today.

# IN A NUTSHELL

Chapter Seven concludes the story of Singapore's history over the past seven centuries by narrating its trajectory in the 20th century. Broadly speaking, it can be divided into two connected halves, examining Singapore's two main roles: first, as Britain's crown jewel and port-city through which the Malay Peninsula's staple products such as tin and rubber were processed for export, which was disrupted and devastated by the Japanese Occupation; and secondly, as a post-war city facing the challenges of seeking a new constitutional arrangement in an era of decolonisation, while continuing its existence as a port-city servicing the region. But separation from Malaysia in 1965 and other regional hostilities scuttled this future, forcing Singapore to de-emphasise its links to the region in favour of internationalising its port-city functions for multinational enterprises.

In the 21st century, the question then becomes: Is such de-emphasising of Singapore's regional connections still viable? Or perhaps it is time to reconnect Singapore's history to the longer stories of the Malay world and the rest of Asia? The threads from each of the separate chapters will be brought together in the final section of this book, its Conclusion.

Staff photograph of the University of Singapore History Department, 1966. (*Front row, from left*) Sharom Ahmat, Jenny Chong (department secretary), C.M. Turnbull, K.G. Tregonning, Eunice Thio, Irene Ee (administrative staff), Wong Lin Ken. (*Back row, from left*) Yeo Kim Wah, Edwin Lee, R. Sunthralingam, Chiang Hai Ding, Yong Chin Fatt, Png Poh Seng, Mat (Mohd. Ibrahim bin Baba, administrative staff).

# CONCLUSION

# Singapore's Challenge

What does the future have in store for Singapore? City-states do not have good survival records. The Greek city-states no longer exist as states. Most have not vanished physically, but have been absorbed by the hinterland in a larger entity.

Singapore's first Prime Minister Lee Kuan Yew
in the concluding passages of his memoirs

### Framing Singapore's History

This history of Singapore – within a lengthy time span of seven centuries beginning with the first material evidence of settlement on the island in the 14th century – is an attempt to contextualise today's dilemmas as recurrences in the long cycles of time. It is a history in which the trajectories of time are disrupted by the turbulence of conflict and wars as well as the competition for trade and commerce. The challenge for Singapore today is to find a way to connect its national narrative of a tangible history of economic progress to the intangible cycles of globalisation.

This volume argues for a linear-cyclical construction of Singapore's history as a harbour settlement or port-city in the past 700 years. The continuity of Singapore's history as a harbour or port may lie less in the presence or absence of settlement on the island, but more in the waters around Singapore, which mariners and traders had to pass en route from the South China Sea to the Bay of Bengal and vice-versa.

As such, a major focus of this long-cycle history of Singapore has been on documenting our knowledge of the waters around Singapore. It is in the archived maps, charts and rutters giving sailing directions for safe passage through the four routes around Singapore – the Tebrau Strait between Singapore and Johor, the Keppel Harbour waterway between Singapore and present-day Sentosa, the fairway south of Sentosa, and the main Singapore Straits (which was earlier known as Governor's Strait) – that a continuous history of Singapore may be found.

What were the critical events that led to the alternating use of these sea lanes? What were the events that led the Portuguese and Dutch to propose constructing forts on Sentosa and at Changi in the 17th century? The history of settlement on Singapore would have pivoted very differently if these proposals had materialised. This history has reviewed the use of the sea lanes around Singapore in the context of the long cycles of European power politics from the 17th century as they played out between the respective East India Companies in the region.

In this respect, Raffles' objective in establishing a "British station" on Singapore was to ensure that the Dutch in Bintan would not be able to block British shippers and merchants from using the sea lanes around Singapore on their way to or from China. He believed the Dutch were evil and threatening, and concluded along with the country traders that they were aiming to close the sea lanes to the British. But Raffles appears to have been unaware or to have forgotten that such a move would have been in violation of the 1784 Treaty of Paris, which assured freedom of passage to all through the waters of the Riaus.

Raffles' station took on a life of its own, transforming into a thriving port-city on the back of Britain's rise to dominance in the long cycle of European power politics in the late 18th century following the French Revolution.

As such, Singapore's history as a port-city, like that of other port-cities, details how the city and land behind the port have been linked and united with the maritime world in front of it. It is also a history of the interaction between Asian and European trading communities that created a viable waterfront to attract and service maritime trade.

### The Long Tail of Pre-colonialism
Within these long cycles of time, 14th-century Temasek rose to eminence at the tail end of what has been termed an "Asian sea trade boom" or an "Asian commercial ecumene" between the 10th and 13th centuries. This upturn in Asian maritime trade was driven by an economic revolution in Song China which continued into the Yuan dynasty. But a series of environmental crises and cycles of climate change in the 14th century forced China and West Asia to turn inwards.

Episodes of climate change wrought drought and famine as well as plagues of locusts on Yuan China from 1324 to 1330 and again from 1339. According to Chinese records, a series of "dragons" brought floods, followed by drought and famine, accompanied by extremely cold winters. A plague pandemic finally ended the Yuan dynasty in 1368. Concurrently, the Black Death decimated an estimated 30 percent of Europe's population and spread to West Asia, which would have depressed trade in the Indian Ocean.

This loss of the China market and the waning of trade in the Bay of Bengal may have led to Temasek's decline at the end of the 14th century. As Chapter Two has demonstrated, Temasek – or Singapura – as an autonomous trading settlement was eclipsed during Melaka's century, when it became a key outpost of the Melaka Sultanate and a base of the sultans' sea nomad warriors.

Singapore's chance for a second rise emerged towards the end of the 16th century, when the island became the gatekeeping port to the riverine economy of the Johor sultans at their peripatetic capitals up the Johor River (Chapter Three). This trading settlement on Singapore – administered by a Shahbandar acting as a proxy for the Johor sultans – thrived on Johor's trade with Ming and Qing China and other Melaka Straits ports.

Singapore was abandoned when a new line of Johor sultans shifted their capital to Bintan island at the beginning of the 18th century. Once again, Singapore was eclipsed, and this time round depopulated by Iranun raiders (Chapter 5).

### Europe's Age of Empire

The Portuguese in the 1500s, and later the Dutch and English in the 1600s, entered an Asian trading world dominated by a series of great Asian empires: the Ming in China, the Mughals in India, the Safavids in Persia and the Ottomans in West Asia. For much of the 16th and 17th centuries, divergent preferences – terrestrial versus maritime conquest, strategies for the localisation of economic competition, and imperatives for war – enabled the Portuguese as well as the Dutch and English East India Companies to compete against each other and co-exist with the Asian empires. But this state of affairs was about to be reconfigured in a new age of empire in the latter half of the 18th century. By then, Dutch domination of European cycles of global power, inherited from the Portuguese cycle in the 16th century, was waning. At the same time, Britain emerged as the rising European power, driving a new cycle of greater technology, connectivity and interdependence in global trade and politics, and thus, creating a "modern" world.

Raffles arrived on a depopulated island and accelerated Singapore's third cycle of settlement. A century later, the island's residents hailed him as the hero to whom they owed everything. Raffles was the archetype of the mythical champion who envisioned turning the East Indies British, and he battled the odds to realise that dream by taking a calculated risk to establish a British station on the island. Sadly, Singapore, as Raffles' "child", was unappreciated, if not unwanted; it might not have survived had it not been for the "trader-statesmen" and "trader-fighters" to whom the Singapore residents of 1919 were the heirs.

Raffles, in chess-speak, would be more of a knight, effective in close encounters because of his exceptional ability to hurdle past obstacles – human, natural or contrived. It was the shifts in global power in the late 18th century that provided him with the opportunities to manoeuvre and succeed in his efforts (Chapter Five). The cycles of trade and commerce underpinning the structure of power in the Indian Ocean were on the cusp of major shifts.

The British station that Raffles established survived and thrived because of the shift in trade dominance from the merchant empires of Portugal's Estado da India, Holland's VOC and the British EIC to the private or country traders. Singapore rose to pre-eminence within 30 years of its establishment in spite of the lack of support from the EIC, which provided minimal administrative help and funds. But unlike the earlier two cycles of settlement, it not only survived its centenary and a further 50 years, it also survived a turbulent crisis to transition into a fourth cycle of settlement as a modern Asian city-state.

### The Arrows and Cycles of British Rule

On a unilineal timescale, only the third settlement of Singapore as a British colonial port-city connects to its fourth settlement as a modern city-state. The absence of any micro-changes that can be linked as events to connect the third and fourth settlements of Singapore to the earlier pair of settlements does not lead to the conclusion of a discontinuous history. Rather it points to the limitations of viewing Singapore's history within the linear trajectory of "time's arrow".

Time's arrow does not solely arc upwards towards progress, but can also curve downwards into decline and decadence, as happened with

14th-century Temasek and the 16th- and 17th-century Shahbandaria. The idea that societal cohesion can disintegrate because of the loss of economic "fortune" or the breakdown of political order is widespread among many societies. It pre-dates European Enlightenment ideals of progress. Arguably, it was these concerns about the possible decay of the *polis* or city-state, and how to arrest it, that preoccupied Plato in his best-known work, the *Republic*. Decline was established as a recurring theme in European history from early modern times in the works of Giambattista Vico (1668–1744) and Edward Gibbon (1737–94). In contrast to the optimism of the British in 1919 (albeit short-lived), the Germans appeared more pessimistic of their future, as reflected in the work of the philosopher Oswald Spengler on the decline of the West.

Time's arrow, as analysed by Isaac Newton at the start of his *Principia*, is "absolute, true and mathematical time, of itself, and from its own nature flows equably without relation to anything external". The issue with this understanding is that if time flows without relation to anything external, how is it to be sensed and measured? This was an issue Newton recognised, and he expended the last 30 years of his life trying to anchor the flow of time to specific events in space. Restated, the flow of time as an arrow has to be fixed to a point in space if it is to be sensed. Newton tried to link the abstract physical world of his *Principia* to the world of men in his posthumously published *Chronology of Ancient Kingdoms* and *Observations upon the Prophecies of Daniel and the Apocalypse of St. John*.

The implication of this physical conception of time on our understanding of Singapore's past is that unless there is an action or activity that can be fixed in the space associated with Singapore, then time and history flow equably past a depopulated island until Raffles arrives to start a chronology.

But there is an alternative experience of time underlying the history of Singapore – one that starts in 1819 and moves through a series of connected events to today. Time, as we experience it, also moves in cycles, when events from our past are perceived to recur, and the rhythms of intangible forces from the past continue into the present.

The events of the past seven centuries do not link up to form a continuous causal sequence leading to our present. Instead, these events oscillate in cycles of episodic settlement, alternating uses of the sea lanes to sail past Singapore, and recurring cycles of trade and commerce. Framing Singapore's past this way may facilitate a keener understanding of how the periods when events were taking place on the island can be connected on a linear timescale to the "empty" phases when nothing seems to have happened.

As Mircea Eliade explicates in *The Myth of the Eternal Return,* his landmark study of time's arrow and time's cycle, most cultures have traditionally envisaged events not as a linear and progressive historical construct, but simply as the sum total of creative recurrences of primordial archetypes. Cyclical time leads to a more stable and reassuring future, whereas with progressive time, the human race may believe it can steer the course of history, but in reality cannot anticipate the disruptive forces its actions may unleash, leading to terrifying futures. For Eliade, this is the "terror of history".

Singapore's British residents in 1919 premised their optimism of achieving another century of prosperity on their perception of the thriving present being the outcome of a century of improvement and progress, with Singapore evolving from a Dependency of the government of India in 1824 to a Crown Colony in 1867.

### Pax Britannica's Rude Awakening

So it was that in 1919, British merchants, bankers and colonial officials in Singapore could, with justifiable pride, celebrate the centennial of Raffles' arrival in Singapore. Britain had just emerged victorious from World War I, and four years earlier, had scuttled a mutiny by Indian troops that threatened the colony. Singapore had risen to the status of capital and crown of British Malaya. It was the staple port through which not only the tin, rubber and other produce of the peninsula were processed and exported, but also the oil of Riau and east Sumatra.

A celebratory tome, *One Hundred Years of Singapore,* was published – dedicated to "the race of trader-statesmen and the clan of trader-fighters" who "sowed the seed of Empire in a rudely furrowed sod". Singapore's British residents could, from their point in time, look forward to ushering in a second prosperous century. For the editors and contributors of *One Hundred Years of Singapore*, the colony was racing towards a bright future as part of a resurgent British Empire "upon which the sun never sets".

This view of history as a process of continuous improvement in human society was a principal assumption of European worldviews associated with the Age of Enlightenment, beginning in the 18th century. It was based on a belief in the primacy of reason and experience, which led to a utilitarian approach to society and ethics, and an optimism that such an approach would bring about the society's intellectual and material advancement.

Education was the key to achieving this, and within such a view of human society, promotion of education became a principal theme of the centennial celebrations. One of the things which emerged from the celebrations was the proposal for a college of higher education, which was realised when the Raffles College of Arts and Sciences was established in 1928. After World War II, the college would merge with the King Edward VII Medical College established in 1905 to form the University of Malaya.

In hindsight, the optimism in 1919 about Singapore's future was in part driven by the rising cycle of global trade and technological innovation which had begun in the last decade of the 19th century. But that virtuous cycle of global trade was disrupted by a series of unexpected micro-events surrounding the assassination of the Austrian Archduke Franz Ferdinand, unleashing deep turbulent forces which erupted in World War I. The end of that war was the start of the sunset on Pax Britannica and the transfer of global political and economic power to America.

However, Malaya's British residents in 1919 could not foresee that their trajectory had reached its zenith and was plunging towards its nadir. The sun was starting to set on the British Empire. The British residents of Malaya may have been aware of the fact-finding mission undertaken that year by Viscount John Jellicoe to assess Japan's threat to the British Empire. But they could not have anticipated that Jellicoe's then-controversial recommendations, that a rising Japan should be countered with a massive naval build-up in the Far East, would lead to the construction of a naval base on Singapore to defend not only the capital and crown of British Malaya, but also the dominions of India, Australia and New Zealand.

These plans and preparations for Singapore's defence came to a traumatic and catastrophic end on 15 February 1942. For Singapore residents, their trajectory of time's arrow disintegrated at 1730 hours when General Arthur Percival arrived at the Ford Factory at Bukit Timah to surrender to General Yamashita Tomoyuki. Singapore entered a liminal period, in which time had no significance, for the next three years and six months.

The lead-up to World War II confirmed the delegitimisation of Pax Britannica and marked the start of a new cycle of global power, connectivity and economics, with the United States dominating the global institutions it led, particularly the Bretton Woods system and the World Bank, for the next 30 years. It is this cycle, of a declining Pax Britannica and rising US hyper-power competing with the Soviet Union in the Cold War, which frames and shapes the competing narratives of Singapore's search for its future in the 1950s and eventually the formation of Malaysia in 1963.

### Untangling a Post-war Conundrum

The British returned to Malaya in 1945 with the intention of resuming colonial rule. But the trauma of 42 months of Japanese Occupation, when time stopped and the future was opaque to the residents of Singapore, had wrought massive changes.

The challenge for Singapore was to work out new futures that would recognise its historical continuity as the peninsula's staple port but at the same time reject colonial assumptions of decolonisation. And so, it was a British "Grand Design" for a federation of its former colonies on the peninsula and Sarawak and Sabah with Singapore that came to be adopted to reconcile the two goals. The hope was that the new Federation would ride on time's arrow to a glorious future. For Singapore, that future came crashing down on 9 August 1965.

That Singapore was able after 1965 to survive and prosper was in large part due to its successful alignment with the cycle of US hyper-power. But the 1986 Plaza Accord that allowed the Japanese yen to float free of the US dollar was a sign that even this cycle of US hyper-power was starting to weaken. However, this is hindsight wisdom, as the collapse of the Soviet Union in 1989 was hailed as the triumph of the US liberal order and, as American public intellectual Francis Fukuyama declared, "the end of history".

As an economist, Goh Keng Swee was well aware of the cyclical nature of the economy. In one of his more theoretical pieces of economic analysis ("Some Unsolved Problems of Economic Growth") in 1975, he turned to Russian economist N.D. Kondratieff's analysis of the capitalist economy wheeling in 60-year cycles. The Austrian political economist Joseph Schumpeter modified Kondratieff's analysis into a theory of business cycles driven by entrepreneurship and technological innovation.

Goh was able to follow the Schumpeter/Kondratieff analysis of a new business cycle starting in the last decade of the 19th century. Hence, a new cycle of business would begin after World War II, subsequently downswinging in 1975. But Goh in 1975 could not sense where he was on the downswing of this Kondratieff cycle, and could not perceive the emergence of any technological innovations or cycle of entrepreneurship, as predicted by Schumpeter, that would drive a new cycle of development. It was only in the 1990s that this Schumpeter cycle of technological innovation emerged, with the advent of new information and communications technologies and the development of the internet, and launched a new Kondratieff cycle.

The intriguing question is whether, during these 60 years of what is now labelled "globalisation", the US, since the 1990s and into the 21st century, has been experiencing a new upswing of its cycle of power, riding on the information and communications technologies it dominates; or whether, like Britain after World War I, it has entered a lengthy decline, making way for an Asian Renaissance, with China rising and India looking east. Or, was the Asian Financial Crisis in 1997 and the financial crisis following the collapse of Lehman Brothers in 2008 the beginning of a cycle of "deglobalisation"?

The vision of Singapore continuing as the staple port with some common-market-like mechanism within Malaysia had to be dismantled, as a Singapore bereft of its hinterland was believed to be doomed to failure. It was a future that Lee Kuan Yew starkly spelt out in the first volume of his memoirs. Singapore might have to crawl back to Malaysia, Lee wrote, and that was a future he and his colleagues rejected resolutely.

Singapore had to forget, and decouple itself from, its colonial and precolonial past, as S. Rajaratnam reflected in 1987:

> Until very recently Singapore's past was a matter of supreme indifference for most Singaporeans simply because they believed this island never really had a history worth remembering… [P]atriotism required that we perform some sort of collective lobotomy to wipe out all traces of 146 years of shame.

### Rajaratnam's Raffles, Goh's Forgotten Gem

Elsewhere, Rajaratnam also explained why he and his colleagues opted to elevate Raffles as the founder of Singapore instead of "contriv[ing] a more lengthy and eye-boggling lineage by tracing our ancestry back to the lands from which our forefathers emigrated – China, India, Sri Lanka, the Middle East and Indonesia":

> *The price we would have to pay for this more impressive genealogical table would be to turn Singapore into a bloody battleground for endless racial and communal conflicts and interventionist politics by the more powerful and bigger nations from which Singaporeans had emigrated.*

Without a past they could link their present to, Rajaratnam and his colleagues had no option but to look to the future to prime the hope for a positive arc of time's arrow. The two decades after 1965 were spent constructing new futures for Singapore as a city-state that could stand alone. Singapore's founding fathers sought historical analogies for its future in the early modern Venetian city-state and the ancient Greek city-state of Athens. In 1988, Brigadier-General George Yeo, in his farewell speech on resigning from the Singapore Armed Forces to enter politics, exhorted his colleagues to consider Venice – a city-state which survived the flight of time – as a lesson on how to defend Singapore.

The study of Venetian history had largely been helmed by Goh Keng Swee in the seminars he conducted at the Civil Service College. Goh also examined more recent analogies for Singapore's future as a city. In a largely forgotten 1967 article, he offered a counter-intuitive argument against the conventional view that hinterlands created cities. He suggested that the reverse was equally true: it was cities that created their hinterlands. He recounted how the development of the Malay Peninsula as Singapore's economic hinterland "was financed by Singapore capital and nurtured by Singapore management skills" – something that Singapore was continuing to do in 1967 as "the natural trading centre" for Malaysia and Indonesian Kalimantan and Sumatra. He stated:

> *It is the role of the cities in Asian countries, established as beach-heads of Western imperialism, to transform themselves under their independent national governments into beach-heads of a dynamic modernisation process to transform the countryside.*

Whereas Singapore's colonial governors and officials in 1919 were able to link their present to their past, half a century later Goh and his colleagues could not do so. Instead, they had to couple their present with possible futures. In 1972, Rajaratnam argued that the pessimistic historical logic of Singapore's imminent doom, predicated upon its dependence on a peninsular hinterland, was being disproved by Singapore's new future as a global city. He was two decades ahead of his time. It was only at the end of the Cold War that Singapore was able to regionalise its economy and join the new global network of trade, finance and services led by cities such as London, New York and Tokyo.

The Singapore story as it has evolved since 1997 is about the progressive development of the British station established by Raffles in 1819 that traversed linearly in time to grow, by 1919, into the capital and crown of British Malaya. It then transformed 50 years later into a city-cum-nation state that was expected to fail but instead survived and prospered, and despite the odds, became an aspiring global city.

**The Second-last Word**
Lee Kuan Yew postulated this sobering hypothesis in the final pages of his memoirs:

> *The city-state of Athens has disappeared. But the city of Athens survives in Greece, with the Parthenon to bear witness to the achievements of the original Athenians. Other cities in big countries have been sacked and destroyed, their people decimated or dispersed, but the nations they were part of have endured and new people have repopulated and rebuilt them. Will Singapore the independent city-state disappear? The island of Singapore will not, but the sovereign nation it has become, able to make its way and play its role in the world, could vanish.*

In Lee's framing of Singapore's postcolonial fate within a Eurocentric *telos* of progress and development on a linear timescale, Singapore could indeed falter, stumble and vanish, never to rise again. This seven-century history has collated sufficient evidence indicating that Singapore emerged as a port and city and vanished on at least three occasions.

Within these long cycles of history, Singapore may yet plunge into another decline, as Lee feared, but it may also subsequently rise again, at some point in time, in some other form, when another group of elites re-establishes the island's centrality as a service centre and trading state in a future cycle of globalisation.

# BIBLIOGRAPHY

## Introduction

Ban, Kah Choon, Anne Pakir, & Tong Chee Kiong. (2004). *Imagining Singapore*. Singapore: Eastern Universities Press.

Borschberg, Peter. (2017). Singapore in the cycles of the longue durée. *Journal of the Malaysian Branch of the Royal Asiatic Society, 90*(1), 29–60.

Borschberg, Peter. (2019). The strategic location of Singapore in the longue durée (c. 1290–1824): An alternative analytical framework. In Hui Y.F. & Linda Y.C. Lim (Eds.), *Singapore: The future of a legacy*. Singapore: ISEAS-Yusof Ishak Institute.

Borschberg, Peter, & Benjamin Khoo. (2018). Singapore as a port city, c.1290–1819: Evidence, frameworks and challenges. *Journal of the Malaysian Branch of the Royal Asiatic Society, 91*(1), 1–27.

Chew, Ernest Chin Tiong, & Edwin Lee. (1996). *A history of Singapore*. Singapore: Oxford University Press.

Chiang, Hai Ding. (1978). A history of Straits Settlement foreign trade 1870–1915. *Memoirs of the National Museum* (No. 6). Singapore: National Museum.

Cleary, Mark, & Goh Kim Chuan. (2000). *Environment and development in the Straits of Malacca*. London: Routledge.

Coclanis, Peter A. (2006). *Time's arrow, time's cycle: Globalization in Southeast Asia over la longue durée*. Singapore: Institute of Southeast Asian Studies.

Hack, Karl, Jean-Louis Margolin, & Karine Delaye (Eds.). (2010). *Singapore from Temasek to the 21st century: Reinventing the global city*. Singapore: NUS Press.

Heng, Derek. (2009). From political rhetoric to national narrative: Bi-culturalism in the construction of Singapore's national history. In Derek Heng, & Syed M. Khairudin Aljunied (Eds.), *Reframing Singapore: Memory, identity and trans-regionalism*. Amsterdam: Amsterdam University Press.

Heng, Derek. (2010). Casting Singapore's history in the longue durée. In Karl Hack, Jean-Louis Margolin, & Karine Delaye (Eds.), *Singapore from Temasek to the 21st century: Reinventing the global city*. Singapore: NUS Press.

Hong, Lysa, & Huang Jianli. (2008). *The scripting of a national history: Singapore and its past*. Singapore: NUS Press.

Kwa, Chong Guan. (2004). From Temasik to Singapore: Locating a global city-state in the cycles of Melaka Straits history. In John N. Miksic, & Cheryl-Ann Low Mei Gek (Eds.), *Early Singapore, 1300s–1819: Evidence in maps, text and artefacts*. Singapore: Singapore History Museum.

Kwa, Chong Guan. (2006). Writing Singapore's history: From city-state to global city. In Kwa Chong Guan, *S. Rajaratnam on Singapore: From ideas to reality*. Singapore: World Scientific & Institute of Defence and Strategic Studies.

Kwa, Chong Guan. (2018). Introduction. In Kwa Chong Guan & Peter Borschberg (Eds.), *Studying Singapore before 1800*. Singapore: NUS Press.

Kwa, Chong Guan, & Peter Borschberg (Eds.). (2018). *Studying Singapore before 1800*. Singapore: NUS Press.

Lee, Geok Boi. (1998). *Singapore: Journey into nationhood*. Singapore: National Heritage Board.

Lee, Kuan Yew. (2015). *From third world to first: The Singapore story, 1965–2000: Memoirs of Lee Kuan Yew*. Singapore: Marshall Cavendish Editions & Straits Times Press.

Rajaratnam, S., Chan Heng Chee, & Obaid ul Haq. (1987). *The prophetic & the political: Selected speeches & writings of S. Rajaratnam*. Singapore: Graham Brash.

Reid, Anthony. (2010). Singapore between cosmopolis and nation. In Karl Hack, Jean-Louis Margolin, & Karine Delaye, *Singapore from*

*Temasek to the 21st century: Reinventing the global city.* Singapore: NUS Press.

Reid, Anthony. (April 2014). Cosmopolis and nation in central Southeast Asia (ARI Working Paper, No. 22). Retrieved from www.nus.ari.edu.sg/pub/wps.htm.

Tarling, N. (Ed.). (2012). *Studying Singapore's past: C.M. Turnbull and the history of modern Singapore.* Singapore: NUS Press.

Tregonning, K.G. (1969). The historical background. In Ooi Jin Bee, & Chiang Hai Ding (Eds.), *Modern Singapore.* Singapore: University of Singapore Press.

Turnbull, Constance Mary. (2009). *A history of modern Singapore, 1819–2005.* Singapore: NUS Press.

Wee, C.J. W.-L. (2003). Our island story: Economic development and the national narrative in Singapore. In Abu Talib Ahmad & Tan Liok Ee (Eds.), *New terrains in South East Asian history.* Singapore: Singapore University Press. Also in Wee, C.J. W.-L. (2007), *The Asian modern: Culture, capitalist development, Singapore.* Singapore: NUS Press.

Wong, Lin Ken. (1981) A view of our past. In Lee Yik, & Chang Chin Chiang (Eds.), *Singapore in pictures.* Singapore: Sin Chew Jit Poh & Ministry of Culture.

Wong, Lin Ken. (1991). Commercial growth before the Second World War. In Ernest C.T. Chew, & Edwin Lee (Eds.), *A history of Singapore.* Singapore: Oxford University Press.

**Chapter One: The 14th Century**

Bellina, Berenice, et al. (2014). The early development of coastal polities in the upper Thai-Malay peninsula. In Nicolas Revire, & Stephen A. Murphy, *Before Siam: Essays in art and archaeology.* Bangkok: River Books, The Siam Society.

Bronson, Bennet, & Jan Wisseman. (1976). Palembang as Srivijaya: The lateness of early cities in Southeast Asia. *Asian Perspectives: The Bulletin of the Far-Eastern Prehistory Association, 19*(2), 221–39.

Brown, C.C. (1970). *Sejarah Melayu; or Malay annals.* London: Oxford University Press.

Buckley, Brendan M., Roland Fletcher, Wang Shi-Yu Simon, Brian Zottoli, Brian, & Christophe Pottier. (2014). Monsoon extremes and society over the past millennium on mainland Southeast Asia. *Quaternary Science Reviews, 95,* 1–19.

Crawfurd, John. (1830). *Journal of an embassy from the Govenor-General of India to the courts of Siam and Cochin China.* London: H. Colburn and R. Bentley.

Hall, Kenneth R. (2011). *A history of early Southeast Asia: Maritime trade and societal development, 100–1500.* Lanham: Rowman & Littlefield.

Heng, Derek. (1999). Temasik as an international and regional trading port in the thirteenth and fourteenth centuries: A reconstruction based on recent archaeological data. *Journal of the Malaysian Branch of the Royal Asiatic Society, 72*(1), 113–24.

Heng, Derek. (2001). The trade in lakawood products between South China and the Malay world from the twelfth to fifteenth centuries AD. *Journal of Southeast Asian Studies,* vol. 32, no. 2, 133–49.

Heng, Derek. (2002). Reconstructing Banzu, a fourteenth-century port settlement in Singapore. *Journal of the Malaysian Branch of the Royal Asiatic Society,* vol. 75, part 1, 69–90.

Heng, Derek. (2004). Economic exchanges and linkages between the Malay region and the hinterland of China's coastal ports during the 10th to 14th centuries. In John N. Miksic, & Cheryl-Ann Low (Eds.), *Early Singapore 1300s–1819: Evidence in maps, text and artefacts.* Singapore: Singapore History Museum.

Heng, Derek. (2006). Export commodity and regional currency: The role of Chinese copper coins in the Malacca Straits region, tenth to fourteenth centuries. *Journal of Southeast Asian Studies, 37*(2), 179–203.

Heng, Derek. (2011). Situating Temasik within the larger regional context: Maritime Asia and Malay state formation in the pre-modern era. In Derek Heng, & Syed Muhd Khairudin Aljunied (Eds.), *Singapore in global history.* Amsterdam: Amsterdam University Press.

Heng, Derek. (2012). *Sino-Malay trade and diplomacy from the tenth through the fourteenth century.* Singapore: Institute of Southeast Asian Studies.

Hsu, Yun-Tsiao. (1948). Notes on the Malay Peninsula in ancient voyages. *Journal of the South Seas Society, 5*(2), 1–16.

Lim, Chen Sian. (2017). Preliminary report on the archaeological investigations at the National Gallery Singapore. *Nalanda–Sriwijaya Centre Archaeology Unit Archaeology Report Series* (No. 5).

Lim, Chen Sian. (2019). Preliminary report on the archaeological investigations at the Victoria

Concert Hall. *Nalanda-Sriwijaya Centre Archaeology Unit Archaeology Report Series* (No. 9).

Low, James. (1848). An account of several inscriptions found in Province Wellesley, on the peninsula of Malacca. *Journal of the Asiatic Society of Bengal, 17*(2), 62–66.

Manguin, Pierre-Yves. (2002). The amorphous nature of coastal polities in insular Southeast Asia: Restricted centres, extended peripheries. *Moussons: Recherche en sciences humaines sur l'Asie du Sud-Est, 5*, 73–99.

Miksic, John N. (2013). *Singapore and the Silk Road of the sea, 1300–1800*. Singapore: NUS Press.

Perret, Daniel, & Heddy Surachman. (2014). *History of Padang Lawas, North Sumatra: I, The site of Si Pamutung (mid-ninth–thirteenth century CE)*, (Cahier d'Archipel 42). Paris: Association Archipel.

Robson, Stuart (Trans.). (1995). *Desawarnana (Nagarakrtagama) by Mpu Prapanca*. Leiden: KITLV Press.

Su, Jiqing. (1981). *Daoyi zhilue jiaoshi*. Beijing: Zhonghua shuju.

Wheatley, Paul. (2010). *The Golden Khersonese: Studies in the historical geography of the Malay Peninsula before A.D. 1500*. Singapore: NUS Press.

Winstedt, R.O. (1928). Gold ornaments dug up at Fort Canning, Singapore. *Journal of the Malayan Branch of the Royal Asiatic Society, 6*(4), 1–4.

**Chapter Two: The 15th Century**

Ahmat Adam. (2016). *Sululat u's-salatin yakni per[tu] turan segala raja-raja: Dialih aksara dan disunting degan kritis serta diberi anotasi dan pengenalan*. Kuala Lumpur: Yayasan Karyawan.

Ahmat Adam. (2016) *Antara Sejarah dan mitos: Sejarah Melayu & Hang Tuah dalam historiografi Malaysia*. Petaling Jaya: Strategic Information and Research Development Centre.

Andaya, L.A. (2008). *Leaves of the same tree: Trade and ethnicity in the Straits of Melaka*. Honolulu: University of Hawai'i Press.

Barnard, T.P. (2007). Celates, Rayat-Laut, Pirates: The orang laut and their decline in history. *Journal of the Malayan Branch of the Royal Asiatic Society, 80*(2), 33–50.

Brown, C.C. (Trans.). (1952). Malay Annals: A translation of Raffles MS 18 in the Library of the R.A.S. London. *Journal of the Malayan Branch of the Royal Asiatic Society, 15*(2–3), 1–276.

Cheah, Boon Kheng (compiler), & Abdul Rahman Haji Ismail (transcriber). (1998). *Sejarah Melayu: The Malay Annals* (Ms Raffles No. 18, new romanised edition, reprint No. 17). Kuala Lumpur: Malaysian Branch of the Royal Asiatic Society.

Dunn, F.L. (1975). *Rain-forest collectors and traders: A study of resource utilization in modern and ancient Malaya* (Monographs No. 5). Kuala Lumpur: Malaysian Branch of the Royal Asiatic Society.

Cheah, Boon Kheng. (1998). The rise and fall of the great Melakan empire: Moral judgement in Tun Bambang's 'Sejarah Melayu'. *Journal of the Malayan Branch of the Royal Asiatic Society, 71*(2), 104–21.

Cortesao, A. (Ed. and trans.). (1944). *The Suma Oriental of Tome Pires: An account of the East, from the Red Sea to Japan, written in Malacca and India in 1512–1515 and the Book of Francisco Rodrigues: Rutter of a voyage in the Red Sea, Nautical rules, almanack and Maps, written and drawn in the east before 1515*. London: Hakluyt Society. New Delhi: Asian Educational Services (1990 reprint).

Hashim, Muhammad Yusoff. (2018). The Seri Bija Diraja in the tradition of the Great Lords of Melaka in the fifteenth and sixteenth centuries. In Kwa Chong Guan & Peter Borschberg (Eds.), *Studying Singapore before 1800*. Singapore: NUS Press.

Hooker, Virginia M., & M.B. Hooker (2001). Introductory essay, John Leyden's *Malay Annals* (Reprint 20). Kuala Lumpur: Malaysian Branch of the Royal Asiatic Society.

Kwa, Chong Guan. (2010). Singapura as a central place in Malay history and identity. In Karl Hack, Jean-Louis Margolin, & Karine Delaye (Eds.), *Singapore from Temasek to the 21st century: Reinventing the global city*. Singapore: NUS Press.

Kwa, Chong Guan, & Peter Borschberg (Eds.). (2018). *Studying Singapore before 1800*. Singapore: NUS Press.

Lapian, A.B. (1979). Le role des orang laut dans l'histoire de Riau. *Archipel, 18*, 215–22.

Lombard, D. (1988). Le sultanat malaise comme model socio-économique. In D. Lombard & J. Aubin (Eds.), *Marchands et homme d'affaires asiatiques dans l'Océan Indien et la Mer de Chine, XIII–XXe siècles*. Paris: École des Hautes Études en Sciences Sociales.

Lowey-Ball, ShawnaKim. (2015). *Liquid market, solid state: The rise and demise of the great global emporium at Malacca, 1400–1641.* Unpublished Yale University doctoral dissertation, 2015. Ann Arbour, MI: ProQuest.

Raimy Che-Ross. (2004). The 'Lost City' of Kota Gelanggi: An exploratory essay based on textual evidence and an excursion into 'Ariel archaeology'. *Journal of the Malaysian Branch of the Royal Asiatic Society, 77*(2), 27–58.

Reichle, N. (2007). *Violence and serenity: Late Buddhist sculpture from Indonesia.* Honolulu: University of Hawai'i Press.

Rouffaer, P.G. (2018). Was Melaka an emporium named Malayur before 1400 CE? And where was Wurawari, Ma-Hasin, Langka and Batu Sawar? In Kwa Chong Guan & Peter Borschberg (Eds.), *Studying Singapore before 1800.* Singapore: NUS Press.

Salleh, Muhammad Haji (Ed.). (1997). *Sulalat al-Salatin ya'ni perteturan segala Raja-Raja (Sejarah Melayu).* Kuala Lumpur: Yayasan Karyan & Dewan Bahasa dan Pustaka.

Sinclair, W.F., & D. Ferguson (Eds.). (1967). *The travels of Pedro Teixeira; with his "Kings of Harmuz" and extracts from his "Kings of Persia".* Nendeln: Kraus Reprint.

Snellgrove, D. (2010). *The Hevajra Tantra: A critical study* (2nd ed.). Bangkok: Orchid Press.

Sopher, D.E. (2018). Boat people in the western archipelago during the Portuguese period. In Kwa Chong Guan & Peter Borschberg (Eds.), *Studying Singapore before 1800.* Singapore: NUS Press.

Thomaz, Luis F.F.R. (1993). The Malay sultanate of Melaka. In A. Reid (Ed.), *Southeast Asia in the early modern era; Trade, power, and belief.* Ithaca: Cornell University Press.

Virunha, Chuleeporn. (2002). Power relations between the orang laut and the Malay kingdoms of Melaka and Johor during the fifteenth to seventeenth centuries. In Sunait Chutintaranond and C. Baker (Eds.), *Recalling local pasts: Autonomous history in Southeast Asia.* Chiang Mai: Silkworm Books.

Wolters, O.W. (1967). *Early Indonesian commerce: A study of the origins of Srivijaya.* Ithaca: Cornell University Press.

Wolters, O.W. (1970). *The fall of Srivijaya in Malay history.* London: Lund Humphries; Kuala Lumpur: Oxford University Press.

## Chapter Three: The 16th Century

Albuquerque, B. de. (1875–95). *The commentaries of the great A. Dalboquerque, second viceroy of India* (tr. Walter de Gray Birch, 4 vols.). London: Hakluyt Society.

Albuquerque, B. de. (1973). *Comentarios de Afonso d'Albuqerque* (J. Veríssimo Serrão, ed. and int., text of the 2nd edition of 1576, 2 vols.). Lisbon: Imprensa Nacional-Casa de Moeda.

Alves, J.M. dos Santos. (1999). *O domínio do norte de Samatra: A história dos sultanatos de Samudera-Pacém e de Achém, e das suas relações com os Portugueses (1500–1580).* Lisbon: Sociedade Histórica da Independência de Portugal.

Barnes, W.D. (1911). Singapore Old Straits and New Harbour. *Journal of the Straits Branch of the Royal Asiatic Society, 60,* 24–34.

Bausani, A. (Ed.). (1970). *Lettera di Giovanni da Empoli.* Rome: Istituto Italiano per il Medio ed Estremo Oriente, Centro Italiano di Cultura, Jakarta.

Bittner M., & W. Tomaschek (Eds. and trs.). (1897). *Die Topographischen Capitel des Indischen Seespiegels Mohit.* Vienna: Verlag der Kaiserlich-Königlichen Geographischen Gesellschaft.

Borschberg, P. (2003). Portuguese, Spanish and Dutch plans to construct a fort in the Straits of Singapore, ca. 1584–1625. *Archipel, 63,* 55–88.

Borschberg, P. (2004). Remapping the Straits? New insights from old sources. In P. Borschberg (Ed.), *Iberians in the Singapore-Melaka area (16th–18th centuries).* Wiesbaden: Harrassowitz.

Borschberg, P. (2008). Jacques de Coutre as a source for the early 17th-century history of Singapore, the Johor River, and the Straits. *Journal of the Malaysian Branch of the Royal Asiatic Society, 81*(2), 71–97.

Borschberg, P. (2011). *Hugo Grotius, the Portuguese and free trade in the East Indies.* Singapore and Leiden: NUS Press and KITLV Press.

Borschberg, P. (2017). Singapore and its Straits, c. 1500–1800. *Indonesia and the Malay World, 45,* issue 133, 373–90.

Borschberg, P. (2018). Three questions about maritime Singapore, 16th and 17th centuries. *Ler História, 72,* 31–54.

Borschberg, P. (Ed.). (2015). *Jacques de Coutre's Singapore and Johor.* Singapore: NUS Press.

Corrêa (also Correia), G. (1858–66). *Lendas da Índia* (ed. R.J. de Lima Felner, 7 vols.). Lisbon: Academia Real das Sciences.

Cortesão, A., & A. Teixeira da Mota. (1987). *Portugaliae Monumenta Cartographica* (9 vols.). Lisbon: Imprensa Nacional-Casa da Moeda.

Dam, P. van. (1931–43). *Beschryvinge van de Oostindische Compagnie* (ed. by F.W. Stapel, 8 vols.). The Hague: Martinus Nijhoff.

Gibson-Hill, C.A. (1954). Singapore: Note on the history of the Old Straits, 1580–1850. *Journal of the Malayan Branch of the Royal Asiatic Society, 27*(1), 165–214.

Gibson-Hill, C.A. (1955). Johore Lama and other ancient sites on the Johore River. *Journal of the Malayan Branch of the Royal Asiatic Society, 28*(2), 126–99.

Gibson-Hill, C.A. (1956). Singapore Old Strait and New Harbour, 1300–1870. *Memoirs of the Raffles Museum, 3*, 11–115. Reprinted in Kwa C.G., & P. Borschberg (Eds.), (2018) *Studying Singapore before 1800*. Singapore: NUS Press.

Han, Wai Toon. (1948). A study on Johore Lama. *Journal of the South Seas Society, 5*(2), 17–34.

Heeres, J.E. (Ed.). (1907). Corpus Diplomaticum Neërlando-Indicum: Verzameling van politieke contracten en verdere verdragen door de Nederlanders in het Oosten gesloten, van privilegiebrieven, aan hen verleend, enz. (eerste deel, 1596–1650). *Bijdragen tot de Taal-, Land- en Volkenkunde, 57*, 1–586.

Jack-Hinton, C. (1963). Further investigations at Johore Lama: Preliminary notes. *Federation Museum Journal* (new series), *8*, 24–31.

Jack-Hinton, C. (1963). A note on a Ch'eng Hua Nien Hao from Kampong Makam, Kota Tinggi, and some remarks on the Johore River trade in the fifteenth century. *Federation Museum Journal* (new series), *8*, 32–35.

Jonge, J.K.J. de. (1866). *Opkomst van het Nederlandsch gezag in Oost-Indië: Verzameling van onuitgegeven stukken uit het oud-coloniaal archief* (eerste reeks). The Hague: Martinus Nijhoff.

Kathirithamby-Wells, J., & John Villiers (Eds.). (1990). *The Southeast Asian port and polity: Rise and demise*. Singapore: Singapore University Press.

Kwa, C.G. (2017). *Precolonial Singapore*. Singapore: IPS and Straits Times Press.

Kwa, Chong Guan. (2004). 16th-century underglazed blue porcelain sherds from the Kallang River. In John N. Miksic & Cheryl-Ann Low M.G. (Eds.), *Early Singapore 1300s–1819: Evidence in Maps, text and artefacts*. Singapore: Singapore History Museum, 2004.

Kwa, Chong Guan. (2018). Kallang estuary: A 17th-century port city. *Cultural Connections 3*. Singapore: Cultural Academy Singapore.

Kwa, C.G., & Borschberg, P. (Eds.). (2018). *Studying Singapore before 1800*. Singapore: NUS Press.

Lamb, A. (1964). Notes on beads from Johor Lama and Kota Tinggi. *Journal of the Malayan Branch of the Royal Asiatic Society, 37*(1), 92–97.

Liaw, Y.F. (Ed. and tr.). (1976). *Undang-undang Melaka. A critical edition* (Proefschrift Leiden). The Hague: De Nederlandsche Boek- en Steendrukkerij/Verlagshuis S.L. Smits.

Linschoten, J.H. van. (1939). *Itinerario: Voyage ofte Schipvaert van Jan Huygen van Linschoten naer Oost ofte Portugaels Indien, 1579–1592*, and *Reys-geschrift vande navigatiën der Portugaloysers* (ed. H. Kern and J.C.M. Warnsinck, 2nd ed.). The Hague: Martinus Nijhoff.

Lobato, M. (1999). *Política e comércio dos Portugueses na Insulíndia: Malaca e as Molucas de 1575 a 1605*. Lisbon: Instituto Português do Oriente.

Loureiro, R.M. (Ed.). (1996). *O Manuscrito de Lisboa da 'Suma Oriental' de Tomé Pires (Contribuição para uma Edição Crítica)*. Macau: Instituto Português do Oriente.

Macgregor, I.A. (1955). Notes on the Portuguese in Malaya. *Journal of the Malayan Branch of the Royal Asiatic Society, 28*(2), 5–47.

Macgregor, I. (1956). A sea fight near Singapore in the 1570s. *Journal of the Malayan Branch of the Royal Asiatic Society, 29*(3), 5–21.

Matos, L.J.R. Semeado de. (2015). *Roteiros e rotas portuguesas do Oriente nos séculos XVI e XVII* (doctoral dissertation, University of Lisbon).

Maxwell, W.G. (1911). Barretto de Resende's Account of Malacca. *Journal of the Straits Branch of the Royal Asiatic Society, 60*, 1–24.

Meilink-Roelofsz, M.A.P. (1962). *Asian trade and European influence in the Indonesian Archipelago between 1500 and about 1630*. The Hague: Martinus Nijhoff.

Mills, J.V.G. (1930). Report on the Golden Chersonese. *Journal of the Malayan Branch of the Royal Asiatic Society, 8*(1), 228–55.

Mills, J.V.G. (1937). Malaya in the Wu-Pei-Chih charts. *Journal of the Malayan Branch of the Royal Asiatic Society, 15*(3), 1–48.

Mills, J.V.G. (1951). Notes on early Chinese voyages. *Journal of the Royal Asiatic Society*, 3–25.

Mills, J.V.G. (1954). Chinese coastal maps. *Imago Mundi, 11*, 151–68.

Mills, J.V.G. (1974). Arab and Chinese navigators in Malaysian waters in about A.D. 1500. *Journal of the Malaysian Branch of the Royal Asiatic Society, 47*(2), 25–32.

Mills, J.V.G. (1979). Chinese navigators in Insulinde, about A.D. 1500. *Archipel, 18,* 69–93.

Muhammad Yusof Hashim. (1992). *The Malay Sultanate of Malacca* (tr. D.J. Muzzafar Tate). Kuala Lumpur: Dewan Bahasa dan Pustaka.

Münster, S. (1978). *Cosmographia oder Beschreibung der gantzen Welt etc.* (facsimile reproduction of the Basel edition of 1628). Lindau: Antiqua Verlag.

Noonan, L.A. (1989). *John of Empoli and his relations with Afonso de Albuquerque.* Lisbon: Instituto de Investigação Científica Tropical.

Obdeijn, V. (1942). De oude zeehandelsweg door de Straat van Malaka in verband met de geomorfologie der Selat-Eilanden. *Koninklijk Nederlands Aardrijkskundig Genootschap* (II serie), *59,* 742–70.

Perret, D. (2000). Les stele funéraires musulmanes dites batu Aceh de l'État de Johor (Malaisie). *Bulletin de l'École française d'Extrême-Orient, 87*(2), 579–607.

Perret D., & Kamarudin Ab. Razak. (2004). *Batu aceh Johor dalam perbandingan.* Johor Bahru: Yayasan Warisan Johor.

Pintado, M.J. (Ed. and tr.). (1993). *Portuguese documents on Malacca* (I: 1509–1511). Kuala Lumpur: National Archives of Malaysia.

Pinto, P.J. de Sousa. (2012). *The Portuguese and the Straits of Melaka, 1575–1619.* Singapore: NUS Press; Kuala Lumpur: Malaysian Branch of the Royal Asiatic Society.

Pires, T. (1944). *Suma Oriental: An account of the East from the Red Sea to Japan; written in Malacca and India in 1512–1515* (trans. and ed. by A. Cortesão, 2 vols.). London: Hakluyt Society.

Pires, T. (1978). *A Suma Oriental de Tomé Pires e o Livro de Francisco Rodrigues* (ed. by A. Cortesão). Coimbra: Por Ordem da Universidade.

Quaritch Wales, H.G. (1940). Archaeological researches on ancient Indian colonization in Malaya. *Journal of the Malayan Branch of the Royal Asiatic Society, 18*(1), 57–63.

Rouffaer, G.P. (1921). Was Malaka Emporium vóór 1400 A.D. genaamd Malajoer? En waar lag Woerawari, Ma-Hasin, Langka, Batoesawar? *Bijdragen tot de Taal-, Land- en Volkenkunde, 77,* 1–174 and 359–604.

Santos, J. dos. (1999). *Etiópia Oriental e Vária História de cousas Notáveis do Oriente* (ed. M. Lobato and M. do Carmo Guerreiro Vieira). Lisbon: Comissão Nacional para as Comemorações dos Descobrimentos Portugueses.

Serrão, J. Veríssimo (Ed. and int.). (1973). *Comentarios de Afonso d'Albuqerque* (text of the 2nd edition of 1576, 2 vols.). Lisbon: Imprensa Nacional-Casa de Moeda.

Sopher, D.E. (1965). *The sea nomads: A study based on literature of the maritime boat people of Southeast Asia.* Singapore: National Museum of Singapore.

Spallanzani, M. (1999). *Giovanni da Empoli: Un mercante fiorentino nell'Asia portoghese.* Florence: Studio per Edizioni Scelte.

Subrahmanyam, S. (1993). *The Portuguese empire in Asia 1500–1700: A political and economic history.* London: Longman.

Thomaz, F.L.R. (1991). *Nina Chatu and the Portuguese trade in Malacca* (tr. by M.J. Pintado). Melaka: Luso-Malaysian Books.

Thomaz, F.L.R. (1994). *De Ceuta a Timor.* Lisbon: Difel.

Thomaz, F.L.R. (n.d.). *Early Portuguese Malacca.* Macau: Commisão Territorial de Macau para as Comemorações dos Descobrimentos Potugueses, Instituto Politécnico de Macau.

Tibbetts, G.R. (1979). *A study of the Arabic texts containing material on South-East Asia.* London and Leiden: E.J. Brill.

Varthema, L. de. (1928). *The Itinerary of Ludovico di Varthema of Bologna from 1502 to 1508* (tr. and ed. by J. Winter Jones). London: Argonaut Press.

Veen, E. van. (2000). *Decay or defeat: An inquiry into the Portuguese decline in Asia, 1580–1645.* Leiden: Research School of Asian, African and Amerindian Studies.

Winstedt, R.O. (1953). The date of the Malacca legal codes. *Journal of the Royal Asiatic Society of Great Britain and Ireland, 1–2,* 31–33.

Winstedt, R.O. (1979). *A history of Johore* (Reprint No. 6). Kuala Lumpur: Malaysian Branch of the Royal Asiatic Society.

## Chapter Four: The 17th Century

Andaya, L.Y. (1975). *The Kingdom of Johor 1641–1728: Economic and political developments.* Kuala Lumpur: Oxford University Press.

Andrews, K.R. (1964). *Elizabethan privateering: English privateering during the Spanish War, 1585–1603.* Cambridge: Cambridge University Press.

Booy, A. de (Ed.). (1970). *De derde reis van de V.O.C. naar Oost-Indië onder het beleid van Admiraal Paulus van Caerden, uitgezeild in 1606* (2 vols.). The Hague: Martinus Nijhoff.

Borschberg, P. (2002). The seizure of the Sta. Catarina, revisited: The Portuguese empire in Asia, VOC politics and the origin of the Dutch-Johor alliance. *Journal of Southeast Asian Studies*, *33*(1), 31–62.

Borschberg, P. (2004). Luso-Johor-Dutch relations in the Straits of Malacca and Singapore, ca. 1600–1623. *Itinerario, 28*(2), 15–33.

Borschberg, P. (2010). *The Singapore and Melaka Straits: Violence, security and diplomacy in 17th-century Southeast Asia*. Singapore and Leiden: NUS Press and KITLV Press.

Borschberg, P. (2013). From self-defence to an instrument of war: Dutch privateering around the Malay Peninsula in the early seventeenth century. *Journal of Early Modern History, 17*, 35–52.

Borschberg, P. (2014). Left holding the bag: The Johor-VOC alliance and the Twelve Years' Truce (1606–1613). In R. Lesaffer (Ed.), *The Twelve Years Truce (1609): Peace, truce, war and law in the Low Countries at the turn of the 17th century*. Leiden: Brill-Nijhoff.

Borschberg, P. (Ed.). (2015). *Jacques de Coutre's Singapore and Johor*. Singapore: NUS Press.

Borschberg, P. (Ed.). (2016). *Admiral Matelieff's Singapore and Johor*. Singapore: NUS Press.

Boxer, C.R. (1965). *The Dutch seaborne empire, 1600–1800*. London: Hutchinson.

Boyajian, J.C. (1993). *Portuguese trade in Asia under the Habsburgs, 1580–1640*. Baltimore and London: Johns Hopkins University Press.

Cortesão, A., & A. Teixeira da Mota. (1987). *Portugaliae Monumenta Cartographica* (9 vols.). Lisbon: Imprensa Nacional-Casa da Moeda.

Dam, P. van. (1931–43). *Beschryvinge van de Oostindische Compagnie* (ed. by F.W. Stapel, 8 vols). The Hague: Martinus Nijhoff.

Draeger, D.F. (2000). *Weapons and fighting arts of Indonesia*. North Clarendon: Tuttle Publishing.

Erédia, M. Godinho de. (1882). *Malaca L'Inde Méridionale e le Cathay: Manuscrit original autographe de Godinho de Erédia appartenant à la Bibliothèque Royale de Bruxelles* (tr. by M.L. Janssen). Bruxelles: Librairie Européenne C. Muquardt.

Erédia, M. Godinho de. (2008). *Informação da Aurea Quersoneso, ou Península, e das Ilhas Auríferas, Carbúculas e Aromáticas* (ed. by R.M. Loureiro). Macau: Centro Científico e Cultural de Macau.

Foreest, H.A. van, & A. de Booy (Eds.). (1980–81). *De Vierde Schipvaart der Nederlanders naar Oost-Indië onder Jacob Wilkens en Jacob van Neck (1599–1604)* (2 vols.). The Hague: Martinus Nijhoff.

Foster, W. (Ed.). (1934). *The voyage of Thomas Best to the East Indies 1612–1614*. London: Hakluyt Society.

Gaastra, F.S. (2003). *The Dutch East India Company: Expansion and decline*. Zuphen: Walburg Pers.

Grotius, H. (2006). *Commentary on the law of prize and booty* (ed. by M.J. van Ittersum). Indianapolis: Liberty Fund.

Hutterer, K.L. (Ed.). (1977). *Economic exchange and social interaction in Southeast Asia: Perspectives from prehistory, history and ethnography*. Ann Arbor: Center for South and Southeast Asian Studies.

Jacobs, H. (Ed.). (1980–84). *Documenta Malucensia* (3 vols.). Rome: Jesuit Historical Institute.

Jonge, J.K.J. de. (1866–1925). *Opkomst van het Nederlandsch gezag in Oost-Indië: Verzameling van onuitgegeven stukken uit het oud-coloniaal archief* (eerste reeks). The Hague: Martinus Nijhoff.

Keuning, J. (Ed.). (1938–49). *De Tweede Schipvaart der Nederlanders Naar Oost-Indië onder Jacob Cornelisz van Neck en Wijbrant Warwijck, 1598–1600* (8 vols.). The Hague: Martinus Nijhoff.

Klerk de Reus, G.C. (1894). *Geschichtlicher Überblick der Administrativen, Rechtlichen und Finanziellen Entwicklung der Niederländisch-Ostindischen Compagnie*. Batavia and The Hague: Albrecht & Rusche and Martinus Nijhoff.

Kwa, C.G. (2017). *Precolonial Singapore*. Singapore: IPS and Straits Times Press.

Kwa, C.G., & P. Borschberg (Eds.). (2018). *Studying Singapore before 1800*. Singapore: NUS Press.

Lombard, D. (1967). *Le Sultanat d'Atjéh au temps d'Iskandar Muda 1607–1636*. Paris: École Français d'Extrême-Orient.

Lopes de Mendonça, H., & R.A. de Bulhão Pato. (1884–1935). *Cartas de Afonso de Albuquerque* (7 vols.). Lisbon: Academia das Ciências de Lisboa.

Luard, C.E., & H. Hosten (Eds.). (1927). *Travels of Fray Sebastien Manrique, 1629–1643: A translation of the Itinerario de las Missiones Orientales* (2 vols.). Oxford: Printed for the Hakluyt Society.

Maxwell, W.G. (1911). Barretto de Resende's account of Malacca. *Journal of the Straits Branch of the Royal Asiatic Society, 60*, 1–24.

Meilink-Roelofsz, M.A.P. (1962). *Asian trade and European influence in the Indonesian archipelago between 1500 and about 1630.* The Hague: Martinus Nijhoff.

Mills, J.V. (1930). Eredia's Description of Malacca, Meridional India, and Cathay, translated from the Portuguese, with notes, by J.V. Mills. *Journal of the Malayan Branch of the Royal Asiatic Society, 8*(1), 1–288.

Moreland, W.H. (Ed.). (1934). *Peter Floris: His voyage to the East Indies in the Globe, 1611–1615.* London: Hakluyt Society.

Muhammad Y.H. (1992). *The Malay Sultanate of Malacca: A study of various apsects of Malacca in the 15th and 16th centuries in Malaysian history.* Kuala Lumpur: Dewan Bahasa dan Pustaka/ Ministry of Education.

Münster, S. (1978). *Cosmographia oder Beschreibung der gantzen Welt etc.* (facsimile reproduction of the Basel edition of 1628, 4 vols.). Lindau: Antiqua Verlag.

Naber, S.P. l'Honoré. (1930–33). *Reisebeschreibungen von Deutschen Beamten und Kriegsleuten im Dienst der Niederländisch West- und Ost-Indischen Kompanien, 1602–1797* (13 vols.). The Hague: Martinus Nijhoff.

Netscher, E. (1870). *De Nederlanders in Djohor en Siak.* Batavia: Bruining & Wijt.

Noonan, L.A. (1989). *John of Empoli and his relations with Afonso de Albuquerque.* Lisbon: Instituto de Investigação Científica Tropical.

Opstall, M.E. van (Ed.). (1972). *De reis van de vloot van Pieter Willemszoon Verhoeff naar Azië, 1607–1612* (2 vols.). The Hague: Martinus Nijhoff.

Rietbergen, P.J.A.N. van. (1987). *De Eerste Landvoogd Pieter Both (1568–1615): Gouverneur-Generaal van Nederlandsch-Indië* (2 vols.). Zutphen: Walburg Pers.

Sinclair, W.F., & D. Ferguson (Eds.). (1967). *The travels of Pedro Teixeira; with his "Kings of Harmuz" and extracts from his "Kings of Persia".* Nendeln: Kraus Reprint.

Sopher, D.E. (1965). *The sea nomads: A study based on literature of the maritime boat people of Southeast Asia.* Singapore: National Museum.

Teixeira, M. (1961). *The Portuguese missions in Malacca and Singapore* (vol. 1). Lisbon: Agência Geral do Ultramar.

Temple, R.C. (Ed.). (1919). *The travels of Peter Mundy in Europe and Asia, 1608–1667* (vol. III). London: Hakluyt Society.

Tiele, P.A., & J.E. Heeres (Eds.). (1886–95). *Bouwstoffen voor de Geschiedenis der Nederlanders in den Maleischen Archipel* (3 vols.). The Hague: Martinus Nijhoff.

Veen, E. van. (2000). *Decay or defeat? An inquiry into the Portuguese decline in Asia, 1580–1645.* Leiden: Research School of Asian, African and Amerindian Studies.

## Chapter Five: The 18th Century

Ali al-Haji ibn Ahmad. (1982). *The precious gift/ Tuhfat al-Nafis* (ed. and tr. by V.M. Hooker and B.W. Andaya). Kuala Lumpur and New York: Oxford University Press.

Andaya, L.Y. (1975). *The Kingdom of Johor 1641– 1728: Economic and political developments.* Kuala Lumpur: Oxford University Press.

Andaya, L.Y. (2008). *Leaves of the same tree: Trade and ethnicity in the Straits of Melaka.* Honolulu: Hawai'i University Press.

Assey, C. (1819). *On the trade with China and the Indian archipelago, with observations on the insecurity of the British interests in that quarter* (2nd ed.). London: Printed for Rodwell and Martin.

Barnard, T.P. (2003). *Multiple centres of authority: Society and environment in Siak and Eastern Sumatra, 1674–1827.* Leiden: KITLV Press.

Bassett, D.K. (1958). English trade in Celebes, 1613–1667. *Journal of the Malayan Branch of the Royal Asiatic Society, 31*(1), 1–39.

Bassett, D.K. (1964). British trade and policy in Indonesia, 1760–1772. *Bijdragen tot de Taal-, Land- en Volkenkunde, 120*(3), 197–223.

Bassett, D.K. (1965). Anglo-Malay relations, 1786– 1795. *Journal of the Malaysian Branch of the Royal Asiatic Society, 38*(2), 183–212.

Bastin, J. (2012). *The founding of Singapore 1819.* Singapore: National Library of Singapore.

Chijs, J.A. van der (Ed.). (1885–1900). *Nederlandsch-Indisch Plakaatboek, 1602–1811* (17 vols.). Batavia: Landsdrukkerij; and The Hague: Martinus Nijhoff.

Chijs, J.A. van der, & H.T. Colenbrander (Eds.). (1896–1931). *Dagh-Register gehouden int Casteel Batavia vant passerende daer ter plates als over geheel Nederlandts-India.* The Hague: Martinus Nijhoff.

Colombijn, F. (2003). The volatile state in Southeast Asia: Evidence from Sumatra, 1600–1800. *Journal of Asian Studies, 62*(2), 497–529.

Cowan, C.D. (Ed.). (1950). Early Penang and the rise of Singapore, 1805–1832: Documents from the manuscript records of the East India Company.

*Journal of the Malayan Branch of the Royal Asiatic Society, 23*(2).

Dampier, W. (1906). *Dampier's voyages, consisting of a new voyage around the world* (ed. J. Masefield, 2 vols). London: E. Grant Richards.

Gaastra, F.S. (2002). *De Geschiedenis van de VOC* (4th ed.). Zutphen: Walburg Pers.

Gaastra, F.S. (2003). *The Dutch East India Company: Expansion and decline.* Zutphen: Walburg Pers.

Gibson-Hill, C.A. (1954). Singapore: Note on the history of the Old Straits, 1580–1850. *Journal of the Malayan Branch of the Royal Asiatic Society, 27*(1), 165–214.

Gibson-Hill, C.A. (1956). Singapore Old Strait and New Harbour, 1300–1870. *Memoirs of the Raffles Museum* (No. 3). Singapore: Government Printing Office. Reprinted in Kwa Chong Guan, & Peter Borschberg (Eds.), (2018) *Studying Singapore before 1800.* Singapore: NUS Press.

Irwin, G.W. (1956). Governor Couperus and the surrender of Malacca in 1795. *Journal of the Malayan Branch of the Royal Asiatic Society, 37*(1), 86–133.

Ismail Hussein (Ed.). (1979). Hikayat Negeri Johor: A nineteenth-century Bugis history relating events in Riau & Selangor. In R.O. Winstedt, *A history of Johore* (Reprint No. 6). Kuala Lumpur: Malaysian Branch of the Royal Asiatic Society.

Kemp, P.H. van der. (1898). De Singapoorsche Papieroorlog. *Bijdragen tot de Taal-, Land- en Volkenkunde, 49*, 389ff.

Kemp, P.H. van der. (1902). De Stichting van Singapore, de Afstand ervan met Malakka door Nederland, en de Britische Aanspraaken op den Linga-Riouw-Archipel. *Bijdragen tot de Taal-, Land- en Volkenkunde, 10*, 313–476.

Kemp, P.H. van der. (1904). *Geschiedenis van het Londensch Tractaat van 17 Maart 1824.* The Hague, Martinus Nijhoff.

Kemp, P.H. van der. (1910). *De Teruggave der Oost-Indische Koloniën, 1814–1816.* The Hague: Martinus Nijhoff.

Klerk de Reus, G.C. (1894). *Geschichtlicher Überblick der Administrativen, Rechtlichen und Finanziellen Entwicklung der Niederländisch-Ostindischen Compagnie.* Batavia and The Hague: Albrecht & Rusche and Martinus Nijhoff.

Kratz, Ernst Ulrich (Ed.). (1973). *Peringatan Sejarah Negeri Johor: Eine Malaiisch quelle zu geschicte Johor sim 18.jahrhundert.* Wiesbaden: Otto Harrassowitz.

Lewis, D. (1970). The growth of the country trade to the Straits of Malacca, 1760–1777. *Journal of the Malaysian Branch of the Royal Asiatic Society, 43*(2), 114–130.

Lewis, D. (1995). *Jan Compagnie in the Straits of Malacca, 1641–1795.* Athens, OH: Ohio University Centre for International Studies.

Lewis, D. (1997). British policy in the Straits of Malacca to 1819 and the collapse of the traditional Malay state structure. In B. Barrington (Ed.), *Empires and imperialism in Southeast Asia.* Clayton, Vic.: Monash Asia Institute.

Malchow, H.L. (1991). *Gentlemen capitalists: The social and political world of the Victorian businessman.* Palo Alto: Stanford University Press.

Marks, H. (1959). *The first contest for Singapore.* The Hague: Martinus Nijhoff.

Matheson, V. (Ed.). (1982). *Tuhfat al-Nafis: Raja Haji Ahmad dan Raja Ali Haji.* Kuala Lumpur: Fajar Bakti.

Milner, Anthony. (2016). *Kerajaan: Malay political culture on the eve of colonial rule* (2nd ed.). Petaling Jaya: Strategic Information and Research Development Centre.

Mohd. Yusof Md. Nor (Ed.). (1984). *Salasilah Melayu dan Bugis.* Petaling Jaya: Fajar Bakti.

Muhammad Yusoff Hashim (Ed.). (1992). *Hikayat Siak.* Kuala Lumpur: Dewan Bahasa dan Pustaka.

Netscher, E. (1870). *De Nederlanders in Djohor en Siak.* Batavia: Bruining & Wijt.

Ng, C.K. (2015). *Trade and society: The Amoy network on the China coast, 1683–1735* (2nd ed). Singapore: NUS Press.

Ng, C.K. (2017). *Boundaries and beyond: China's maritime Southeast in late Imperial times.* Singapore: NUS Press.

Ng, C.K., & Wang, G.W. (Eds.). (2004). *Maritime China in transition, 1750–1850.* Wiesbaden: Harrassowitz.

Paulus, J. (Ed.). (1917–39). *Encyclopaedie van Nederlandsch-Indië* (2nd ed., 8 vols.). The Hague and Leiden: Martinus Nijhoff and E.J. Brill.

Schilder, G., J. Moerman et al. (2006–10). *Grote Atlas van de Verenigde Oost-Indische Compagnie. Comprehensive Atlas of the Dutch United East India Company* (7 vols.). Voorburg: Uitgeverij Asia Maior.

Shaharom Husain. (1995). *Sejarah Johor: Kaitannya dengan Negeri Melayu.* Kuala Lumpur: Fajar Bakti.

Sirtema de Grovestius, C.F. (Ed.). (1852). *Notice et souvenirs biographiques du comte Van der Duyn de Maasdam et du baron de Capellen.* Saint-Germain-en-Laye: H. Picault.

Sopher, D.E. (1965). *The sea nomads: A study based on literature of the maritime boat people of Southeast Asia.* Singapore: National Museum of Singapore.

*Surat-surat perdjandjian antara kesultanan Riau dengan pemerintahan-pemerintahan VOC dan Hindia-Belanda, 1784–1909.* (1970). Jakarta: Arsip Nasional Republik Indonesia.

Tarling, N. (1962). *The Anglo-Dutch rivalry in the Malay world.* Brisbane: Cambridge University Press.

Tarling, N. (1978). *Piracy and politics in the Malay world: A study of British imperialism in nineteenth-century South-east Asia.* Nendeln: Kraus Reprint.

Tregonning, K.G. (1965). *The British in Malaya: The first forty years, 1786–1826.* Tucson: University of Arizona Press.

Trocki, C. (1977). *Prince of pirates: The Temenggongs and the development of Johor and Singapore.* Singapore: Singapore University Press.

Vlielander Hein-Couperus, C.R.G. (1915). *De overgave van Malakka aan de Engelschen door den Gouverneur Abraham Couperus.* Amsterdam: Bussy.

Vos, R. (1993). *Gentle Janus, merchant prince: The VOC and the tightrope of diplomacy in the Malay world, 1740–1800.* Leiden: KITLV Press.

Vries, D. de. (1996). *Uit de Kaartenwinkel van de VOC: Cataloges van zeekarten van de Verenigde Oostindische Compagnie in de Collectie Bodel Nijenhuis.* Alphen aan den Rijn: Canaletto.

Warren, J.F. (2002). *Iranun and Balangigi: Globalization, maritime raiding and the birth of ethnicity.* Singapore: Singapore University Press.

Warren, J.F. (2007). *The Sulu zone, 1768–1898: The dynamics of external trade, slavery, ethnicity and the transformation of a Southeast Asian maritime state* (reprint of 1981 ed.). Singapore: NUS Press.

Winstedt, R.O. (1979). *A history of Johore* (Reprint No. 6). Kuala Lumpur: Malaysian Branch of the Royal Asiatic Society.

Wright, N. (2017). *William Farquhar and Singapore: Stepping out of Raffles' shadow.* Penang: Entrepot Publishing.

**Chapter Six: The 19th Century**

Aiza Maslan. (2014). Hajj and the Malayan experience, 1860–1941. *Kemanusiaan, 21*(2), 79–98.

Amrith, Sunil S. (2013). *Crossing the Bay of Bengal: The furies of nature and the fortunes of migrants.* Cambridge, Massachusetts: Harvard University Press.

Arudsothy, Ponniah. (1968). *The labour force in a dual economy.* PhD dissertation, University of Glasgow.

Birch, E.W. (1879). The vernacular press in the Straits. *Journal of the Straits Branch of the Royal Asiatic Society, 4,* 51–55.

Carey, Hilary M. (Ed.). (2008). *Empires of religion.* UK: Palgrave Macmillan.

Chiang, Hai Ding. (1978). *A history of Straits Settlements foreign trade 1870–1915* (Memoirs No. 6). Singapore: National Museum.

Drabble, John H. (2003). Technology transfer in Singapore/Malaya during the colonial period: Some further comments. *Journal of the Malaysian Branch of the Royal Asiatic Society, 76*(2), 81–85.

Evers, Hans-Dieter, & Jayarani Pavadarayan (1980). *Asceticism and ecstasy: The Chettiars of Singapore.* Working paper, no. 79. Bielefeld: Forschungsschwerpunkt Entwicklungssoziologie, Fakultat fur Soziologie, Universitat Bielefeld.

Farwell, Byron. (1991). *Armies of the Raj: From the mutiny to independence, 1858–1947.* New York: Norton.

Goh, Chor Boon. (2013). *Technology and entrepôt colonialism in Singapore, 1819–1940.* Singapore: Institute of Southeast Asian Studies.

Harfield, A.G. (1984). *British and Indian Armies in the East Indies, 1685–1935.* Chippenham: Picton.

Megat Muhammad Nuruddin Muhammad Yunis. (1956). *Mecca pilgrim traffic, 1868–1897.* AE Department of History, University of Malaya.

Miller, Michael B. (2006). Pilgrims' progress: The business of the Hajj. *Past & Present, 191*(1), 189–228.

Rai, Rajesh. (2014). *Indians in Singapore, 1819–1945: Diaspora in the colonial port city.* New Delhi: Oxford University Press.

Riddell, Peter G. (2001). Arab migrants and Islamization in the Malay world during the colonial period. *Indonesia and the Malay World, 29*(84), 113–28.

Roff, William R. (1964). The Malayo-Muslim world of Singapore at the close of the nineteenth century. *The Journal of Asian Studies, 24*(1), 75–90.

Sandhu, Kernial Singh. (2010). *Indians in Malaya: Some aspects of their immigration and settlement (1786–1957).* Cambridge: Cambridge University Press.

Savage, Victor R., & Brenda S.A. Yeoh. (2013). *Singapore street names: A study of toponymics* (updated and expanded edition). Singapore: Marshall Cavendish Editions.

Schrader, Heiko. (1996). Chettiar finance in colonial Asia. *Zeitschrift für Ethnologie, 121*(1), 101–26.

Siebel, M. (1961). *A study of the changes in the Malaysian population of Singapore, 1819–1959.* BA Hons academic exercise, University of Singapore.

Solomon, John. (2016). *A subaltern history of the Indian diaspora in Singapore: Gradual disappearance of untouchability, 1872–1965* (Intersections: Colonial and Postcolonial Histories 12). London: Routledge/Taylor & Francis Group.

Song, Ong Siang. (1923). *One hundred years' history of the Chinese in Singapore.* London: Murray.

Spaan, E. (1994). Taikongs and calos: The role of middlemen and brokers in Javanese international migration. *The International Migration Review, 28*(1), 93–113.

Tan, Tai Yong. (2005). Early entrepot portal: Trade and the founding of Singapore. In Aileen Lau & Laure Lau (Eds.), *Maritime heritage of Singapore.* Singapore: Suntree Media.

Tan, Tai Yong. (2005). Early Southeast Asian maritime trade and historical overview of pre-colonial Singapore. In Aileen Lau & Laure Lau (Eds.), *Maritime heritage of Singapore.* Singapore: Suntree Media.

Tan, Tai Yong. (2005). The Indian Ocean: Arab and Indian traders. In Aileen Lau & Laure Lau (Eds.), *Maritime heritage of Singapore.* Singapore: Suntree Media.

Turnbull, Constance Mary. (2009). *A history of modern Singapore, 1819–2005.* Singapore: NUS Press.

Wong, Lin Ken. (2003). *The trade of Singapore 1819–1869* (Reprint No. 23). Bandar Puchong Jaya, Selangor: Malaysian Branch of the Royal Asiatic Society.

Yen, Ching-hwang. (1986). *A social history of the Chinese in Singapore and Malaya, 1800–1911.* Singapore: Oxford University Press.

## Chapter Seven: The 20th Century

Abdul Rahman, Tunku, Putra Al-Haj. (1977). *Looking back: Monday musings and memories.* Kuala Lumpur, Pustaka Antara.

Bradbury, Malcolm. (1991). The cities of modernism. In Malcolm Bradbury & James McFarlane (Eds.), *Modernism: 1890–1930.* London; New York: Penguin Books.

Chanderbali, David. (2008). *Indian indenture in the Straits Settlements: 1872–1910.* Leeds: Peepal Tree.

Chua, Ai-Lin. (2012). Nation, race and language: Discussing transnational identities in colonial Singapore, circa 1930. *Modern Asian Studies, 46*(2), 283–302.

Fischer-Tiné, Harald. (2007). Indian nationalism and the 'world forces': Transnational and diasporic dimensions of the Indian freedom movement on the eve of the First World War. *Journal of Global History, 2*(3), 325–44.

Huff, W. Gregg. (1997). *The economic growth of Singapore: Trade and development in the twentieth century.* Cambridge: Cambridge University Press.

Ismail Abdullah Umar Effendi. (1924). *Melawat ke Melaka 1920 dan 1921.* Singapore: Balai Pustaka.

Kaur, Amarjit. (2006). Indian labour, labour standards, and workers' health in Burma and Malaya, 1900–1940. *Modern Asian Studies, 40*(2), 425.

Lee, Edwin. (2008). *Singapore: The unexpected nation.* Singapore: Institute of Southeast Asian Studies.

Louis, William Roger. (1984). *The British Empire in the Middle East, 1945–1951: Arab nationalism, the United States, and postwar imperialism.* London: Oxford University Press.

Manring, T.A. (1968). National integration and legal systems: Malaysia. *Malaya Law Review, 10*(1), 29–54.

Murfett, Malcolm H., John N. Miksic, Brian P. Farrell, & Chiang Ming Shun. (2011). *Between two oceans: A military history of Singapore from 1275 to 1971* (2nd ed.). Singapore: Marshall Cavendish Editions.

Nik Ahmad Bin Haji Nik Hassan. (1963). The Malay press. *Journal of the Malayan Branch of the Royal Asiatic Society, 36*(1), 37–78.

Noor, Farish A. (2011). 'Racial profiling' revisited: The 1915 Indian sepoy mutiny in Singapore and the impact of profiling on religious and ethnic minorities. *Politics, Religion & Ideology, 12*(1), 89–100.

Ooi, Keat Gin. (2014). Between homeland and 'ummah': Re-visiting the 1915 Singapore Mutiny of the 5th Light Infantry Regiment of the Indian Army. *Social Scientist, 42*(7/8), 85–94.

Sood, Malini. (1995). *Expatriate nationalism and ethnic radicalism: The Ghadar Party in North America, 1910–1920.* PhD dissertation, State University of New York at Stony Brook.

Streets-Salter, Heather. (2013). The local was global: The Singapore Mutiny of 1915. *Journal of World History, 24*(3), 539–76.

Suppiah, Ummadevi, & Sivachandralingam Sundara Raja. (2016). *The Chettiar role in Malaysia's economic history.* Kuala Lumpur, Malaysia: University of Malaya Press.

Taagepera, Rein. (1997). Expansion and contraction patterns of large polities: Context for Russia. *International Studies Quarterly, 41*(3), 475–504.

Tan, Tai Yong. (2008). *Creating Greater Malaysia: Decolonisation and the politics of merger.* Singapore: Institute of Southeast Asian Studies.

Tan, Tai Yong. (2009). Singapore's story: A port city in search of hinterlands. In Arndt Graf and Chua Beng Huat (Eds.), *Port cities in Asia and Europe.* New York: Routledge.

Tyers, Ray K., & Jin Hua Siow. (1993). *Ray Tyers' Singapore: Then and now.* Singapore: Landmark Books.

Yeo, Kim Wah, & Albert Lau. (1991). From colonialism to independence, 1945–1965. In Ernest Chew & Edwin Lee (Eds.), *A history of Singapore.* Singapore: Oxford University Press.

Zainul Abidin bin Rasheed, Norshahril Saat, & Norshahril Saat. (2016). *Majulah!: 50 years of Malay/Muslim community in Singapore.*

## Conclusion

Borschberg, Peter. (2017). Singapore in the cycles of the longue duree. *Journal of the Malaysian Branch of the Royal Asiatic Society, 90*(1), 29–60.

Brooke, J.L. (2014). *Climate change and the course of global history: A rough journey.* New York: Cambridge University Press.

Coclanis, Peter A. (2006). *Time's arrow, time's cycle: Globalization in Southeast Asia over la longue durée* (Raffles Lecture Series). Singapore: Institute of Southeast Asian Studies.

Corfield, Penelope J. (2007). *Time and the shape of history.* New Haven/London: Yale University Press.

Corfield, Penelope J. (2013). Conclusion: Cities in time. In P. Clark (Ed.), *The Oxford handbook of cities in world history.* Oxford: University Press.

Eliade, Mircea. (1954). *The myth of the eternal return; or, cosmos and history* (Bollingen Series, XLVI). Princeton, N.J.: Princeton University Press.

Goh, Keng Swee. (1967). Cities as modernisers. In Goh Keng Swee, *The economics of modernisation and other essays.* Singapore: Asia Pacific Press.

Hack, Karl. (2010). The Malayan trajectory in Singapore's history. In Karl Hack, Jean-Louis Margolin, & Karine Delaye (Eds.), *Singapore from Temasek to the 21st century: Reinventing the global city.* Singapore: NUS Press.

Hack, Karl. (2012). Framing Singapore's history. In N. Tarling (Ed.), *Studying Singapore's past: C.M. Turnbull and the history of modern Singapore.* Singapore: NUS Press.

Hack, Karl, & Jean-Louis Margolin. (2010). Singapore: Reinventing the global city. In Karl Hack, Jean-Louis Margolin, & Karine Delaye (Eds.), *Singapore from Temasek to the 21st century: Reinventing the global city.* Singapore: NUS Press.

Hopkins, A.G. (Ed.). (2001). *Globalization in world history.* London: Pimlico.

Kwa, Chong Guan. (2006). Writing Singapore's history: From city-state to global city. In Kwa Chong Guan (Ed.), *S. Rajaratnam on Singapore: From ideas to reality.* Singapore: World Scientific & Institute of Defence and Strategic Studies.

Kwa, Chong Guan. (2013). The Singapore story: The writing and rewriting of a history. *Commentary 22.* Singapore: National University of Singapore Society.

Kwa, Chong Guan. (2018). From Temasek to Singapore: Locating a global city-state in the cycles of Melaka Straits history. Reprinted in Kwa Chong Guan & Peter Borschberg (Eds.), *Studying Singapore before 1800.* Singapore: NUS Press.

Preston, Peter. (2007). *Singapore in the global system: Relationship, structure and change.* London: Routledge.

Tan, Tai Yong. (2002). Surviving globalisation: An historical perspective. *Commentary 18.* Singapore: National University of Singapore Society.

Tregonning, K.G. (2010). *Merdeka and much more: The reminiscences of a Raffles Professor, 1953–1967.* Singapore: NUS Press.

Wee, C.J. W.-L. (2007). *The Asian modern: Culture, capitalist development, Singapore.* Singapore: NUS Press.

Zerubavel, Eviatar. (2003). *Time maps: Collective memory and the social shape of the past.* Chicago: University of Chicago Press.

# IMAGE CREDITS

Jacket: Singapore from space. Astronaut photo from Expedition 47 of the International Space Station. Courtesy of the Earth Science and Remote Sensing Unit, NASA Johnson Space Center.

Fold-out: (a) Reconstruction of 14th-century Singapore. Illustration by Cheng Puay Koon. (b) Google Earth 3D image of Fort Canning Hill. © 2019 DigitalGlobe. (c) Artist's impression of John Crawfurd. Illustration by Cheng Puay Koon.

Page 1 (facing page): S. Rajaratnam addressing University of Singapore History Society. Ministry of Information and the Arts Collection, courtesy of National Archives of Singapore.

Page 18: Gold armlet and earrings. Courtesy of the National Museum of Singapore, National Heritage Board.

Page 23: *Jewel of Muscat*. Jewel of Muscat website: http://jewelofmuscat.tv/images/preparing-for-sea/nggallery/page/3

Page 24: Song dynasty junk. Reproduced from Kwa Chong Guan, Derek Heng, & Tan Tai Yong (2009), *Singapore: A 700-Year History* (Singapore: National Archives of Singapore).

Page 26: Stone inscription. Courtesy of the National Museum of Singapore, National Heritage Board.

Page 29: (a) Glass globules. Courtesy of National Parks Board. (b) Glass beads. National Parks Board. Photograph reproduced from Mark Ravinder Frost & Yu-Mei Balasingamchow (2009), *Singapore: A Biography* (Singapore: Editions Didier Millet).

Page 31: Hypothetical reconstruction of temple on Fort Canning Hill. Adapted from drawing by Glenn Lim.

Page 32: Duku. William Farquhar Collection of Natural History Drawings. Courtesy of the National Museum of Singapore, National Heritage Board.

Page 33: Untitled Chart of Southern Singapore from Sentosa to Tanjong Rhu, 1825 (detail). © The British Library Board (IOR/X/3346).

Page 35: Fragments of celadon platter and Bodhisattva figure. Courtesy of Lim Chen Sian.

Page 36: (a) Fragment of stem-cup excavated from Fort Canning Hill. Reproduced from Kwa Chong Guan, Derek Heng, & Tan Tai Yong (2009), *Singapore: A 700-Year History* (Singapore: National Archives of Singapore). (b) Blue-and-white stem-cup (top and side views). Collection of the Asian Civilisations Museum, Singapore.

Page 37: Small-mouthed jar. Courtesy of the National Museum of Singapore, National Heritage Board.

Page 39: Plan of Singapore Harbour by Captain Daniel Ross (1819). © The British Library Board (Maps 147.e.18.154).

Page 40: Earthenware sherds. Reproduced from Kwa Chong Guan, Derek Heng, & Tan Tai Yong (2009), *Singapore: A 700-Year History* (Singapore: National Archives of Singapore).

Page 43: Figurine of horse and rider. Courtesy of the National Museum of Singapore, National Heritage Board.

Page 44: Rhinoceros hornbill. William Farquhar Collection of Natural History Drawings. Courtesy of the National Museum of Singapore, National Heritage Board.

Page 50: Statue of Avalokitesvara. Collection of the Asian Civilisations Museum, Singapore.

Page 53: Pages from the *Malay Annals*. Reproduced from Munshi Abdullah (Ed.), *Sejarah Melayu*, printed in Singapore, c. 1840. Collection of National Library, Singapore (Accession no.: B03014389F).

Page 55: Jimmy Ong, *Offering at Temasek Stone* (2011). Reproduced with permission of the artist; collection of Sotheby's.

Page 57: Postage stamp of Tomé Pires. Source: https://nenotavaiconta.wordpress.com/2012/11/02/selos-postais-comemorativos-da-fundacao-de-macau-1955/

Page 58: Zai Kuning, *Dapunta Hyang: Transmission Of Knowledge* (2017). Singapore Pavilion in the Arsenale, 57th Venice Biennale. Photograph courtesy of National Arts Council.

Page 62: Seated Guanyin riding *qilin* with acolytes. Collection of the Asian Civilisations Museum, Singapore.

Page 63: Guanyin seated on lion. Collection of the Asian Civilisations Museum, Singapore.

Page 64: Zheng He treasure boat. Wikimedia Commons: https://commons.wikimedia.org/wiki/File:Nanjing_Treasure_Boat_-_P1070978.jpg

Page 65: The Way of Trafficking by Exchange. Reproduced from Johan Nieuhof, *Voyages & Travels* to the East Indies, 1653–1670 (Oxford in Asia 1988 reprint, 1704 edition of English translation), p. 184. Courtesy of National University of Singapore Libraries.

Page 66: Double *ikat* textile. Collection of the Asian Civilisations Museum, Singapore.

Page 67: (a) A Marchant of Java. Reproduced from Johan Nieuhof, *Voyages & Travels to the East Indies, 1653–1670* (Oxford in Asia 1988 reprint, 1704 edition of English translation), p. 276. Courtesy of National University of Singapore Libraries. (b) Malay *lancaran* and Chinese junk. Reproduced from G. de Erédia, C. Ruelens, & L. Janssen (1881), *Malaca, L'Inde Orientale et le Cathay; Malaca, L'Inde Méridionale et le Cathay* (Bruxelles: Librairie Européenne C. Muquardt). Collection of National Library, Singapore (Accession no.: B03013605G).

Page 68: Scale model of 15th-century Chinese vessel. Photograph by Nick Burningham.

Page 69: New Geographic Map of the Interior of Malaca (Godinho de Erédia, 1602). Wikimedia Commons: https://commons.wikimedia.org/wiki/File:New_Geographic_Map_of_the_Interior_of_Malaca_WDL972.png. Collection of National Library of Brazil.

Page 71: A Melaya Captain. Reproduced from Johan Nieuhof, *Voyages & Travels to the East Indies, 1653–1670* (Oxford in Asia 1988 reprint, 1704 edition of English translation), p. 27. Courtesy of National University of Singapore Libraries.

Page 73: Orang Laut families on board their houseboats (1950s). Ivan Polunin Multimedia Lab, courtesy of National Archives of Singapore.

Page 76: John Turnbull Thomson (1821–1884), *Seletars of Singapore*. Watercolour on paper, 23.5 x 31.5cm. Hocken Collections, Uare Taoka o Hākena, University of Otago (gifted by the Hall-Jones family, Invercargill, 1992, Accession no.: 92/1259).

Page 78: Map of Singapore and the Johor River to Batu Sawar, by Manuel Godinho de Erédia (c. 1613). Reproduced (with colour added) from G. de Erédia, C. Ruelens, & L. Janssen (1881), *Malaca, L'Inde Orientale et le Cathay; Malaca, L'Inde Méridionale et le Cathay* (Bruxelles: Librairie Européenne C. Muquardt). Collection of National Library, Singapore (Accession no.: B03013605G).

Page 80: Portrait of Alfonso de Albuquerque. Museu de Arte Antiga, Lisbon. Wikimedia Commons: https://commons.wikimedia.org/wiki/File:Retrato_de_Afonso_de_Albuquerque_(ap%C3%B3s_1545)_-_Autor_desconhecido.png

Page 81: Reconstructed map of Malay Peninsula based on the *Muhit*. Peter Borschberg, private collection.

Page 82: Portrait of Manuel Godinho de Erédia. Reproduced from G. de Erédia, C. Ruelens, & L. Janssen (1881), *Malaca, L'Inde Orientale et le Cathay; Malaca, L'Inde Méridionale et le Cathay* (Bruxelles:

Librairie Européenne C. Muquardt). Collection of National Library, Singapore (Accession no.: B03013605G).

Page 83: Overlay of Erédia's *Atlas Miscelânea* map on modern topographic map. Graphic courtesy of Mok Ly Yng.

Page 84: Sherds from Johor River. Collection of Heritage Conservation Centre, National Heritage Board. Photograph by Kwa Chong Guan.

Page 86: Sketch of a Malay woman. Image reproduced from J. Crawfurd (1828), *Journal of an embassy from the Governor-General of India to the courts of Siam and Cochin China* (London: Henry Colburn). Collection of National Library, Singapore (Accession no.: B20116740J).

Page 87: Drawing of clove plant. Reproduced from Kwa Chong Guan, Derek Heng, & Tan Tai Yong (2009), *Singapore: A 700-Year History* (Singapore: National Archives of Singapore).

Page 88: Bird's-eye view of the city of Aceh (Johannes Vingboons, c. 1665). Wikimedia Commons: https://commons.wikimedia.org/wiki/File:AMH-6132-NA_Bird's_eye_view_of_the_city_of_Atjeh.jpg

Page 90: Gold coins. Courtesy of the National Museum of Singapore, National Heritage Board.

Page 93: Chorographic Description of the Straits of Sincapura and Sabbam. Reproduced from G. de Erédia, C. Ruelens, & L. Janssen (1881), *Malaca, L'Inde Orientale et le Cathay; Malaca, L'Inde Méridionale et le Cathay* (Bruxelles: Librairie Européenne C. Muquardt). Collection of National Library, Singapore (Accession no.: B03013605G).

Page 94: Map of the Singapore and Melaka Straits, by Andre Pereira dos Reis (c. 1654). W.A. Engelbrecht Collection, Maritime Museum, Rotterdam.

Page 95: Porcelain vase, plate and sherds. Courtesy of the National Museum of Singapore, National Heritage Board.

Page 96: *Rochor, Singapore* (1866). Courtesy of the National Museum of Singapore, National Heritage Board.

Page 97: Mao Kun map, published in *Wu Bei Zhi*. Retrieved from the Library of Congress: https://www.loc.gov/item/2004633695/

Page 98: Selden map. Photo: Bodleian Libraries, MS. Selden Supra 105, Map recto.

Page 99: Overlay of Selden map with Erédia's maps of overland routes. Graphic by Mok Ly Yng.

Page 100: Sketch of Batu Berlayar (Lt. Jackson, 1823). © The British Library Board (WD 2972).

Page 101: *Batu Blair or Sail Rock, Old Straits of Singapore* (Charles Dyce). National University of Singapore Museum Collection.

Page 102: Map of Singapore and Johor River (redrawing of Erédia map, c. 1616–22). Reproduced with permission from NUS Press, publisher of Peter Borschberg (Ed.), *Journal, memorials and letters of*

*Cornelis Matelieff de Jonge: Security, diplomacy and commerce in 17th-century Southeast Asia.*

Page 103: Portrait of Linschoten. Reproduced from Jan Huyghen van Linschoten (1595), *Itinerario* (Amsterdam: C. Claesz). KB – Nationale Bibliotheek, The Hague (1702 b 4 [1]).

Page 104: Map of Singapore and Johor River region. Reproduced and adapted with permission from NUS Press, publisher of Peter Borschberg (Ed.), *Journal, memorials and letters of Cornelis Matelieff de Jonge: Security, diplomacy and commerce in 17th-century Southeast Asia.*

Page 106–7: *Exacta & accurata delineatio cum orarum maritimdrum tum etjam locorum terrestrium quae in regionibus China, Cauchinchina, Camboja sive Champa, Syao, Malacca, Arracan & Pegu.* Collection of National Library, Singapore.

Page 109: *Gezigt van het meer op de Negory Tondano en het daarachter gelegen gebergte* (1677). Collection of Foreign Maps Leupe, National Archives of the Netherlands, The Hague.

Page 112: A view over Malacca shortly after its conquest by the Portuguese. Gaspar Correia (1858–1863), *Lendas da Índia.* Wikimedia Commons: https://commons.wikimedia.org/wiki/File:Malacca_in_1511.png

Page 115: Hand-coloured etching of junk. Reproduced from Jan Huyghen van Linschoten (1595), *Itinerario* (Amsterdam: C. Claesz). KB – Nationale Bibliotheek, The Hague (1702 B 4 [1]).

Page 116: Etching depicting arrival of Raja Bongsu. Theodor de Bry, Johann Theodor de Bry, & Johann Israel de Bry (1607). Photo courtesy of the Bibliotheca Thysiana, Leiden.

Page 119: (a) VOC logo. Wikimedia Commons: https://commons.wikimedia.org/wiki/File:VOC.svg. (b) EIC coat of arms (1600–1709). Wikimedia Commons: https://commons.wikimedia.org/wiki/File:Coat_of_arms_of_East_India_Company_1600-1709.jpg

Page 120: Bazaar at Banten, 1596. Collection of Rijksmuseum, Amsterdam.

Page 122: (a) Portrait of Jacob van Heemskerk. Reproduced from Emmanuel van Meteren, *Commentarien ofte Memorien van den Nederlandschen Staet, Handel en Oorlogen* (Commentaries or Memories Concerning the Dutch State, Trade and Wars), 1637 edition. Peter Borschberg, private collection. (b) Maurice of Nassau receiving Acehnese ambassador. Collection of Rijksmuseum, Amsterdam.

Page 123: Cover of pamphlet, *Corte ende sekere Beschrijvinge* (1603). Allard Pierson, the Collections of the University of Amsterdam.

Page 124: Portrait of Hugo Grotius. Reproduced from Hugo Grotius, *Annales et Historiae de Rebus Belgicis* (Annals and Histories of the Low Countries), 1658 Latin edition. Peter Borschberg, private collection.

Page 125: Contrafactur des Scharmutz els der Hollender wider die Portigesen in dem Flus Balusabar. Theodor

de Bry, Johann Theodor de Bry, & Johann Israel de Bry (1607). Collection of National Library, Singapore.

Page 127: Printed etching of landing of VOC troops at Melaka. Reproduced from Johan Isaksz Pontanus, *Historia urbis et rerum Amstelodamensium* (History of the City and Affairs of Amsterdam), first published in 1611.

Page 128: Portrait of Cornelis Matelieff de Jonge. Collection of Rijksmuseum, Amsterdam.

Page 131: *Cosmographia* title page. Source: http://www.columbia.edu/itc/mealac/pritchett/00generallinks/munster/munster.html

Page 133: Pepper plant. William Farquhar Collection of Natural History Drawings. Courtesy of the National Museum of Singapore, National Heritage Board.

Page 135: Coloured sketch of Palembang. National Archives of the Netherlands, The Hague.

Page 137: Portrait of Pieter Willemszoon Verhoeff. Collection of Rijksmuseum, Amsterdam.

Page 139: View of entrance to port of Batavia. Wikimedia Commons: https://commons.wikimedia.org/wiki/File:AMH-6135-NA_View_of_Batavia.jpg

Page 140: View of the Island of Ternate. Johannes Kip, 1682. Collection of Rijksmuseum, Amsterdam.

Page 142: Portrait sketch of Sir Francis Drake. Reproduced from William Cullan Bryant & Sydney Howard Gay (1876–81), *Popular History of the United States,* 4 vols. (New York: Scribner, Armstrong & Co.). Peter Borschberg, private collection.

Page 143: Bird's-eye view of the city of Banten. Collection of Rijksmuseum, Amsterdam.

Page 144: View of Fort Concordia at Kupang on Timor. Wikimedia Commons: https://commons.wikimedia.org/wiki/File:AMH-4677-NA_View_of_Fort_Concordia_at_Coupan.jpg

Page 146: *Carte réduite des détroits de Malaca, Sincapour, et du Gouverneur, dressée au dépost des cartes et plans de la Marine* (Jacques Nicolas Bellin, 1755). Peter Borschberg, private collection.

Page 148: Sultan Mahmud Mangkat di Julang Mausoleum. Wikimedia Commons: https://commons.wikimedia.org/wiki/File:Sultan_Mahmud_Mangkat_Di_Julang_Mausoleum.jpg

Page 149: Hand-drawn chart of southern portion of Malay Peninsula and Singapore Strait, by Thomas Bowrey (1690). © The British Library Board (Add. 5222 f.10).

Page 150: *A Map of the Dominions of Johor and of the Island of Sumatra with the Adjacent Islands.* Reproduced from Alexander Hamilton (1727), *A New Account of the East Indies.* Leiden University Libraries.

Page 153: A Bugis or Boekjes. Reproduced from Johan Nieuhof, *Voyages & Travels to the East Indies, 1653–1670* (Oxford in Asia 1988 reprint, 1704 edition of English translation). Courtesy of National University of Singapore Libraries.

Page 155: Hand-drawn Map of Riau Straits. Leiden University Libraries.

Page 158: Map of Singapore Straits (1680). © The British Library Board (Add. 15737 f.9v–10).

Page 160–1: *Carte réduite des détroits de Malaca, Sincapour, et du Gouverneur, dressée au dépost des cartes et plans de la Marine* (Jacques Nicolas Bellin, 1755). Peter Borschberg, private collection.

Page 162: Map of Singapore and the Straits (Dupré Eberard, 1700). © The British Library Board (Add. 15738 f.29).

Page 163: Singapore's many names in historical maps. Graphic by Peter Borschberg.

Page 164: *A Large Chart Describeing the Streights of Malacca and Sincapore.* Sam Thornton (c. 1711). Collection of National Library, Singapore.

Page 167: *Fort of Rhio from the Roads* (Charles Dyce). National University of Singapore Museum Collection.

Page 168: Iranun *lanon* warship, by Rafael Monleón (1890). Wikimedia Commons: https://commons.wikimedia.org/wiki/File:Iranun_lanong_warship_by_Rafael_Monle%C3%B3n_(1890).jpg

Page 169: Iranun pirate of Borneo. Reproduced from Frank Marryat (1848), *Borneo and the Indian Archipelago: with drawings of costume and scenery* (London: Longman, Brown, Green, and Longmans).

Page 171: Watercoloured sketch of Dutch Melaka (Jan Keldermans, 1764). Collection of Rijksmuseum, Amsterdam.

Page 172: Portrait of Baron Godert van der Capellen. Wikimedia Commons: https://commons.wikimedia.org/wiki/File:Godart_Alexander_Gerard_Philip_Baron_van_der_Capellen_(1778-1848)._Gouverneur-generaal_(1816-26)_Rijksmuseum_SK-A-3795.jpeg.

Page 173: Portrait of Francis Rawdon-Hastings. Wikimedia Commons: https://commons.wikimedia.org/wiki/File:Francis_Rawdon-Hastings_(1754-1826),_2nd_Earl_of_Moira_(later_1st_Marquess_of_Hastings),_Governor-General_of_Bengal_and_Commander-in-Chief_of_the_Forces_in_India.jpg

Page 177: *Malay Perahu.* Thomas and William Daniell (1769–1837), 1800s, Singapore. Courtesy of the National Museum of Singapore, National Heritage Board.

Page 180: Map of Singapore 1819–20. The Bute Collection at Mount Stuart, Isle of Bute, Scotland.

Page 183: Horsburgh chart (1824). James Horsburgh; engraved by John Bateman. Collection of National Library, Singapore.

Page 185: *Sketch of the Land Round Singapore Harbour.* The National Archives of the UK (Ref. ADM344/1307).

Page 187: Raffles' ship *Indiana.* Courtesy of the National Museum of Singapore, National Heritage Board.

Page 189: Treaty of 1819. Courtesy of the National Museum of Singapore, National Heritage Board.

Page 190–1: *Singapore Waterfront, 1861* (W. Gray). Courtesy of the National Museum of Singapore, National Heritage Board.

Page 192: Portrait of Munshi Abdullah by Harun Lat. Collection of Perbadanan Muzium Melaka.

Page 193: (a) William Farquhar. Lithograph, c. 1830. Wikimedia Commons: https://commons.wikimedia.org/wiki/File:WilliamFarquhar.jpg (b) Portrait of Stamford Raffles. Painted by James Lonsdale, 1817. Courtesy of the Zoological Society of London. (c) Portrait of John Crawfurd. Courtesy of the National Museum of Singapore, National Heritage Board.

Page 194: *The River From Monkey Bridge* (Charles Dyce). National University of Singapore Museum Collection.

Page 195: View of Boat Quay from Fort Canning. August Sachtler of Sachtler & Co. (1860–70), 1860s. Courtesy of the National Museum of Singapore, National Heritage Board.

Page 196–7: Plan of Singapore Town and Adjoining Districts, from an Actual Survey by John Turnbull Thomson (1844). © The British Library Board (Maps.60020.1).

Page 199: Singapore stamps of ships. Reproduced with permission from Singapore Philatelic Museum.

Page 200: *Siamese Junks Moored in Singapore* (1842). Courtesy of the National Museum of Singapore, National Heritage Board.

Page 201: *Chinese Junk in Singapore.* Louis Le Breton, 1839. Courtesy of the National Museum of Singapore, National Heritage Board.

Page 202: Alexander Guthrie. Courtesy of National Archives of Singapore.

Page 203: (a) View of para rubber plantation, Singapore. Courtesy of National Archives of Singapore. (b) Henry Nicholas Ridley. Courtesy of National Archives of Singapore.

Page 204: *Coaling by Night at Singapore* (1876). Courtesy of the National Museum of Singapore, National Heritage Board.

Page 205: Tanjong Pagar docks. Courtesy of the National Museum of Singapore, National Heritage Board.

Page 206: View of Battery Road and Tan Kim Seng Fountain. Courtesy of the National Museum of Singapore, National Heritage Board.

Page 208: Kampong Bugis (1890s). G.R. Lambert, *Streets and Places.* Lee Kip Lin Collection. All rights reserved, Lee Kip Lin and National Library Board, Singapore.

Page 209: Office staff of Alkaff and Co. Reproduced from Arnold Wright & H.A. Cartwright (Eds.) (1908), *Twentieth-century impressions of British Malaya: Its history, people, commerce, industries, and resources* (London: Lloyd's Greater Britain Publishing Company, Limited).

Page 210: Pilgrims on the Hajj on board a ship. Ministry of Information and the Arts Collection, courtesy of National Archives of Singapore.

Page 212: Sri Mariamman Temple (c. 1890). Courtesy of the National Museum of Singapore, National Heritage Board.

Page 213: (a) Chettiars (studio shot from the 1920s). Nachiappa Chettiar Collection, courtesy of National Archives of Singapore. (b) Rm. V. Supramanium (1920s). Nachiappa Chettiar Collection, courtesy of National Archives of Singapore.

Page 214: P. Govindasamy ("Early Singaporeans" stamp issue, 2001). Reproduced with permission from Singapore Philatelic Museum.

Page 215: Tan Tock Seng ("Early Singaporeans" stamp issue, 2001). Reproduced with permission from Singapore Philatelic Museum.

Page 217: Hokkien Street (1890s). Courtesy of the National Museum of Singapore, National Heritage Board.

Page 218: The first committee of the Straits Chinese British Association. Courtesy of National Archives of Singapore.

Page 220: Suez Canal. Wikimedia Commons: https://commons.wikimedia.org/wiki/File:SuezCanal-Kantara.jpg

Page 221: Two Means of Conveyance in the Straits Settlements. Courtesy of the National Museum of Singapore, National Heritage Board.

Page 222: Electric tram at Collyer Quay (c. 1905). Koh Seow Chuan Collection, courtesy of National Archives of Singapore.

Page 224: *Hikayat Abdullah*, published by Mission Press, Singapore, 1849. Collection of National Library, Singapore (Accession no.: B03014389F).

Page 226–7: Waterworks and Boat Quay (C.J. Kleingrothe, 1907). Courtesy of the National Museum of Singapore, National Heritage Board.

Page 228: Chang Chin Fai, *Changing Cityscape* (1992). Reproduced with permission of the artist; reproduced from *Singapore: Places, poems, paintings* (Singapore: Art and Artist Speak).

Page 230: Ferryboat between Singapore and Johor. Arshak C. Galstaun Collection, courtesy of National Archives of Singapore.

Page 231: Singapore-Johor Causeway. Courtesy of National Archives of Singapore.

Page 233: (a) Pillbox at Labrador. Photograph by Marshall Cavendish International (Asia). (b) General Archibald Wavell inspecting Singapore's fortification. Reproduced from Kwa Chong Guan, Derek Heng, & Tan Tai Yong (2009), *Singapore: A 700-Year History* (Singapore: National Archives of Singapore).

Page 235: Execution of mutineers of 5th Light Infantry at Outram Road (c. March 1915). Wikimedia Commons: https://commons.wikimedia.org/wiki/File:1915_Singapore_Mutiny.jpg

Page 236: Singapore Volunteer Corps, Seletar Camp (1928). Reproduced from Ministry of the Interior and Defence (1969), *Our Security, 1819–1969:*

*Nation-building through service in the armed forces and the police* (Singapore: Printed by the Govt. Print. Off.). Collection of National Library, Singapore.

Page 237: Tan Kah Kee at Ee Hoe Hean Club. Tan Kah Kee Memorial Museum Collection, courtesy of National Archives of Singapore.

Page 239: (a) Japanese tanks rolling past Supreme Court, 1942. Courtesy of Lim Shao Bin, collection of National Library, Singapore (Accession no.: B29245901J). (b) Japanese soldiers in Singapore. Reproduced from Liu Kang (1946), *Chop Suey*, Vol. II (Singapore: Eastern Art Co.). Collection of the National Library, Singapore (Accession no.: B02901746G).

Page 240: Saburo Miyamoto, *The Meeting of General Yamashita and General Percival* (1942). The National Museum of Modern Art, Tokyo © Mineko Miyamoto 2019/JAA 1900027.

Page 241: Subhas Chandra Bose declaring the formation of the provisional government of Azad Hind. Nirvan Thivy Collection, courtesy of National Archives of Singapore.

Page 242: Chin Peng as MPAJA commander. Imperial War Museum Collection, courtesy of National Archives of Singapore.

Page 243: Emergency regulations pamphlet. Reproduced with permission from SGM Herbert A. Friedman (Ret.).

Page 244: Sir Gerald Templer at Kallang Airport (1952). Ministry of Information and the Arts Collection, courtesy of National Archives of Singapore.

Page 245: David Marshall. Source: *The Straits Times* © Singapore Press Holdings Limited. Reprinted with permission.

Page 246: Tan Tee Chie, *On Strike* (1955). Oil on canvas, 66 x 86.5 cm. Collection of National Gallery Singapore

Page 247: Ho Chi Minh. Bettman/Bettman Collection/Getty Images.

Page 248: Malcolm MacDonald greeting widow of Lim Bo Seng. Source: *The Straits Times* © Singapore Press Holdings Limited. Reprinted with permission.

Page 249: (a) PAP members campaigning (1959). Ministry of Information and the Arts Collection, courtesy of National Archives of Singapore. (b) Lim Chin Siong's release from Changi Prison. Ministry of Information and the Arts Collection, courtesy of National Archives of Singapore.

Page 251: *Swearing-in of Lee Kuan Yew as Prime Minister of Singapore,* Lai Kui Fang (1994) Oil on canvas. Reproduced with permission of the artist; courtesy of the National Museum of Singapore, National Heritage Board.

Page 252: Chua Mia Tee, *National Language Class* (1959). Oil on canvas, 112 x 153 cm. Collection of National Gallery Singapore.

Page 255: Lee Kuan Yew and Tunku Abdul Rahman, 1962. Source: *The Straits Times* © Singapore Press Holdings Limited. Reprinted with permission.

Page 256: Sukarno declaring Konfrontasi, September 1963. https://penasoekarno.wordpress.com

Page 257: MacDonald House bombing. Ministry of Culture Collection, courtesy of National Archives of Singapore.

Page 258: Tan Siew Sin and Goh Keng Swee. Ministry of Information and the Arts Collection, courtesy of National Archives of Singapore.

Page 260: Syed Ja'afar Albar. Source: *The Straits Times* © Singapore Press Holdings Limited. Reprinted with permission.

Page 261: Confronting rioters. Singapore Press Holdings Collection, courtesy of National Archives of Singapore.

Page 263: Raising of Singapore flag. Reproduced with permission from *Ren min xing dong dang, 1954–1979* (People's Action Party 25th anniversary publication). Collection of National Library, Singapore.

Page 264: Smelted tin, Pulau Brani (1952). Ministry of Information and the Arts Collection, courtesy of National Archives of Singapore.

Page 265: Transforming Jurong. Ministry of Information and the Arts Collection, courtesy of National Archives of Singapore.

Page 266: Albert Winsemius. Ministry of Information and the Arts Collection, courtesy of National Archives of Singapore.

Page 269: Au Yee Pun, *The Conventional Way* (1992). Reproduced with permission of the artist; reproduced from *Singapore: Places, poems, paintings* (Singapore: Art and Artist Speak).

Page 270: Thang Kiang How, *World's Busiest Port* (1993). Reproduced with permission of the artist; reproduced from *Singapore: Places, poems, paintings* (Singapore: Art and Artist Speak).

Page 271: Lai Kui Fang, *Construction of Sheares Bridge* (1976). Oil on canvas, 202 x 132 cm. Istana Art Collection.

Page 272: Lee Boon Wang, *Shipyard*. Oil on canvas, 84 x 123 cm. Collection of National Gallery Singapore.

Page 273: Ong Kim Seng, *Moonlit Night in an HDB Estate* (1999). Acrylic on canvas, 213.8 x 132.4 cm. Istana Art Collection; image courtesy of National Heritage Board.

Page 274–5: Port of Singapore. Photo credit: Maritime and Port Authority of Singapore.

Page 276: University of Singapore History Department, 1960. Courtesy of Department of History, National University of Singapore. Reproduced with permission from NUS Press, publisher of Kwa C.G. & P. Borschberg (Eds.), *Studying Singapore before 1800*.

# INDEX